DESOCIALISATION
THE CRISIS OF POST-MODERNITY

To all those Italians who helped me

DESOCIALISATION
THE CRISIS OF POST-MODERNITY

'It is not good that man should be alone' (Gen 2:18)

MATTHEW FFORDE

GABRIEL

Desocialisation
The Crisis of Post-Modernity

A catalogue record for this book is available from the British Library.

Published by Gabriel, 4th Floor, Landmark House,
Station Road, Cheadle Hulme, Cheshire SK8 7JH
www.totalcatholic.com

Publication date: April 2009

ISBN: 978-1-904657-54-5

Typeset in Times New Roman by Rob Beswick

Printed in the UK by CPI William Clowes Beccles NR34 7TL

Contents

Preface

This book was long, indeed very long, in the making. It began some twenty-five years ago when I became aware in Great Britain of the dynamics described in its pages. At that time the ideas I present in this volume, and the warnings I offered, were received in my professional, social and personal life with keen opposition, if not outright aggression. I found myself in the unenviable position of belonging, to employ the phrase of P.L. Berger, to a 'cognitive minority';[1] it was as though I was seeing ghosts or tilting at windmills. In my own way I was a cultural dissident and in line with what that condition often brings, much of what I had to endure was severe in the extreme; on occasions, in truth, unspeakable. However, *ex malo bonum*. An aspirant Johann Georg Elser (1903-1945) of cultural politics, I decided to leave England and to move to Rome, the ancient centre of Christianity, with the aim of writing on desocialisation from a distance (even though Italy, like other countries of the Western world, has been experiencing these dark trends in which the United Kingdom has been a notable pioneer). My aim was to demonstrate that mechanisms are now at work in Great Britain which act like crowbars to prise people apart, and that this is happening because the spiritual pillars of community have been severely weakened or knocked away. It would be interesting to know how many of the two million Britons who have emigrated over the last ten years have done so out of a similar rejection of cultural conditions in their own country, constituting thereby a further indicator of our national malaise.

Since moving to Italy I have received great kindness from many Italians who helped me as I walked along my path, often with a very unsteady step. I am thus naturally drawn to the sentiments of P.B. Shelley (1792-1822) who declared that Italy was the 'paradise of exiles'[2] and the reader will readily understand why it is that I have dedicated this work to all these Italians, far too many to mention by name here: 'I was a stranger, and you welcomed me' (Mt 25:35). People from other nationalities also helped me greatly and they are always remembered. Special reference must be made here to my late aunt, Patricia Cooper, who saved me from a most unwelcome fate; to my cousin William McEnchroe, a rare spirit; and to Clarisse Faugeron, who showed me that I did not want the impossible. Lastly, two Christians no longer on this earth constantly illuminated my path through their writings and their pronouncements and my debt to them is immense: John Paul II (1920-2005) and Alexander Solzhenitsyn (1918-2008).

Since my youthful decision to leave my country there has been growing realisation in Great Britain (and the West) that post-modernity increasingly means a loss of ties for contemporary man. For example, on 2 September 2007 *The Sunday Times Magazine* blazoned its front cover with the following lines: 'By 2021 a third of us will live alone. How many will die alone too?'[3] and in January 2008 *The Independent on Sunday* published an article under the headline 'Community? We Don't Know Our Neighbours' which contained the following chilling lines:

> A third of people are predicting the death of their communities, according to a report by the Prince's Trust. Traditional social networks are becoming a thing of the past…The crisis is exacerbated by a climate of fear that is making old people afraid of the young and adults reluctant to intervene when confronted by anti-social behaviour.
>
> One in three of those surveyed agreed that Margaret Thatcher's notorious statement – "there is no such thing as society" – will come true in the near future.
>
> Most people believe the days of face-to-face contact are numbered, with 65 per cent saying that people in the future will have more contact through the internet than in person. Almost one in 10 Britons, nine per cent, admits to failing to meet other people socially on a weekly basis. And 15 per cent go a week without speaking to any of their neighbours.[4]

And has not the leader of one of the principal parties of state recently told us that we have now to address the realities of a 'broken society'?[5] Some twenty-five years on there is now a veritable flood of comments and statistics on the breakdown of community, and as the reader will be aware when turning over the pages of this volume I have tried to keep up with them (and interpret them) as best I can. Equally, there is increasing awareness that a whole series of developments cannot be understood without reference to this breakdown. For example, as this book illustrates, the contemporary economic crisis, set in motion by the credit crunch and the banking meltdown, must also be understood against the background of the dissolving effects of post-modern culture. Much the same may be said about the catastrophic fall in the legitimacy and authority of politicians, political parties and political institutions.

The field where perhaps the greatest divergences now exist is that of the reasons for this phenomenon. This book, in offering its own explanation, may be seen as a Christian critique of our present predicament, perhaps a late-personalist interpretation of late-modernity. At a time when identity is being assaulted from all sides, this volume seeks to affirm the fundamental identity of man – the soul – and its supreme value: 'For what will it profit a man, if he gains the whole world and forfeits his soul?' (Mt 16:26). It goes on to argue that the attack on this identity and its dictates now means not only that authentic spiritual life and its community-engendering effects are inhibited but also that individuals are increasingly the unwilling victims of cultural conditions which systematically impose upon them a loss of ties. At the same time, it proposes a hypothesis as to what the essential contents of these conditions now are (and here, peering deep into changes that have taken place at the heart of our national life, it pays particular attention to what has entered the gap left behind by deChristianisation), and in understanding these it proposes what the real contents of human culture should be and thus should become.

For all its focus on negative developments, which at times spill into what can only be seen as horror (regretfully, a recurrent theme of this volume), this is thus a work of purpose and hope. In believing in the imitation of Christ, it calls for healing; in appealing for a return to authentic spiritual health and therefore the regeneration of community, it expresses my faith that we will not be destroyed by the void. Furthermore, in contemplating the future struggle to reverse these negative developments, and in reflecting on those who will have to play a leading part in that struggle and on what they may have to endure, it pays great attention to a recent statement of Benedict XVI: 'those who believe are never alone'.[6]

The subject of desocialisation was touched on in my monographic work *Conservatism and Collectivism 1886-1914*[7] and explored at greater length in my textbook for Italian universities, *Storia della Gran Bretagna 1832-2002*.[8] It also crops up in some of my other academic publications[9] and in my articles for the Vatican newspaper *L'Osservatore Romano*.[10] The first real attempt at an overall analysis was my *Desocialisation: the Crisis of the Post-Modern. A Spiritual Critique*,[11] published in a limited edition in 2000 as work in progress to crystallise my ideas and invite the opinions of others. That work, flawed from many points of view, must now be considered completely superseded. However, it formed the point of departure for *Desocializzazione. La crisi della post-modernità*, published by Cantagalli of Sienna in 2005,[12] which was awarded the Capri San Michele prize – to whose committee I express my profound gratitude – in 2006. The present volume is essentially a version of that publication with a series of additions and the up-dating of statistics.

M. Fforde,
Rome,
1 December 2008

Glossary

The following is a brief list of key terms used in this book, some of which are new or are used in a new way.

Animalism: the belief that human nature is to be chiefly explained with reference to man's animal inheritance and his biological evolution.

Anomic condition: that state marked by anonymity which is brought about in an individual by desocialisation.

Anthropology: (a) the discipline which studies human culture; (b) the cultural system of a group or groups of people; (c) a model of man proposed by a specific doctrine or philosophy.

Collectivism: the creed which believes that the existing economic system and propertied order is unjust and regressive, and proposes large-scale state intervention, principally in favour of the less-advantaged, to promote the collective good.

Culture: (a) that set of causally interconnected systems of ways of perceiving and forms of behaviour which characterises a group or groups of people; (b) that reality of the human experience which is studied by the discipline of anthropology.

Deculturalisation: a process involving the impoverishment and depletion of the cultural inheritance of a group of people or a people.

Desocialisation: a cultural condition or process that attacks humanity where (a) the mechanisms of social cohesion are severely compromised; (b) the soul's potential to form authentic community is heavily frustrated; (c) the kingdom of heaven in its cultural expression is strongly repudiated; (d) love for love and for truth is weak in human relationships; and (e), there are strong pressures to make the individual live in an anomic condition.

Determinism: the doctrine that the individual does not have free will in the spiritual, moral, ethical and behavioural spheres.

Economism: the belief that human nature is to be chiefly explained with reference to an innate propensity to the acquisition and accumulation of material wealth.

Feelingism: the belief that human nature is to be chiefly explained with reference to the feeling faculties of man.

Humanism: the belief that God does not exist and that man has no soul, and that humans are the supreme beings of the universe.

Life according to the Spirit: (a) that which a soul gives rise to when it is in a healthy condition; (b) that which conduces to authentic human community; (c) that obtained by the soul through true adherence to the teachings and example of Christ.

Marketism (or market correctness): the doctrine that asserts that the free market is the principal way forward for the improvement and progress of society.

Materialist matrix: a specific grid of twelve separate models of man all of which (with the exception of relativism which has special features of its own) are united in the belief that there is no supernatural presence in the cosmos and no spiritual presence in man.

Physiologism: the belief that human nature is to be chiefly explained with reference to the character and working of man's body, and especially his brain.

Post-modernity: the late-twentieth century and the early twenty-first century.

Powerism: the belief that human nature is to be chiefly explained with reference to an innate propensity within man to the acquisition and maintenance of power.

Psychism: the belief that human nature is to be chiefly explained with reference to an inner 'psyche' to be found within each individual.

Rationalism: the belief that human nature is to be chiefly explained with reference to man's rational faculties

Relativism: the belief that there is no such thing as objective truth and that everything, including questions of ethics and morality, is merely a matter of a point of view.

Rightsism: the belief that human nature is to be chiefly explained with reference to an innate package of rights which men (who are said not to have souls and to live in a Godless universe) bear within them from birth, prior to entering human society.

Sameism: the doctrine that human beings are, in essentials, the same. This doctrine at times has the appellation 'egalitarianism'.

Selfish individualism: a style of life based upon the pursuit of personal gain and gratification, especially in relation to power, money, rank   and pleasure.

Sexualism: the belief that human nature is to be chiefly explained with reference to the sexual and reproductive impulse in man.

Societalism: the belief that human nature is to be chiefly explained with reference to the conditioning effects on man of human society.

Spiritualism: the belief that human nature is to be chiefly explained with reference to a non-material presence within man placed there by God – the soul.

Introduction

Our Post-Social Future?

This book is an exploration of the contemporary cultural crisis in Great Britain: its characteristics, its causes, and its cure. Although there are wider references to the West and beyond, this volume focuses on the United Kingdom and should always be read in that light. A central thesis in the analysis is that the past four decades or so (the era of post-modernity) have witnessed a form of cultural collapse. A whole host of phenomena indicate that in post-modern society people are increasingly faced with a loss or impoverishment of ties, a decline in community. Whether we look, for example, at the institution of the family or the number of people living alone, the high incidence of crime or low turnouts at elections, the changing character of civil society or alienation from political institutions, we constantly encounter the same theme: the trend is towards a desocialisation of contemporary man. Yet this process, which is an overall cultural movement that at times resembles a veritable juggernaut, does not seem to be conducive to the well-being of those who fall victim to its impact. Indeed, abundant evidence indicates that the various forms of isolation that are involved in this trend provoke suffering. To adjust a famous phrase (Marx), a spectre is haunting England – the spectre of loneliness. This book, therefore, shares the concerns of those who perceive the 'increasingly atomised culture of late modernity' in which human beings are 'cut off from the saving grace and presence of their fellow human beings',[1] with all the deleterious consequences that this condition involves.

This book proposes that the central factor behind this cultural crisis is

a revolution in models of man (or 'anthropologies') that has taken place
during the modern age. It thus agrees with the judgement of the Swiss
theologian Georges Cottier:

> In reality the cultural situation in which we find ourselves is
> characterised by a conflict between anthropologies...The rooting
> of man in the transcendent has been lost from view...there can be
> no doubt that we are on a dangerous downward slope. The
> banalisation of abortion and euthanasia are worrying signs of a
> negating process where in the end man in his humanity is
> threatened...This is perhaps our first task, namely to help in the
> discovery or rediscovery of the beauty of the human calling within
> a civilisation which, by exalting and exciting selfish appetites and
> the spirit of competition, nourishes the subtle feeling of the
> insignificance of human existence...The negation or the
> condemnation to oblivion of the transcendent can lead to the bitter
> experience of the emptiness and the vanity of everything.[2]

It is advanced in this volume that during post-modernity a set of false
anthropologies have become increasingly entrenched in people's minds,
a collection of models of man that do not recognise the soul in man, an
authentic 'materialist matrix'. This book argues that this matrix has
increasingly displaced and worked against the contents and the
consequences of the Christian (and not only Christian) model of what
we are as humans, which perceives a soul within man, created by God,
which must be stewarded with due care. This 'spiritualist' model (which
recognises the centrality of the spiritual element in man), by stressing
the vital importance of love for love and love for truth, if followed
establishes the basis for authentic community at all levels. The materialist matrix, on the other hand, works against such community, in
particular through the promotion of a lifestyle of selfish individualism.
But such an outcome should not surprise us. As the French philosopher
Jacques Maritain (1882-1973) observed:

> Materialistic conceptions of the world and life, philosophies which
> do not recognise the spiritual and eternal element in man, cannot
> escape error in their efforts to construct a truly human society
> because they cannot satisfy the requirements of the person, and, by
> that very fact, they cannot grasp the nature of society.[3]

This volume examines this materialist matrix and its presence in
contemporary British society (a by no means easy undertaking), and
explores in detail the ways it acts to bring about a loss of ties. This work

thus stresses with great emphasis that spirituality has its social aspects; what a man does to his soul has consequences for other people. In following the historical rise of this materialist matrix the analysis also examines at length the impact of mass society and the consequences of deChristianisation – a vital subject which deserves far more attention than it has received. Indeed, this book suggests that there is a close connection between secularisation and desocialisation and that in studying the loss of ties we are focusing, in part, on one of the primary consequences of the decline of Christian culture – one of the great developments of recent British history.

Although this book is an analysis, it is also a warning. What is being studied in Great Britain (which is held up as a case study, a veritable laboratory, of post-modern developments) in this volume is part of a far wider movement. What one eminent academic body has described as 'a crisis in human ecology, a deterioration of the social environment evidenced by a widespread breakdown of social norms',[4] is not a feature of Great Britain alone in the Western hemisphere. Indeed, there is growing evidence that the phenomenon of desocialisation is increasingly afflicting the countries of the Western world and in this sense studying what has taken place in Great Britain – which seems well advanced down this road and has often been a vanguard nation in terms of modern developments – could well mean studying in one way or another the future of Western man.

Other societies of the world are also threatened by the drive towards non-belonging and disaffection. The countries of Central and Eastern Europe, for example, after the fall of Communism, now find themselves much more exposed to the influence of Western (and British) culture, and will have to think very seriously about what this influence will mean, especially if they want to defend themselves against those of its aspects that are pernicious.[5] In addition, of course, there is the whole question of what Westernisation, not least through globalisation, will mean for the countries of the so-called third and fourth worlds. The Western world, obviously enough, has many positive aspects, but at the same time the ideas and attitudes which lie behind desocialisation in our hemisphere (and especially the notion that man does not have a soul or that truth is relative) now seem to be being spread far and wide by the many potent mechanisms of Western influence. Economic ascendancy (expressed, for example, through the mighty multinationals) and technological advance; the world of the United Nations and similar international bodies (e.g. the IMF, the World Bank); the impact of Hollywood and the realm of learning and thought – such are some of the instruments of a continuing Westernisation of the globe. By such paths the integrity of the cultural patrimony of many a people of the earth is now threatened by the dangers of first-world neighbours who have drawn ever nearer with the creation of the global village, neighbours who bring with them societies which are increasingly characterised, in reality, by an absence of 'neighbours'.

In addition, this volume is an invitation not only to recognise and understand the phenomenon of desocialisation, it is also an invitation to try to look into the future and to foresee where it will lead. Clearly, we are not dealing with a static process that will run down predictable tramlines and we should be prepared to speculate on what the future might bring. Some questions now appear ineluctable. For example, will practices in the bioethical sphere and the creation of humans outside the natural processes lead us to cross a fateful threshold in human identity and eliminate traditional kindred ties? Will the triumph of the ideology of the free market lead to a breakdown of the social state and its core principle of people's responsibility for the welfare of their fellow citizens through social transfers by means of taxation? Will the imposition of 'political correctness' in the key power points of cultural formation bring about widespread censorship and the elimination of alternative viewpoints that work for true community? Will the creation of a European super-State engender processes of engineered cultural homogenisation in order to create greater political unity that will, in fact, lead to the 'deculturalisation' of the European peoples? Will the processes of globalisation lead to the construction of a gigantic and universal mass society that will spread anonymity everywhere? And lastly, given that culture has a major impact on the individual, will deeply desocialised cultures, which are characterised by their capacity to inhibit the development of the human in people, create a kind of 'new man', a sort of 'cultural mutant', who is increasingly unable to grasp what it is to be truly human and truly social – and also to become such? Overall, as we look into what the post-Christian era will bring, are we peering into a kind of post-social future? All these questions, and many others, naturally pose themselves as we survey desocialisation – a process that appears to be undergoing rapid acceleration.

So first of all, this book is an attempt to contribute to the shaping of understanding, orientations and priorities. Its perspective focuses on our cultural crisis and the drive towards desocialisation, and it argues that this is the single most important challenge that now faces post-modern man. For this reason, it is a call for the establishment of a new national (and not only national) agenda. At the same time, by providing an analysis of what has happened, this volume contributes to a growing (although not yet sufficiently widespread) debate in Great Britain and other parts of the West, engaged in by thinkers of a wide spectrum of intellectual and ideological perspectives (e.g. Bauman, Etzioni, Fukuyama, Houellebecq, Putnam, Touraine), about what increasingly appears to have all the characteristics of an epoch-making development. At a more specific level, because of its orientations, it seeks to contribute to the debate in Christian circles about how Christianity should understand and react to post-modernity, and does this within the context of the projected 'new evangelisation' of the Catholic Church.[6]

Necessarily, this book also seeks to invite the exponents and followers of the dominant currents of thought of post-modernity to reflect on the validity of their approaches in the light of the negative developments that this volume describes in detail. Given that a broad range of statistics (many of which are cited in this volume) now clearly demonstrate the phenomena of cultural breakdown, does it not behove such figures to ask themselves whether their ideas and beliefs really function? In related fashion, should not British society more generally take a step back and ask whether it has not gone down wrong roads in recent times, and thereby question the validity of those roads?

However, the principal aim of this work is to propose a solution. Few dispassionate observers would now deny that contemporary British man is often a creature who suffers, afflicted by a constellation of symptoms that derive from the frustration, deprivation and pain of a lack of ties and belonging, and that this is a situation which is getting worse. What Michel Houellebecq writes about the France of the chief protagonist of one of his novels certainly has relevance to contemporary Britain:

> the men of his generation lived out their lonely, bitter lives. Feelings such as love, tenderness and human fellowship had, for the most part, disappeared; the relationships between his contemporaries were at best indifferent and more often cruel.[7]

Faced with such an absence of fulfilment, unhappiness and distress we are called upon to engage in a project of healing. This book is above all else a small contribution to that undertaking.

In proffering a perspective, an analysis and a response this work seeks to fulfil another purpose. Social decay also carries within it the very dangerous propensity to eliminate elements – feelings, sensibilities and forms of behaviour – from people's experience which, when lost, no longer provide evidence of alternative ways of being and living that could serve as signposts forward by which to escape malaise and error. This volume, not least because of its historical perspective, seeks to correct that tendency by stressing that it is clearly possible to live in ways that are not desocialised and permeated by selfish individualism. What it proposes is that in addressing the way we are now it is essential to bear in mind that in defining realities with reference to what is not present, we must also have an idea of what could be present.

The above paragraphs describe what this book is, but it is also necessary to describe what this book is not. Because this book goes against the tide, pronounces strong judgements and deals with sensitive areas, it can be easily misunderstood or misrepresented. First of all, this is not a condemnation of post-modern culture *tout court*. To adjust a famous Shakespearean phrase, there is something rotten in the state of Great Britain – but not everything. Thus, for example, although this book explores the negative consequences that derive from some phenomena, it does not declare that these phenomena are without positive aspects. For example, modern science has generated enormous benefits for humanity; one need, for example, only refer to the great advances in combating illness. Equally, market structures, and this is especially evident after the fall of the state control of the economy in the countries, for example, of Communist Eastern Europe, can do much to develop human potential. The state can intervene to very beneficial effect, as the popularity of the principle of a national health service in contemporary Britain well testifies. In addition, the development of the modern secular theory of human rights has done a great deal to create a system of international law and rights designed to combat dictatorship and tyranny. What this book necessarily suggests, however, is that with advancing desocialisation there is an increasing risk that the possible negative consequences of these phenomena, and others like them, will no longer be checked by dehumanised societies that do not perceive and respect man for what he is.

Equally, this volume does not declare that the whole of British society has sunk into alienation and anonymity. Although there has been a breakdown in community, many components of community still remain. Not all people adhere to models of man that are dehumanising; not all subscribe to selfish individualism; not all are desocialised. Indeed, significant sections of the population view others in human terms, are animated by good will and have a whole series of ties through their families, friends, neighbours, work colleagues, the associations they belong to and the realities of civic and public participation. I also believe that the kind of developments I am describing in this book are less present in some areas of the United Kingdom than others: Scotland, Wales, Northern England, Northern Ireland and the rural areas, for example. Yet this volume does suggest that we are still in a period of transition and that these positive features appear to be threatened. For this reason it concentrates on the dynamics of desocialisation, on specific trends that are growing in importance. As a result, it does not concentrate on those parts of post-modern British society that are healthy. But there again, when a physician examines a sick patient it is the illness and its effects that command his attention; he has a natural eye for the morbose.

In addition, this book should not be seen as belonging to that well-known lineage that looks back to an imaginary golden age when everything was positive. Although this work may refer, for example, to the strong religiosity of our Victorian forefathers, to the strength of the institution of the family before the Great War, to low levels of crime during the 1930s or to high levels of electoral turnout in the decades following the Second World War, this does not mean to say that I am proposing that much was not wrong in the past or that many of the changes that have been brought about have not been constructive. At the same time, however, it would be equally mistaken to assert, as many do – and often from a relativistic perspective – that decline or decay do not take place in the history of peoples. What is required is a clear assessment based on reason and evidence of those features of a society that display health and those that do not. This volume concentrates on the latter category of features of contemporary British society, but this does not mean to say that it denies the presence of the former.

In related fashion, despite its focus, this work is not an exercise in pessimism. It is certainly true that these pages highlight negative developments and focus on dark aspects of the human experience. But this does not mean that the author belongs to that category of observers who declare that nothing can be done, that we should throw in the towel and retreat into fatalistic resignation: this is not the manifesto of a latter-day *secessus*. In truth, there are two chief reasons for thinking that the processes in this book can be reversed by the *human* hand. Firstly, much remains that is positive within British society and these aspects can be drawn upon, built upon and developed – the healthy parts of the organism can be employed to counter those parts afflicted by malaise. Secondly, man is born with potential for good within him. Indeed, those of faith not only see this reality as part of a wider design but also as a source of objective grounds for hope. By proposing a return to the soul and its stewardship, this volume requests an activation of this potential. This dual source of optimism may prove appealing to the increasing number of people who recoil from what post-modernity imposes.

Furthermore, this volume does not seek to give an exhaustive account of the causes of desocialisation in Great Britain. It readily recognises that the movement towards the loss of ties is also rooted in causal factors that lie outside the impact of the materialist matrix. Many of these factors have been, or are being, analysed by other authors, although perhaps not with the intensity that they merit. What this book proposes is that the false anthropologies of post-modernity are the central culprits, and that without an analysis of them a solution to our cultural crisis is not possible. Given the empirical obstacles now existing in the way of proving this thesis, and for other reasons as well, this volume should to a certain extent also be seen as a hypothesis and be read in that sense.

At the same time, although this work is a critique of post-modern culture written from a Christian perspective, it does not exclude the value of perspectives that do not specifically share its doctrinal bases. It recognises that often the same truths thread through different religions and outlooks, albeit expressed in different languages and concepts. Indeed, this volume invites those who have, for example, visions of the world that perceive the transcendent, the presence of an immaterial spirit within individuals, the link between spirituality and community, the existence of objective ethics and morality, or the importance of creating a culture that encourages the positive potential within man, to consider how far their own visions of the world, when applied to post-modern society, can produce a similar critique to that offered in this book. This could lay a shared basis for dialogue and discussion with the perspective it employs with a view to addressing daunting problems that are perceived in common. Indeed, the recognition of the presence of these shared truths, and the fact that they can be arrived at through rational paths of inquiry as well, also means that this work, although it presents the doctrines that form the basis for this critique with reference to Revelation,[8] has implicit in its pages the assumption that 'Faith and reason are like two wings on which the human spirit rises to the contemplation of truth'.[9]

Some words are also required on what kind of a book this is in terms of *genre*. It is clearly not an academic monograph or the outcome of detailed empirical research (hence, in part, the attempt to keep the footnotes down to a minimum); if anything it is an essay that presents a thesis and propounds a critique. Its purpose, therefore, is to offer a general argument, to contribute to debate, to sketch a programme. And because it crosses so many fields of study (for example, theology, sociology, politics, economics, anthropology), it necessarily runs the risk of over simplification or neglect of areas that require more detailed analysis. But the author hopes that this inherent weakness is obviated by the fact that the aim of the book is to provide an overall view of a distinct trend and that he has managed to furnish a picture of the overall topography even though many parts of the landscape have not been sufficiently mapped in detail. To put the point another way, this book is much more of an impressionist painting than a product of the school of Tintoretto. Lastly, for this reason as well, this volume is most emphatically not some definitive statement. If anything it is a first attempt, a probe, a work of exploration that invites comment and criticism, a hypothesis. Knowledge is a progressive debate that becomes revised with new discoveries and understandings: the author, therefore, would be very grateful for any correction of fact or interpretation.

To provide this, however, the reader must first read the book. The first chapter explores the general contours of the loss of ties in contemporary British society. The second sets out doctrines by which the materialist matrix and its consequences can be understood and judged. The third provides a taxonomy of the false anthropologies of post-modernity and comments on their features. The fourth explains how they are necessarily desocialising in impact at a direct and personal level. The fifth rounds off the survey of the materialist matrix by concentrating on relativism – an anthropology with special characteristics – and its acidic effects. The sixth argues that the rise of this materialist matrix has been favoured by the advance of deChristianisation in contemporary Britain. The seventh surveys mass society and stresses that it, too, works to generate alienation. The eighth explores how the materialist matrix and contemporary mass society interact at a number of specific levels to promote a loss of ties on a wider canvas. The ninth explores how desocialised culture, although it generates unhappiness, is endowed with potent mechanisms of self-reproduction. The tenth emphasises that a broad range of voices have predicted or observed the arrival of desocialisation both in Great Britain and the West, a development that leads credence to one of the central theses of this volume. The conclusion, invoking Christian renewal, argues that in order to escape our present predicament we must return to a complete model of man and engage in a regeneration of the human spirit.

Chapter One

Our Cultural Crisis

In the past, disorientated Aborigine tribes or Polynesian islanders have presented a sorry picture of what happens when peoples are no longer able to sustain community. The traditional mechanisms of integration and cohesion break down; individuals become detached from each other, deprived of a common project, lost in a disengaged state, unsure as to how to act towards others and disturbed in their identity. Generations are no longer able to hand down those learned methods and practices by which a culture holds a people together. A society becomes drained of its tradition and emptied of its inheritance, and individuals increasingly cease to belong.

Cultural breakdown takes a whole host of forms but the familiar contours can be gleaned from the many studies of the devastating impact of Western life on indigenous peoples over the last few centuries. Daisy Bates (1863-1951), the heroic and humanitarian champion of the Australian aborigines, wrote how:

> On their own country they were trespassers. There was no more happy wandering in the interchange of hospitality. Sources of food supply slowly but surely disappeared, and they were sent away to unfamiliar places, compelled to change their mode of life, to clothe themselves in the attire of strangers, to eat foods unfitted for them, to live within walls.
>
> Their age-old laws were laid aside for the laws they could not understand. The young generation, always wilful, now openly

flouted the old, and defied them, and haunted the white man's homes, protected by his policemen. A little while and they resorted to thieving – where theft had been unknown – and sycophancy, and they sold their young wives to the depraved and foreign element. Half-castes came among them, a being neither black nor white, whom they detested. They died in their numbers of the white man's diseases, measles, whooping-cough, influenza and the results of their own wrong-doing.[1]

The French painter Paul Gauguin (1848-1903) described similar horrors in Tahiti. In his paintings the islanders are portrayed in a listless state where all hope has vanished. He recorded in his journals:

The natives, having nothing, nothing at all to do, think of one thing only, drinking...Many things that are strange and picturesque existed here once, but there are no traces of them left today; everything has vanished. Day by day the race vanishes, decimated by the European diseases...There is so much prostitution that it does not exist...one only knows a thing by its contrary, and its contrary does not exist.[2]

Similar things are happening to us in Great Britain today. But in proposing that we are undergoing a cultural crisis, and in analysing its causes and symptoms, this work does not suppose that our culture is uniform and homogenous – we have before us a complex and variegated reality. Many people, for example, do not in the least subscribe to the materialist matrix; many others live happy and fulfilled social lives. There is no single machine producing identical outcomes, even though there are major forces working for a shared cultural experience and across the differences there is much common ground: the institutions of mass society – an increasingly uniform language, the mass media, and recreational activities, for example – are some elements behind this outcome; such realities as shared systems of law, administration, and government are others. Yet what this book proposes is that there is an increasingly influential pattern (favoured by these major forces) within our cultural system based upon a distinctive matrix of ways of seeing man, society and the human experience, which acts to desocialise people. This, of course, does not rule out – and the point cannot be stressed too forcefully – the presence of other patterns. However, it seems likely that in studying this pattern and its effects we are examining the 'dominant culture',[3] to employ the phrase of Paul Poupard, of post-modern British society – or at least the culture that is becoming preponderant.

This matrix of desocialising anthropologies increasingly encourages a loss of ties which takes three interacting forms: personal loneliness, relationships lacking in authentic contents, and a general weakening of the institutions and mechanisms of community. In such a context it is hardly surprising that many people feel out on their own. In 1993, for example, the Department of Health conducted a survey in England into whether people believed they were receiving 'social support': 48% of men and 39% of women replied that they experienced either a moderate lack or a severe lack.[4]

The Tangibles

Since the 1960s there has been a marked intensification of phenomena connected with these three forms and in this chapter a general overview is offered. Their increasing presence at the same time, the very speed of their advance and the fact that they revolve around the loss of ties indicate that we are dealing with a single development. When we survey such phenomena of our post-modern period we encounter elements which point to a single conclusion – we are face-to-face with an authentic cultural breakdown. In their own way, albeit with the special features of their condition and the continuing presence of positive aspects, the British have become disorientated Aborigine tribes or Polynesian islanders. By adopting this perspective we can also place a number of disparate elements in their rightful context and understand that they are the interconnected symptoms of a wider malaise. Indeed, we can achieve a more penetrating reading of a variety of phenomena which are often not linked together at all. Thus it becomes possible to see such apparently distant elements as the suffering of children, the fall in membership of trade unions, the growth of minor political parties or the rise in violence as part of a distinct cultural development. Indeed, the thesis of 'desocialisation' proves an incisive key for the interpretation of a broad swathe of realities. One may think of how people increasingly die alone in hospitals or similar institutions rather than at home surrounded by those nearest to them, with a concomitant distancing of death from social horizons. Or of how meals seem to be increasingly taken alone rather than in company, with a concomitant removal of eating from the social context. Or of how literature and cinema are increasingly concerned with the realities of the loss of ties, with a concomitant emergence of a distinct lineage within these two art forms. Equally, a long-term historical perspective enables us to achieve a similar understanding of what is happening now with reference to processes which have been working themselves out within British civilisation for centuries.

  This crisis has both tangible and intangible aspects, and the first lend themselves more easily to empirical description. The family is the basic unit of society, the place where affections are learnt, love expressed, relationships ensured, tradition imparted and social cohesion promoted. The success of the family is essential to the success of community. Yet over the last forty years the family has entered into very troubled waters. Commenting on the family in a wider context, John Paul II referred to how 'this fundamental institution is experiencing a radical and widespread crisis'.[5] In Great Britain divorce rates have risen greatly; the percentage of adults who marry has declined; the number of single mothers has boomed; and the proportion of children born outside marriage has grown enormously. Increasing homosexuality and bisexuality challenge this institution from another angle. In addition, wider kinship patterns beyond the 'nuclear' family have been weakened and constitute another expression of malaise.[6]

  Such developments suggest an increasing inability of people to live together and the presence of a spreading rift between men and women. They also point to the absence or disruption of intimate relationships at a key point of potential social interaction. It is a striking statistical fact that in Great Britain the number of households composed of only one person rose from 14% in 1961 to 22% in 1981[7] to 29% in 2006,[8] and it is estimated that in England and Wales by 2016 '36 per cent of all households will consist of a single person', largely 'due to an increase in the number of men aged under 65 who live alone'.[9] 'It seems the UK is becoming a nation of loners', declared A. Leve in an article for *The Sunday Times Magazine* in September 2007: 'In 2004 there were 7m people living alone in Britain – nearly four times as many as in 1961'.[10] Here we are dealing with a glaring reality of desocialisation which is intimately linked to the travails of the family. It comes as no surprise that in November 1999 a leading national newspaper, in an article entitled 'Lonely Britons', reported that 'four out of ten British adults are single, and more than half of them are looking for a partner'.[11]

  Entering into this world of loneliness one often encounters major suffering (often of a hidden kind) and destinies that can at times only be described as horror. The following comes from a newspaper article written by Jan Masters published in August 2006:

> Feeling lonely? You're not alone. With seven million people living on their own, Britain is turning into a nation of loners – and it's making us ill…I remember a particular visit to my GP some years ago, when I'd been living on my own for quite a while. The ailment was minor: a twisted ankle. But as the doctor crouched down, asking me all relevant medical questions, he gently cradled my foot in his hand and without warning (and as much to my surprise as to his) I burst into tears. It was the concerned touch that did it, the uncomplicated physical connection. And in that moment I realised that no matter how many friends were at the end of a phone, how many stellar events studded my diary, however much I knew it was better to live solo than in a sour relationship (something I still wholeheartedly believe) and however well I was coping (which was pretty damn well, as it happened), it was possible to feel lonely. And never admit it to others. Not even to oneself.[12]

To take a more extreme example, the above-cited article from *The Sunday Times Magazine* centred around the fate of one Andrew Smith, 'one of thousands of people who die alone and unmourned in the UK every year':

> When Andrew Smith died, nobody noticed. His flat, No 171, was at the end of the row on the second floor. His body was discovered when a neighbour, someone he had never talked to, smelt something off and phoned the police. Andrew Smith had been dead for two months…There were no details on record of next of kin, and nothing in his flat to identify family or friends…he had nobody.[13]

The rise of crime – and especially of violent crime – is another symptom of our present predicament, and here, too, horror is more than present. The European Crime and Safety Survey, the work of the United Nations, the European Commission and the Gallup polling organisation, found in 2007 that Britain had 'one of the worst crime rates' in the European Union, and the highest level of assaults and burglaries.[14] Crime rates and violent crime have risen notably during the post-modern period, and attest to deep assaults on relationships and fracture between people. There was roughly one offence for every 100 persons in England and Wales in 1951, four in 1971 and ten by 1994,[15] and recorded crime doubled between 1979 and 1992.[16] Notwithstanding a subsequent sizeable decrease, the number of crimes committed every year remains high from a twentieth-century perspective.[17] In 2007 the British Crime Survey reported that the risk of becoming a victim of crime in England and Wales was 24 per cent.[18] In this context, it is not surprising that the prison population of England and Wales was at an all-time high at the beginning of the new millennium.[19]

Violent crime has been a particular feature of post-modernity; its symbol, the ever-increasing presence of the knife.[20] Violent crimes increased almost twofold every decade from the 1960s to the early 1990s. For example, in 1981 there were 100,000 acts of violence against the person in England and Wales – ten years later there were 220,000.[21] Violence at the workplace rose by 100% between 1981 and 1991.[22] Such realities mean that those working with the public run great risks. In London at the end of the previous century one could come across a sign which read: 'Our Staff are Entitled to Carry Out their Duties Without Fear of Attack'. Affirming that there had been a diminution of violent crime since the peak in the mid-1990s, the British Crime Survey (BCS) nonetheless estimated that by 2005/6 there were as many as 2.4 million violent incidents every year against adults in England and Wales.[23] There is much to indicate, however, that this is an underestimate. Research by two criminologists, Graham Farrell and Ken Pease, suggests that 'because of the way the BCS counts (or rather fails to count) crimes where the same person is repeatedly the victim of violent crime, the number of violent crimes committed against the over-16s is likely to be 80 per cent higher than that recorded by the BCS'.[24] In October 2008, indeed, the Home Office conceded that it been significantly underestimating serious violent crime for a decade.[25] Violence is felt in many areas and contexts, from the workplace to the television programme and from the football stadium to the family. Indeed, research indicates that one woman in every four will be subjected to violence within the walls of the home during her lifetime,[26] and according to a BCS study carried out a few years into the new millennium there were a million victims each year of domestic abuse, with 15.4 million incidents involving threats or force happening each year in England and Wales.[27] And like crime, violence renders society ever less a shared home and ever more a place of danger, menace and horror. Indeed, who can but be horrified in the face of such terrible events as the shooting of the eleven-year-old Rhys Jones in Liverpool?

The rise of anti-social behaviour has formed a part of this distressing picture and has itself become the object of statistical inquiry. The Crime and Disorder Act of 1998 defined anti-social behaviour as 'acting in a manner that caused or was likely to cause harassment, alarm or distress to one or more persons not of the same household (as the defendant)'.[28] Between 1992 and 2005/6 the proportion of respondents in England and Wales saying that forms of anti-social behaviour such as noisy neighbours or loud parties, people being drunk or rowdy in public places, people using or dealing in drugs, teenagers hanging around the streets, or vandalism, graffiti and other deliberate damage to property, were a very or fairly big problem increased significantly.[29] It is an instructive fact that in 2005/6, 17% of those questioned asserted that they perceived a high level of anti-social behaviour in their local area.[30] 'The U.K. has the worst problem with anti-social behaviour in Europe, fuelled by alcohol and a lack of discipline in homes and schools', a study by the Jill Dando Institute of Crime Science of University College, London, was reported as observing in 2006. This survey of 7,000 people in EU countries found that '76 per cent thought Britain had more of a problem with anti-social behaviour than any other country in the region, and 83 per cent of Britons thought the problem was growing'.[31]

The changes in this whole field (as the above-mentioned statistics indicate) have indeed been dramatic. In his book *Exploring English Character* (1955), the anthropologist G. Gorer gave the following picture of the way things used to be:

> In public life today the English are certainly among the most peaceful, gentle, courteous and orderly populations that the civilised world has ever seen...the control of aggression has gone to such remarkable lengths that you hardly ever see a fight in a bar (a not uncommon spectacle in most of the rest of Europe or the USA), football crowds are as orderly as church meetings.[32]

And a decade earlier George Orwell (1903-1950) had referred to the 'gentle-mannered, undemonstrative, law-abiding English':[33]

> An imaginary foreign observer would certainly be struck by our gentleness; by the orderly behaviour of English crowds, the lack of pushing and quarrelling, the willingness to form queues...And except for certain well-defined areas in half-a-dozen big towns, there is very little crime or violence.[34]

It should be stressed that violence and crime are factors which make people retreat into their own private worlds and are intimately connected to other configurations of our disrupted way of life, as R. Weatherill observes in *Cultural Collapse* (1994):

> The private security business has been a growth industry in recent years. The number of those employed by security firms in Britain

now actually exceeds the total size of the police force...Feelings of helplessness are induced by rising crime statistics, and we are inclined to lock ourselves into our homes, workplaces and offices with security devices, alarm systems, vicious dogs and the like. This is the culture of retrenchment: each against the other. With the loss of historical community and the collapse of the public domain, we limit our horizons to consideration of our own and our children's survival. We protect ourselves and watch out for the other. Our personal and professional relationships are especially affected. Whereas formerly we emphasised obligations, now we emphasise 'rights'. Our social relations have become increasingly legalistic. We can no longer rely on the goodwill of the other.[35]

Political institutions, for their part, were for long an essential and valued feature of British national identity. They were shared points of reference which underpinned membership of the community and secured bonds at a collective level. It should not surprise us that the positive phrase 'our national institutions' was for so long on the lips of politicians. The development of democracy was a special element in securing social cohesion and was living proof of participation in a shared project of being a nation. In the 1940s Orwell observed that 'democracy' was the only abstract political term which was widely used and well-understood and reported that 'the English do feel that they live in a democratic country'.[36] The contrasting travails of authoritarian or totalitarian Europe acted to reinforce this keenly-felt aspect of the national participatory polity.

Such institutions were the natural outcome of the organic growth of the nineteenth century when major reforms secured change in harmony with inherited practices and customs. The advance of democracy at both national and local levels, for example, took place within a framework of tradition and, being rooted in the bedrock of national culture, was thus built on very solid foundations. Foreigners were often impressed by the success of political institutions of British society and our systems of government and politics frequently served as models for foreign imitators. In the late 1950s two American scholars conducted an inquiry into the 'civic cultures' of Great Britain, America, Germany, Italy and Mexico. Almond and Verba had very high praise for what the British had achieved and through the jargon expressed this admiration in almost lyrical terms:

The political culture in Great Britain also approximates the civic culture. The participant role is highly developed. Exposure to politics, interest, involvement, and a sense of competence are relatively high. There are norms supporting political activity, as well as emotional involvement in elections and system affect. And the attachment to the system is a balanced one: there is general system pride as well as satisfaction with specific governmental performance...the political culture is permeated by more general attitudes of social trust and confidence...the British have maintained a strong deference to the independent authority of government. Thus the British political culture, like the American, approximates the balanced civic culture.[37]

But as in the cases of the family and crime, here, too, there has been very rapid change.

Recent decades have witnessed rising levels of popular disenchantment with political institutions and politicians. This is a phenomenon to be found throughout the West and is a part of the general crisis of authority. A widening fracture has grown up between the governed and their governors; alienation between individuals has been matched by alienation from institutions. This is exemplified in Great Britain by changing attitudes towards politicians, the political parties, local government and the Union. We are dealing here in very tangible form with fault lines and fissures which have grown up within a national polity that was once the envy of the Western world and exported its models for imitation far and wide. Detailed statistics illuminate the picture.

In April 1995 a survey found that more than a half of British people believed that the honesty and ethical standards of MPs were 'low' or 'very low'. Ten years earlier that figure had been only a third.[38] In 1973, 49% of those questioned in a survey said that the British system of government could be improved 'quite a lot' or a 'great deal' – by 1994 that figure had shot up to 69%.[39] In 1974, 57% of those questioned in an opinion poll said that the government put the needs of the nation above the interests of party 'only some of the time' or 'almost never' – by 1994 that figure had risen to 73%.[40] In 1993 an ICM poll found that 43% of those interviewed believed that none of the three major parties were 'trustworthy'; 40% thought none of them were 'sincere'; 31% believed them to be not in 'touch with ordinary people'; and the same percentage thought none of them were 'fair with people'. A very high 77% dissented from the proposition that the government of the day told the truth. To complete the melancholy picture, 59% said politicians were the least trustworthy of the professions – close to car salesmen in the rankings.[41] In addition, whereas in 1974 39% of those polled declared that they trusted the government almost always or most of the time, in 2000 only 16% answered in the same way.[42] In 2007 a Communicate Research poll showed that fewer than one in five (18%) of those interviewed thought the Labour Party could be trusted to keep its promises, compared to 26% for the Conservatives; 59% said they saw Labour as 'sleazy', compared to 47% for the Conservatives.[43]

In a further sign of popular disaffection the two major political parties have witnessed a substantial erosion of electoral support over the past three decades. People seem less willing to trust themselves to bodies which once exercised a near hegemony at the polls and could count on deeply-rooted loyalty, participation and support. In 1970 the Conservative and Labour Parties polled 89.5% of the total UK vote; by 1983 that figure was down to 70% and at the general election of 2005 it hit a low of 67.6%.[44] In addition, turnout at general elections has fallen in a dramatic fashion, a further sign of popular disaffection and of fracture between the governed and their governors: from 1945 to 1997 the number of voters going to the polls at general elections always exceeded, and often by a great deal, 70%; in 2001 and 2005 it was down to 59.4% and 61.2% respectively.[45]

Concurrently, there has been an increasing disillusionment with local government – a vital focus point of civic identity and participation during the Victorian period. In 1965, 77% of people interviewed agreed with the statement that the 'way people vote in local elections is the main thing that decides how things are run in this area' – by 1994 that figure had fallen to 54%.[46] Town hall polls in England in 1994 secured a 42% turnout; by 1996 that figure had fallen to 37%, and in December 1997 a national newspaper reported that two-thirds of voters stayed at home and did not take part in local elections.[47] Worse was to come: the local election turnout in May 1999 was 29% – 'the lowest-ever figure recorded for any election in living memory'.[48] The figure in England for the local elections of May 2003 was only 34% and in London, a major electoral basin, turnout hit a modern record low.[49] And all this in a country where democratisation had been firmly built upon local government energy and participation. In this general context it comes as no surprise that *The World in 2007*, published by *The Economist*, referred to 'a shocking decline in political participation'[50] in the United Kingdom.

The rise of the Scottish and Welsh nationalist parties since the 1960s completes this picture of disenchantment. There has been a mounting rejection of the inherited national community and the political processes by which it is governed – the traditional polity has lost many a regional adherent. An opinion poll in late 1999 revealed that 72% of Scots and 81% of the Welsh identified with their own nations compared with 'only 18 per cent in Scotland and 27 per cent in Wales who identified with Britain'.[51] In 2006 an ICM opinion poll found that 52% of Scots and 59% of English voters wanted Scottish independence and 48% of English voters also wanted independence from Wales and Northern Ireland.[52]

The crisis of political institutions seems to have been accompanied by a hollowing of 'civil society'. Indeed, the phrase 'civil society' may have begun to be used in Britain in the 1990s in part because this reality had encountered serious difficulties. The British appear to have increasingly withdrawn from organisations and associations, based upon social interaction and active participation, situated between the state and the family. Membership of political parties has experienced a notable fall: in 1975, for example, the Conservative and Labour Parties had together about 1.7 million members; by 1997 that figure had fallen to about 650,000.[53] The trade unions, which were always much more than economic interest groups and offered a broad gamut of activities that ranged from the political to the recreational, fell from 13 million members in 1980 to 10 million in 1990 and to fewer than 7 million in 1997.[54] Other organisations have also witnessed a decrease in their membership: the number of the members of the Mother's Unions and Women's Institutes, which was nearly 800,000 in the early 1970s, was reduced to about half of that figure by the mid-1990s, and the membership of similar associations such as friendly societies, the Red Cross, the Royal British Legion, the Hospital Friends' Leagues and various kinds of youth organisations all followed a downward path from 1980 onwards.[55]

A detailed study of the phenomenon of civil society concludes that although participation in organisations dedicated, for example, to the defence of the environment, has increased over recent decades, participation in organisations of a more traditional and social nature has declined: 'Associations that involve people in the kind of face-to-face interaction thought to build social capital may have been replaced by others that involve little such interaction'.[56] Overall, therefore, there seems to have been a desocialisation of civil society in line with more general developments within post-modern society: 'These figures lend credence to concerns that the overall character of civic engagement in Britain may have shifted away from organisations dedicated to the public interest in favour of those that serve more narrow individual purpose'.[57]

The Intangibles

So much for the more tangible features of our crisis. At a more intangible level one perceives a society increasingly coming apart at the seams because of the advance of a lifestyle of 'selfish individualism'. The trend appears for life to be ever more a process of seeking personal gain in various forms which centres around a massive emphasis on material wealth, social prestige, the acquisition of power and the pursuit of pleasure. Interaction between people becomes increasingly motivated by egotism and self-interest increasingly pervades points of contact. In an opinion poll of 1984 about 40% of those questioned thought that their own neighbourhood was one in which people 'go their own way', a figure equal to those who thought that people 'helped each other'; in 2000 36% thought that people 'helped each other' and 49% thought that people 'go their own way'.[58]

Society is thus moving down the road (although only a part of that journey has been travelled so far) of becoming an aggregation of separated individuals where dominant rules come to be informed by the idea that people are to follow their own personal gain. In this way of living, people tend to act in competition with each other, use each other, and in a way which involves treating their fellows as objects. There is thus encouraged a process of friction, hostility and aggression at points of contact between members of society, and the vision that people have of each other tends to become based upon opposition and conflict. In this context, ever more individuals become locked up in their own defensive bastions, much moved by fear and suspicion of others, and deprived of vast areas of potential authentic interaction. It should not, therefore, surprise us that distrust has become an increasingly marked feature of social life. In 1959, 56% of adults agreed that 'most people can be trusted'; by 2000 this figure had fallen to 45%.[59]

There increasingly emerges not so much the practice of responsibility and concern but the realities of neglect and indifference. In such circumstances the idea that society is a shared task designed to work to the benefit of all and to express and promote 'spiritual health'[60] declines in importance. Individual projects come to replace a common project. By all these paths fractures grow up between people and loneliness in its various forms extends its grip. External observers of our way of life often comment on such increasingly present realities. Ashis Nandy is one of them:

> Many non-Western observers of the culture of the modern West – its lifestyle, literature, arts and its human sciences – have been struck by the way contracted competitive individualism – and the utter loneliness that flows from it – dominates Western mass society... what once looked like independence from one's immediate authorities in the family, and a defiance of the larger aggregates they represented, now looks more and more like a Hobbesian worldview gone rabid.[61]

Desocialised man is also deculturalised man. This is a primary reason why we have been witnessing 'traditions in turmoil',[62] to employ the phrase of M.A. Glendon. With the decline of an effective context of community the cultural inheritance, with all its mechanisms by which to guarantee social cohesion, becomes weakened and dispersed. The morals, mores and manners of that cohesion – and the virtues and principles of life in community – experience a process of enfeeblement. In the face of such 'deculturalisation', of culture loss, individuals increasingly lack the agreed instruments by which to relate to each other. As things have turned out, this deculturalised context tends more and more to fail to provide those essential inputs into the experience of those who come into contact with it which work to their well-being. This 'absent input' encourages a lack of growth and development, a failure to acquire certain truths in thought and behaviour, the absence of sound guidance, and high levels of depersonalisation. There is a tendency for people to become moulded in such a way that they no longer know how to live with each other; they lose their social dimension and become what by their natures they are not – non-social.

An 'anomic condition' thus emerges. Lack of support with all its myriad consequences, high levels of stress, feelings of insecurity, expressions of aggression, the presence of distrust, confusion over identity, the suffering of loneliness, a retreat into subjectivity, the adoption of a siege mentality, the pains of disorientation, mental malaise – such are the products of a cultural context which increasingly fails to provide man with what he needs. A disturbed culture is creating disturbed people. Man, both spiritually and biologically, was not made for such a process and it brings him no happiness. Many of the children of post-modernity are not happy children. In the economically highly-developed countries, Benedict XVI recently observed, at the origin of new forms of mental illness 'we may also find the negative impact of the crisis of moral values. This increases the feeling of loneliness, undermining and even breaking up traditional forms of social cohesion, starting with the family institution'.[63] Since 1994 in the United Kingdom the number of people 'consulting their GP for depressive disorders has more than doubled, from four million to nine million', it was reported in 1999, and given that 'only half of depressed people actually consult their GP, the real figure is probably even higher'.[64] Concurrently, the number of medical prescriptions for anti-depressants in England rose from nine million in 1991 to 24 million in 2001.[65] Once again the chronology says everything and we are reminded that decadence is often an accelerating process.

Perhaps the key dynamic of this whole development is an impulse towards nothingness. Atomisation and separation, distance and detachment, isolation and alienation, fracture and dislocation, impersonality and anonymity – these are the goals towards which desocialisation works. Here we have the prospect of an absence, a lack, an emptiness – we are face-to-face with the increasing diffusion of what is not present. What is loneliness, anyway, but not having certain necessary social inputs? The danger is that what should be there becomes removed and the individual has to face a context which begins with the starting point of deprivation. Yet the drive is not only towards the creation of nothingness outside man – the move is also towards the extension of its realm deep within him. When subject to this dynamic the individual becomes the subject of a process of emptying, of depletion, of impoverishment – within desocialised man a black hole is encouraged to expand. In addition, the consequences of deprivation are matched by the cancelling of what man is called to be; whole areas of potentiality of his inner self run the risk of being destroyed at their point of departure. As will be observed in this study, desocialised man thus faces a context whose trajectory is towards making him de-responsibilised, de-culturalised, de-identified, de-moralised, de-sexualised, de-aestheticised, and de-feelingised – to name only the more obvious. Faced with the extension of absence outside him and nothingness within him, the post-modern victim of the anomic condition increasingly comes to experience a world drained of light: the void abounds. But to understand why British society has gone down the wrong path it is necessary to establish what the right path should have been. To begin with, therefore, a statement of essential doctrines.

Chapter Two

Spirituality and Community

The official exposition of doctrine of the Catholic Church rightly affirms that man is called to community and that there is a direct link between spiritual well-being and the shared well-being of humans living together in society:

> The vocation of humanity is to show forth the image of God and to be transformed into the image of the Father's only Son. This vocation takes a personal form since each of us is called to enter into the divine beatitude; it also concerns the human community as a whole...
>
> All men are called to the same end: God himself. There is a certain resemblance between the union of the divine persons and the fraternity that men are to establish among themselves in truth and love. Love of neighbour is inseparable from love of God.
>
> The human person needs to live in society. Society is not for him an extraneous addition but a requirement of his nature. Through the exchange with others, mutual service and dialogue with his brethren, man develops his potential; he thus responds to his vocation.
>
> A *society* is a group of persons bound together organically by a principle of unity that goes beyond each one of them. As an assembly that is at once visible and spiritual, a society endures through time; it gathers up the past and prepares for the future. By means of society, each man is established as an 'heir' and receives certain 'talents' that enrich his identity and whose fruits he must develop.[1]

What, therefore, is the direct link between spirituality and community?

Christianity is not only a moral proposal, it is also a way of interpreting man, society and the cosmos. The analysis of this book is rooted in the axioms of the Christian world-view and the tenets of its teachings. Indeed, the critique that it presents – and the very concept of desocialisation itself – cannot be understood without a grasp of these axioms and tenets. Alexander Pope (1688-1744) wrote that 'the proper study of Mankind is Man'[2] and in his *Logic* (1800) Immanuel Kant (1724-1804) declared that the three great questions – what can I know? What ought I to do? What may I hope? – ultimately depend on the question: what is man?[3] At the core of this analysis, as at the centre of this critique, is a specific understanding of what we are as humans. In this humanistic age attention is constantly paid to these special inhabitants of the planet and so here, at least, it is possible to conform to the spirit of the times. This book thus argues that it is only by providing a satisfactory answer to the question 'what is man?', and by understanding his vocation, that we can really understand the nature of the predicament of post-modern society and produce a solution. Although reference is made to British people living at the beginning of the third millennium – with all the social, economic, political and cultural baggage that such a status implies – a much broader frame of reference is taken into consideration. Our crisis cannot be explained without an understanding of man – his origins, his nature, and his purpose – and without effective knowledge of the supernatural world.

Christian Spiritualism

The 'spiritualist' model of man adopted by this work is that of the Christian world-view. This perspective is more than familiar to Western man and can be summed up in a paragraph. God is the divine force of the universe, the supreme expression, source and promoter of truth and love; the devil in hell is the fallen angel, the father of all lies, and the enemy of love. Both of these supernatural polarities are connected with the human world and in especial fashion with its spiritual dimension. Man is not mere matter (whatever that may be), but has a non-material presence within him created by God – the soul.[4] The soul on earth is engaged in only one stage of its journey, an eternal voyage which after death involves an ultimate union with God or a descent into the abyss. The destiny of that soul depends upon the actions of its bearer during its terrestrial life – its fate hinges upon the nature of its earthly relationship to these supernatural polarities. The soul is non-material in character and is thus a reflection and expression of the good or evil of these polarities beyond us, to which by various routes and mechanisms it is sensitive and responsive. The soul of man thus constitutes that principal human point where the kingdoms of heaven and of hell, the kingdoms of God and of Satan, extend beyond their non-terrestrial boundaries. Jesus of Nazareth is the Son of God and his teachings not only throw light on the true nature of the cosmos and man but also provide essential lessons upon how the soul should be stewarded. The Gospels contain an exposition of the divine law necessary to the achievement of that spiritual health which both constructs the kingdom of heaven here on earth and leads to celestial life in eternal union with God above.

The Christian world-view thus has a spiritualist vision of *homo sapiens*. It believes that the most important thing about man is that he has a soul and asserts that this gift is the central reality of his existence – it is what distinguishes him from the other creatures. Human history has been powerfully shaped by the spiritualist understanding of what we are and this kind of vision of man has been constantly advanced by religious thought down the ages. It is probably safe to say that wherever there has been a system of religious belief in human culture there has also been the notion that man has a non-material content – a 'spirit' or a 'soul'. Today this conviction is the great binding belief which links the world's major religions and attitudes towards the existence of this entity mark one of the great points of fracture within contemporary Western thought. An obvious question naturally poses itself: if man throughout his history has repeatedly sensed this reality, might that fact not suggest that the soul is actually there? However, in the West and Great Britain today we are increasingly faced with a break with this past. The decline of religious thought has been accompanied by the rise of alternative visions of man which reject such a spiritualist perspective. In this secular age diminishing credence is given to the contention that humans have an immaterial spirit. At the end of the nineteenth century Friedrich Nietzsche (1844-1900) sensed the demise of religious belief and declared in a famous phrase: 'God is dead'.[5] Could we not proclaim in similar vein today: 'the soul has perished'?

At this point a linguistic observation should be made. The recognition of the soul within us has also been sabotaged during our epoch by changes in the meaning attributed to that term – an example of a more than familiar tactic. In the West in modern times there have been frequent attempts to undermine Christianity by altering the definition of God. During the seventeenth and eighteenth centuries the Deists (e.g. Collins, Herbert, Tindal, Toland) were engaged in exactly such an endeavour and in more recent times one often encounters the view that God is somehow a construct of the human mind, or a general 'life force', or the principle of order in the universe. Exactly the same process of linguistic redefinition has been at work in relation to the soul. Two rival concepts now seem to hold sway. On the one hand, there is the religious view that the soul is a non-material presence which animates individual human behaviour and continues after physical death. On the other, there is the secular approach which employs the term in a metaphorical sense to refer to the inner essence of man. This second definition is now widely employed by the intellectual classes in our hemisphere. 'Many educated people, especially in the Western world, also share the belief that the soul is a metaphor', observes one opponent of the religious view, 'they may call themselves atheists, agnostics, humanists or just lapsed believers, but they all deny the major claims of the traditional religions'.[6] However, this book upholds the validity of these claims and in its pages employs the religious – indeed, the Christian – meaning of this increasingly unused term.

The Stewardship of the Soul

But the Christian world-view does not only perceive this presence within man – it also has much to say about its nature and experience. It asserts that the soul comes from God and is therefore sacred, making the human being sacred at the same time. It is also that which constitutes the true dignity of man – it dignifies him above the rest of the Creation and sets him apart from the rest of life or earth. Being the most important feature of his make up, it also constitutes his fundamental identity – when a man is asked who he is, he could well reply: 'I am a soul'. This spiritual reality also has innate characteristics which reveal its purpose. When the soul draws in alignment towards the supernatural polarities of good or evil, it necessarily comes to display rival clusters of characteristics which reflect the nature of these opposing supernatural forces – an important doctrinal background to the famous traditional schema of 'vices' and 'virtues'. In particular – and the point cannot be stressed enough – when the soul is aligned with God it displays *love for love and love for truth*. In contrary fashion, its alignment with the devil produces opposite propensities. Thus it is that each person is called to dedicate himself to the stewardship of his soul and should so exercise his free will as to decide in favour of the right directions to be taken. He should be an aware and responsible agent in the safeguarding of this divine gift, for upon this depends his ultimate future. To alter a famous phrase (Freud), the soul is destiny.

The correct stewardship of the soul means bringing the good side of the spirit to life, a process which opens up the prospect of eternal life. It requires giving true vitality to the soul within us. This means that individuals should live 'according to the Spirit' (Rom 8:5) and thereby achieve spiritual health, true spirituality, authentic spiritual life. The contrary path of action promotes the dark side of the soul, its state of ill-health and the absence of spiritual life. The notion of the life according to the Spirit – a central concept of this work – requires clarification. First and foremost, it involves the recognition of the soul and of its special relationship with God. This, in turn, requires love of God and openness and adherence to what He wants. The will of God requires that we express love for love and for truth in our relationships with other people, for in adopting such a stance towards others we also adopt such a stance towards God. This love takes many forms and expresses itself in a variety of ways – the cultivation of virtue being of especial importance. For these reasons, other people can never be 'objects' to be used or towards whom we are indifferent. They must be 'subjects' of our care and concern to whom we cannot be indifferent. The life according to the Spirit further requires that we employ our free will to steward our souls and to ensure the expression of love for love and for truth in our relationships with others. In this endeavour, as in others, we must defend a vital faculty of the soul – the conscience. There may be a price to pay in the performance of these duties, and so the authentic spiritual life also involves a readiness to accept suffering and sacrifice. It is clear, therefore, that living according to the Spirit involves very marked responsibilities towards others, in the discharge of which the stewardship of the soul plays an essential part.

The Soul and Culture

In order to see the human soul and authentic spiritual life in their true perspective, it is necessary to examine another key feature of *homo sapiens*. To alter another famous phrase (Aristotle): man is a cultural animal. Man has a soul but he is also the bearer and generator of culture and these characteristics of the human experience should always be considered in harness. A Christian theory of culture is thus a necessity and an imperative. The Oxford Dictionary describes culture as 'the customs or civilisation of a particular people or group'[7] and R. Nisbet referred to 'the totality of norms, ideas, techniques, skills, and values, transmitted socially from generation to generation, that is the substance of what we call culture'.[8] Starting with these definitions, it is possible to understand the culture of a group of people as a set of characteristic modes of thought and feeling which find expression in shared patterns of activity. This is in line with R. Williams's 'social' definition of culture – 'a description of a particular way of life, which expresses certain meanings and values not only in art and learning but also in institutions and ordinary behaviour'.[9] Here we are referring to connected systems of perception and conduct which arise more from learning and transmission than from biological programming or instinctive impulse. Indeed, one of the great features of culture is that it goes backwards and forwards in time – it is bequeathed by ancestors and outlives those who die. Thus culture may be compared to a book handed down by a family whose text is marked, changed and altered as it is passed down the generations. Understood in these terms, society is much more than the sum of its members, as Edmund Burke (1729-1797) was only too aware:

> A nation is not an idea only of local extent, and individual momentary aggregation; but it is an idea of continuity, which extends in time as well as in numbers and space. And this is a choice not of one day, or one set of people, not a tumultuary and giddy choice; it is a deliberate election of the ages and of generations; it is a constitution made by what is ten thousand times better than choice, it is made by the peculiar circumstances, occasions, tempers, dispositions, and moral, civil and social habitudes of the people, which disclose themselves only in the long space of time.[10]

It is highly suggestive that human cultures usually seem to have at their centre a distinct constellation made up of understandings of man which are connected to related morals and ethics, visions of the human experience, and ideas about the role and purpose of the group or people bearing that culture. As Joseph Ratzinger observed: 'In all known historical cultures, religion is an essential element of culture, is indeed its determinative center; it is religion that determines the scale of values and, thereby, the inner cohesion and hierarchy of all these cultures'.[11]

It was once widely supposed that culture, like the soul, distinguishes man from the animal kingdom. It was observed, for example, that soldier ants always behave in the same way but that humans vary from society to society. Yet zoological studies have demonstrated that a capacity for rudimentary culture is also present in certain higher animals, most notably the primates. However, humans are different from such other tenants of this planet in that the culture they produce is vastly more sophisticated. Nobody would deny, for example, that the special gift of language, and the capacity to express it in written form, provides us with an unbeatable advantage over other competitors in the race to be the premier cultural being. Furthermore, humans produce culture in great abundance and far outstrip other creatures in the quantity and volume that they generate. And in being so central to the human experience, culture is also highly influential in its impact on those individuals who participate in it – it enters deeply into the tissue of personal experience and reaches far and wide into the workings and configurations of society. But it must be recognised that because only man has a soul, and because the soul expresses itself in thought and behaviour, the culture generated by humans is *qualitatively* different from that produced within the animal kingdom. So because humans are some of the very few creatures on earth to produce culture; because they give it an unrivalled complexity and richness and generate it on a grand scale; because it exercises a massive influence on their experience and lives; and above all, because they give it a unique *spiritual* character, this central feature of *homo sapiens* is *a priori* of vital importance in understanding the sad condition of contemporary Britain.

As is clear from what has been observed in this section, a cultural perspective is essential to a comprehension of the Christian message. When Jesus of Nazareth affirmed the need to construct the kingdom of heaven he was at one level calling for the creation of a culture which would express and promote the spiritual health of its members. Seen in these terms, human culture emerges as a 'moral entity' all of its own. On the one hand, there is a spiritual input into the culture produced by a human society. The souls of individuals express themselves in behaviour towards other members of society, they shape the way people treat each other, and they leave an imprint on the shared experience. Yet this process is not merely one way, and here we come to one of the key observations of this book. The habits of mind and ways of living typical of a people can in turn mould the spiritual experience of its individual members. Thus these two vital characteristics of the human condition are intertwined and interacting – souls are of great importance for the character of culture and culture has major consequences for the condition of souls. Furthermore, just as the soul conforms to the characteristics of the two supernatural polarities, so a culture does exactly the same. When acting together as a group, healthy and unhealthy souls will produce divergent sets of cultural forms characterised by predictable sets of features which align with these polarities. Equally, the spiritual character of a culture can play an important role in shaping an individual's alignment with these contrasting points. It follows that just as the individual spirit is a field of battle between light and dark, so there is an inevitable constant struggle to determine the spiritual character of a people's cultural system. The soul and culture thus emerge as great interacting areas of terrestrial contention between the kingdom of heaven and the kingdom of hell. Christ's ministry was devoted to securing victory for the positive polarity.

Thus we come to the guiding principle of how humans should live together to mutual benefit in society – a question which in these days of intensifying selfish individualism is increasingly neglected. Since the age of the Enlightenment great attention has been devoted to establishing which basic agreements and accords should underlie human society. In his contribution to the debate, Jean-Jacques Rousseau (1712-1778) employed the famous phrase 'social contract'.[12] Some thinkers, especially those belonging to the liberal tradition, have imagined some kind of pre-civic or pre-political state of man – hence the phrase 'state of nature' – and then asked what principles individuals would insist upon before acceding to or creating a full society – detect these pre-conditions, it is supposed, and you have teased out the clauses of the true social contract.[13] But, of course, the great point is that man is not born into such a hypothetical state – he is born into cultural contexts with all their roles and traditions, beliefs and conventions, habits of mind and forms of conduct, patterns of power and structures of authority. He has to deal with what he has before him and in what he is enmeshed. 'In the strict anthropological sense', Nisbet observed, 'there cannot of course be any escape from culture'.[14] Rousseau declared in a famous phrase: 'Man is born free, but everywhere he is in chains'[15] and so illuminated the error: in reality, as is often pointed out, children are born, for example, within a relationship to their parents and are subject to all that this condition implies. Moreover, even if you imagine such a state, you still have to define what man is in order to decide what is best for him – a consideration which takes us the vital step backwards to what we are.

The Common Project

And here we encounter the Christian vision of man. If the fundamental reality of man is his soul, and if his first priority is the achievement of spiritual health for himself and for others – for no greater goal could we have for our fellow-men than that they should achieve eternal life – it follows that men in society (both personally and culturally) must act together to express and engender spiritual health. This is the real social contract and its clauses are composed of divine (or natural) law – those injunctions which, if obeyed, guarantee spiritual health. Such is the 'common project', or 'common purpose', which should form the basis for our living together in society. Thus it is that true community exists where individuals and their shared culture work to express and generate love for love and love for truth. If an individual fails to express and promote spiritual health, he is neglecting his duty to himself, to his fellow men and to God. When a culture engages in a similar failure, it has torn up this social contract and thrown it into the wastepaper basket. It should not be thought, however, that spiritual health is separate from material well-being – that was one of the major errors of the late-medieval epoch. On the contrary, it complements it and assists in its achievement. To conclude this analysis and to answer the question posed at the beginning of this chapter, the direct link between spirituality and community is to be found in the personal and cultural promotion of the well-being of the soul.

All these are perhaps rather difficult concepts, not least because in these deChristianised times they are so unfashionable. They may be illuminated with reference to the thought of Jacques Maritain, the French Christian and personalist philosopher whose in many respects ultramodern views linked up with and developed the pre-Enlightenment lineage. Maritain stressed that man is a 'being made of matter and spirit, whose body may have emerged from the historical evolution of animal forms, but whose immortal soul directly proceeds from divine creation'.[16] The end of terrestrial life is to achieve eternal life, and people should 'commune with one another as much as possible here below, before perfectly communing with one another and with God in life eternal'.[17]

A society, therefore, should involve the 'common work' of promoting this end:

> And from this point of view – that is to say, with regard to the things that involve the absolute in man – it is to the perfect fulfilment of the person and his supra-temporal aspirations that society itself and its common good are indirectly subordinate, as to an end of *another* order, which transcends them. A single human soul is of more worth than the whole universe of bodies and material goods. There is nothing above the human soul except God. In the light of the eternal value and absolute dignity of the soul, society exists for each person and is subordinate thereto...The aim of political society, as of all human society, implies a certain work to be done in common...Men assemble for a reason, for an object, for a task to be done...above all for the development of the life of the spirit within us...there is, by virtue of human nature, *an order or disposition which human reason can discover and according to which the human will must act in order to attune itself to the necessary ends of the human being. The unwritten law, or natural law, is nothing more than that.*[18]

At the same time a 'culture or civilisation' should favour 'whatever material development may be necessary and sufficient to enable us to lead an upright life on this earth'.[19] Indeed, Maritain wanted to 'being back to the order of the spirit all the riches of life the modern world contains'.[20] To achieve all these ends 'the religion of Christ should penetrate culture to its very depths'.[21]

*

In the Christian world-view man is thus called to community. By the very fact of possessing a soul we are by definition neighbours; we have a responsibility towards our fellow-men; and we cannot be indifferent towards other people or treat them as objects. We are called not to selfishness but to self-giving; to act together and not against each other; and to work in favour of the highest well-being of other people. Such is the core of love. The Christian message thus emerges as a pre-eminently *social* message, and the correct stewardship of the soul is the key to its practical realisation. A direct link runs from the life according to the Spirit, authentic spiritual life, to the achievement of community. There is thus an implicit connection between what man should be spiritually and what he should be socially. In cultural terms, the healthy soul and its expressions should be the central shaping forces of the cultural system of each society. Equally, this system should itself conduce to the well-being of each participating soul. Here we encounter a vital dual route to the terrestrial expression of the kingdom of heaven. Indeed, by definition real community can only exist when there is love for love and for truth – this, indeed, is man's vocation for authentic life, and also achieves community with God – alignment is achieved with Him, and His kingdom is entered into. To repudiate this vocation, to abandon this project, which is written into the human condition, and to go against divine law (and to promote another kingdom – indeed let it be remembered that hell is perfect desocialisation), is to court disaster – we risk massive disorder in the way we live as individuals and together as a people. Our present crisis is to be understood in exactly such terms. The causes of that crisis form the subject of the next chapters.

Chapter Three

The False Anthropologies of Post-Modernity

A succession of modern theologians and philosophers have observed the modern move towards social isolation. Buber, Brunner, Demant, Maritain and Niebuhr all recognised 'the atomizing effects of the long tradition of Western individualism upon man's relation to both society and God'.[1] Maritain, for his part, correctly perceived that dominant models of man have shaped the modern experience and stressed that in modern times there has been a major move towards seeing ourselves in secular terms:

Every great period of civilisation is dominated by a certain peculiar idea that man fashions of man. Our behaviour depends on this image as much as on our very nature – an image which appears with striking brilliance in the minds of some particularly representative thinkers, and which, more or less unconscious in the human mass, is none the less strong enough to mold after its own pattern the social and political formations that are characteristic of a given epoch.

In broad outline, the image of man which reigned over medieval Christendom depended upon St. Paul and St. Augustine. This image was to disintegrate from the time of the Renaissance and the Reformation – torn between an utter Christian pessimism which despaired of human nature and an utter Christian optimism which counted on human endeavor more than on divine grace. The image of man which reigned over modern times depended upon Descartes, John Locke, the Enlightenment and Jean-Jacques Rousseau.

Here we are confronted with the process of secularization of the Christian man which took place from the sixteenth century on.[2]

Maritain believed that this development had had disastrous consequences:

> The great undertaking of secularized Christian man has achieved
> splendid results for everyone but man himself; in what concerns man
> himself things have turned out badly – and this is not surprising.
>
> The process of secularization of the Christian man concerns above
> all the idea of man and the philosophy of life which developed in
> the modern age?[3]

This chapter discusses the various forms of the 'idea of man' that
seem to have become established in contemporary Britain, their
interconnections, their historical-cultural supports and their evident
historical function (although relativism is subject to a special analysis
in chapter five), and also argues that these false anthropologies constitute
a natural set, an authentic matrix, which appears to be becoming
increasingly ascendant in British culture. In the next chapter their
'atomising effects' will be investigated, that is to say 'how things have
turned out badly'.

In analysing these visions of man and their injurious consequences
we seem to enter into the heart of contemporary materialism. However,
it should be stressed that within post-modern British culture there are
other models of man that do not recognise the existence of the soul
within man (and in this sense may be termed 'materialist') but which
are worthy of respect and conduce to ways of living and forms of
behaviour that are certainly positive.

Introductory Observations

Shakespeare had Hamlet declare (II, 2, 309-14):

> What a piece of work is a man.
> How noble in reason, how infinite in faculties.
> In form and moving how express and admirable,
> In action how like an angel,
> In apprehension how like a god.
> The beauty of the world.
> The paragon of animals.
> And yet, to me what is this quintessence of dust?

The post-moderns have their own views on the subject. However, before
presenting a taxonomy of the false anthropologies of post-modernity it
is necessary to make some introductory observations.

First of all, it should be stressed that this chapter does not assert that these false visions of man – in the definition of which neologisms have at times been coined or standard terms employed in new ways (see glossary) – are exclusive to the post-modern age (that is to say, the last forty decades or so). Indeed, they often go back to the modern age, to the medieval period and to antiquity. But here the intention is to stress that these false anthropologies appear to be increasingly characteristic of post-modern British culture and the contemporary mentality. Thus the subject of the analysis is a matrix that seems to increasingly mark out a specific historical period. In the same way, the terms 'post-modern' and 'post-modernity' are here employed in a chronological sense and should not be confused with specific currents of thought or philosophical approaches which employ such terms in different ways and with different purposes.

Secondly, in exploring these false anthropologies of British society this chapter does not present a survey of contemporary philosophy or theory nor does it seek to explore the influence of important intellectual movements or prominent thinkers. Instead, what it seeks to do is to illustrate the various approaches that seem to be deeply ingrained in people's minds; it engages in an attempt to describe how men and women think today.

But how do we know that these materialist visions of man are present in post-modern minds? It is certainly true that they are often to be found – implicitly or explicitly – in the pages of theoretical writings or in the volumes of specialists in certain disciplines – zoology, psychology or economics, for example – or in the publications of popularisers. Each specialisation, indeed, tends to produce a vision of man natural to its province of knowledge. And this chapter draws freely upon such sources of both British and Western provenance for *illustrative* purposes. But it would be a mistake to fall into the easy trap of scanning the works of thinkers and academics to uncover the patterns of ascendant contemporary thought. We live in a rationalist age when intellectuals and their like have acquired great influence and prestige and part of their power is reflected in a tendency to look at what they do and say rather than to discuss ideas and attitudes which are diffused widely within the population. For this reason, and for others, the analysis presented in this chapter is that of an amateur anthropologist. It is based upon personal observations and inquiries, on listening and talking, and on impression and inference. In addition, because this work, with all its innumerable defects, is a pioneering work, maps of the terrain produced by previous explorers do not exist. The risks of a virgin survey are evident and the coining of neologisms forms a part of such risks. The reader should bear in mind that this book is written on the assumption that the materialist matrix analysed below not only exists widely in men's minds but also exercises a major influence on their behaviour. *Henceforth this volume takes this assumption as being true.* It will be necessary in the future to demonstrate empirically that this assumption is correct. Certainly there is an urgent need to explore in a scholarly way people's conceptions of man during the post-modern age (just as it is also necessary to construct a set of indicators of desocialisation) and the impact of those conceptions. This volume, therefore, is also a call for the advance of such a sociological undertaking which hitherto has been far too neglected.

It should also be emphasised that a shared characteristic of this set of models of man is their membership of the dominant trends of modern thought. Indeed, many of the principal currents of modern philosophy and theory in Great Britain (and of the West more generally) have united in an attempt to remove the soul from the mindset of man. At the same time they have done a great deal to promote materialist (and also relativist) perspectives on man and human society. A survey of key thinkers and currents of thought over the last three hundred years from the perspective of the materialist models of man outlined below would perhaps provide a new approach to modern theory and philosophy and open up innovative paths of investigation and classification. That undertaking, however, may be left to far more expert scholars. Suffice to say here that when we cast our eyes over such key modern intellectual movements as rationalism and romanticism, positivism and utilitarianism, Marxism and Freudianism, existentialism and verificationism, structuralism and deconstructionism, we encounter creeds which have acted to shift man away from a belief in God and the soul. What is now termed in Great Britain 'postmodernism', the latest in the long line of such movements, brings much of this trajectory to fruition in concentrated form.

Against such a background it comes as no surprise that the head of the Catholic Church should have declared in the 1990s that modern history in the West may be seen as a *'struggle against God, the systematic elimination of all that is Christian'* which 'has to a large degree dominated thought and life in the West for three centuries'.[4]

Another shared feature of these models of man lies in their having many of the characteristics of heresies. On the one hand, they take one real or purported aspect of what man is and hold it up (usually in deformed fashion) as the key to his identity; on the other, they often replace the soul with this single feature. In addition, they frequently do this in a very simple and convincing way. T.S. Eliot (1888-1965) offered us the following prescient observations on heresy some seventy years ago:

the essential of any important heresy is not simply that it is wrong: it is that it is partly right. It is characteristic of the more interesting heretics, in the context in which I use the term, that they have an exceptionally acute perception, or profound insight, of some part of the truth; an insight more important often than the inferences of those who are aware of more but less acutely aware of anything... we must remember too, that an heresy is apt to have a seductive simplicity, to make a direct and persuasive appeal to intellect and emotions, and to be altogether more plausible than the truth.[5]

The human being is certainly many things and is multifaceted. Man has the faculties of his soul, his intellect, and his senses; he has both will and instinct; he is a fusion of spirit and of his body; he is the creation of biology and of paradise; he experiences emotions and lives in society; he is a bearer of rights and a being endowed with sexuality; he aspires to power and strives for resources; and he both feels and perceives. But the false anthropologies of post-modernity listed below all disregard the spiritual dimension to man and instead direct attention towards other real or purported aspects of his identity – usually erecting them into a supreme truth, often deforming their true nature, putting them in the place of man's spirituality, and presenting them with great plausibility. Reductionism is one of their greatest characteristics.

One aspect of this shared heretical appeal requires emphasis. Part of the allure of these visions of man lies in their frequent claim to be 'scientific'. From this point of view the modern assault on the soul has in part been an exercise in the application of science (even though many scientists have a spiritualist approach). 'Why, then, should this basic concept of the soul be doubted?', asks Francis Crick. 'The main reason for this radical change of opinion', he answers, 'is the spectacular advance of modern science'.[6] Crick is of course referring here to the exact sciences. How far these disciplines really do invalidate the religious concept of the soul is a very open question but, living as we do in a heavily scientific age, there is now a natural receptivity amongst people to accept what scientists affirm. They seem to be experts whose voice carries the weight of authority.

Indeed, what seems to be happening is that men from the world of the exact sciences are now often extending their range into new regions, and in particular into those connected with ethics and morals – rushing in, as it were, where before they feared to tread. Many a television programme, newspaper article or paperback bestseller of recent decades attests to this development. For example, Crick himself declares that only 'scientific certainty (with all its limitations) can in the long run rid us of the superstitions of our ancestors'.[7] And this application of science seems to have had major consequences for modern man's belief in the soul and God. 'Religious beliefs just do not seem to fit into the scientific world-view', observes K. Ward, 'so they are either repressed, or they are adopted for purely emotional reasons'.[8] Yet there are reasons for doubting the grounds for such 'scientific certainty'. There are signs that the exact sciences themselves may be entering into troubled waters the more they advance down the path of knowledge. This is not a fact which should surprise us – the more you know, the more you realise how little you know.

Furthermore, the history of the exact sciences has been repeatedly marked by the radical overturning of previous certitudes, as Einstein's revision of Newtonian physics in the first decades of the last century demonstrated only too clearly. A whole host of factors are now working to create what may be, in the words of one authority, 'the crisis of modern science':[9] the difficulties in verifying advanced physical theories; alarm over the seemingly endless depth of matter; worries over the extent to which knowledge is the product of conditioning paradigms; and the unanswered questions raised by quantum mechanics. There is also the question of how much the human mind can really understand. As the physicist P.W. Bridgman (1882-1961) was moved to declare: 'the structure of nature may eventually be such that our processes of thought do not correspond to it sufficiently to permit us to think about it at all'.[10] It is possible that the scientistic critique of religion may itself be being undermined by increasing doubts about the theoretical bases of the exact sciences themselves.[11]

But it is not only the exact sciences which vaunt the title 'scientific' and have often used this claim to sustain an assault on the soul. From the age of the Enlightenment onwards a number of other disciplines have arisen which sport the title, many exponents of which have often asserted that man and the human condition are materially measurable and function in ways commensurate with the mechanisms of the physical universe. The 'social sciences' sometimes belong to this image, as does psychology in its many forms and offshoots, not to mention the followers of Marxism and Freudianism.

The trappings of scientific discourse and method which mark these disciplines in reality often conceal an evident lack of agreement about their theoretical bases – one factor which explains the heated internal controversy and the flourishing of divergent schools which have so characterised their existence.[12] Such disciplines are now often in a condition of uncertainty as well. The discipline of psychology may be taken as a case in point. One of its founding fathers believed that it was following in the tracks of the exact sciences. In 1892 William James (1842-1910) declared that 'the Galileo and the Lavoisier of psychology will be famous men indeed when they come, as come they some day surely will'.[13] But this has proved very far from the case. Indeed, in the 1970s B.A. Farrell declared: 'it is quite wrong to think of contemporary psychology as being like physics, or any other post-paradigmatic natural science. Here the sceptics are right; this traditional picture of psychology has indeed broken down'.[14]

The Materialist Matrix

Humanism

'Humanism' – a concept not understood here in the sense of Renaissance 'humanism' – is the creed which sees man as the crowning glory of the cosmos. It is pre-eminently a philosophy of this world. Humanism recognises no God and detects no spirit. It affirms that our innate value derives not from the divine bestowal of a soul but from the mere fact of our being human. This materialist vision of man believes that *homo sapiens* – defined in non-spiritual terms – is what really matters in the Creation; that our well-being – understood without reference to the soul – is the primary imperative of the universe; and that it is to ourselves alone – seen from a material perspective – that we must look for our success and salvation. This adoration of soulless man within a Godless universe, and this emphasis on the need to satisfy what is material within him, are linked to immense faith in his non-spiritual capacities – humanism praises man's will, admires his qualities and trusts to his invention.

In this sense humanism is the pride of man erected into a philosophy of existence; the self-importance of the premier species of the globe transformed into an ideology. Western history is replete with warnings about such an approach. The Book of Genesis contains the event of the Garden of Eden. The Greeks narrated the fate of Icarus. The Faust myth continued the theme. But such warnings do not seem to have been heeded – in Great Britain today the great tendency is to look and trust to man alone, and to man seen from a very narrow and impoverished perspective. The German philosopher Leo Strauss (1899-1973) believed that this approach to ourselves is what has really characterised the modern mind:

> The first characteristic feature of modern thought as modern thought, one might say, is its anthropocentric character...The underlying idea, which shows itself not in all places clearly but in some places very clearly, is that all truths, or all meaning, all order, all beauty, originate in the thinking subject, in human thought, in man...One must not forget that even the atheistic, materialistic thinkers of classical antiquity took it for granted that man is subject to something higher than himself, e.g., the whole cosmic order, and that man is not the origin of all meaning.[15]

'The spiritual dominant of modern culture', observed Maritain, 'is an anthropocentric culture'.[16]

The humanist outlook, with its associated faith in man and his capacities, has been powerfully promoted by the astonishing scientific, technological and economic achievements of the last three centuries. It is a creed which has gained massive credibility and legitimacy from modern human advance. Amazing wealth, incredible machines, landing on the moon, the conquest of diseases, the micro-chip, jet-planes, the mapping of the human genome, vast cities – all these successes, and many others, have given man immense belief in himself and his abilities. Moreover, such advance has been very much a phenomenon of Western man, whose supremacy in such areas has marked him out from the other peoples of the earth and lain behind his planetary ascendancy – a process which has added further lustre and prestige to such achievements. Nowadays what can man not do? He seems, indeed, the master of his own destiny, Hamlet's 'beauty of the world'. This self-admiration has been especially encouraged by apparent success in the enterprise of dominating nature – an ancient ambition. For millennia man was heavily subordinated to the natural world and thus constantly reminded of his limits. His scientific successes during the modern age have revolutionised this relationship, as Hans Jonas well emphasises in his work *The Imperative of Responsibility.*[17]

Through genetic engineering man now has the prospect of even being the master of the physical processes which govern his very make-up. He seems to have broken some of the final bonds of nature's dominion. Man has achieved the power to be his own creator, or so it might appear – in this area, too, perhaps his own god. All this is of a piece with the faith in himself so greatly encouraged by these conspicuous leaps forward. And let us not forget that Great Britain, not by chance the nation of Francis Bacon (1561-1626), was the first industrial nation and a central force behind this explosion in human capacity and audacity.

One testimony to the growth of humanism is to be found in the success of one of its principal offshoots – faith in men who appear to carry human capacities to their highest point. Belief in *homo sapiens* became naturally transmuted into a concomitant trust in those who seemed to be supermen. The path of humanity was to be lit up by trail-blazing superior beings endowed with special powers of action, insight and comprehension. This attitude and hope was propelled forward by the figure of 'Renaissance man' and carried on by the idea of the 'genius' which took off in Europe (and particularly in France) in the second part of the eighteenth century. Perhaps it is artists and writers who have been the greatest champions of the idea of the genius – often presenting themselves as the seers, mystics or prophets of deep truths hidden to ordinary mortals. A series of self-confident intellectuals and thinkers have also promoted the modern idea of the genius, ranging from Rousseau to Voltaire, from Marx to Sartre, and from Russell to Foucault – figures who have been ever-ready to regale mankind with grand schemes of improvement. In the political province this idea found monstrous fruition in the totalitarian dictators of the twentieth century. Lenin, Stalin, Hitler, Mao Tse Tung and Pol Pot (atheists all) led a long list of hideous demi-gods who promised the earth only to poison it. With their pragmatic and common sense inheritance, the British proved rather resistant to this offshoot of humanism – the French were far more susceptible. Yet in the long term the idea of the genius came to form a fixed part of their mental horizons, in particular within the various highways and byways of the artistic and literary world.

Rationalism

The term 'rationalism' is usually employed to describe a distinct philosophical approach to the world, but this book goes further and defines it as the creed which believes that man can be chiefly understood with reference to his rational faculties. This version of rationalism sees man primarily as a creature endowed with the capacity to reason. *Homo sapiens* is seen first and foremost as a kind of walking intellect. Where the Christian world-view believes that what raises man above the animals is his possession of a soul, rationalism asserts that it is his reason which provides him with this superiority. Here there is an important crossover with humanism in that human reason is perceived as the only reason in the cosmos – it is believed that above man there is no superior mind and below him there are the unthinking beasts. Concurrently, rationality, not the soul, is what is held to be the great common denominator of mankind. This perspective also holds that all things in the final analysis are accessible to rational investigation and goes on to assert that the rational faculties of man are the primary path to knowledge and progress in all spheres. From this point of view, rationalism should be seen as an expression of supreme faith in the human intellect, and for this reason 'intellectualism' would be just as suitable an appellation. Much of the rationalist perspective is described in the definition of the more conventional meaning of the term supplied by a standard work of reference:

> Rationalism is the philosophical view that regards reason as the chief source and test of knowledge. Holding that reality itself has an integrally logical structure, the Rationalist asserts that a class of truth exists that the intellect can grasp directly...In ethics, Rationalists hold the position that reason, rather than feeling, custom, or authority, is the ultimate court of appeal in judging good and bad, right and wrong.[18]

The positive connotations of such terms as 'rational' or 'logical' attest to the grip that rationalism now exercises on the contemporary mind. Similarly, and in telling fashion, we are constantly encouraged to value 'intelligence' much more highly than truthfulness or virtue, and this quality is habitually (and quite wrongly) defined in narrowly intellectual terms – as witness the spread, influence and prestige of the ridiculous IQ test. At times in post-modern Britain it seems better to be intelligent than to be good.

Rationalism's immense confidence in human reason not only neglects other features of man, and downplays the inherent limits to rational analysis and related initiative, but leads off into a readiness to impose highly rationalised structures (often of a distinctly mechanistic character) on realities which do not lend themselves to such an approach. Such a tendency is linked to a propensity to believe that major advance can be achieved through the application of rationally-based programmes of reform to man and to human society. Rationalism also has an impulse to subject everything to debate and to believe that such debate both has a value inherent in itself and is the key to future progress. Furthermore, there are strong individualist overtones in this creed in that each specific individual's rationality is given prominence and the committed rationalist trusts greatly in his own personal reason. At the same time, rationalism tends to downplay the value and reliability of inherited belief and wisdom, and has the arrogant habit of rejecting that which cannot be rationally explained or justified at any given moment. Rationalism also tends to bestow a premium of importance on those who dedicate great time and effort to the cultivation of their intellects and lay commensurate claims to wield power within society and to the right to change society. Many of these features were captured by the English Conservative philosopher Michael Oakeshott (1901-1990). 'The general character and disposition of the Rationalist are, I think, not difficult to identify', he maintained:

> At bottom he stands (he always *stands*) for independence of mind on all occasions, for thought free from obligation to any authority save the authority of 'reason'. His circumstances in the modern world have made him contentious. He is the *enemy* of authority, of prejudice, of the merely traditional, customary or habitual. His mental attitude is at once sceptical and optimistic: sceptical, because there is no opinion, no habit, no belief, nothing so firmly rooted or so widely held that he hesitates to question it and to judge it by what he calls his 'reason'; optimistic, because the Rationalist never doubts the power of his 'reason' (when properly applied) to determine the worth of a thing, the truth of an opinion or the propriety of an action. Moreover, he is fortified by a belief in a 'reason' common to all mankind, a common power of rational consideration which is the ground and inspiration of argument: set up on his door is the precept of Parmenides – judge by rational argument...He believes of course in the open mind, the mind free

from prejudices...the character which the Rationalist claims for himself is the character of the engineer...the morality of the Rationalist is the morality of the self-made man and of the self-made society.[19]

The rationalist perspective has been strengthened in a variety of ways and on a broad range of fronts by the fact that much of modern and contemporary British history has been an exercise in laying stress upon the rationality of human beings. An important self-fuelling process has been at work at the heart of our civilisation. Rationalism emerged with full force during the age of the Enlightenment, giving rise to its own specific philosophical tradition, and during that period gained major impetus from the scientific study of the physical universe. The telescope was turned from the stars and the planets to man and his activities. It was believed that the methods employed in studying the natural world could also be applied to understanding and improving the human world. During the last three centuries such methods, in one form or another, have been embraced and applied far and wide, and the contemporary world bears the marks of the massive impact and power of the human intellect. Indeed, the application of the rational faculties of man has so shaped our vision of our realities and so moulded their character that when we look at ourselves and our environment we are naturally led back to a consideration of our own rationality. In this way the observer is spontaneously encouraged to believe that what really matters in man is, indeed, his reason, and by such a mechanism the rationalist perspective has gained self-generating force and credibility.

This massive impact of the rational faculties on the modern age has operated at two principal levels. On the one hand, they have left a deep imprint on the shape of our surroundings and the form of our society. Advances in science and technology have permeated our human environment with the products of these faculties and have permitted an unprecedented management and exploitation of nature. In particular, we have filled our lives with machines – those quintessential products of the human intellect and the fitting symbols of our ever-more mech-anistic way of life. Furthermore, over the last two hundred years the state has dedicated enormous energy, through government and legis-lation, to achieving an elaborate organisation and direction of society to an extent which would never have been imaginable during the medieval era. To echo the thinking of Max Weber (1864-1920), there has been a long-term 'rationalisation' of the way we live. This process has been accompanied by similar changes in how we create, use and manage material resources. The advance in science and technology has been bound up with the growth of highly organised and systematic forms of economic activity – a development in which machines have played an integral part. For example, one of the great features of the industrial revolution was a much more rigid use of time, and who now amongst us fails to wear a wristwatch? Today's visitors to the West (and thus also to Great Britain) frequently comment upon our attachment to timetables, our liking for organisation and our frenetic rhythms – to the detriment, it is said, of the quality of human relations. Equally, we have dedicated ourselves to the systematic organisation, storing and retrieval of knowledge.

On the other hand, the application of the rational faculties has favoured new approaches to understanding man and his experience, as a whole range of disciplines well testify. The advances of medical science and biology have provided a highly rationalised picture of ourselves as organisms and this has had a marked impact on our self-identity. These branches of knowledge have acted to reveal, and draw attention to, the ordered functioning and organisation of our physiological processes. There has been a parallel attempt to approach our minds and emotions from the same perspective. Thus psychology often provides highly rationalised and at times mechanistic visions of what constitutes the inner man. One offshoot of this discipline even believes that this part of us is fully accessible to rational investigation – hence the highly significant term 'psychoanalysis'. There have also been attempts to study human society along such lines. The more than aptly named 'social sciences', and the assumptions which often underpin them, are a perfect expression of the contention that the methods of the exact sciences can be applied to the world of man and his activities – what humans do in society is held to be accessible to disciplines which claim that they are based upon 'scientific' method.

At times these two principal levels, which so stress and encourage the rational dimension of man and his experience, overlap. In recent decades we have encountered a perfect example of this process which also illustrates the continuing tension and conflict between materialism and spiritualism. Proximity breeds comparison, and the mechanistic model of man has gained ground with the advance of the machine age. Our constant nearness to computers, for example, frequently encourages us to liken ourselves to these constructs of the human intellect. How many people seated in front of their video screens (and their number increases every day) have not been led to believe that in essence they are really sophisticated computers in flesh and blood, the bearers of natural rather than merely 'artificial' intelligence?

Indeed, the present heated debate about what computers are and the extent to which they can resemble man is highly controversial precisely because of the presence of rival visions of man, as William Barrett well illustrates in his work *Death of the Soul*.[20] Materialists tend to argue that it is possible to reproduce man in machine form; spiritualists, naturally enough, maintain the opposite. At times the debate parallels that about UFOs and has similar attendant anxieties. If aliens exist, might this not disprove the assumption that humans are unique in the universe in possessing souls? Computers and Martians touch on very sensitive nerves in a centuries-old debate about man which still gives rise to major demarcation lines within British thinking.

Rightsism

'Rightsism' is the creed which believes that man (conceived as not having a soul) should primarily be seen as the bearer of a set of innate rights – 'natural rights' or 'human rights' to use the standard phrases. The guiding idea is that all men by the very fact of being human carry within them the same bundle of entitlements. It is argued that such rights are an inherent part of our nature, that they are written into the human condition, and that they are not present within the animal kingdom. It is also stressed that the function of society is to ensure that such rights are upheld, and government is said to have a special role in ensuring their realisation. Here is one enthusiast of the modern secular theory of rights, C.B. Macpherson, explaining the doctrine in order to apply it far and wide:

> The problem we now face is created by the fact that any doctrine of human rights must be in some sense a doctrine of natural right. Human rights can only be asserted as a species of natural right, in the sense that they must be deduced from the nature (i.e., the needs and capacities) of men as such, whether of men as they now are or of men as they are thought capable of becoming. To say this, is simply to recognize that neither legal rights nor customary rights are a sufficient basis for human rights.
>
> The problem, then, is whether there can be found a doctrine of

human rights which is a doctrine of natural rights but which does not contain the factors which have made the early doctrine of natural rights unacceptable. The problem is not insoluble in principle.[21]

At the end of the eighteenth century Edmund Burke observed that the concept of natural rights was 'metaphysical',[22] and indeed in a whole host of ways this creed puts rights in the place of the soul. In rightsist thinking such rights are invisible and cannot be measured but are nevertheless powerfully present and discernible. They also characterise *homo sapiens* alone and serve to distinguish him from the animal kingdom. In addition, the achievement of these rights is the central purpose of existence, and each individual is to be chiefly seen in relation to their realisation. His life, as it were, can be understood in terms of what happens, or what does not happen, to these inner entitlements.

This creed also argues that the defence and promotion of these rights should be the governing principle of social experience, the central determinant of how a community should be organised. The enforcement and realisation of natural rights is thus seen as the regulating factor of how individuals should treat each other, the governing moral and ethical imperative of the world of men. In this perspective, the social contract or common project should be understood in terms of a shared and enforced upholding of certain innate rights to be found within the (soulless) human person. To put it another way – man has within him not a soul, with all that that implies, but a bundle of theoretical entitlements, with all that they imply.

Seen in historical terms, modern secular natural rights theory is a break with a more ancient approach which affirmed that innate rights and duties derive from divine or 'natural' law ordained by God – a lineage belonging to the heritage of Christian thought and which can be traced back, in recent times, not only to the personalism of the twentieth century and the affirmations of the Constitution of the United States of America, but also more remotely to 'Grotius, and before him Suarez and Francisco de Vitoria, and further back to St Thomas Aquinas; and still further back to St. Augustine and the Church Fathers and St. Paul'.[23]

In Great Britain the modern theory of natural rights (which has both Christian and secular roots) was certainly given great lift-off during the seventeenth century by the English thinkers Thomas Hobbes (1588-1679) and John Locke (1632-1704), but this theory found its most fertile terrain elsewhere – most notably in the United States of America, France and Germany. In 1791 the American Constitution incorporated the Bill of Rights into its clauses. In this lineage there were still links with the more traditional religious conception of rights and natural law, something which cannot be said of the 'Declaration of the Rights of Man and the Citizen' proclaimed by the new French Republic in 1797, with its references to the 'natural and inalienable rights of man'. During the nineteenth century and the first half of the twentieth, the modern theory of natural rights made especial headway in America, and the refrain 'I've got my rights' became a commonplace of transatlantic discourse.

After the Second World War – in part in an attempt to provide a philosophical underpinning to condemnation of the horrors of Nazism – the theory found much wider adherence in the West. In 1948 the Universal Declaration of Human Rights of the United Nations was passed amidst general acclamation; in 1949 West Germany incorporated certain guarantees of human rights into its 'Basic Law'; and in 1950 the European Convention for the Protection of Human Rights and Fundamental Freedoms was presented to the world. These latter-day affirmations of modern natural rights theory have since been powerfully developed by the Europeanist movement and a continuing American commitment.[24] For this and other reasons this theory now exercises a major influence on Western political discussion. 'In the years since the end of World War II', observes M.A. Glendon, 'rights discourse has spread throughout the world'.[25]

From the eighteenth century until recently, Great Britain diverged from this tradition. The English utilitarian thinker Jeremy Bentham (1748-1832) even went so far as to reject the notion out of hand: '*Natural rights* is simple nonsense...*Right*...is the child of law; from *real* laws come *real* rights, but from *imaginary* laws, from laws of nature...come *imaginary* rights'.[26] In reality, the common contemporary invocation of 'rights' is really a new departure in Great Britain.

In political discussion during the Victorian period there was instead emphasis on the certitudes of tradition, habit and precedent. Change and reform largely took place within a pragmatic and adaptive framework. Organic development along Burkean lines was the keynote. This can be seen in one of the major achievements of British society during the years 1830-1918 – the advance of democracy. From on high, for example, democratisation was sustained not so much out of an impulse to the realisation of abstract theoretical rights but more out of a readiness to incorporate what were deemed to be the responsible sections of society into a polity which was naturally receptive to reform and adjustment.

Similarly, whereas on the Continent justice was increasingly based upon rationalised legal codes and concepts of 'right' (*droit, diritto*), the English continued to adhere to their common law tradition (with all its faith in precedent and custom) and liked to talk in terms of 'law'.

Both these features of our national evolution provide an important clue as to the British idea of what rights were. They were largely seen as entitlements conferred by the Constitution (which significantly enough remained unwritten and open to change), by legislation, and by the precepts of custom. They sprang from practical human arrangements – and from the principles and values which underlay such arrangements – and not from an alleged bundle of entitlements carried within each human from birth. They were, so to speak, conferred by the way things were.

In recent decades there has been a major shift within British political culture in relation to modern natural rights theory. For example, in 2000 the Human Rights Act was passed which incorporated the European Convention on the Protection of Human Rights and Fundamental Freedoms into British law.

At the same time rightsism, which does not see innate rights with reference to divine law, has reached a position of strength within British culture. In part, this may stem from the twentieth-century collectivist impulse to ensure certain basic economic and social guarantees for the citizenry – at an implicit level there is the idea that individuals have a 'right' to certain forms of government help and assistance. In part, it is one of the more conspicuous results of the Americanisation of our national culture. But in part, also, it derives from the process of Europeanisation created by our membership of the European Union (within which France and Germany exercise notable influence). For these reasons, and others, British political debate is now increasingly coloured by rightsist thinking and terminology, not only in relation to personal rights, which tend to be conceived in political and economic terms, but also in relation to the rights of groups. Such phrases as 'students' rights', 'workers' rights', 'gay rights' or 'women's rights', with all their implicit repudiation of the previous universalism of natural rights theory, express the presence of an approach which would not have been possible a hundred years ago. Yet, in Great Britain, as in many other Western countries, there is now a reaction against many of the philosophical bases and practical implications of modern natural rights theory. As some students of our national political culture have recently observed: 'In the mid-1990s leading politicians on the left have joined those on the right in alleging that there is 'too much emphasis on rights' in today's Britain'.[27] Much must have taken place for such a reaction to have occurred.

Societalism

'Societalism' is the creed which believes that man should principally be seen as a product of society. He is a kind of *tabula rasa* upon which the human environment writes its words. It is argued that an individual is chiefly what society makes him, and that it is in terms of society that he is largely to be understood. Thus it is often argued that there is no such thing as human nature (a doctrine which has gained increasing ground in recent decades), and thus necessarily, as well, no such thing as human spiritual nature. 'The Blank Slate', declares S. Pinker, 'has become the secular religion of modern intellectual life':[28]

> During the past century the doctrine of the Blank Slate has set the agenda for much of the social sciences and the humanities…The social sciences have sought to explain all customs and social arrangements as a product of the socialisation of children by the surrounding culture: a system of words, images, stereotypes, role models, and contingencies of reward and punishment. A long and growing list of concepts that would seem natural to the human way of thinking (emotions, kinships, the senses, illness, nature, the world) are now said to have been "invented" or "socially constructed"…The Blank Slate has also served as a sacred scripture for ethical and political beliefs. According to the doctrine, any differences we see among ethnic groups, sexes, and individuals come not from differences in innate constitution but from differences in their experiences.[29]

Of the false anthropologies of post-modernity (with the exception of relativism), societalism is perhaps the most widely rooted of them all and contains some of the great assumptions of the post-modern mentality. Indeed, it is so deeply embedded that its axioms are often taken for granted and its perspectives rarely called into question. For example, it is commonly believed that our characters and personalities, and our beliefs and ideas about right and wrong, are shaped, if not actually determined, by 'society'; that a great deal of our life experience is the outcome of our societal context (indeed, it is this approach to man which often lies behind the widely used phrase 'social conditioning');

and that our happiness and well-being are largely dependent on how society is organised and directed.

This creed not only disregards the spiritual and supernatural, but even sees society, rather than God or the soul, as the prime determiner, animator and mover of man. In a way, society acquires semi-divine characteristics, after a fashion being held responsible for matters which medieval man once attributed to supernatural forces. Once the devil was invoked; today one hears that 'society is to blame'. And as the alleged source of human ideas about right and wrong, society takes the place of our spiritual impulse. In this creed there are two chief overlaps with the rest of the materialist matrix. An intersection with humanism exists – human reality is taken as the pre-eminent point of reference. Rightsism also enters the picture because 'society' is said to be the proper guarantor of certain inherent entitlements.

Language reflects culture and one of the great features of contemporary discussion is the repeated use of the terms 'society' and 'social' – a tell-tale sign of the penetrating influence of this post-modern model of man. Such terms have acquired a powerful positive charge and at times bear the moral connotation that the word 'good' once enjoyed. F.A. Hayek (1899-1991) noticed this striking phenomenon and testimony to the power of societalism a few decades ago:

I doubt whether there exists a better example of the little understood influence that may be exercised by a single word than that afforded by the role which for a hundred years the word 'social' has played in the whole sphere of political problems – and is still playing. We are so familiar with it, we accept it so much as a matter of course, that we are hardly conscious of any problem regarding its meaning. We have accepted it for so long as the natural description of good behaviour and sincere thinking, that it seems almost sacrilege even to ask what this word really means which so many men consider as the guiding star of their moral aspirations.[30]

But the actual meaning of the word 'society' – one of the most frequently used and influential terms of contemporary thinking – is far from clear. The British prime minister of the 1980s even went so far as to declare that no such thing existed[31] – a sure sign of modern-day ideological controversy. The meaning of the term in the societalist scheme of things is rather nebulous and is certainly far less tangible than 'nation' or 'community', but four principal features stand out. First of all, society, seen as the cumulative outcome of a specific human population, is conceived as a kind of separate and autonomous entity. Although composed of individuals, it is somehow assigned a life and existence all of its own. It is also given an independent will – something which is frequently identified with the wishes and decisions of government. At the same time this purported entity is frequently approached from an economic perspective and defined with reference to the world of wealth – in societalist thought, indeed, 'society' seems to be predominantly 'economic society'. Lastly, and as befits a materialist vision of the human universe, society is usually seen as an entity which is fully accessible to rational analysis (an important intersection with rationalism); something which has a distinctly mechanistic character; and as a reality which as a consequence can be examined, represented, reformed and reorganised. However, whether society conceived in these above-mentioned terms really exists, whether such an entity is anything more than the mental construct of a specific vision of the human experience, remains a very open question.

Various historical developments have aided the rise of societalism in Great Britain over recent centuries. The creed received a great impulse from the humanist and rationalist irruption of the seventeenth and eighteenth centuries. The desire to apply the methods of the natural sciences to the world of men naturally became bound up with the idea that the human experience produced a reality ('society') which could be measured and analysed. This impulse was carried forward into the contemporary period with great force by the 'social sciences', disciplines which were to prove of great influence in a variety of spheres. Political radicalism increasingly employed the guiding concepts of societalism from the late-nineteenth century onwards as a point of departure in its critique of existing economic and societal arrangements, and the whole collectivist trajectory was to become permeated with the societalist perspective. Indeed, the history of the Liberal and Labour Parties during the last hundred years cannot be understood without grasping the meaning and appeal of the modern notion of 'society'. The large-scale intervention of the state over the last hundred years, very much the work of such radicalism, has also given practical encouragement to much of the contours of this perspective. The rise of mass society has been a further factor. The decline of small-scale horizons which were characteristic of life before the industrial revolution necessarily opened up far broader frames of reference. The mass experience naturally led people to move from identifying with a personal world of villages, towns or counties towards seeing themselves in relation to a much wider and less tangible entity – 'society'.

One strand of societalism has had a special role and history all of its own. Marxism and its various expressions have had a massive (and at times catastrophic) impact on the modern world. It is true that Communist practice has been distant from the British experience, but this does not mean to say that the Marxist model of man has not entered into our cultural bloodstream. It acquired significant influence from the 1930s onwards, not least within the intelligentsia, and despite the fall of the Berlin Wall Marxist thought continues to exercise a notable influence within our universities. Karl Marx (1818-1883) believed, or said he believed, that he was constructing a 'science' of the social world. In 1859 the scholar of the British Museum gave a good account of his own version of the societalist creed:

> In the social production of their existence, men inevitably enter into definite relations, which are independent of their will, namely relations of production appropriate to a given stage in the development of their material forces of production. The totality of these relations of production constitutes the economic structure of society, the real foundation, on which arises a legal and political superstructure and to which correspond definite forms of social consciousness. The mode of production of material life conditions the general process of social, political and intellectual life. It is not the consciousness of men that determines their existence, but their social existence that determines their consciousness.[32]

This heavily economic view of what society is, and therefore of what humans are and do, overlaps with another post-modern vision of man.

Economism

'Economism' is the creed which sees man as a being primarily engaged in a constant striving for economic resources. It believes that what really motivates man, and what determines the essential shape and character of his society, is his innate drive towards the acquisition, conservation and accumulation of material wealth. In this scheme of things *homo sapiens* is really *homo oeconomicus*. Consequently, it is assumed that society is really to be understood in economic terms. Marx belonged to this lineage in extreme form:

upon the different forms of property, upon the social conditions of existence, rises an entire superstructure of different and distinctly formed sentiments, illusions, modes of thought and views of life.[33] As this affirmation suggests, economism, like societalism, is strongly deterministic – there is a frequent emphasis on the role of economic realities in shaping and moulding the collective and personal human experience.

A number of intersections exist with the rest of the materialist matrix. Economism has much in common with societalism's frequent assumption that society is essentially economic society; rationalism overlaps with economism in seeing the pursuit of economic resources as a rational process natural to man which takes place within a context – the economy – which follows rational processes that are accessible to rational analysis (hence the discipline of economics); and rightsism now lays increasing emphasis on man's 'rights' in the economic field. Perhaps there is also a humanistic input – during the modern age Western man has demonstrated astounding abilities in the economic field, expressing to the full his inventiveness and his power to manage nature.

A number of historic developments have encouraged the economistic perspective. Over recent centuries the Western world has devoted immense energy to economic growth. One of the great features of our modern experience has been the gigantic expansion and development of our national economies. Great Britain has been a full participant in this process – indeed, it was the first nation to embark on industrialisation. The increased importance of this sector has naturally promoted the idea that such activity is what really matters in man. In connected fashion, the academic discipline of economics has risen to dizzy heights. This purported science, which has gained great influence (not least within government), has often had a natural tendency to see individuals and societies in terms of the economic dimension of man. Furthermore, from the late-nineteenth century onwards national politics has become increasingly dominated by economic issues. Religion, the Constitution and international affairs have declined in importance as politicians have increasingly presented themselves as the operators of economically beneficial state levers. As a part of this process, general elections today are increasingly dominated by promises to the electorate about the economy and wealth. This 'materialisation' of politics has been matched by, and bound up with, major changes in the responsibilities and function of the state. During the modern era government has greatly extended its role in spheres such as the management of the economy, the social distribution of wealth and the regulation of property relations. Both these developments have powerfully acted to stress, and to draw attention to, the economic dimension of what man is and what he does.

Party ideological orientations have played an important role in these two developments and have joined them in helping to propel economism into its position of modern-day prominence. On the British Left from the late-nineteenth century onwards there has often been a tendency to lay emphasis upon economic realities within society and to argue that the primary purpose of politics is to employ the state to alter economic arrangements. Whether justified or not, this approach has involved a marked stress on our economic activity and conditions, and on the role of the economy in shaping our relationships with others and in determining the destiny of our personal lives. It has often been the economic route which has been held up as the primary path to our future well-being. On the Right, and especially in recent decades, there has often been the belief that a correct management of the 'market', and the defence and promotion of a 'free' economy, is one of the primary tasks of politics and that the correct functioning of this market is a vital key to the happiness of the people. A great deal of emphasis is placed upon the correct workings of this market and upon the benefits which it is said to produce. In this way of thinking, it is almost as though the success of the free economy is the great aim of civilisation. Once again, the economic path is that which is pointed out to contemporary man. Whether well-conceived or not, this approach – like its ideological counterpart – has proved a major promoter of economism.

Powerism

'Powerism' is the creed which believes that man is chiefly the expression of an inner impulse to power and that human society should primarily be seen as a place where people struggle for dominance and control, rank and position, wealth and command. At times, emphasis is placed upon how individuals are animated by this will to power; at others, we are presented with a vision of societal conflict between different interests, groups or classes. The idea becomes transferred onto the international scene with the assertion that ethnic groups, peoples or nations are engaged in a similar process of conflict for ascendancy and dominion. Hitler, as is well known, erected this vision of man into a diabolical ideology: 'God...casts the masses of humanity on the earth and each one has to look after himself and how he gets through. One person takes something away from another and you can only say that the stronger wins'.[34] Indeed, he appears to have replaced the soul with the will. And in his novel *The Devils* (1871), the great Russian writer Fyodor Dostoevsky (1821-1881) has one of his characters declare: 'For three years I have been searching for the attribute of my divinity, and I've found it: the attribute of my divinity is – Self-Will'.[35]

Powerism, too, has a strong determinist element. It is argued that this drive to power is an innate force which propels man forwards in his actions; it is said to be an inescapable and impelling dynamic which moulds his entire experience. For powerism, therefore, *homo sapiens* is not animated by the soul or to be understood in terms of his relationship to supernatural realities – he is to be seen first and foremost as a striver after power, and his condition is to be analysed primarily in terms of how much power he holds and with reference to the power structures to which he belongs. In this vision, will-power seems to take the place of spirituality.

Within the West this approach to man and the human experience has a distinct philosophical pedigree which stretches back through such milestones as Nietzsche's 'will to power', Marx's class struggle, and the insights of Nicolò Machiavelli (1469-1527). In the seventeenth century the Englishman Thomas Hobbes gave forceful expression to the powerist perspective:

> It is true, that certain living creatures, as Bees, and Ants, live sociably one with another, (which are therefore by Aristotle numbered amongst Political creatures) and yet have no other direction, than their particular judgements and appetites; nor speech, whereby one of them can signify to another, what he thinks expedient for the common benefit: and therefore some man may perhaps desire to know, why Man-kind cannot do the same. To which I answer:
>
> First, that men are continually in competition for Honour and Dignity, which these creatures are not; and consequently amongst men there ariseth on that ground, Envy and Hatred, and finally Warre; but amongst these not so.
>
> Secondly, that amongst these creatures, the Common good difference not from the Private; and being by nature enclined to their private, they procure thereby the common benefit. But man, whose Joy consists in comparing himself with other men, can relish nothing but what is eminent.[36]

In recent times we find much of the powerist perspective expressed in the opinions of the European 'New Left', as witness the following reflections of one of its leading torchbearers, Michel Foucault (1926-1984):

> It seems to me that power is 'always already there', that one is never 'outside' it, that there are no 'margins' for those who break with the system to gambol in...I would suggest rather (but these are hypotheses which will need exploring): (i) that power is co-extensive with the social body; there are no species of primal liberty between the meshes of this network; (ii) that relations of power are interwoven with other kinds of relations (production, kinship, family, sexuality) for which they play at once a conditioning and a conditioned role.[37]

Powerism has various crossovers with the other materialist visions of man. It has gained great force and credibility from one way of understanding the animal kingdom (see below under 'animalism') and thus intersects with the idea that in essentials man is the outcome of a process of biological development. It is often assumed that nature revolves around a system of the 'survival of the fittest' and that within and between species there is a constant struggle for supremacy. Whether this idea is correct or not, it acts to give marked reinforcement to the powerist perspective – it is asserted that man belongs to the animal kingdom and thus reflects and expresses this central and governing principle of life on earth. Powerism also interacts with economism. Money and wealth are an expression of power, and the impulse to their acquisition – which is alleged to be the great feature of *homo oeconomicus* – is seen as a part of this more general drive to power. There is also a tie-up with humanism. The emphasis of this creed on power is strengthened by the belief that human power is supreme within the universe (there being no God) and by the enormous increase in man's domination of nature during the modern era – a thought-world emphasis on power has been encouraged by its massive human acquisition.

Animalism

'Animalism' is the creed which holds that man should really be seen as a member of the animal kingdom and perceived as the outcome of a process of biological evolution. Man, it is said, is certainly a highly developed and advanced animal, but he remains an animal, and there is nothing which separates him in fundamental terms from the animal kingdom. It is believed that there are no grounds for supposing that man has a soul, and it is asserted that he should be placed within the framework of these natural and material processes of earth and the universe which produce and condition biological life.

A powerful determinist element is conspicuous by its presence. It is maintained that man, like the animals, is propelled forward by a biological pre-programming, and for this reason his actions, thoughts and feelings are to be understood with reference to the inheritance of millennia of evolution. He merely does and thinks what is natural to a species marked out from the others merely by a higher stage of development.

But it is not just individual man who is seen in these terms. Human society receives the same perspective, as the doctrines of sociobiology at times illustrate only too well.[38] Thus it is argued that human communities have shared characteristics which are determined by biological moulding. Evolution, it is said, leaves inevitable marks on the way we live together, and these forms should not be understood with reference to some mythical soul or God but in terms of the conditioning produced by our biological inheritance. Culture, for this reason, cannot have a spiritual content. Lions and baboons in their societies do what they have to do, and in ours we do what we have to do. The conclusion is obvious: in this schema, biological pre-programming and nature take the place of the soul and the supernatural.

Much of this line of thought is well expressed by two contemporary authors who believe, like so many others, that the key to understanding what we are lies in probing into our biological past. In the premise to their *Shadows of Forgotten Ancestors,* Sagan and Druyan ask:

Who are we? Where do we come from? Why are we *this* way and not some other? What does it mean to be human?...When, beginning in 1859, our very origins, it was suggested, could be understood by a natural, unmystical process – requiring no God or gods – our aching sense of isolation became nearly complete...The study of the history of life, the evolutionary process, and the nature of the other beings who ride this planet with us has begun to cast a little light on those past links in the chain. We have not met our forgotten ancestors, but we begin to sense their presence in the dark. We recognize their shadows here and there. They were once as real as we are. We would not be here were it not for them. Our natures and theirs are indissolubly linked despite the aeons that may separate us. The key to who we are is waiting in those shadows.[39]

Later, predictably enough, these authors also pose the following question: 'When we consider the kinship of all life on Earth, is it plausible that humans have immortal souls and all other animals do not?'[40]

Animalism's centrality in the materialist matrix is evident. It has a whole series of overlaps with the other false anthropologies of post-modernity. The false but widespread idea that the natural world is a harsh world of strife, teeth and blood is transposed onto the experience of the individual and human society, and here we encounter an important intersection with powerism. Humanism is connected to a perspective which excludes the existence of the soul and God and sees man as the supreme animal, the highest of the high, the princely primate at the pinnacle of the universe. For all its emphasis on primordial instincts and impulses, animalism also has an overlap with rationalism – man's biology and his evolution are said to be the outcome of rational, almost mechanistic, processes; what he is and does follow certain discernible patterns; and he is made up of, and produces, evident structures. It is thus asserted that he is fully accessible to scientific analysis. Economism, too, works its way in – primordial man, like modern-day animals, was constantly engaged in the search for food and we are said to continue to bear within us this determining impulse to acquisition. An element of societalism is also present – it is argued that human society, like the society of other higher species, is biologically determined and produces a separate entity (marked by certain predictable characteristics) which exercises a great influence on its participants.

During the modern era the creed of animalism has received impetus from the impact of such disciplines as biology, zoology and botany. Under the influence of these branches of study the idea has gained ground that man can be approached much as one would approach a plant or an animal. The age of the Enlightenment wanted to apply the methods employed in the study of physical phenomena to the understanding of man; an analogous later belief was that *homo sapiens* was accessible to the techniques of inquiry applied to the planet's flora and fauna.

The British themselves have done a great deal to promote this development and have displayed a noted liking for the animalist perspective. During the nineteenth century the British led the world in such disciplines – in part because the growth of their empire stimulated an intense interest in what were the rapidly expanding horizons of the natural world. The great English naturalist Charles Darwin (1809-1882), who participated to the full in this development, located man firmly within the animal kingdom and sought to understand human nature with reference to biological dynamics of evolution which followed rational patterns of development. His ideas spread far and wide and have since been carried forward by the disciplines to which he made such an important contribution. In Great Britain these branches of knowledge have achieved an especial purchase on popular culture, as the endless flow of television wildlife programmes well demonstrates – broadcasts which often place man fairly and squarely within the animal world. A cursory reading of the works of such writers as Desmond Morris well illuminates how this historical trajectory has led to a rooting of the conviction that man is, in reality, a 'naked ape':

> There are one hundred and ninety-three living species of monkeys and apes. One hundred and ninety-two of them are covered with hair. The exception is a naked ape, self-named *Homo sapiens*. I am a zoologist and the naked ape is an animal. He is therefore fair game for my pen and I refuse to avoid him any longer simply because some of his behaviour patterns are rather complex and impressive. My excuse is that in becoming so erudite Homo sapiens has remained a naked ape nevertheless; in acquiring lofty new motives, he has lost none of the earthy old ones. This is frequently a cause of some embarrassment to him but his old impulses have been with him for millions of years, his new ones only a few thousand at the most – and there is no hope of quickly struggling off the accumulated genetic legacy of his whole evolutionary past. He would be a far less worried and more fulfilled animal if he would only face up to this fact. Perhaps this is where the zoologist can help.[41]

There is another element behind the British embrace of the animalist perspective which requires comment. Ever since the nineteenth century Continental visitors have frequently commented on the English sensitivity to animals. This sensitivity grew up against a background of a constant attachment within British culture to nature, an attachment which has been expressed in such disparate elements as Romantic poetry, a passion for gardening and the presence of town parks. It may be remembered that pushed forward by such organisations as the Royal Society for the Prevention of Cruelty to Animals (1824), the Victorians paved the way at a European level in ensuring humane treatment for animals.

Animals have also been central to many areas of recreational activity, as greyhound racing, pigeon-flying and horse-racing well illustrate, and have formed the central focus of field sports, conservation movements and wildlife associations. Animals have also had a high profile in a long chain of children's books from Beatrix Potter (1866-1943) to C.S. Lewis (1898-1963) and beyond – works which have formed many a young British mind. But the real great point of contact, and the principal site for this sensitivity, is probably to be found in an intense attachment to domestic pets (often provoked by personal loneliness) – a practice in which Great Britain seems to have led the West. Around half of households in the United Kingdom are now said to own a pet.[42] As is the case with computers, in this whole area, too, nearness breeds comparison. In close proximity to animals, whether in recreational activity, childhood reading or within the home, how many people are not led to perceive a difference only of degree? The recent (and highly symptomatic) idea of extending natural rights to animals – and in particular to the primates – is one theoretical expression of this removal of an ancient barrier between humans and animals which was previously defended by the spiritualist perspective.[43]

Sexualism

In part the creed of 'sexualism' is a variant of animalism and has been promoted by similar factors, but it also has a specific autonomy and profile all of its own. Sexualism believes that man is fundamentally a reproductive creature whose primary purpose and goal is to continue his line, to extend his genetic inheritance and to promote what he is through time, both as an individual and as a species. To this end what really matters, it is argued, is his sexual nature – that aspect of his identity which is dedicated to his reproduction. In this outlook an individual's actions and experience are primarily understood and perceived in relation to his sexuality, and it is assumed that the sexual realm, with all its impulses, configurations and forms of expression, is the great motivator and animator of what he is. In this schema the existence and the functions of the soul of man become replaced by sex and sexual activity. Human communities also come to be seen from the point of view of their impulse to self-reproduction and demographic expansion – a perspective evident in various types of racist theory.

In this creed, too, determinism is powerfully present – man is perceived as being driven forward by a biological impulse and moulded in what he is and does by a constant drive to self-reproduction. All sorts of parallels with the animal kingdom are employed to support this approach and this creed intersects with animalism in many ways. The powerist and economist perspectives are also present in that the impulse to reproduce is often placed within the context of a struggle for the power and the economic resources necessary to guarantee the survival and success of offspring. Humanism also enters the picture – does not man's domination of the planet and his surpassing of the other species bear witness to a supremacy rooted in a highly successful form of sexuality?

Much of this line of approach, albeit with evident variations, is espoused by the contemporary best-selling author, ethnologist and philosopher Richard Dawkins. Men are defined by this Oxford academic as 'gene machines' – this is said to be the great reality of the human experience. The emphasis of this writer on the selfishness innate to our condition, and its endemic barriers to love, is highly significant:

> I shall argue that a predominant quality to be expected in a successful gene is ruthless selfishness. This gene selfishness will give rise to selfishness in individual behaviour. However, as we shall see, there are special circumstances in which a gene can achieve its own selfish ends best by fostering a limited form of altruism at the level of individual animals. 'Special' and 'limited' are important words in the last sentence. Much as we might wish to believe otherwise, universal love and the welfare of the species as a whole are concepts which simply do not make evolutionary sense...My own feeling is that a human society based simply on the gene's law of universal ruthless selfishness would be a very nasty society in which to live. But unfortunately, however much we may deplore something, it does not stop it being true...Be warned that if you wish, as I do, to build a society in which individuals co-operate generously and unselfishly towards a common good, you can expect little help from biological nature.[44]

The perception of conflict which is central to the animalist vision of what we are is expressed in many of the chapter headings of Dawkins' book – 'aggression: stability and the selfish machine'; 'battle of the generations'; 'battle of the sexes'; and 'you scratch my back, I'll ride on yours'.

Physiologism

'Physiologism' is the creed which believes that man is in essential terms his material make-up. This perspective asserts that his personality, perceptions, feelings, and even his ideas of right and wrong, derive largely from his physical frame, and in particular from the structures, composition and workings of his brain. When this organ is altered by surgery or drugs, it is observed, an individual's behaviour and character change – is one not thus dealing, it is asked, with what really determines what man is? For physiologism it is the body – not the soul – which is the great animator of *homo sapiens*. This approach also stresses that the body comes from evolutionary, biological and genetic origins – from material forces, that is to say, which have nothing to do with the divine. Here we have an example of materialism in very pure form, and no doubt part of the appeal of this creed lies in the fact that our bodies are highly tangible and visible entities. This creed certainly has high levels of plausibility and has placed its roots very deep in the contemporary mind. 'Modern psychologists have catalogued at length the assumptions of orthodox Western psychology, the assumptions that often form the nature of the modern reader's selfhood and its perception', write two experts on the English poet and mystic William Blake (1757-1827), a thinker who was a vehement anti-physiologist:

> The chief of these may be summarized as follows: a person is his body and nothing more; each person is isolated from all others, locked in his nervous system; consciousness is identical with the activity of the brain; death is the termination of human consciousness; a person perceives the physical world and obtains sensations from the internal operations of his body and nervous system; a person can trust his senses to inform him accurately about the nature of the physical world. It is crucial to reading Milton for us to understand that these assumptions of the modern world view were developed as a direct result of the scientific revolution of Blake's time, and that they are the assumptions underlying what may be called a worship of the physical world or what Blake, in fact, called Natural Religion... Those of us educated in this scientistic world view – who earn our livings through the advanced technologies developed from it, and enjoy comfort as a result of its radical transformation of daily life – constantly dwell in an environment fabricated out of these assumptions. Our laws, our institutions, our understandings of sanity and insanity, and many of our basic cultural codes and social conventions imply the "truths" of this Natural Religion.[45]

Much of the physiologist position is expounded by Francis Crick, the world-famous neurobiologist. Crick is yet another modern thinker who wishes to reject the validity of the religious concept of the soul and invokes the full force of scientific authority to support this undertaking:

> "You", your joys and your sorrows, your memories and your ambitions, your sense of personal identity and free will, are in fact no more than the behaviour of a vast assembly of nerve cells and their associated molecules. As Lewis Carroll's Alice might have phrased it: "You're nothing but a pack of neurons." This hypothesis is so alien to the ideas of most people alive today that it can truly be called astonishing...A modern neurobiologist sees no need for the religious concept of a soul to explain the behaviour of humans and other animals...It is not that they can yet prove the idea to be false. Rather, as things stand at the moment, they see no need for that hypothesis.[46]

Physiologism, too, has a strong determinist content. It habitually argues that the way we are, and the way we see the world, are the direct outcomes of our physical structures; that all this is fixed, as it were, by our bodies much as a robot is determined by its programming; and that our selves are in reality our material processes. Predictably enough, in this creed there are reinforcing overlaps with a number of the other post-modern visions of man. Animalism emphasises the biological and evolutionary origins of man's body; humanism lays stress upon how our physical – and especially our cerebral – capacities place us at the pinnacle of the universe; rationalism stresses the rational and mechanistic nature of our physical structures; and sexualism draws attention to one of the great features of the human corporeal identity.

Of course, the idea that man is his body, for all its post-modern clothing, is not new. The ancient Greeks, for example, believed that the 'humours' were major determinants of our consciousness. But this vision of man has received major new impetus during the modern era, most notably from important advances in knowledge about our material selves. The Darwinian exploration of our evolutionary and biological origins, and the many other inquiries which followed on from that point of departure, have proved one powerful factor in promoting physiologist thought. Mandel's discovery of the mechanisms of genetic inheritance, and subsequent research carried out in the wake of that breakthrough – not least as regards the nature and role of DNA – have constituted another. Medical science, especially as regards its great advances in relation to the processes of the brain, is the third great force which has delved deep into the mechanisms of our bodies, drawn attention to our physical dimension, and thereby fuelled the physiologist approach. The ascendancy and authority of the exact sciences has interwoven with these three factors to provide further support. In particular, they have attributed value and importance to that which can be measured and examined in concrete terms – in this case the human body. Are we not repeatedly encouraged by these disciplines to think that we are mechanistic entities, the expression of physical systems and processes which work their way out in a tangible frame of flesh and blood?

Feelingism

'Feelingism' is closely related to animalism, sexualism and physiologism in its stress and emphasis upon what man feels. This creed sees the individual as primarily a bearer and expression of feelings which shape and direct his perceptions and behaviour, and which act as a powerful arbiter of his moral and ethical attitudes and beliefs. In essence, feelingism maintains that it is man's feeling systems (understood in a very wide sense) which really animate what he is and does. It advances the idea that such systems and the perceptions which spring from them are the principal source of action within the human frame and that beneath this basic level nothing else is to be found – here, too, we encounter a substitute for the soul. Such systems are often held to derive from man's evolutionary programming and physiological structures, and here we encounter notable points of intersection with animalism, sexualism and physiologism. A strong determinist element is evident. Feelingism frequently asserts that an individual is driven forward by what he feels and that he responds and reacts to what his feeling systems experience and promote much as animals obey instinct and natural impulse. The common (and monstrous) contemporary refrain – 'I felt like it' – both bears witness to the influence of this post-modern model of man and illustrates its deterministic content. Much of the orientation of feelingism is expressed by another best-selling author, Daniel Goleman:

A view of human nature that ignores the power of emotions is sadly shortsighted. The very name *Homo Sapiens*, the thinking species, is misleading...As we all know from experience, when it comes to shaping our decisions and our actions, feeling counts every bit as much – and often more – than thought...But while our emotions have been wise guides in the evolutionary long run, the new realities civilization presents have arisen with such rapidity that the slow march of evolution cannot keep up...Despite these social constraints, passions overwhelm reason time and time again. This given of human nature arises from the basic architecture of mental life...For better or for worse, our appraisal of every personal encounter and our responses to it are shaped not just by our rational judgements or our personal history, but also by our distant ancestral past.[47]

A number of key factors have helped to promote the feelingist perspective in Great Britain over recent centuries. There has certainly been a strong theoretical and artistic background and input. From the eighteenth century onwards, in part as a reaction to philosophical rationalism and as a support to empiricism, emphasis has been repeatedly laid upon the senses as a source of knowledge. This is more than evident in the writings of such thinkers as David Hume (1711-1776), in the highly influential stress on 'pleasure or pain' as a basis for moral decision which was promoted by Utilitarianism in the early nineteenth century, or more generally in the philosophical movement known as Sensism. In addition, the artistic intelligentsia from the Romantics onwards has repeatedly laid emphasis on the value of feelings, frequently endowing them with a quasi-sacral quality and constantly stressing the legitimacy of engaging in their almost limitless exploration. From the statement of the Romantic painter John Constable (1776-1837), 'painting for me is another word for feeling',[48] to the affirmations of the exponents of the 1960s' counter-culture, and on to today's rock singers, British artists of various hues and colours have frequently been committed proponents of the feelingist perspective. Advances in medical science, especially in relation to the workings of the nervous system and the brain, have also drawn attention to the inner world of feelings and sensations, probing their mechanisms, stressing their impact and emphasising their importance. And contemporary society itself, with its massive emphasis on consumption, stimulation and excitement, and its world of the video screen and cars, food and sex, images and dreams, is engaged in an unceasing process of emphasis on what we feel. With such intense pressures is it really surprising that post-modern man is constantly led to believe that *homo sapiens* is really *homo sentiens*?

Psychism

'Psychism' is the creed which holds that at the guiding centre of every individual there is a 'psyche'. Rightsism asserts that man is the bearer of a set of rights, but this outlook perceives an alternative presence. Despite psychism's frequent claims to 'scientific' validity, what this purported psyche really is, where it is located and how it functions, are by no means clear. The central notion is that each person is the carrier of an internal system composed of impulses and perceptions, memories and emotions, desires and fears, in part conscious and in part unconscious, which is the great animator of what he is and does.

This highly influential creed has replaced the soul with the psyche in very effective fashion and now exercises an extraordinary grip on Western and British culture and thought. Such terms and disciplines as 'psychology' (and its adjective 'psychological'), 'psychiatry' and 'psychoanalysis' all attest, at times, to the power and impact of the psychist perspective. This creed has a number of overlaps with the rest of the materialist matrix. Psychism has a strong rationalist (and at times mechanistic) impulse – inner man is said to be organised according to fixed patterns and arrangements which are accessible to rational analysis; its emphasis on the primitive and primordial springs of human action derives great force from the animalist, sexualist and feelingsist perspectives; and societarism enters the picture through psychism's stress on the alleged conditioning effects of an individual's childhood experience. With its belief that man is controlled and driven by 'sub-conscious' or 'unconscious' forces, this post-modern vision of man, too, clearly has a strong determinist dimension.

The rise of psychism owes much to the impact of the thought of one of its founding fathers – Sigmund Freud (1856-1939). With his theories about the 'ego' and the 'id', the 'conscious' and the 'unconscious', and 'complexes' and 'neuroses', Freud believed that he had laid bare the real inner machinery of what we are and of what it is to be human. His notion of 'psychoanalysis' was a further expression of this conviction that man could be explained in rational and measurable terms – inner 'laws' were said to be at work which could be understood and analysed. Freud, it must be recognised, neglected the contribution of genetics to the understanding of personality, and the exact sciences have never been able to corroborate his theories. 'The impact of psychoanalysis on the West cannot be justified on the ground that it contains a body of reasonably secure or established knowledge about human nature', wrote B.A. Farrell in 1981, 'analysis does not contain any such body of knowledge'.[49] Another authority, P.B. Medawar, puts psychoanalysis on the same level as Mesmerism and phrenology and declares that its ruins 'will remain for ever one of the saddest and strangest of all landmarks in the history of twentieth-century thought'.[50]

But this fact has not inhibited the immense diffusion and influence in Great Britain of the model of man that Freud proposed. The 'psychoanalytic movement' which he helped to set in motion, with its vast army of practitioners, has been one influential promoter; the intellectual, academic and artistic classes, who have always proved a fertile field for his notions and beliefs, another. The disciplines of psychology and psychiatry, in all their various forms and expressions, although of course not necessarily 'Freudian' in approach, have sometimes promoted the same kind of model of man. And whoever encounters one of the mass of 'counsellors' which government (and others) have seen fit to introduce into the texture of social life (occupying the space filled previously by family, priests, neighbours and friends), may often have to endure – explicitly or implicitly – the tenets, principles and practices of the psychist world-view.

A historian of the psychoanalytic movement spawned by Freud and others tells us a great deal about the character of this salient expression of the psychist outlook. Ernest Gellner observes that this system of ideas was able to conquer much of Western thought in the space of a few decades, thereby becoming 'the dominant idiom for the discussion of the human personality and of human relations',[51] and stresses that an analysis of this movement is of the 'utmost importance for the understanding of our society and its intellectual and moral climate'.[52] His summarising description of this movement's essential beliefs is instructive:

> The key doctrines of the Psychoanalytic Movement may be summed up as follows:
>
> There is a realm known as the Unconscious, which is reasonably similar in much of its contents to the conscious mind and continuous with it...
>
> Many, perhaps most, or perhaps all, important turning-points in a person's life – which determine his basic attitudes, emotions, orientation – occur within this realm.
>
> Many of these crucial decisions – or predetermining events – occur very early in a person's life...
>
> Though this realm is not accessible to consciousness or common sense, its general laws are the subject of an autonomous science, namely psychoanalysis.[53]

Their Historical Function

The false anthropologies of post-modernity make up a natural matrix for a number of reasons. First of all, they are united in attacking the Christian vision of the world and the practical expression of that vision. In this sense they have had a shared aim and have performed a distinct historical function. 'Let us renounce the ridiculous theory of the immortality of the soul, made to be scorned as relentlessly as that of the existence of a God as false and as ridiculous as it is', declared the Marquis de Sade (1740-1814), 'let us abjure with equal courage both of these absurd fables, the fruits of fear, ignorance, and superstition'.[4] In conformity with the intentions of these sentiments the primary historical function of these false anthropologies has been to eject the Christian world-view from the formative core of British culture. Their purpose has been pre-eminently anti-theological and anti-religious. This elaborate and far-ranging matrix provides a whole number of perspectives which constantly deny the existence of the spiritual and the supernatural – the first step to the undermining of Christian teachings. If the various contentions of these different ways of looking at ourselves and our world are right, there can be no soul, idea of the life according to the Spirit, concept of spiritual health or ill-health, kingdom of heaven or of hell, the afterlife in the abyss or paradise, or the devil and God. If they are correct, we must look at the human condition and the cosmos in very different terms.

In a further demonstration of their historical function, these materialist visions of man counter the Christian world-view by providing substitute means by which to satisfy man's religious needs and impulses. They provide a pseudo-religious framework which undercuts the appeal of their adversary. They invite the journeying individual down wrong paths marked by erroneous signposts. There are all kinds of forces which are said to command us (determinism, indeed, powerfully permeates these false anthropologies): our animal inheritance, society, sexuality and the will to power, to name just a few of these surrogates for the supernatural; there are a number of substitutes for the soul – the psyche, innate rights, the rational faculties, our physiological processes, our feelings – and so the dire list goes on; and there are a variety of related ideas about our purpose in life and what our behaviour should be – notions which supplant spiritualist concepts of good and evil, shape personal conduct and mould the culture to which we belong.

In this context it would be very surprising if such materialist thought did not have its specific machinery of support within society, and at times we encounter a veritable priesthood composed of intellectuals, academics, psychist practitioners, social scientists and political activists, all of whom are engaged in the promotion of an orthodoxy which is often expressed in writings and publications strongly reminiscent of sacred texts. In this post-modern clerisy we appear to have before us much of what is condemned in organised religion – dogmas and certitudes, totems and superstitions, unfounded fears and tenacious prejudices, censorship and intimidation, the promotion of orthodoxy and corporate self-serving. All these various elements constitute salient features of the pseudo-religious appeal of the materialist matrix, and are an integral part of its anti-theological and anti-religious function.

This historical function is also borne out by the tendency of these materialist visions of man to be held up as positive new departures which have lifted humanity out of the dark ages. They are often presented as the essential ingredients of latter-day civilisation; the components of contemporary enlightenment; the expressions of what is modern, pro-gressive and scientific. This line of presentation aims at a repudiation and cancellation of the pre-modern Christian tradition, which in corresponding fashion is often held up as being out-of-date and 'unscientific'. One can thus readily understand the frequent polemical emphasis of the supporters of the components of this matrix on the witchcraft, superstition, mysticism, prayers against diseases, biblical myths, and Galileo trial of the Christian medieval period.

The apparent success of this materialist matrix in imposing itself during the contemporary era has acted to reinforce this line of reasoning. Given the way things have actually gone, given how we think now, are we not, it is argued, really dealing with progress, the modern, and with what science approves? This line of attack also means that opponents can be ridiculed as the benighted adversaries of a development which constitutes the authentic and perhaps even inevitable advance of man. Those who go against the trend can be dismissed as members of an ignorant and out-dated past. Notions of the soul and of God become stigmatised as anachronisms and adherence to them deemed a mere cultural throw-back. And who nowadays does not want to be 'modern'?

Moreover, as has been demonstrated, these visions of man frequently intersect; they often reinforce each other and provide important reciprocal support. In this way these visions lead back and forth to each other by a number of routes, setting up powerful mechanisms of credibility and persuasion. They naturally lead on to each other and back to each other through an intricate series of paths of connection. So it is that in a variety of ways animalism is linked to powerism, which is connected with economism, which intersects with societalism, which overlaps with rightsism, and so on. The individual becomes entrapped within their encompassing confines. His mind moves from one explanation of what we are to another without ever escaping. He is like a rubber ball which bounces from wall to wall and from floor to ceiling without ever leaving the darkened room.

The contradictory quality of this matrix brings out the extent to which in its workings it is a made-to-measure destructive device. Its lack of internal coherence illustrates the extent to which it is an instrument, a means to an end, a functional phenomenon. Looked at closely, these false anthropologies frequently contradict each other and are often in marked opposition. For example: can man be essentially cerebral and the product of his feelings at the same time? If his psyche is what counts, how is it possible that it is the human body that matters? Is it likely that we are both formed by society and moulded by our sexual impulses? How can the notion that we are primarily the bearers of a bundle of innate rights be reconciled with the belief that we are chiefly biological creatures shaped in our natures by a process of natural evolution? But in practice these questions are not often raised by the proponents of these models – a fact which in itself is highly suggestive. It is almost as though the actual truthfulness of these creeds is not what really matters. What seems to be of primary importance is that they attack the cosmological validity of the Christian world-view and thereby inhibit its practical implementation. We are dealing with an authentic devil's brew – potent in its acidic and destructive effects but lacking in internal consistency.

The great point about all these approaches to man, what provides them above all else with homogeneity and unity, is that they take away that which makes him truly human – his divinely-bestowed soul. That is their fundamental cutting edge. The soul is what makes us human, 'all too human'. What guarantees our humanity is our spirit – it is the force which marks us out from the rest of the Creation; it is what raises us above the animal kingdom; it is the determining factor of the specifically *human* experience; the central feature of the human vocation. In short, it is the key to understanding what we are, what we undergo and what we should be and do. Yet the materialist matrix not only dehumanises man at the level of definition, it also works to dehumanise his personal experience and human society. Authentic individual fulfilment and the achievement of true community are impeded and their inverse is promoted. This outcome should not surprise us. Given the nature of the cosmos and the purpose of man, it is more than predictable that an assault on the concept of the soul leads to a negation of what the soul is called upon to create and what the life according to the Spirit is capable of sustaining. This very reality lends credence to the Christian world-view – we grasp its validity by understanding what happens when it is repudiated: *per opposita cognoscitur*. Attention must now be turned to the various mechanisms of this dehumanisation. The fatal impact of these eleven false anthropologies, of which a taxonomy has just been presented, now becomes the subject of our concern.

Chapter Four

Their Fatal Impact

How have these materialist visions of man brought about desocialisation in a direct and personal fashion? The thesis proposed here is the following. On the one hand, they have attacked the idea that man has a soul. A powerful philosophical and intellectual assault has sought to distance man's spiritual presence from the contemporary thought-world. In this way an attempt has been made to displace the Christian world-view from the way we think and perceive – at the level of the deepest knowledge about ourselves there has been an impulse towards the spreading of ignorance. But of course we are not dealing here with a mere matter of mind – action and behaviour are also affected. This assault on the idea of the soul has involved an attempt to discourage the life according to the Spirit and an accompanying attack upon its essential features. By this route there has been a move towards inhibiting the release of the socialising potential of the soul of man into our national culture. On the other hand, these false anthropologies have actively promoted the dark side of man's inner being – that potential side of the human soul which lacks true life. They have acted to generate the spiritual ill-health which is always possible within us; they are powerful generators of selfish individualism and the lifestyle based upon it. Following the structures of the human condition and the cosmos ordained by God, this promotion of the dark side can only induce disorder and disruption, fracture between individuals, and the dissolution of social ties. The materialist matrix, we begin to perceive, is *an assault on love* and therefore involves a terrible imposition of social poverty. What are the detailed contours of this assault?

The Attack on the Life According to the Spirit

> For those who live according to the flesh set their minds on the
> things of the flesh, but those who live according to the Spirit set
> their minds on the things of the Spirit. To set the mind on the flesh
> is death, but to set the mind on the Spirit is life and peace. For the
> mind that is set on the flesh is hostile to God; it does not submit to
> God's law, indeed it cannot; and those who are in the flesh cannot
> please God. But you are not in the flesh, you are in the Spirit, if the
> Spirit of God really dwells in you (Rom 8:5-14).

Going against the words of St. Paul, these post-modern visions of man
do not only drive out a way of looking at things, a perspective on life, a
way of understanding humans and the universe, in short a distinctive
cosmology. They also involve an assault on the life according to the
Spirit and on that positive social expression of the soul which is vital to
the achievement of authentic community. This is the greatest single
force behind our contemporary state of desocialisation. How does this
assault operate? First of all, men become convinced that they do not
have souls and the stewarding of these souls is thereby systematically
discouraged. Without the concept of the soul its guardianship becomes
undermined. Thus the socialising role and potential of authentic spiritual
life becomes compromised and the undermining of social cohesion is
the inevitable result. In this way a denial of the soul of man removes the
philosophical bases of a process which leads to the construction of an
integrated and integrating culture.

But it is not only the theoretical starting point of true spirituality which
is removed. Just as the materialist matrix is tailor-made to displace the
Christian world-view, so many of the features of these visions of man are
perfectly designed to launch a *direct* attack on the essential features of
the authentic spiritual life. The presence of such symmetries brings out
the extent to which we are dealing here with a conflict innate to the human
condition. We are touching on that struggle to control the spiritual
character of culture which forms such a characteristic part of our life on
earth. What are the principal features of this *direct* attack? The life
according to the Spirit becomes checked and cancelled at its key points.
Firstly, there is a discouragement of a relationship of the soul with its
maker and an undermining of the openness and receptivity of man to
God. This is accompanied by an intense encouragement of selfish
individualism – that great cause and symptom of desocialisation – which

is marked in particular by a propensity to keen if not fierce competition with other people. Linked to this element is a constant readiness to define and perceive other individuals as objects. Indeed, no account of the impact of the materialist matrix would be complete without an understanding of its 'objectification' of humans. These attacks on the springs of authentic community are accompanied by the deleterious results of a strongly promoted determinism – namely the abandonment of the conscience, the promotion of amoralism, the refusal to accept personal responsibility, and a reluctance to adopt a moral stance. At the same time there is an associated disinclination to accept the suffering that loyalty to true spirituality often requires. All these aspects of this direct attack are major factors behind our present plight, and will now be considered in the order in which they have just been adumbrated.

The philosophical denial of the spiritual presence within us undermines the guardianship of the soul's relationship with God. How is it possible to steward a relationship which by definition cannot exist? Here authentic spiritual life receives a strong blow. Communion with God by a variety of mechanisms – prayer in a host of forms; sensitivity to vocation; obedience to divine law; openness to supernatural direction; and love for other souls – becomes discouraged. In extreme form individuals come to construct a kind of cement bunker which shuts them off from the reception of divine light. Because communion with God is of vital help in ensuring authentic spiritual life, it is obvious that the constraints on this process promoted by the false anthropologies of post-modernity are a direct route to the loss of ties.

In addition, the refusal of the relationship with God impedes the reception of personal vocation willed by the Almighty for the benefit of individuals and society, and as God is the constant promoter of love and truth, a potent source of benefit for a people's culture is thereby countered – a vital conduit is blocked in its personal channels. The removal of this feature of the life according to the Spirit is supported by the tendency of the materialist matrix to place the individual not within the context which contains supernatural realities but inside a framework which is all too human – perhaps the central purpose of humanism. People, for example, are to see themselves in relation to society, or to the evolution of their species, or to their own internal physical processes. The human world replaces God as the principal point of reference for each individual; and as a result, naturally enough, the positive social expression of the healthy soul is discouraged.

Secondly, authentic spiritual life involves a communitarian perspective, a concern with one's neighbour and an awareness that love is our fundamental purpose. But from the materialist matrix there emerges a movement in the other direction – away from a spirit of community towards individualism; away from giving towards selfishness; and away from generosity towards egocentricity. There is an emphasis on thinking about ourselves and our personal satisfaction to the detriment of concern for others. A lifestyle of selfish individualism is engendered and it is here that we encounter the 'philosophy of life' of Maritain's modern man. Indeed, John Paul II referred to a 'society which is often lost in agnosticism and individualism and which is suffering the bitter consequences of selfishness and violence'.[1]

The materialist matrix enormously encourages and legitimates selfishness by arguing that man is by his nature a selfish creature. In being concerned only with ourselves, it is argued, we merely do that which is in our nature – we should not be blamed; life is like that; we are doing that which is natural. Thus rightsism encourages us to think of the satisfaction of our personal needs and wants; societalism leads us to think that the human environment owes us certain things; econom-ism lays stress upon our personal striving for wealth; powerism does the same with regard to power; animalism likes to argue that individuals struggle for resources and self-reproduction; sexualism emphasises personal sexual gratification; physiologism and feelingism encourage us to seek out pleasure and comfort. With such an emphasis on self-interest, self-seeking and self-serving, an orientation towards acting for the benefit of others – either directly at an interpersonal level or indirectly through a positive input into our cultural environment – becomes marginalised or removed. The idea of the common project gets thrown out of the window. Society becomes desocialised by a refusal to look anywhere but at ourselves, and at ourselves understood in narrow and very impoverished terms.

The materialist matrix imparts a specific character to this lifestyle – a strong competitiveness and a marked emphasis on 'winning'. As was emphasised in chapter three, a large number of the false anthropologies of post-modernity involve a model of social life where strife and struggle between competitive individuals have a high profile: rightsism promotes a vision of society where individuals and groups engage in conflict to obtain certain entitlements; societalism perceives the human environ-ment as a place where each person strives for position, money and prestige; economism and powerism understand society as a place where people wrestle for power and wealth; animalism evokes a competitive world of the survival of the fittest; and sexualism detects a fight to promote one's own genes.

Under the impact of this way of approaching things, co-operation and collaboration become submerged by the encouragement of struggle and tension; peace and harmony become pushed aside by the promotion of strife and discord. The propensity to act with one's neighbour – which so characterises authentic spirituality – is elbowed aside by an impulse to act against him and in some way to 'beat' him. He is no longer a neighbour but something (indeed, almost an object) to be defeated and subordinated. Concomitantly, a whole host of aggressive methods by which to achieve personal advance are promoted and justified. In this context of competitive selfish individualism, the authentic spiritual life – and thus the prospects for authentic community – becomes chilled by very icy blasts.

Thirdly, let it be recalled that because of the existence of the soul men are subjects, not objects – the presence of the spirit bestows a unique value on man which means that he cannot be placed on the level of other living creatures or mere things; there is a sacredness within the human person which commands our concern; we are bound to other people by the common possession of a spiritual nature; and we are called by vocation to engage in love and thereby join with others in the construction amongst us of the kingdom of God on this earth. But the false anthropologies of post-modernity work in the opposite direction by encouraging the conversion of our fellow men into mere objects. By denying that men have a soul these perspectives devalue individuals and help to put them on the same level as things. They thus knock away the fundamental principle of the brotherhood of man.

In addition, the selfish individualism encouraged by materialist thinking promotes the idea that other people are objects to be used, means to an end, or instruments to a purpose. They are to be employed to achieve power or money, self-importance or sexual pleasure, the continuation of one's genetic code or the attainment of certain alleged rights – to name only the more obvious. In other words, people exist for oneself, rather like machines or beasts of the field. Here, too, highly aggressive methods of selfish advance receive sanction and encouragement. Yet such an objectification of humans is incompatible with the creation of authentic human community because it rules out the reality of love.

Fourthly, the materialist matrix has a strong content of determinism and this is one of its most important and destructive features. In this matrix's various expressions the individual is often perceived not as a spiritual being with a conscience and the capacity for moral choice but as an entity propelled forward by inner or external forces over which he has no control. Societalism encourages the idea that what we are and do is the outcome of societal forces; economism sees man as driven forward by an impulse to the acquisition of wealth; powerism holds him to be impelled by a will to power; animalism understands man as shaped and driven forward by his evolutionary programming; sexualism defines him as a creature spurred forward by an impulse to self-reproduction; physiologism and feelingism see individuals as determined in their lives and actions by their physical and emotional states; and psychism rounds off the barrage with the assertion that in essentials man is shaped, conditioned and controlled by the workings of his inner psyche. Not only does the materialist matrix replace the soul with a range of substitutes of what really animates man, but it also cancels or severely weakens the idea of effective personal choice by assuming the existence of a range of forces which mean that man cannot help what he does – he is conceived as a kind of puppet dancing on strings which are not in his hands. Such determinism amounts to a major attack on the idea and practice of free will, and is thereby a powerful factor working in favour of the loss of ties. By what routes?

One of the primary features of the life according to the Spirit is defence of the conscience and respect for its dictates. The conscience is that central faculty of our spiritual existence which helps to guide us in deciding between right and wrong and in choosing between the kingdom of God and the kingdom of Satan. It is an essential element in the employment of free will, the cultivation of virtue and the exercise of personal responsibility. Yet this integral feature of living according to the Spirit is attacked at two key points by the materialist matrix. The conscience, like God and the soul, indeed, seems to be one of the casualties of the modern world. Certainly references to it in daily conversation are becoming ever rarer. On the one hand, the denial of the soul involves the denial of the existence of this principal faculty or perceives it in such a light as to betray its real significance and purpose. On the other, determinism renders the conscience superfluous by arguing that there can be no room for its purported guidance and reflection because what happens occurs inevitably anyway. If everything is determined, moral choice and its primary seat within the human frame become irrelevant. The false anthropologies of post-modernity on the whole have no space for this vital feature of what we are, this truly sublime gift. From what has been said above, it is more than obvious that the abolition or neglect of the conscience compromises or even annuls a potent instrument by which the socialising potential of the soul is injected into the human environment.

The materialist matrix works against the authentic spiritual life in another way – through the systematic promotion of amoralism. The common contemporary desire to create a kind of morally 'neutral' society, a terrain where in some way all 'values' are possible, an environment which is somehow 'beyond good and evil', can often be directly traced to this aspect of the materialist matrix. These post-modern models of man frequently refuse objective points of moral reference – indeed are often not interested in ideas of right and wrong at all – and tend to see man as a programmed being who is not capable of other directions and thus lacks a capacity for choice – the fundamental point of departure for any moral stance. Similarly, the denial of the soul promotes a detachment from the perceptions of good and evil, and of supernatural realities, which are an integral feature of the authentic spiritual life. By these routes man becomes 'de-moralised' and consigned to a world of amorality, a context with no fixed points of moral reference, a limbo on earth. Views to the effect, for example, that man is an animal, a seeker after wealth or power, a reproductive machine, or a mere satisfier of his physical feelings, with all their powerful amoralist implications, counter the life according to the Spirit at a key point. There is an attack on our responsibility to think and act in moral terms. And this deprives society of essential binding cement.

The assault on the conscience and the promotion of amoralism are flanked by a parallel attack on virtue. In such a context it is hardly surprising that a movement has grown up in Great Britain and the United States of America in recent years dedicated to a restoration of the virtues. How does this attack operate? First of all, the absence of the concept of the soul abolishes the idea that its correct guardianship will naturally give rise to its positive expression in attitudes and behaviour – no spirit, no virtues. In addition, the determinism present in the materialist matrix discourages us from embracing the idea that certain virtuous paths should be followed. There is no impulse towards the conscious and deliberate development of certain attributes and features of our characters and behaviour which would conduce to our own spiritual health and to that of society around us. Not only, it is argued, is what we are and do in large measure determined for us and beyond the control of any purported free will, but we are actually impelled towards an existence based upon competitive selfish individualism. In such a schema the concept and practice of virtue fast become redundant, and it comes as no surprise that a whole series of terms are now heard less and less in daily conversation. The thinning of language reflects the depletion of society. How many now speak of perseverance, rectitude, constancy, patience, integrity or fortitude? But such neglect is to ignore a vital category of personal qualities which act to bind individuals together into a viable common project.

The materialist matrix also attacks the concept and exercise of personal responsibility. The authentic spiritual life requires an active exercise of free will in favour of the truth in all its forms. This is an integral part of the stewardship of the soul and an essential factor in the creation of authentic community. Moreover, by the natural order of things we necessarily impinge on the experience of others and contribute to the shaping of their context. In having free will we are called upon to assume personal responsibility for the consequences of our actions for other people. Such a recognition of responsibility is a component feature of the authentic spiritual life and forms a necessary feature of love for one's neighbour. But the materialist matrix by a number of routes launches an attack on this essential component of life in society – it 'de-responsibilises' man.

In the first place its determinism acts to shut down the idea of free will and thereby cancels a pre-condition to awareness of personal responsibility. The very concept becomes impracticable. If my actions are determined how can I be held responsible for them? In addition, the idea that other people are objects of no concern to us undermines the principle that we should be moved by considerations as to what the possible impact on others of what we say and do might be. Thirdly, the realities of selfish individualism encourage us to disregard the welfare of others in thinking about our conduct – our orientations are towards our world and our interests, not theirs. The attitude of not caring about what the direct or indirect impact of our conduct might be, the opinion that the devil can take the hindmost, and the lack of concern for personal responsibility can only act to weaken the bonds which bind a community together.

These four forms of attack on the authentic spiritual life are connected to another – the discouragement of an active moral stance in relation to the human environment. Living according to the Spirit must involve guidance and criticism, the constant input of truth into the tissue of our social context, and the adoption of a moral position. We have a duty to ensure that what is right is upheld, respected and debated. Such an attitude acts as a check on injurious behaviour and an encouragement to virtue. Indeed, a people's culture should be constantly regulated and safeguarded by this vital expression of the healthy soul. But this essential component of true community is undermined by the deterministic notion that we are not really responsible for our actions (and certainly not responsible for the welfare of others) and that a moral stance is largely irrelevant to a human condition which is in large measure shaped by forces beyond our control. There is thus an impulse towards indifference in relation to essential spiritual, moral and ethical questions which strikes deeply at the source-springs of social cohesion. For a society to be safeguarded, we must care. But if there is no sustained and constant concern to promote the vital principles of true community, how can this goal ever be really achieved? In this light one can readily understand why the contemporary Communitarian movement has called for the activation of 'moral voices'.[2]

To conclude this survey of the attack on the authentic spiritual life we may refer to the words of Dietrich Bonhoeffer (1906-1945) who observed that 'To be as free from pain as possible was unconsciously one of our guiding principles'.[3] 'To renounce a full life and its real joys in order to avoid pain', he added, 'is neither Christian nor human'.[4] Living according to the Spirit requires a readiness to endure hardship for the sake of the truth; to dissent from erroneous thought and action and to accept the consequences; and to suffer for adherence to beliefs and principles. Such a stance is a necessary part of the stewardship of the soul. Indeed, suffering is at times an important route to nobility – it can lead to knowledge, then to wisdom, and on to the capacity to do good. But within the materialist matrix there is an attempt to deny the value of suffering and to persuade people that it is an illegitimate feature of the human condition. Indeed, there is a tendency to discourage suffering and even to anaesthetise it wherever possible. The readiness to suffer, and the practical implementation of such readiness, thus become constantly countered. This rejection of suffering has been helped by advances in the medical sphere which have acted to reduce physical suffering – there is now a natural propensity to wish to do the same in the realm of the psychological and spiritual suffering. Hence, for example, the widespread promotion of psychotropic drugs to impinge on moods and feelings – a practice which often constitutes a dangerous interference with the spiritual faculties. Furthermore, the materialist matrix lays immense emphasis on comfort, pleasure and ease in all their forms, and this is an emphasis which invites the individual to refuse the option of risking injury and pain in fighting the proverbial good fight. By such routes moral cowardice becomes legitimised and sanctioned. How many now, it might be asked, are willing to take up their cross?

The Encouragement of the Dark Side

However, the materialist matrix does not only deny the soul and counter the authentic spiritual life at key points. It also actively encourages the dark side of human nature – it promotes and legitimises the negative potential of man's spirituality with all its desocialising consequences. It should be recalled, during this secular epoch, that one of the purposes of religion down the ages has not only been to promote the spiritual welfare of the individual but also to guarantee social cohesion. The elimination of the dark side of man's inner self, whether discussed in terms of 'sin', 'vice', 'wickedness', or a variety of other ways, has also been animated by a desire to contain the 'anti-social'. Today's insistent exponents of the 'social', who disregard the soul, would do well to bear this fact in mind. This centuries-old twin endeavour and its impact have been weakened by the modern undermining of the philosophical bases of religion and its associated systems of comprehension. But more specifically the false anthropologies of post-modernity actively favour spiritual ill-health which in turn undermines community. No comprehensive account of this process is possible here, but perhaps it is possible to capture the salient features of the topography. Attention must be paid to the encouragement given to such elements as pride, avarice, envy, lust, gluttony and wrath – terms which we now seem to hear less and less. What we have before us is a system which works in favour of the cancellation of love at a whole host of points.

At the outset two general observations about how these visions of man encourage the void within us and around us. Firstly, they promote a spiritual ignorance which produces an inability to understand that the dark side damages both the individual soul and human society. With the soul left out of the equation, and with the life according to the Spirit ignored, there is little recognition of the damaging negativity of certain courses of action. There is a blindness, a lack of consciousness, which means that certain ways of thinking and actions are not repudiated. In this way the living of an individual's life becomes powerfully conditioned by an absence. When, for example, these visions of man encourage the selfish pursuit of money, of power, of rank or of sexual pleasure, there is no perception that such activity should be understood with reference to the soul and to God. Such behaviour is not seen as damaging to ourselves and the culture around us. Thus approaches to spiritual, ethical and moral areas become conditioned by a fundamental lack of awareness. A void grows up, a great gaping hole, within the way we live and think. This means that the rejection of the dark side becomes impeded by false systems of comprehension which engender ignorance about its presence and workings. Blindfolded, people fall into pits in front of them that they are no longer able to see – and much gets broken in the process.

Secondly, there is a strong tendency to self-exculpation which is rooted in an insistent determinism. This is something which gives free rein to the embrace and expression of the dark side of our inner selves. The argument goes that if what I do is the result of internal or external forces which are outside my control, then I cannot be blamed or reproved for my thoughts or actions – it is not really 'I' who am doing the acting or thinking. Everything that I do or say can be attributed, for example, to my body or to society, to my feelings or to evolution, to my unconscious or to my drives, to something else but never to 'me'. This constitutes a veritable rogue's charter; a *carte blanche* for the practice of immorality. By this route internal checks on wrong-doing are removed and external rebukes and controls become countered and neutralised. When practised on a grand scale, such an approach to life means that real social cohesion no longer becomes tenable. Much of this is described by Roger Scruton, who here, however, employs the word 'soul' in its secular sense:

> More subtle ways are available, however, whereby the sense of the soul's priority is lost. Perhaps the most important – and characteristically modern – of these is through the great scientific illusion according to which the source of human life is hidden from us: in the unconscious, in the 'material conditions' of economic life, in our history, our instincts or our genes. Such an idea – associated with every pseudo-science of man, from Marx to Freud to socio-biology – severs us more effectively than any superstition from our

purposes and fulfilment. For it fosters the master thought of crime: the attribution of my life and actions to something that is not myself, and for which I cannot answer.[5]

Pride

One of the increasing features of contemporary life is a constant striving for self-importance. Medieval man would have employed the term 'pride' and probably referred to 'vanity' as well. Selfish individualism is powerfully encouraged by this menacing denizen of the dark side. The mentality of self-importance is easily outlined. The only thing that matters is myself, and what is of primary concern to me is my own importance, especially in relation to others. There is a social frame of reference but only in an anti-social sense. I must be seen, and see myself, as being superior, better, a winner; what I need is rank, prestige, position. I must always strive in all things to be important, regardless of whether I actually deserve such importance. All in all, my own importance is what really matters, and my wider responsibilities and duties are of secondary consequence – if of any relevance at all. The dark methods I employ to achieve importance can be justified on the grounds that they are necessary to this end. Indeed, other people may be used as objects in this endeavour – mere instruments by which I achieve what I see, or what others see, as my importance. 'You know that those who are supposed to rule over the Gentiles lord it over them, and their great men exercise authority over them. But it shall not be so among you' (Mk 10:42-43) we were told. But in our contemporary culture how many now adhere to such humility?

Pride or self-importance is promoted by the materialist matrix in a number of ways. First of all, the societalist-economist-powerist-animalist cluster sees the human environment as a place where people struggle to obtain supremacy in a variety of spheres. The human being is held up as a creature who by his very nature is called to pride – such is said to be his vocation. The pursuit of self-importance is thus justified and encouraged with reference to visions of man which seek to persuade people that this is what life is inevitably like. Secondly, the constellation of internal sensations and sentiments associated with pride and vanity are not condemned by feelingism. On the contrary – this model of man declares that individuals by their nature are made in this way and that in sustaining and expressing pride people are merely being themselves.

Thirdly, to a substantial extent self-importance (rather like relativism) is the humanist perspective run riot. The pride of man within the cosmos becomes very easily translated into the pride of men within society. The idea that man is the most important thing in the universe naturally leads on to the opinion that each individual is the most important thing in the universe. In lacking humility towards God, the human person is led to lack humility towards his fellow men. Equally, if the individual's frame of reference is the human world alone, there is a natural receptivity to the idea that life is really about acting within a context of human society where being important is the true name of the game.

Self-importance is one of the greatest of all desocialising forces. It promotes struggle between people and acts to drive them apart through a process of conflict. Individuals become competitors and not co-operators, rivals within an impersonal conglomerate and not builders of real community – hostile beings engaged in a fight to subordinate each other. The lifestyle of overbearance is incompatible with social union. Secondly, pride acts as a potent mechanism of objectification, thereby eating away at the binding ties of community and turning people into non-neighbours. It acts to convert other people into objects, separate units, who are to be used to achieve the self-importance of a single individual. They are means to be used to his end, mere instruments to a selfish personal goal. Thirdly, pride submerges a whole range of potential mechanisms of social cohesion by directing attention away from the many pre-requisites of community towards the world of personal gain and advantage – a desocialising misorientation is thereby promoted.

The pursuit of self-importance also combats and works against the spiritually healthy individual, the man of virtue, by denying him the role and influence within society that he deserves and which society requires. The drive to self-importance acts to deprive him of importance, to weaken his position, and by this mechanism his integrating input into the surrounding culture becomes diminished or nullified. That he can do good to society as a whole does not matter – what matters to the selfish individual is that he himself achieves importance, and in this process the good man can be thrust aside.

Avarice

The materialist matrix systematically encourages a massive emphasis on material possessions. There is a legitimation and promotion of the dedication of the individual's life to the acquisition of wealth. Medieval man would have used the concepts 'avarice' or 'greed', and these impulses now constitute some of the chief features and pillars of the lifestyle of selfish individualism. The belief, almost the faith, in material wealth and the idea that people should be judged in relation to what they possess and not according to their spiritual qualities – that is to say, with reference to what they have and not what they are – is one of the great characteristics of contemporary culture. What is now termed 'consumerism'– a phenomenon which now so disfigures the face of the Western world – is merely one of the most obvious manifestations of this unremitting concern with the pursuit of riches. Such an approach is closely bound up with pride – individual self-importance is gained from the possession of material wealth.

Economic resources are certainly important and should be seen as a means to an end – property exists to defend love and truth – but what has happened is that riches have often become an end in themselves, the very alpha and omega of a person's life. Emphasis is placed not upon the health of the soul but upon the health of a bank account; not upon the well-being of the community, but upon the accumulation of personal property. The modern rejection of God has been accompanied by a frequent return to the worship of Mammon; 'how hard it is for those who have riches to enter the kingdom of God' (Mk 10:23-24) we were told. But how many now heed this warning?

This other denizen of the dark side is also strongly encouraged by the societalist-economist-powerist-animalist cluster. The central notion is that human life is in essentials a struggle for money and possessions, and for the power and rank that these bring in their wake. In striving to acquire wealth, this cluster argues, an individual is merely doing that which his innermost nature commands and engenders. Feelingism offers further support by arguing that the pleasure of riches, and the enjoyment that their acquisition and use involves, are part of the natural world of human sentiments and experiences. Their selfish pursuit is not to be condemned or upheld, but merely accepted as an inevitable fact of the human condition.

Greed and avarice clearly desocialise the human environment in a variety of ways. Other people become instruments, nothing but objects, to be employed in the acquisition of personal wealth – thus social relationships become reduced to a mere economic nexus and drained of their other contents. The idea of giving to others and of helping one's fellow man, and thereby extending and deepening human contact, becomes submerged by the drive to accumulate ever more possessions. The virtue of generosity becomes driven out by the vice of meanness; other people are simply ignored in the headlong rush for gold; and the authentic spiritual life with all its socialising potential becomes trampled beneath the imperatives of bank balances, share certificates, and title deeds.

Envy

These two denizens are closely linked with a third which is perhaps the most destructive and dangerous of them all. We live in an age characterised by the rise of envy – that sentiment which St. Augustine believed was '*the* diabolical sin'.[6] Envy involves resentment of those who have something which you do not have; it is a refusal to accept any kind of superiority on the part of others; and it is a rejection of the feelings of inferiority caused by comparison with those who have more. That 'more' can take many forms ranging from money to beauty, and from talent to prestige, but the great point is that it is 'more'. Needless to say, envy is closely bound up with pride and avarice – an individual's importance and possessions become automatically diminished when someone else has more than he does. Today envy in Great Britain appears often legitimised; something which is acceptable if not inevitable; just another part of human nature not to be condemned or kept in check but accepted. All the visions of man which bring about and sustain selfish individualism also encourage and support envy. After all, at a general level, if what really matters is the individual and what he has, then anything which threatens his own standing or importance must be rejected. In being hostile to others who have more, it is argued, he is merely expressing his nature; it is asserted that envy between people is simply a part of the human social experience; and it is proposed that the inner reactions and propensities connected with it are somehow an inevitable feature of our feeling systems.

Envy is particularly promoted by a lack of an awareness of God and by the absence of a communitarian perspective. It is greatly facilitated by the neglect of those aspects of the life according to the Spirit and is also a very natural feature of the individual who suffers from spiritual ill-health. All this is especially evident when we come to consider the question of quality. Talents, capacities and abilities are in themselves valuable and draw near to the characteristics of God, who is indeed the supreme expression of quality. For this reason, quality in others should be respected for its own sake. It also forms a part of the vocation given by God to each individual and this is another reason why it should be defended. In addition, the qualities of others should be welcomed as contributing to the well-being of the community and as elements which work indirectly to the benefit of each of its members. What conduces to the common good conduces to the individual good. But, of course, if there is no vision or reality of community then this process is neither perceived nor appreciated. The quality of others is, in addition, a major object of attack by the unhealthy soul. The talents, abilities and capacities of another person may well lead to that person acquiring greater money, power or prestige, but this is not to be allowed by the spiritually unhealthy – such things are desired by the envious individual. Similarly, the envious person resents the fact that other people are born with greater talents than he – this is seen as an injustice which must be corrected by worldly mechanisms. As a result, attempts are made by that person to ensure that the gifted individual does not gain advantage within society because of his quality. Like the white hart pulled down by hounds in the famous medieval painting, the man of quality must be brought to his knees.

Envy, too, is a constant and ceaseless desocialiser. It is a pre-eminent destroyer of the key source of community between men – love. It drains a relationship of its proper content, replacing good will with ill-will, happiness at another's well-being with pleasure at his misfortunes, and delight at his achievement with resentment at his success. Where there is envy, true love cannot exist. In addition, envy often hides itself, conceals its presence, awaits its moment for its victim to weaken before it attacks – it thus deprives a personal relationship of honesty and sincerity. All in all, it establishes distances between people, driving them apart and placing them in conflict. When widely established and legitimised, envy constitutes a constant acid which ceaselessly erodes social bonds and prevents new ones from forming. It is also a characteristic of the unhealthy soul which, when once embraced, can never be sated. There can never be true satisfaction for those who are wrapped in its coils – there will always be somebody who in one way or another has 'more'. For this reason it is a force of great intensity and persistence whose power and influence are reinforced by its innate propensity to grow. The danger of envy to the health of individuals and of societies has been recognised for millennia. Bonhoeffer had distinctly incisive observations to make:

> There is a kind of evil satisfaction in knowing that everyone has his failings and weak spots. In my contacts with the 'outcasts' of society, its 'pariahs', I've noticed repeatedly that mistrust is the dominant motive in the judgement of other people. Every action, even the most unselfish, of a person of high repute is suspected from the outset. These 'outcasts' are to be found in all grades of society... The more isolated a man's life, the more easily he falls a victim to this attitude...A basic anti-social attitude of mistrust and suspicion is the revolt of inferiority.[7]

Lust and Gluttony

The materialist matrix also promotes a headlong rush to hedonism – the pursuit of pleasure and the gratification of our senses. Medieval man employed the terms 'lust' and 'gluttony' to refer to such impulses. Today we are often encouraged to believe that the great thing is to satisfy our own feelings, and feelings defined in rather narrow terms. The human frame is seen as an entity which exists to be gratified, to be pleased, and to experience comfort. Today an increasing imperative of life is not so much that we should be good but that we should feel good. The important thing, we are frequently told, is to 'enjoy yourself', to 'have a good time', and to 'seize the day'. *Carpe diem* has become almost a post-modern motto. It should be stressed, however, that hedonism has a very circumscribed definition of the world of the feelings and the senses. It involves a highly impoverished vision of our potential inner experience – the many joys of the life according to the Spirit are neglected. It usually upholds the pleasures of the body – food, sex, drugs, drink; the stimulation of the mental world – entertainment, excitement, thrills; and the gratification of desires – possessions, power, prestige. It is thus an integral part of selfish individualism in that it asserts that personal pleasure is the great purpose of human existence – the welfare of others, adherence to divine law, love for the truth, or spiritual happiness are simply shunted to one side. Hedonism's great philosophy is not that we should steward our souls but that we should indulge our feelings and pander to our senses.

Many of the false anthropologies of post-modernity give force and vigour to hedonism. Feelingism lays great emphasis upon the feelings – they are said to be what really count in our experience. This creed encourages the view that the pursuit of their satisfaction is merely an inevitable part of being human – to seize the day is to be what we are. Exactly the same occurs with physiologism – an outlook which sees the feelings as bodily sensations. Sexualism legitimates the unthinking desire for sexual pleasure. Animalism provides a blanket coverage for the pursuit of what pleases us – are we not mere advanced beasts and, like our cousins of the animal kingdom, entitled to do what gives us pleasure? Powerism and economism legitimate and promote the desire for money and wealth, dominance and command. Rightsism weighs in by asserting that it is somehow our right to receive these pleasures and that the impeding of their pursuit is an interference with our freedom. The mental massaging which is present in much of psychist practice, and the goal of a pain-free psychic life which is often propounded by psychist theory, illuminate the links between hedonism and psychism. Furthermore, who would deny that the intellectual proponents of rationalism often search not for truth but for the stimulation of their intellects? In reality, debate and inquiry are frequently mere forms of entertainment. Humanism, for its part, has the effect of directing attention away from what God wants to what man wants, and without a spiritual dimension to the cosmos and to what we are as humans it becomes very easy to lapse into a facile emphasis on our feelings.

Hedonism promotes the loss of ties in a number of ways. In the first instance, it works against the socialising impact of the authentic spiritual life by directing attention towards other areas of our inner experience. Indeed, it corrupts and pollutes that life by seeking to make us understand its workings with reference to false perspectives. Is it not often suggested, for example, that we are committed to love because it gives us pleasure? What is noble is frequently debased and discouraged by being attributed to a selfish wish for gratification. Similarly, the suffering which is often required in the fight for what is right is countered by the hedonist refusal of pain. Hedonism also encourages us to direct all our attention towards ourselves – our own pleasure is what is said to really count in this life. A wider concern for others, not to mention our responsibilities and our duties towards them, becomes submerged and subsumed. At the same time, we are encouraged to compete with others to obtain the means by which to experience pleasure. We, not they, must possess the instruments to this sacred end. Our attitude towards them thus becomes not one of co-operation but of competition. Hedonism also leads us to see other people as mere objects in the achievement of our gratification. They are to be used by us to satisfy our feelings, whether in the pursuit of power or the acquisition of wealth, the gaining of sexual pleasure or the achievement of self-importance. During the present high summer of the 'me' generation hedonism encourages the exploitation of our fellow-man for our own personal gain. And what could be more desocialising than this?

Hedonism lays especial emphasis upon sexual pleasure, and here we encounter a part of the dark side which requires special examination. Nowadays there is a growing encouragement to indulge our sexual impulses without reference to wider considerations. It is urged that we should achieve pleasure and gratification from our sexuality. We are told that it is part of our freedom, our way of expressing ourselves, perhaps even our 'right'. Sex at any cost, sex whatever the price, sex before anything else, sex however you like it ('whatever turns you on') – the message is on a myriad of lips, shouted from a thousand billboards, expressed in a host of television programmes, communicated unceasingly by the cinema. Not to indulge is even said to be dangerous, a practice which may lead to disturbance through deprivation. Science, it is argued, has even liberated us from its 'dangers' through the invention of contraceptive devices or the cure (before AIDS) of its diseases. And abortion is proposed as a further safety net. Current culture often hands sex to us on a plate – and large numbers are ready to accept the invitation.

As is to be expected, many of the false anthropologies of post-modernity encourage this attitude. Sexualism and animalism, feelingism and physiologism – all these creeds have powerful impulses in this direction. If I engage in sex (in whatever context or form), am I not following my evolutionary programming, or obeying my body, or expressing my feelings, or giving free rein to my sexuality? In addition, am I not entitled to pursue such a line of conduct because of my freedom or the innate rights I bear within me? Furthermore, does not psychism, and in particular its Freudian version, inform me that without such activity I might damage my mental health or risk the penalties of repression? Here is Marlon Brando expressing some commonly held views on the subject:

> I don't think I was constructed to be monogamous. I don't think it's the nature of any man to be monogamous. Chimps, our closest relatives, are not monogamous; neither are gorillas or baboons. Human nature is no more monogamous than theirs. In every human culture men are propelled by genetically ordained impulses over

which they have no control to distribute their seed into as many females as possible. Sex is the primal force of our and every other species. Our strongest urge of all is to replicate our genes and perpetuate our species. We are helpless against it, and are programmed to do as we do. There may be variations from culture to culture, but whether it is in Margaret Mead's Samoa or modern Manhattan, our genetic composition makes our sexual behaviour irresistible.[8]

The increasing cult of sexual licence, and more especially of sex without love, drives people apart in a whole host of ways. First of all, it encourages men and women to treat each other as objects to be utilised in the gaining of physical pleasure. Hence the revealing current phrase 'sex object'. This readiness to use can only further sow distrust between men and woman. Indeed, around us we often see people who are hesitant and suspicious in their relationship with the opposite sex precisely because of some previous painful experience which involved being used. In the same way, different kinds of 'conquests' are often no more than the acquisition of trophies, of status and of self-importance – a process which is deeply objectifying.

Secondly, this cult strikes a mighty blow at that great force for social union – love between a man and a woman. The sexes come to understand their differences in the wrong way. Rather than realising that sexual activity exists to take place within a context of love – which involves both the spirit and the body – and which provides a spiritually healthy environment for the upbringing of children and the happiness of the marriage partners, people adopt a very mistaken approach: sexual activity is seen to exist for physical pleasure. A deep ignorance thus grows up which places a thousand explosive charges under the family – that essential cement of any human community. There is also a lack of a readiness to wait for love (which is disregarded or not understood) and a frequent propensity to engage in a series of relationships which often pass as rapidly as they have come. Thus sexual hedonism creates confusion about one of the most fundamental features of our human identity. And love between a man and a woman, with all its massive socialising potential, is the most conspicuous casualty.

Wrath

Lust, like pride, envy and greed, helps to engender that climate of hostility, violence and aggression which so marks the contemporary period. 'Outwardly bland, submissive, and sociable', C. Lasch wrote of his contemporaries, 'they seethe with an inner anger'.[9] Indeed, rage, not peace, is ever more the keynote of post-modern culture. Medieval man would have used the term 'wrath' to describe this emotional state of mind. The statistics on violence outlined in chapter one illustrate many of the realities of this climate. Yet the presence of anger is not solely to be found in statistics on violence. It spreads far and wide, into the family and traffic, at work and in public places, in political speeches and in the factory. Wrath is not only the horrific 'girl gangs' attacking old ladies, youth gangs with all their violence or 'hoodies' and their aggression; it is also 'road rage', 'cinema rage', and 'toddler rage'; not only hooliganism, but backbiting and betrayal; not only wife and child beating (seemingly much on the increase), but barely concealed hostility in shops, banks and public offices; not only murder, but resentment and spite.

As has been observed, conflict pervades many of the false anthropologies of post-modernity: it is perceived as playing a vital role in the achievement of power, the obtaining of economic wealth, the reproduction of one's genes, the gaining of pleasure, the upholding of natural rights, and Darwinian survival – to name the more obvious. And these visions of man have played an important part in creating this climate of wrath. Much of animalism suggests that nature is a struggle of tooth and claw – what is this if not an invitation to anger? Societalism, economism and powerism all see man and human society in terms of strife and combat. Sexualism, for its part, often evokes the notion of forced possession, and it should not surprise us that modern cinema often portrays sexual encounters as a sort of quasi-violent mauling. 'Life is horrible',[10] declared Hitler, and well do we know what that monster did. In truth, no community can stand for long if permeated by such hostility, violence and aggression.

*

To summarise the argument of this chapter, the Christian message makes clear that love is the key force in the achievement of community. But, as we have seen, the false anthropologies of post-modernity outlined in chapter three assault love in a whole variety of ways and thereby impede community. They abolish the idea of the soul in men's minds and thus work against its stewardship. This abolition works through providing alternative and false visions of what we are. They also counter the life according to the Spirit by promoting approaches which negate and work against a number of its essential components. Selfish individualism thus increasingly emerges as the way of life of contemporary man. All this takes place within a context where spiritual ignorance has been created and sanctions on wrong-doing weakened or removed. The promotion of pride and vanity, avarice and greed, envy and covetousness, hedonism and lust, aggression and wrath (in whatever terminology they may be described), can only further drive love from men's hearts. Those who succumb to, or participate in, this assault have reneged on the social contract which lies at the basis of life together in society – the commitment to express and promote authentic spirituality. With such a contract repudiated, society itself is encouraged to wither and desocialisation rears its ugly head. This massive attack is flanked by relativism, another contemporary creed, which, however, *chooses truth more than love as its target*. Here we encounter one of the authentic horrors of post-modern culture.

Chapter Five

Relativism:
an Authentic Philosophy of the Void

Dostoevsky had one of the protagonists of his novel *The Devils* declare:

> I formulated for the first time in my life what appeared to be the rule of my life, namely, that I neither know nor feel good or evil and that I have not only lost any sense of it, but that there is neither good nor evil (which pleased me), and that it is just a prejudice: that I can be free from any prejudice, but that once I attain that degree of freedom I am done for.[1]

Dostoevsky was referring to a state where there is no longer any recognition of objective ethical or moral truth. He accurately perceived that this was a freedom which condemned man. In contemporary culture we are now faced with a potent creed which promotes exactly such a state. Moreover, its most conspicuous champions argue that liberty is what it really confers. 'The dominant modern tendency is not to search for absolute moral standards at all', observes Paul Johnson, 'but to insist that all codes are relative and subjective'.[2] This creed is 'relativism' ('subjectivism' would be just as good a term) – the twelfth of the materialist matrix, but in reality a force with an autonomy and particularities all of its own. Relativism holds that there is no objective truth and that everything is dependent on point of view. There is no separate and independent reality, but only that of our perception. The world we see exists in our mind or senses – we are the creators of what we behold. In essence, everything which is believed must be related to the believer – 'truth' is held to be 'relative' to the perceiver. As the sociologist E. Gellner observes:

> Relativism is basically a doctrine in the theory of knowledge: it asserts that there is no unique truth, no unique objective morality. What we naively suppose to be such is but the product – exclusively, or in some proportion, which varies with the particular form the relativism takes – of the cognitive apparatus of the individual, community, age or whatever.[3]

This perspective is powerfully present – and at its most dangerous – in the ethical and moral province. It is asserted that there is no such thing as objective right and wrong and that the only thing that matters in this vital area is the personal opinion we hold. One person (or group of people) believes one thing, another another, and there's an end to it. In the relativist outlook, each individual (or group of individuals) is a little republic of decision and each point of view is of equal worth. 'There are no objective values', proclaims J.L. Mackie, illuminating a central feature of this outlook,

> the claim that values are not objective, are not part of the fabric of the world, is meant to include not only moral goodness, which might be most naturally equated with moral value, but also other things that could be more loosely called moral values or disvalues – rightness and wrongness, duty, obligation, an action's being rotten and contemptible, and so on. It also includes non-moral values, notably aesthetic ones, beauty and various kinds of artistic merit.[4]

Necessarily in the relativist scheme of things nothing fixed can be said about *homo sapiens* (an idea that links up powerfully with the frequent post-modern assertion that there is no such thing as human nature). He, too, becomes relativised. Hence we encounter the final and most hideous of the false anthropologies of post-modernity – that there can be no certain point of departure by which to understand what we are and guide what we do. This anti-vision well completes the assault on the soul begun by the rest of the materialist matrix. In the end, we are left with nothing.

Alexis de Tocqueville (1805-1859), when writing about the United States in the middle of the nineteenth century, sensed that relativism would be the philosophy of the future – modernity would mean the triumph of the subjective. He predicted that a flight from shared agreement would be accompanied by the sanctification of personal opinion; the atomisation of society would involve the atomisation of truth:

Where the citizens are all placed or an equal footing and closely seen by one another, and where no signs of incontestable greatness or superiority are seen in any of them, they are constantly brought back to their own reason as the most obvious and reliable source of truth. It is not only confidence in this or that man which is destroyed, but the disposition to trust the authority of any man whatsoever. Everyone shuts himself tightly within himself and insists on judging the world from there.[5]

Today in post-modern Great Britain the individual increasingly maintains that he is sovereign in relation to truth, and especially in matters relating to right and wrong. We are now increasingly faced with a do-it-yourself approach to ethics and morality where the claims of the home-grown are paramount. There is an emphasis not on divine law, absolute points of reference, the certitudes of inherited wisdom or the tenets of cultural tradition, but on the primacy of individual subjective perception. It should be stressed that although relativism is applied as a creed to all forms of truth it is especially insistent in relation to moral and ethical questions – a fact highly suggestive of its central purpose. Indeed, what relativism really wants to do is to destroy all ethical and moral consciousness and commitment. In this it links up in its effects and impact with the promotion of determinism by the other members of the materialist matrix. At a more general level, relativism completes the materialist assault on the Christian world-view but differs in its fundamental strategy. Whereas the other components of the materialist matrix are primarily concerned with the extirpation of love, relativism is principally a device to murder truth. The core of Christian teaching thereby receives a double challenge – love for love and love for truth are subjected to mighty concurrent blows. Relativism is thus yet another potent force for desocialisation and is a principal cause of the expansion of the void both within us and around us. Dostoevsky could feel the future in his bones. An anticipation of this tragedy is also to be found in Plato's *Theaetetus* with the author's opposition to the relativism of Protagoras – 'a man is the measure of all things',[6] and subsequently in the Gospels: '"Every one who is of the truth hears my voice." Pilate said to him, "What is truth?"' (Jn 18:37-8).

Relativism, too, has many of the characteristics of a heresy. It will be recalled that the other models of man of the materialist matrix tend to take one aspect of the human identity and to blow it up out of proportion. A deformation of that feature also usually takes place. What is true becomes utilised in a false fashion as an instrument by which to deny the soul and attack the life according to the Spirit. For its part, what relativism does is to exploit one of the great features of the human experience, namely that man is a perceiving creature and the fact that there is immense variation between individuals in the nature of their perceptions. We are constantly perceiving things but different capacities within people involve varying levels of ability to perceive realities. This is the case wherever we turn. The man with normal sight appreciates colours which cannot be seen by the colour-blind; the musician grasps patterns of notes not accessible to the tone-deaf; the man of artistic sensibility can feel things which are lost on those who do not have such talents; the mother understands the mood of her child by routes not known to the outsider; the man who stewards his soul perceives spiritual and moral realities in ways very different from the sadist; the mystic enters into realms of understanding never to be reached by most of mankind. The great point here is that independent realities are or are not being seen. What relativism does is to call attention to the fact that we are pre-eminently perceiving creatures, observes the immense variations which exist in perception, draws upon the enormous importance of this fact in the human experience, and then twists such elements around to suit its own ends. What happens is that emphasis becomes placed upon the perceiver not the perceived. The fact of the perception is deemed to be what matters, not its actual accuracy. Variation in perception is said to indicate variation in truth and the independent realities get thrown out of the window. For relativism, 'truth' is something which can only be in the eye of the beholder.

Yet relativism is a creed which contradicts itself. It has not the slightest coherence or credibility. It is exclusively destructive and in essence merely promotes the philosophy and lifestyle of nothing. This is immediately evident when we pose a few simple questions. If truth is relative what can we make of the statement 'all truth is relative'? If everything is an opinion is not that very assertion an opinion? If what I perceive is a point of view is that declaration also not a point of view? In reality, relativism relativises itself and thereby disappears into a black hole of its own creation (much as deconstructionism inevitably deconstructs itself). If truth is relative then I can have no trust in what I say or how I behave; there can be no fixed criteria for evaluating what I think and do; and mistakes cannot be corrected nor certainties upheld. There is a paralysis in points of departure and an annulment of all points of arrival. Relativism emerges as a destructive creed which is unable to construct anything at all since the moment it does so it applies its own nullifying line of approach. It is like anti-matter which sweeps away everything before it and leaves nothing in its place, except itself, which is nothing. 'Vulgar relativism has no hope of surviving outside the minds of ignorant rascals', we are told by one contemporary philosopher, 'sophisticated relativism has to be so sophisticated as barely to deserve the name'.[7] 'Notoriously', observes E. Gellner, 'there is no room for the assertion of relativism itself in a world in which relativism is true'.[8] This creed turns out to be nothing else but a creator of emptiness – an authentic philosophy of the void. As King Lear declared: 'Nothing will come of nothing' (I, 1, 91).

However, notwithstanding these glaring features, relativism is one of the great success stories of our times; the central doctrine of contemporary culture; the lode star of post-modernity; the core teaching of the politically correct. On the eve of his election, Pope Benedict XVI was even moved to declare: 'We are building a dictatorship of relativism'.[9] This creed has extended its grip deep into the structures of our thought and mentality, our action and our conduct, and if there is one thing which distinguishes the world-view of British man today from one hundred years ago it is this bizarre self-contradictory approach. Reflecting the historical development of world society, relativism also gives rise to a powerful demarcation line between the West and much of the rest of the globe. It is thus one of the further maladies that in the future we are liable to export far and wide. Indeed, this creed at times seems so deeply ingrained in the British mind as to almost have the status of a received dogma. It is frequently implicitly subscribed to, and a questioning of its legitimacy often meets with an irrational rebuttal, if not outright aggression, and perhaps is even interpreted as an assault on personal worth or freedom. The very fact that we now frequently talk about 'values' – a concept impregnated with relativist connotations – rather than about right or wrong or good and evil is a disquieting sign of our times. The language of moral discourse has become infected with this fatal malady of the contemporary soul.

The cultural analyst Allan Bloom observed of his American teaching experience: 'almost every student entering the university believes, or says he believes, that truth is relative'. 'That anyone should regard the proposition as not self-evident astonishes them', he continued, 'these are things you do not think about'.[10] Much the same may now be said about many young people in Britain today. Yet relativism now seems to extend far beyond the young generation and crosses the various boundaries of age, wealth, class, region, gender, ethnic group or political party. It is almost the dissolving force which unites us. 'Ages which are regressive and in process of dissolution are always subjective', warned the great Goethe (1749-1832), 'whereas the trend in all progressive epochs is objective'.[11] Relativism is to be encountered everywhere, spreading within the fabric of our existence and driving out the religious spirit wherever it can. 'In Hunslet, a working-class district of Leeds', observed Richard Hoggart:

> old people will still enunciate as guides to living, the moral rules they learned at Sunday Schools and Chapel. Then they almost always add, these days: "But it's only my opinion of course." A late-twentieth-century insurance clause, a recognition that times have changed towards the always shiftingly relativist. In that same council estate, any idea of parental guidance has in many homes been lost. Most of the children there live in, take for granted, a violent jungle world.[12]

What has lain behind this remarkable rise of relativism?

The Historical Developments that have Favoured Relativism

Relativism has certainly derived a major impulse from the advance of other members of the materialist matrix but it has also had specific supports all of its own. It seems to have demonstrated a marked ability to fasten onto a number of developments – at times some of the greatest achievements – of modern British history to advance its cause. In this it has often had the heretical touch – exploiting the admired and the valued in perverted form to secure its own success. Thus relativism has acquired noted legitimacy from the theory of relativity formulated by Albert Einstein (1879-1955) to explain the physical world. It also appears to have derived strength from such key principles of our national political culture as democracy, liberty, pluralism and equality. Modern artistic movements – with all their stress on subjective perception – and the Protestant inheritance – with its emphasis on the direct personal relationship with God – have been further realities upon which relativism seems to have fastened much like ivy on an oak strives to make its way to the light. In the same way relativism is surrounded by a cluster of associated tenets, indeed almost advance assault cohorts, which provide it with strength and credibility. This creed has also been propelled forward by a long-standing intellectual project which now wields very great influence within our academic and educated classes. All these elements require detailed discussion.

From the Materialist Matrix to Protestantism

The other part of the materialist matrix – the eleven other partners in cultural crime – prepare the ground for relativism. The two parts are now mutually supporting even though in reality they contradict each other – in itself a highly revealing fact. A strong impulse to relativism threads its way in and out of these other visions of man. Humanism shuts out the absolute truths of God and places truth within a merely human framework. Man is held to be the only real source of knowledge and of ethics and morality. From man as a species it is very easy to go to man as an individual: the belief that mankind's perceptions are sovereign easily prepares the ground for the idea that each person's views are sovereign. Societalism relativises beliefs and convictions by relating them to a community or a culture – they are seen not as truthful or untruthful but as the constructs of a society. It should thus not surprise us if this creed takes two principal forms – individual relativism and cultural relativism. Rationalism has provided another important input. Its constant stress on debate has promoted the idea that one man's opinion is as good as another's – is not truth, it is easily suggested, in fact merely a point of view? Equally, one man's reason is held up as the starting point for the perception of truth, an eminently subjective perspective. Rightsism often confuses a right with rightness. The law may give a man the right to do or say certain things but this does not mean that in speech or conduct he upholds the truth. The rightsist disregard for the moral content of what is said or done once a right has been established often involves the attribution of decision in such a sphere solely to the individual's personal judgement. What matters is that the right has been conceded and everything else becomes relative. The determinism espoused by much of the materialist matrix is a further generator of relativism. Perceptions are seen not as right or wrong, correct or erroneous, but as the products (for example) of psychic, physiological, societal or feeling processes – they are deemed to be the mere constructs of internal or external forces and it is to these that they must be related.

Relativism seems to have taken advantage of a number of other historical developments. In this process it has employed all the cunning of heresy and abused such developments in order to serve its own purpose. The list is brief but instructive. Just as the rational methods of the exact sciences paved the way for the rationalism of the eighteenth century, so Einstein's theories of relativity prepared the ground for the relativism of the twentieth. The great scientist himself protested against his understanding of the physical universe being applied to other spheres of knowledge, most notably the ethical and the moral worlds, but to little avail. It is now often argued that everything in reality is 'relative' and when relativistic arguments about right and wrong are advanced there is frequent reference to the alleged fact that Einstein demonstrated that everything was relative – a suggestion which is in fact completely false. Here, then, it is also alleged, is the answer to why it has never been possible to 'prove' certain truths concerning how man should be and how he should behave. It is asserted that in reality there is no such proof because everything is in essence merely a question of individual or cultural perspective. Relativism has thereby offered a simple answer to those who have perceived difficulty in deciding on great questions, or who wish to dodge them, or who wish to deny them; and Einstein's theory of the physical universe is habitually invoked as a justification for this most outlandish of contemporary assertions.

Relativism also appears to have battened onto the advance of democracy in order to promote its cause. Democracy has been one of the great success stories of modern British history and its achievement one of the boasts of our national civilisation. Great Britain defended democracy in two World Wars and has been a major force behind much of its diffusion throughout the world, not least through the mechanisms of its empire. From the Great Reform Act of 1832 through the legislation of 1867, 1884/5, and on to 1918 and 1928, a policy was pursued of gradually establishing universal suffrage as the basis of the system of parliamentary government. Men and women were to be considered equal at least in this – that they were each to have one vote of the same value in the selection of their governors. The unwritten Constitution – the effective and real bestower of entitlements in this area – came to establish that the political rights of citizens were to be the same. But democracy was not only a matter of electing members of the House of Commons. Local government underpinned the processes of democratisation at a national level during the Victorian period and for many decades thereafter. Such institutions as friendly societies, co-operative societies, trade unions and the whole world of associations and clubs were further integral features of this deeply-rooted democratic culture. All in all it is more than clear that democracy has been a central and lauded part of the modern British identity. Who nowadays denies that they are democratic? The very term has a connotation which is ringingly positive and this is another element which has made democracy especially useful to the relativist offensive.

Relativism seems to have fastened onto democratic development in order to gain credibility for itself even though within the democratic idea there is nothing which could be considered remotely relativistic. Was it not the case, it became insistently proposed, that as each man had a vote of equal value the judgement he expressed was of equal value to that of another elector? And if this was so did it not follow that when it came to the hustings no one judgement could be superior or inferior to another? By this line of reasoning it was asserted that no political opinion could be more true or less true than another. The egalitarianism of the ballot box became transformed into an egalitarianism in the value of political points of view. Today the common statement 'there are always two points of view to any question' bears ample testimony to this perversion of the democratic ideal to promote the contention that truth is many-sided. The practice of majority rule and the reality of party allegiance have lent weight to this process. A decision or a statement is often seen not in relation to whether it is right or wrong, correct or erroneous, but in terms of whether it is approved by a majority or propounded by a party. It becomes relativised to its location and perceived from that perspective alone. It is understood in terms of its origins not in relation to its objective validity. By these two principal routes our deeply-rooted democratic culture, the cornerstone of our national polity, has been quite wrongly exploited to advance the relativist locomotive. But just as ivy chokes its tree, so relativism is now weakening and undermining our democracy by removing its true lymph source – the belief in truth.

Relativism seems to have exploited another great feature of our national inheritance – love of political freedom. Liberty has been another vital element in our common identity and has attained a similar prestige to that enjoyed by democracy. Indeed, long before Great Britain was a democratic country it was the renowned land of freedom. Notwithstanding the imposing aristocratic settlement of the eighteenth and nineteenth centuries, the British state of that epoch was famous throughout the West for the liberties it guaranteed to its citizenry. This was one of the reasons why England became a safe haven for countless European political refugees (Mazzini, Marx, Napoleon III). Such a background also played an important role in securing and consolidating democratic advance. Since the nineteenth century this tradition of freedom has become even more deeply woven into the fabric of national life. Thus the struggle against totalitarianism during the Second World War and the Cold War was very much seen in terms of the defence of a cause of which the British were historic champions. Central to this tradition of liberty was freedom of speech – the right to express in print and by voice one's own opinions and views. Relativism has exploited this inheritance to achieve success, and at the same time, in predictable fashion, it has repaid the compliment by damaging its host. Dangerous questions are now asked which threaten to undermine liberty's rationale. Why should attention be paid to a statement if all truth is relative? What is the use of freedom if it is not used to arrive at the truth? What is the point of exchanging views if objective truth cannot be arrived at? Liberty is now being attacked by the parasite it has inadvertently hosted.

Relativism appears to have exploited the sacred cause of liberty in two major ways. Firstly, freedom of speech and the written word encouraged and favoured debate – from here relativism went on to the 'equal value of each opinion' line of argument. One point of view, it was readily asserted, was as good as another. An equality of the right to expression became quite wrongly transmuted into an equality of value in what was declared. Secondly, and far more importantly, since individuals had equal rights with regard to the expression of their opinions it became very easy to believe that what was of real importance was not the truth of what was said but the fact that it was allowed to be said – that in a sense what really mattered was not the content of the communication but the act of communication itself. Hence those frequent irrelevant assertions of today's world when the truth of a statement is contested such as: 'it's a free country, I can say what I like' or 'everybody has a right to their point of view'. This general approach naturally has a powerful propensity to reduce a statement or an evaluation to an 'opinion', a 'judgement' or a 'point of view' rather than to give rise to an assessment of its actual accuracy. Such notions are strongly relativistic in connotation and direct attention away from the question of whether what is being said is actually true or not.

Relativism also seems to have exploited a feature of our political culture which is intimately bound up with liberty. 'Pluralism' proposes that there is, and that there should be, a plurality of views and ideas within a modern polity. It is argued that this is a positive outcome of political liberty and asserted that this is a highly natural state of affairs which arises from the complexity of society and the inherent differences which exist between people. It is also maintained that in some way the more opinions there are the better and that the greater the plurality the more beneficial our condition. There is even a rationalist input – the more opinions within rational debate there are, it is argued, the greater the statistical probability of getting things right. This line of reasoning is also applied to cultural relativism – the greater the number of cultures or lifestyles within a society, it is proposed, the greater the true or potential wealth of that society. Against this background we can readily understand why one of the key values of pluralism is 'diversity'. Nowadays we are constantly enjoined to accept what is different on the sole grounds that diversity in itself is valuable. What is different is somehow good regardless of the validity of what is being proposed. No doubt plurality, variety and difference can be beneficial and positive, but what relativism does is to convert these features of pluralism into values in themselves without reference to their actual contents. It detaches them from their truthfulness. It exploits them to assert its own contention that what is important is not truth but point of view; not accuracy but perspective. But what is the use of plurality, variety and diversity if they contain errors and falsehood? We could well put Himmler, Charles Manson, the Marquis de Sade and Attila the Hun in a room, and thereby acquire a plurality, variety and diversity of outlook, but it would help us very little.

Egalitarianism appears to have proved a powerful force behind the growth of relativism. A belief in equality is one of the great ideas of our times and permeates deeply into the way we think about ourselves – for many people, indeed, it is a kind of moral postulate. Despite the evident and profound differences which separate us – between children and the elderly, men and women, the good and the evil, the talented and the mediocre, the beautiful and the ugly – the idea that in some way we are 'equal' has become one of the dogmas of our times. Although I could never have the scientific mind of Einstein, the literary genius of Shakespeare or the musical ear of Beethoven, it is nonetheless asserted that I am in some sense their equal. At heart what is being proposed is that we are all in fundamental and essential terms the same and for this reason perhaps it would be more accurate to employ the term 'sameism'. How on earth has this weird notion arisen? Why does the French Revolution slogan 'All Men are Equal' find such sustained consent in the Great Britain of the year 2008? As might be expected, much of the blame can be put at the door of the false anthropologies of post-modernity.

With the removal of the soul (in the possession of which men are indeed equal) there have been attempts to define human nature in egalitarian and universalist terms. Rationalism lays stress upon the common denominator of human reason. Rightsism asserts that all men carry within them the same bundle of entitlements. Psychism has the tendency to assume that at the outset human psychic structures are the same in each person. Animalism perceives a uniform process of biological programming which leaves the same kind of imprint. Economism, powerism and sexualism detect the same kinds of drives within each individual. Feelingism and physiologism tend to understand humans in terms of the same general internal patterns and processes. And much of societalist thought has aimed at achieving equality in terms of material wealth and economic opportunity. In historical terms, the uniform bestowal of political rights and the achievement of equality before the law have been further forces behind this creed. Collectivism has provided further support by seeking to guarantee certain uniform provisions of social assistance. Within such a sameist context it is very easy to embrace the idea that the judgements, the opinions, the very ethics and morals of one man are of equal value to those of another. To argue otherwise, or so it is commonly asserted, would be to deny our fundamental equality or sameness – in this way, once again, truth becomes relativised to its perceiver. The same line of reasoning is applied to different cultures and is used to buttress cultural relativism. The sheer absurdity of this approach staggers belief – are we really to believe that Pol Pot's killing fields or Stalin's camps were the products of perspectives of equal value to our own?

Over the last two hundred years artistic developments also seem to have furnished major support to relativist advance. The idea has increasingly gained ground that all artistic and aesthetic judgement is solely a question of personal perspective. Thus one cannot say that a work of art is good or bad – one either likes it or one does not. The modern world of literature, painting, sculpture, music and architecture has proved an important propulsive force behind relativistic thinking.

This is more than evident in the principal schools of innovation which have passed across the British artistic stage over the last two centuries. The Romantic movement laid great stress on personal feelings and perceptions and thereby placed subjectivity on the highest of high pedestals. The Pre-Raphaelites echoed much of this posture, as did the aesthetic movement of the end of the century. The Bloomsbury Group paid great attention to the world of the inner man and both the Auden group of the 1930s and the Angry Young Men of the 1950s exuded relativistic perspectives. Since that time the snowball has just kept rolling and it seems that within the artistic world today, and its accompanying realm of criticism and assessment, there is a decreasing readiness to contest the commonly accepted proposition that art in all its forms is in essence a matter for the judgement of the observer. The notion that there might be independent or objective sets of criteria has been increasingly weakened. The artistic dimension of the human experience is a major dimension and so in achieving success in this sphere relativism has gained control of very influential terrain.

The idea that there are no fixed guidelines by which to judge objective worth in art is now widely diffused and is one of the reasons for the decline in censorship laws over recent decades – it is frequently asserted that any attempt to impose censorship merely involves a reference to absolute artistic criteria which do not really exist. However in the world of art, in the history of the West, the idea that objective worth is an irrelevant concept is very new and bears witness to the advancing grip of the relativist approach. It is also a wonderful way of defending poor quality. The idea that there are no standards is a great help to those who do not have any but want the prizes which belong to merit. It is almost as if there is now no way of condemning scribbles, daubed sketches, or the horrific buildings of our urban landscape. In its most ludicrous form this refusal of standards can come out in such well-publicised phenomena as piles of bricks in the Tate Gallery or people being given grants to walk around with planks on their heads. It is certainly true, as is often observed in the defence of artistic relativism, that great artists have often not been understood and that men of genius have frequently been attacked. But this does not mean to say that nothing can be condemned because no criteria can possibly exist. Such an attitude would have amazed such figures as Michelangelo, Leonardo da Vinci, or Raphael. Indeed, just as determinism is a rogue's charter so artistic relativism is a charlatan's licence. It is for this reason that relativism, having exploited the world of art, now constitutes a real menace to artistic achievement.

It is probably fair to say that within the Western world desocialisation has advanced with greatest force where there is a Protestant inheritance. There appears to be a causal link. This statement is not a criticism of this branch of Christianity but a further attempt to draw attention to how relativism has exploited the British cultural heritage to advance its cause. From the Reformation onwards, Protestantism has had a marked tendency to emphasise the immediate and direct relationship between the individual and God. Indeed, in its most radical forms this expression of Christianity has even sought to abandon clerical structures altogether. This tendency has frequently led to an emphasis on individual perceptions and judgements, on the need to reflect personally upon the Bible, and on the primacy of the individual conscience. For these reasons there seems to have been a latent impulse within Protestantism in England towards emphasis on subjectivity in religious practice and reflection. Perhaps this was implied in the famous declaration of Luther (1483-1546):

> Unless I am convinced by Scripture and plain reason – I do not accept the authority of popes and councils, for they have contradicted each other – my conscience is captive to the Word of God. I cannot and I will not recant anything, for to go against conscience is neither right nor safe. God help me. Amen.[13]

And let it not be forgotten that after the Reformation Great Britain was the premier Protestant country of Europe, even though it is certainly true that Protestantism came to express itself in a broad variety of often conflicting denominations. Great Britain has a Christian heritage but it must be remembered that this is an inheritance of a strongly Protestant stamp. In 1851, for example, the proportion of the population of England and Wales made up of practising Catholics was in the low percentage points.[14]

Relativism seems to have abused and exploited the Protestant heritage to advance its cause and employed some highly cunning arguments in the process. If the individual is sovereign in decisions as to correct religious belief, the relativist voice argues, then all individuals are equally sovereign; and if such is the case then each religious point of view is of equal value to the next. In the same way it is asserted that just as there are a variety of denominations so also are there a variety of ways of perceiving religious truth. And as each denominational per-spective is of the same worth so no single denomination has the real answer. Thus in the religious sphere as well everything becomes a question of perception – a pre-eminently relativistic position. Of course with its denial of absolutes, relativism flies in the face of Protestantism and all that this branch of Christianity has ever stood for. It seems to have abused this part of our heritage, in the same way as it has abused democracy, liberty, pluralism, equality and artistic expression, and having done so it is now seeking to destroy Protestantism just as it aims to destroy the others. The idea that truth is relative is incompatible with any form of authentic religious belief.

The Relativist Virtues

Relativist thinking bears a very positive charge within British culture – a development which would have amazed our Victorian forefathers. The man who denies the reality of objective truth is often held to be free of prejudice, open-minded, tolerant, modest, liberal and enlightened. He is praised because he believes in 'live and let live'; he is admired because he 'respects' the opinions of other people and other cultures; and he is thought to be modern and progressive. He is today's 'good man' or 'model citizen'. Some of this attitude is expressed in the 1967 Reith lecture given by Dr. Edmund Leach, the Provost of King's College, Cambridge:

Beware of moral principles. A zeal to do right leads to the segregation of saints from sinners, and the sinners can then be shut out of sight and subjected to violence. Other creatures and other people besides ourselves have a right to exist…So long as we allow our perceptions to be guided by morality we shall see evil where there is none, or shining virtue even when evil is staring us in the face, but what we find impossible to see are the facts as they really are.[15]

Conversely (and astonishingly) the man who believes in objective truth is often placed in the same category as religious fanatics or political extremists. He is said to belong to the company of Hitler, Pol Pot, Lenin, Stalin, Robespierre and Torquemada. He is branded as intolerant, arrogant or bigoted, and described as someone who wants to 'impose' his views on others. It is complained that he thinks he is right and that the result of this is that others must suffer. His attitudes are said to be those which have caused wars and persecution down the ages. Such a man is said to belong to an unenlightened past which stretches back through the medieval period, the Dark Ages and beyond. Yet although this line of argument is employed to attack the 'absolutism' of religion it is often forgotten that the mass butcheries of the last century were largely the work of atheistic totalitarian movements characterised by intense hostility to the Judeo-Christian tradition and to organised religion in any form.

This positive evaluation of relativistic thought is expressed in the value frequently attributed to the 'virtues' which belong to its orbit and to the related value of 'privacy'. These virtues are tolerance, the open mind, the balanced view or moderate approach, compromise, and understanding, all of which relativism takes to absurd extremes. Here also a process of exploitation and abuse has been in operation. Such elements can often be valuable – their worth depends on how they are conceived and applied – but this towering creed of our age radicalises them to the point of their becoming indiscriminate in application. All critical assessments based on ideas of objective truth or independent standards become inoperative, as the following survey well demonstrates.

'Tolerance' is now often conceived as an essential feature of civilisation and considered part and parcel of the rejection of 'intolerant' totalitarian regimes or medieval obscurantism. Thus we are frequently told that we must be 'tolerant'. This post-modern virtue was rarely advocated in the eighteenth century ('toleration' was a very different concept) and pre-Enlightenment man would never have listed it amongst the qualities of the holy man. Yet the great thing, it is now argued, is to be tolerant of other opinions and forms of behaviour. We must not condemn or reject but keep an open mind. To do otherwise would be 'arrogant'. As truth is relative we must not pass judgement because we cannot pass judgement. Conceived in such terms the notion becomes indiscriminate and almost meaningless. In reality tolerance is quintessentially contextual – some things should be tolerated and some should not. Everything depends upon the criteria employed in the evaluation. From this point of view 'intolerance' might just as well be considered a virtue. However, in removing any such objective criteria of evaluation relativism succeeds in turning tolerance into a mechanism which encourages us to suspend our critical faculties, avoid an ethical and moral stance, and abandon value judgements. An approach of largely indiscriminate acceptance of what is said and done is what is really being sought. Yet why on earth, we might ask ourselves, should we be tolerant towards Hitler's crematoria?

Intimately linked with tolerance is the other relativist virtue of the 'open mind'. The great notion here is that we should be ready to consider any proposal or practice, almost regardless of what it might be; an attitude which often lies behind the relativistic promotion of 'dialogue'. The most important thing for the proponents of the open mind, indeed the great imperative, is not to be a true believer – who indeed is regarded as a great danger – but to be open to others and to what they think and do, whether they belong to one's own culture or lifestyle or to others. To do the opposite is to be prejudiced, perhaps to be in favour of 'discrimination'. Such a stance is held up as being eminently enlightened and progressive. This approach is frequently supported by the practice of welcoming novel ideas on the grounds that they are 'original' – in reality an exceedingly poor qualification for their acceptance. The rationalist injunction to debate clearly also has an input – everything somehow deserves to be taken into consideration. The 'virtue' of openness, conceived in these terms, is relativist to the core in that it offers no machinery or criteria by which to assess and evaluate what comes into our minds; it involves no attempt to utilise or reject incoming propositions; and it implies no process of evaluation or of sifting. The open mind abolishes the discerning mind. It may also involve a driving out of what is already valuable within our thought-systems, the precious outcome of experience, reflection or inherited cultural wisdom. In reality, the open mind as it is so conceived within the relativist framework is a closed mind – open to everything, it is unable to embrace anything; it lacks the machinery to acquire and retain what is true; and what was received yesterday can just as easily be discarded tomorrow. This is an authentic abdication of the primary purpose of our rational faculties. And why on earth, we might ask, should we have an open mind towards the exploitation of child labour?

There is also the virtue of the 'balanced view' or the 'moderate approach'. This is somewhat of a variant in that at least some points of reference (albeit of a purely functional nature) are taken into consideration – points that tolerance and openness completely lack. The notion here is that we should seek an admirable middle way, a kind of habitable halfway house, between different points of view; a satisfactory average, as it were, between opposing poles of thought. But this approach, which is now so frequently held up as being a hallmark of the civilised mind, does not really help us at all. Moderation and the balanced view (at least in the forms in which they are commonly conceived) are, like the relativist tenet of tolerance, totally contextual in character – they are determined and conditioned by the other views which are being expressed. They do not

attempt to approach a question from the point of view of whether it is true
or not but operate solely in relation to what others say and propose. In this
the balanced view or moderate approach carry on the relativist trajectory,
albeit in rather altered form – truth becomes related to the hats already in
the ring. In this sphere, also, relativist virtues are matched by the
condemnation of non-relativist vices – those who are not 'moderate' or
exponents of the 'balanced view' are condemned for being extremists or
fundamentalists, fanatics or bigots. Yet if some people champion freedom
and others support slavery why on earth should we choose the middle
ground between them?

In the same way we are often encouraged to engage in a policy of
'compromise'. According to the champions of this virtue the great thing
is not to adhere to a truth but to move towards the positions advocated
by others. What we are called upon to do is to adapt and adjust our
views to the points of view of other people. Such a stance is said to
involve tolerance, an open mind, and a liberal and enlightened attitude.
Conversely, if we do not adapt such a stance we are said to be rigid, set
in our ways, arrogant and unyielding. We are deemed to be 'unwilling
to compromise'. This idea of compromise follows much of the line of
argument of the moderate approach or the balanced view, and in the
same way it is a stance which is conditioned by its context. The correct
attitude to be adopted becomes one not based upon right or wrong, or
truth or falsehood, but something which is defined in relation to other
points of view – it, too, becomes relative to the other hats in the ring.
What matters is not the correctness of what you are saying or doing but
whether you have compromised with what others say or do. Compromise,
therefore, like tolerance, is to be seen as a virtue of a thought-world
which does not take objective truth as its point of departure. It is valued
precisely because it does not insist upon such a starting point. However,
compromise, like tolerance and the middle way, can never be a primary
value – it all depends on what one is compromising with. Why on earth,
we might ask, should we compromise with those who want to apply
euthanasia to elderly people because they are no longer able to engage
in productive work?

This brings us to the last virtue of relativism which like the rest has a
superficial attraction but which in reality is profoundly deceitful in
relation to moral questions. Today it is often asserted that we must be
'understanding' and that in some way 'to understand all is to forgive
all'. What we have to do, it is argued, is to realise why people think or

act in a certain way – we are invited to expand our own mental horizons so as to be able to encompass explanations of their thought and behaviour. In so doing, it is suggested, we will not condemn or judge, we will 'understand'. And because there is no objective truth, especially in the ethical and moral sphere, this is the only fitting stance we can take – a stance, moreover, which will make us more tolerant and open-minded. It is also argued that we must 'understand' what is different and thereby reject any attempt at evaluation, which is said to be impossible anyway because objective criteria for such an exercise do not exist. Thus it is suggested that if a person does something for a certain set of motives, whatever those motives may be, then this in itself is a justification which must be understood. This links up with determinism because it is argued that if we manage to perceive the forces which led someone to behave in a certain way then somehow this involves exculpation, understanding and forgiveness. The rationalist emphasis on debate also enters the picture because we are encouraged to 'understand' other points of view which are being put forward. By all those routes 'understanding' fits very neatly into the relativist approach. Objective truth is abandoned and morality becomes related to mere personal perception. Yet why on earth should our first priority be to 'understand' the most pitiless and sadistic murderers? The really important thing is to stop them.

Another notion which is much bound up with relativism, which this creed has fastened onto only to pervert, and which comes close to being a kind of relativist 'virtue' but which really belongs to a category of its own and should more properly be seen as a relativist value, also merits discussion. We now live in an age of 'privacy'. This value is powerfully reinforced by the retreat into the private which now characterises much of the post-modern lifestyle. In part this is a natural response to a human environment which fails to integrate and is frequently hostile. In part, also, it stems from that autonomy in thought and action of the individual which is so promoted by contemporary culture. And in part it is linked to, and derives from, patterns of recreation – expressed in the 'do-it-yourself' movement, TV watching, domestic pets or gardening – which confine people ever more to the home. No doubt there are (and there should be) personal realms into which others should not intrude. Within British traditions much weight has rightly been given to this important aspect of civic life – was not an Englishman's home his castle? But we have now gone far beyond the confines of this traditional notion. Today the idea of privacy is employed to ward off ethical or moral criticism and control and to buttress the claims and practices of selfish individualism.

It is argued in this attitude of mind that others have no right to comment on my personal world – in that private world I am sovereign and I decide. This attitude is often justified in relativistic terms – my point of view is what counts. In this way privacy allows the individual to retreat into a private and egotistical world, to escape his duties towards others, and to pursue his own selfish interests. He is allowed to assert that any opposition to this crab-like way of living is an assault on his 'privacy'. Viewed in such terms, privacy has become a legitimator of the desocialised lifestyle. Thus it is also that people who by force of circumstances live alone, are distant from others, are without real contacts, or who lack authentic social integration, are not to be seen in negative terms. They are not examples of the breakdown of community but of a respect for privacy. To question the way they live, to approach them, perhaps even to help them, is said to constitute an intrusion. How often in Great Britain are we told to shy away from others because to do otherwise would amount to an invasion of privacy? In such a way a powerful barrier is erected to contact; reaching out is warded off by adherence to a tenet which maintains social distance. Indeed, today's potential Good Samaritan would be tempted to pass by on the other side of the road so as not to invade the privacy of the wounded man. The concept of privacy has become both a value of relativism and a legitimator of desocialisation.

The 'Liberationists'

The impulse towards the creation of a relativist culture has also been an inherent feature of a long-term intellectual project of a distinct lineage within modern Western and British thought. This 'liberationist'[16] trajectory has found expression in such major milestones as Marxism, the New Left, postmodernism and 'political correctness'. Through 1789, 1917 and 1968, and on to the present day, this current has shifted and mutated over time but its central aim has always been to remove existing constraints and authority in order to achieve the purported emancipation of modern man. To this end, this lineage has repeatedly affirmed that society's ethics and morals – the very heart of its inherited culture – are mere oppressive constructs lacking in innate validity. This is a pre-eminently relativistic perspective. The principal assertion is that received wisdom and beliefs are creations of an existing power system – mere instruments in the perpetration of domination, oppression and exploitation. There has thus been a constant declaration of an intention to 'liberate' subjected groups and individuals from the binding chains of conventional ideas and attitudes. This long-standing endeavour has been marked by an underlying professed egalitarianism where an alleged belief in human equality goes hand in hand with the rejection of all distinction, especially of class, race or gender, and the conviction that all assertions of objective ethics and morality are merely acts of imposition or 'discrimination'. Surveying the results of the impact of this lineage, it can be seen that liberationism has employed relativism to attempt to 'liberate' people from the received axioms of inherited culture (and especially of Christian culture) but in so doing it has helped to leave the contemporary soul high and dry, stripped of its role and context, lost in a state of nothingness rather like the figures of a theatre of the absurd play.

This project inserted itself into the left-wing part of our political spectrum (fastening onto minority tendencies in its favour) in direct contrast to the very deep impulses towards objective truth which were present within the Labour and Liberal traditions. It has since grown and grown rather like a bulging cuckoo in another's nest. In this it has paralleled the insertion into the political Right of the idea that the great road forward for our national civilisation is to be found in a free market world where individuals pursue their own personal gain in selfish fashion. This cuckoo has found increasing space over the last forty years and in particular received a major impulse from the irruption of 1960s counter-culture. A brief survey of the logic and dynamics of this movement is more than worthwhile because here we are uncovering a significant force behind our present predicament. Indeed, what is most telling about these people, and most revealing about this project, is that they have been very conscious of the need to practice 'cultural politics'. In this they have shown much more acumen than any of their opponents or rivals. The British Conservative Party, for example, the great electoral success story of the last hundred years, has never even considered its role in these terms. Today this project is even very freely admitted to – a sure sign of a sense of security. The ideas of this lineage have filtered down from the intelligentsia into popular culture over recent decades and have now achieved a widespread diffusion.

The *philosophes* formed a part of the background to the French

Revolution; in more recent times the liberationists have played a similar role in relation to desocialisation. In examining this current of thought we are studying a very successful attempt at cultural deconstruction, a project which was understood with perspicacity by Dostoevsky when he described the programme of one of the Russian nihilists in his novel *The Devils*:

> the systematic destruction of society and the principles on which it was based, with the object of throwing everyone into a state of hopeless despair and of bringing about a state of general confusion: so that when society – sick, depressed, cynical, and godless, though with an immense yearning for some guiding idea and for self-preservation – had been brought to a point of collapse, they could seize power, raising the banner of revolt and supported by a whole network of groups of five, which were in the meantime recruiting new members and discovering the best methods of attacking the weak spots.[17]

The promotion of relativism has been more than evident in the Marxist-Leninist tradition. One of the dominant ideas of this trajectory has been that existing shared beliefs are not true in themselves but mere devices of an oppressive class structure. Marx himself argued that the 'ideas of the ruling class are in every epoch the ruling ideas', and in asserting that 'the class which is the ruling material force of society, is at the same time its ruling intellectual force'[18] he sought to strike a mighty blow at ethical and moral certitudes. In this light we can well understand the habitual Marxist contempt for so-called 'bourgeois' thought and morality. Lenin (1870-1924), for his part, rejected 'all morality which proceeds from supernatural ideas or ideas which are outside the class conception' and went on to affirm that 'morality is entirely subordinate to the interests of the class war'.[19] And Mao Tse-Tung (1893-1976) relativised belief by referring it to the social class of its bearer or protagonist – 'in every society everyone lives as a member of a particular class, and every kind of thinking, without exception, is stamped with the brand of a class'.[20] Wherever the Marxist-Leninist (or -Maoist) world-view has penetrated or held sway this impulse to the relativisation of received belief has been very influential.

One of its most notable consequences has been the erosion of traditional cultural mechanisms of social cohesion caused by their being branded as mere instruments of oppression promoted by existing class structures. This is a natural consequence of the perspectives latent in that world-view. Before the Great War Lenin visited London and as he went round he constantly designated features of public life as the work of 'them' – the purported ruling classes. 'In his eyes', reported the person who accompanied him, 'the invisible shadow of the ruling class fell over the whole of human culture and he always saw this shadow as distinctly as daylight'.[21] Existing culture, therefore, was a device to be dismantled or deconstructed. Religion, for example, was to be dismissed as the opium of the people. For this, and other reasons, one of the great features of the Communist experiment in Europe of the twentieth century was the deculturalisation of the peoples upon which it was imposed. Indeed, one of the main difficulties encountered by the nations of Eastern Europe since 1989 has been that they have had to face up to their future handicapped by the previous politically-engineered elimination of vast swathes of their anthropological heritage. In 1998 Vaclav Havel, the President of the Czech Republic, gave an address to the parliament of his country. He lamented the erosion of culture 'in the broadest sense of the word – that is, the culture of human relationships', which had taken place in Czech society. 'You must know that I am talking about what is called a civil society', he continued:

civil society is important for two reasons: in the first place it enables people to be themselves in all their dimensions, which includes being social creatures who desire, in thousands of ways, to participate in the life of the community in which they live. In the second place it functions as a genuine guarantee of political stability...It was no accident that communism's most brutal attack was aimed precisely at this civil society. It knew very well that its greatest enemy was not the individual non-communist politician, but a society that was open, structured independently from the bottom up, and therefore very difficult to manipulate.[22]

Outside the world of 'real socialism' such deculturalisation has been aimed at through the word and the pen.

During the second part of the twentieth century a number of other influences interacted with the Marxist-Leninist tradition to create a new synthesis usually termed the 'New Left'. Once again we encounter a strong propensity to attribute what is held to be true to the workings of impersonal and often hidden forces. It may be observed that the French – the great protagonists of 1789 and 1968 – were in the vanguard. Jean-Paul Sartre (1905-1980) was the guiding light of 'existentialism', a radical creed which rejected ideas of objective right and wrong; stressed the role of subjective perception; and saw in life a vast void of nothingness broken by the sole certainty of existence. Claude Lévi-Strauss detected the presence of 'anthropological structures' which he thought shaped and moulded our actions and thought. In so doing he relativised our certainties to deep and usually concealed underlying forces. Roland Barthes (1915-1980) was the leading spirit of 'structuralism' in literary criticism, a movement which sought to relate what was said and thought not to criteria of objective truth but to purported hidden structures. Herbert Marcuse (1898-1979) grafted Freudianism onto Marxism and expounded the theory of 'social control' – a concept used to describe those mechanisms by which society is said to form and master the individual. Michel Foucault perceived the presence of deep and capillary structures of power within society which he saw as instruments of domination – once again beliefs and outlooks were related to impersonal forces. 'Deconstructionism', another movement within literary criticism (but with far wider applications), led by Jacques Derrida (1930-2004), has carried on this inheritance by undermining all certainties within a literary text and relativising everything about it. This approach has been readily applied to wider social 'texts'. A number of other prominent thinkers have been weakly or strongly connected to this lineage (e.g. McLuhan, Chomsky, Fanon) – far too many to be discussed here. However, the recurrent notion has always been that we think something not because of its objective truth but because it is the outcome of independent forces acting outside us or within us.[23]

The liberationist trajectory, carried forward in the minds of a series of dissenting intellectuals, many of whom belonged to the Marxist-Leninist tradition or the New Left, has acted to challenge and undermine tradition by relativising its essential contents; it has sought to 'de-mystify' conventional belief and morality; and it has constituted an attempt by rebels against Western civilisation to break existing constraints and systems of order in the name of the liberation of culture (and thus of allegedly suffering categories and individuals) from authoritarian and oppressive principles and practices. Today this approach is more than alive and kicking and is expressed in a broad range of priorities. The idea that 'capitalist' society is an attack on the working classes is still widely propounded. Many conserve the ambition to undermine this society by weakening its anthropological joints and joins. Feminism has been a major success story of recent times and has often espoused the view that received ideas about the sexes and their relationships are mere constructs of society which have the aim of oppressing women. Here a relativistic perspective has also been used as a conspicuous weapon of assault on the existing order. The same may be said of the homosexualist movement with its frequent idea that there is no such thing as sexual 'normality' and its contention that existing beliefs in this field oppress a minority and deprive certain individuals of their freedom of self-expression. There is also the purported championing of ethnic groups and an associated support for what is termed 'multicultural-ism'. Employing the tenets of cultural relativism to the full, this last perspective sometimes asserts that specific sub-groups are the victims of a misplaced wider social adherence to values and beliefs which cannot be objectively true. In the light of all these concerns we can well understand the constant liberationist rejection of 'discrimination' (a boom word of the last decades) in relation to class, sex, race and lifestyle. This solid amalgam of priorities now finds expression in what is termed 'postmodernism' although 'hyper-modernism' would per-haps be a more suitable term. Significantly enough, when we study the underlying assumptions of this creed we often return to those material-ist models of man – and most notably societalism – which were outlined in the third chapter. In addition, 'the postmodernist movement', as Ernest Gellner makes clear, is 'a living and contemporary specimen of relativism.'[24]

Postmodernism is now indeed the most vigorous and elaborate theoretical current of thought rooted in the materialist matrix but it is by no means the only such expression, as is evident from a brief *tour d'horizon*. Those who lay immense emphasis on the gains to civilisation to be achieved by a free-for-all market economy energised by the drive for private gain remain an influential force. Radical individualists, with their ceaseless promotion of the construction of a society based on atomised individuals whose secularly-conceived innate rights are upheld by legislation and the state, are also of marked consequence. We are now largely free of racist theory but sociobiology and its offshoots have at times continued some of its dangers. In addition, some now await with enthusiasm the future practice of genetic engineering on human beings in order to achieve a 'better' man and an improved society. Lastly, and despite the fall of the Berlin Wall, a great many unreconstructed Communists still adhere to the dream of a classless society where economic 'exploitation' has been removed and the societal barriers to individual fulfilment dismantled.

However, amongst all these currents it is the postmodernist challenge which now displays the greatest vitality and energy, and it is highly significant that it emerged in the last decades of the twentieth century precisely when Marxist-Leninism entered into major decline. A natural mutation appears to have taken place in the contents of the liberationist trajectory. Postmodernism has strong support in academic, intellectual and artistic circles and in Great Britain it has received a major push forward from developments in the USA. Indeed, in the Western world postmodernism is probably most deeply entrenched within the Anglo-Saxon archipelago. It is in these countries, too, that the 'politically correct' movement has achieved its greatest success – a political movement whose philosophical background is to be firmly located in postmodernism. With its purported concern for working-class interests and the problems of the poor; its support for feminist and homosexualist aspirations; its apparent sensitivity to ethnic groups and sympathy for minorities; its commitment to relativism and its antipathy to religion; its emphasis on freedom of expression and its stress on originality; its seeming championing of the third world and its hostility to Western global ascendancy, political correctness is not only to be located firmly within the postmodernist frame of mind but is also to be placed squarely in the liberationist tradition. Its wish to enforce orthodoxy in thought and conduct (that which is deemed to be 'correct'), which is often expressed in a ruthlessness in seeking to control cultural power-points, is not only an action which is clearly fundamentalist in style but also a stance in line with the historic concern of the liberationist project with the practice of cultural politics, of which indeed it is the culminating expression.

An excellent account of postmodernism is given from the inside by Richard Tarnas, an enthusiastic sympathiser. Relativism is at its core. This thinker observes how a broad variety of modern currents of thought converge to sustain the view that 'human knowledge is subjectively determined by a multitude of factors; that objective essences, or things in themselves, are neither accessible nor positable'.[25] Thus it is that a number of academic disciplines have 'underscored the relativity of human knowledge' and revealed 'the "Eurocentric" character of Western thought, and of the cognitive bias produced by factors such as class, race, and ethnicity'.[26] The study of language, in particular, has produced an approach which 'radically relativizes human claims to a sovereign or enduring truth'.[27] Such is the theoretical background to an assault on the Western tradition launched because of its 'anti-Semitism, its oppression of women, people of color, minorities, homosexuals, the working classes, the poor, the destruction of indigenous societies throughout the world'.[28] Faced with such alleged oppression 'the contemporary academic world has increasingly concerned itself with the critical deconstruction of traditional assumptions through several overlapping modes of analysis'.[29] Yet with all this questioning and discrediting, as Tarnas himself well admits, what seems to be emerging is the insecurity of the void – 'The postmodern human mind exists in a universe whose significance is at once utterly open and without warrantable foundation'.[30] For Tarnas and his kind perhaps this is all very exciting, leading on through 'openness' to who knows what kinds of intellectual thrills and spills. Others may have a very different evaluation.

Much of the neo-Marxist, New Left, postmodernist, politically correct, liberationist project can be found in a most candid publication which presents aims and objects with very little reserve. A close reading of this work is worthwhile because we are able to perceive much of this project in a form presented without any attempt at camouflage. For a long time these dissenters had to be very careful in what they propounded. But here we encounter an openly proclaimed plan of cultural engineering underway for a very long time, albeit often in hidden form; an endeavour which is firmly rooted in the materialist matrix; and an exposition which lays bare many of the ideas and intentions which have lain behind desocialisation. G. Jordan and C. Weedon in *Cultural Politics, Class, Gender, Race and the Postmodern World* (1995) declare that power is their 'central concern'.[31] They see culture as what conserves existing power structures within society – it is a 'key site in the political struggle to reproduce and transform power relations'.[32] The aim of their book, therefore, is to 'contribute to critical cultural inquiry and liberating political practice.'[33] What is of primary concern in this project is the transformation of relationships involving class, gender and race. For these authors the deconstruction of existing cultural patterns will involve liberation through the overcoming of inequality. In this goal they are well aware of the importance of 'controlling the means of cultural production'[34] and of determining how the past is described – hence the title of chapter five: 'Whose History is It? Class, Cultural Democracy and Constructions of the Past'. The authors perceive that culture is a 'contested space',[35] and their book is a contribution to that struggle. Needless to say, the visions of man to be found in the pages of their book contain no reference to the soul. 'What most distinguishes human beings from animals?, they ask, 'Intellect, culture, language, the capacity to reason, the capacity to delay gratification'.[36]

In true liberationist style everything in their analysis is seen in terms of conflict and domination. There is no idea that power, authority or guidance can at times be benevolent or based on consent. No thought is given to the possibility that much of the cultural heritage may actually have a positive role. In striking fashion what will actually be built in the way of anthropological struts and girders when tradition and convention are stripped away is given precious little thought. In short, we are asked to embrace a programme of deculturalisation and to move towards an unpredictable vacuum with no guarantees as to what will result. A perilous venture indeed, but one which belongs to the long-standing liberationist project. In this context let us not forget that the Marxist-Leninist tradition has constantly enjoined the tearing down of an old society and the building up of a new. Similarly there is no idea that many people may not actually want to be subject to a project which seeks to deny them of much of what they hold dear. Such a factor does not seem to matter, indeed it may be an obstacle. The plan must go ahead, conceived by thinkers who believe they have the qualifications to dream up such grand schemes and then carry them out through the wielding of instruments of cultural change. This is part and parcel of the rationalist mind's propensity for engineering detected by Oakeshott. In vain one searches the pages of this book for any proposals for man which go beyond questions relating to wealth or the distribution of power. Edmund Burke, ever hostile to such hazardous projects, must be turning in his grave:

Societies contain social divisions, that is, lines of actual or potential conflict between various social groups. All known societies have contained divisions of age, gender and kinship, that is divisions between young and old, men and women, people from one kinship group and people from another. Further, most societies maintain divisions between themselves and their neighbours. Such divisions are marked by differences in appearance, behaviour and speech. Their reproduction is largely secured through culture, that is, through belief systems, social rituals, ideologies and other modes of intersubjective thinking and acting.

Social divisions rarely divide equals: in any society some groups are more powerful and/or have higher status than others...Very often, social divisions are reflections of *social inequality*, that is, differences of wealth, power and/or status...relations of inequality are closely tied to questions of culture. The relative domination of various groups by other groups is partly secured and reproduced through the practices and products of cultural institutions. Here we are thinking of examples such as language, the family, the educational system, the media, the law, and religious organizations. It is through these institutions that we learn what is right and wrong, good and bad, normal and abnormal, beautiful and ugly...

Suppose that within a given society one poses the question: 'Which cultural practices and products are most valued'? The answer is most likely to be this: those of the dominant group and the past traditions with which it aligns itself. Social inequality is *legitimated* through culture. It is through intersubjective modes of thinking and acting that the relative domination of one group over another is made to appear logical, acceptable, 'natural', perhaps even prescribed by God. This is not all that culture does, but it is no small thing.

Just as group *domination* has its cultural dimensions, so *resistance to domination* must also be rooted in culture and experience, at least, if it is to be successful. Take, for example, the Women's Liberation Movement, or 'Third World' liberation movements. Struggles to achieve political independence or social equality have not been fights simply for formal recognition. They have also been battles to transform the nature of the educational system, to shift the pattern of control in the national media, to rewrite history, to reconstruct human beings. All revolutions – from socialist revolutions to the Women's Movement to Thatcherism – decentre, displace or deconstruct dominant cultural constructions, meanings and values. All seek to realize one aim: to transform human action and being.

The legitimation of social relations of inequality, and the struggle to transform them, are central concerns of CULTURAL POLITICS.[37]

What is worrying is that the proponents of the latter-day liberationist project seem to be strongly entrenched in powerful positions of cultural influence in British society. The postmodernists and the politically correct are now well established in the universities and schools, publishing houses and academic reviews, the press, radio, television and cinema, and are, in one way or another, committed to a far-reaching

project of reform of hearts and minds, much of which has already been
carried out. The successful practice of cultural politics has led to the
capture of important commanding heights. In surveying the activity of
this current we can observe a distinct propensity towards the repeated
expression in debate, print, broadcasts, films and scholarship of the
same concepts, systems of understanding and lexicon; the reproduction
of orthodox lines of interpretation; and the presentation of history in
conformity with a certain set of fixed perspectives.[38] Obviously enough,
irreligiosity, if not anti-religiosity, is conspicuous by its presence. A
conformist tendency to promote the same approach is compounded by
a frequent propensity to exclusion – in a variety of contexts those of a
dissenting viewpoint frequently find their space for manoeuvre checked,
if indeed they are ever allowed such space in the first place. There is a
totalitarian tendency to occupy all of the terrain and to exclude those
who do not conform to the postmodernist agenda. Indeed, the number
of people whose careers have been blasted because of this ideological
filtering would constitute an interesting subject of statistical inquiry.
The much vaunted ideas of tolerance, the open mind, the balanced view
or moderate approach, compromise and understanding, pluralism,
diversity and anti-discrimination here seem to be suspended.

A good example of this process may be found in the imposition of
political correctness in the world of learning and the mechanisms which
lie behind recruitment to the academic profession. Indeed, the universities
exemplify this grip and this project; at times they even seem to perform
the function of postmodernist seminaries. An anti-libertarian system of
screening seems to be at work. It is highly significant that at the 1987
general election, for example, when the Conservatives gained 42% of the
national vote, only 17% of academics voted Tory.[39] Something has gone
very askew. It is as if *The Idea of a University Defined and Illustrated*
(1873) by Cardinal Newman (1801-1890) had never been written. Thomas
Hobbes's warning has not been heeded. For this thinker, universities were
'fountains of Civill and Morall doctrine' which had to be defended 'both
from the Venime of Heathen Politicians and from the Incantation of
Deceiving Spirits'.[40] One commentator has observed the entrenchment of
a 'full-scale left establishment' in our universities (exactly the same thing
has happened in the USA and other Western countries since the 1960s)
and outlined the salient features of its outlook:

> The fundamental belief in human equality, accompanied by a
> hostility to all distinction, whether of class, race or gender. The

suspicion of 'power'; and the absence of any lively sense that the surrounding power might be legitimate, despite being in other's hands than one's own.

The hostility to all that confers power: and especially to enterprise, business, and the market.

The 'critical' approach to society in which 'power' and 'conflict' are everywhere perceived and unmasked.

The paradoxical identification with the external enemies of power: especially with those states which pose a threat to the security of Western nations.

The willingness to believe the bona fides of those who speak the language of 'liberation' and 'struggle'.

Guilt towards one's country and its past – the attitude described in America as the 'liberal cringe': a form of embarrassment at one's ancestors, for having believed in their own superiority and having, through that belief, made themselves superior.

Anti-patriotism; usually accompanied by mockery towards patriotic sentiments in one's own nation – or an open war upon them as forms of 'militarism'.[41]

Here we are not far from the hostility of the Hollywood power barons to patriotism, marriage, religion, self-discipline, hard work, decent manners and non-violence.[42] This is no coincidence – we are dealing with the same general strand and outlook.

Looked at in terms of historical trajectory, however, this form of ascendancy should not surprise us. From the age of the Enlightenment onwards dissenting intellectuals have engaged in a sustained and in recent times successful drive for power. Their claim to rule has often been linked to programmes for the liberation of those they say are oppressed. Given their nature, it is only natural that they should have sought out these special areas of cultural influence and persuasion. Indeed, the enormous emphasis on rationality and knowledge which has so characterised the modern age has frequently served as a method by which the intellectual classes have sought to increase their own importance. But at a much deeper level we are looking at an intellectual attack on Christian civilisation which is bound up with an attempt to supplant the role of the clergy. It is more than symbolic that the universities before the nineteenth century were largely religious institutions – today they are authentic bastions of materialist thought. During the medieval period the Church was the chief guardian of cultural orthodoxy, the principal site of the intelligentsia, and the chief influence on learning. Committed to the promotion of the Christian world-view, ecclesiastical structures exercised a keen grip over key power-points of cultural formation. In promoting materialist thinking and relativist perspectives over recent centuries a large number of intellectuals have not only aimed at the withdrawal of Christian culture but have also sought to entrench themselves in positions of power previously occupied by members of the cloth. As Paul Johnson has observed:

> Over the past two hundred years the influence of intellectuals has grown steadily...With the decline of clerical power in the eighteenth century, a new kind of mentor emerged to fill the vacuum and capture the ear of society. The secular intellectual might be deist, sceptic or atheist. But he was just as ready as any pontiff or presbyter to tell mankind how to conduct its affairs. He proclaimed from the start a special devotion to the interests of humanity and an evangelical duty to advance them by teaching. He brought to his self-appointed task a far more radical approach than his clerical predecessors. He felt himself bound by no corpus of revealed religion. The collective wisdom of the past, the legacy of tradition, the prescriptive codes of ancestral experience existed to be selectively followed or wholly rejected as his own good sense might decide. For the first time in human history, and with growing confidence and audacity, men arose to assert that they could diagnose the ills of society and cure them with their own unaided intellects: more, that they could devise formulae whereby not only the structure of society but the fundamental habits of human beings could be transformed for the better...One of the most marked characteristics of the new secular intellectuals was the relish with which they subjected religion and its protagonists to critical scrutiny...The verdicts pronounced on both churches and clergy were harsh.[43]

Yet when we look at the broad ranks of the postmodernists of various hues and colours with their pseudo-sciences and their frequent control of publications, their sacred texts and quasi-theological denunciations, their orthodox interpretations and rigid dogmas, their university stipends and mass media salaries, their internecine struggles and ferocious polemics, their frequent intolerance for dissent and their promotion of their own, their belief that they have the right to tamper with a community's culture and their frequent disdain for popular opinion, perhaps we are not so far removed from seeing modern versions of what was so vehemently denounced during the upheavals of the late-medieval period – priestcraft. But who now will launch a Reformation against the schemes of the high priests, scribes and Pharisees of this section of the latter-day materialist (and frequently fundamentalist) clergy? Who will correct the politically correct? Who will liberate us from the liberationists?

It should be observed that political correctness exists well beyond these positions of cultural influence and has left its mark on the world of government and law, at both a national and European Union level. In this sphere, too, we may perceive worrying expressions of the totalitarian inheritance of the liberationist movement. Indeed one contemporary observer goes so far as to describe political correctness as 'the most intolerant system of thought to dominate the British Isles since the Reformation'.[44] Thus we encounter attempts to regulate thought, speech, the written word, and behaviour by state or EU decree, in particular in those areas stressed by the liberationists, in line with the tenets of postmodernist thinking carried forward in particular by these positions of cultural influence. This drive towards uniformity is a development full of disturbing implications for the sacred cause of liberty, made all the more worrying by the absence of constitutional safeguards. Indeed, we seem at times to be witnessing the emergence of distinct elements of authoritarianism and what from many points of view appears to be a growing secular (and secularist) theocracy.

Towards Nothing

In what ways does relativism promote desocialisation? By a large number of routes. Like the materialist visions of man outlined in chapter three, relativism involves an assault on the soul and community made up of an attack on the Christian world-view and the life according to the Spirit, in conjunction with a many-sided encouragement of the dark side. In this last endeavour it baits its hooks with the prospect of the attainment of liberty and the enjoyment of the delights of the unhindered pursuit of free inquiry. It also encourages deculturalisation and de-Christianisation – themselves forces behind the establishment of the anomic condition – which in turn are matched by the undermining of the viability of authentic society carried out by means of an assault on the very possibility of a shared project based on common beliefs. Furthermore, both relativism and the other false anthropologies of post-modernity unite to form a very special battering ram against the gates which bar the way to desocialisation, which of course they themselves act to promote in the first place. In reality, however, relativism contradicts these other visions of man – a further sign (in addition to its own self-contradiction) that relativism is largely a destructive device. All of this gives us a clear clue as to the underlying *telos* of this philosophical success story of the post-modern age. Essentially, relativism is a generator of nothingness. Desocialisation itself is characterised by the lack of certain things which should be there (love, community, union, good will); it is an expression of the emptiness created by the many-sided impact of the materialist matrix. And the failure to fulfil man's vocation produces an imposing absence. Relativism participates in the achievement of this outcome by being a remorseless propagator of the void wherever it exercises influence. This interpretation is by no means the idiosyncratic invention of this author. This long-term impulse towards nothingness, which has so stamped its mark on the contours of modernity, has often been sensed and expressed in the thought and works of writers, artists and thinkers. The future diffusion of the void has had its latter-day heralds. These various elements will now be analysed in the order in which they have been adumbrated in this paragraph.

The Attack on the Life According to the Spirit

Certainly relativism is the deadly enemy of the Christian world-view and the Christian life, which is why political correctness is inevitably in overall terms an anti-Christian movement. Notions of relative truth (which in reality murder the very concept of truth) confront ideas of objective truth. This is one of the great fields of battle of our times and it has to be acknowledged that the tide has turned strongly – indeed very strongly – in favour of the former. On the one hand, relativism attacks any certainties which an individual may have about himself and the cosmos. It is therefore a direct assault on the perception of the soul and God. On the other, it undermines beliefs about how an individual should live and act – there is thus an intense assault on the life according to the Spirit. The principles and virtues, morals and ethics, and convictions and rules, which arise from a stewardship of the soul are all belittled or dismissed. It is asserted that there can be no certainties in this sphere. Thus the most essential truths about what we are and what we should do become removed by the simple declaration that there is no objective truth. In related fashion there is a propensity to relate what is said and done to certain alleged 'causes'. It is almost as though by explaining something the truth of that something is discredited. By this primary route relativism strikes at the very heart of everything that is most important and most valuable in human existence. The entire edifice of the construction of the kingdom of heaven has a charge of dynamite placed at one of its cornerstones – love, respect and search for truth.

The dark side of man's spirituality is also promoted. There is a devilish cunning in relativism. Although it denies all certainties it also discourages rejection. It does not uphold anything but equally it is loath to condemn. It replaces guidance by licence. 'Beyond good and evil',[45] to use Nietzsche's famous phrase, there is freedom to do as you please. This is a mighty method by which to encourage and legitimate spiritual ill-health. Indeed, relativism emerges as a wonderful support for the practice of selfish individualism in all its forms. As you decide what truth is, and as you can never by definition be 'wrong', you can twist it and deform it, change it and bury it, marginalise it and invert it, to suit your own interests and selfishness. You can justify everything and ward off all reproaches. You are the arbiter of what is true. Here relativism turns post-modern man into a god because he can never be in 'error'. This not only provides *carte blanche* to egoism, it is also an immoral man's *passe partout*, an indulgence granted to the criminal. There are no obstacles placed in the way of wrong-doing and no checks on the embrace of the dark side – one of the great goals of the assault launched by the materialist matrix. You can say and do whatever you like except talk and act to the effect that there are some things you should not say or do; in typical self-contradictory form, prohibitions are prohibited. Everything is accepted except the idea that some things cannot be accepted. Contemporary man is to look for points of departure other than objective morality by which to govern society. Hence the contemporary frequent refusal to disapprove or to judge – we encounter here a principal root of the frequent condemnation of being 'judgemental' – and the great quest to discover and promote the 'neutral'. We also gain insight into why the much vaunted tenets of tolerance, openness, moderation, compromise and understanding become suspended in relation to ideas of objective truth and morality – such ideas alone are to be condemned because they believe in condemnation. This in itself is a classic example of relativism's constant capacity for illogicalness.

This creed goes beyond a refusal to condemn to arrive at the encouragement of a stance which is another ally of the dark side.

Relativism is a major engine of indifference – which indeed is what 'tolerance' often really amounts to. Relativism promotes a propensity to be unconcerned about the ethical and moral behaviour of others – what they do is up to them, for them to decide. This attitude is closely bound up with notions of liberty – it is not for me to interfere in the freedom of others – and is also supported by notions of privacy: it is not for me to interfere in what is essentially a private question. This is to draw back from ideas that a community should be based upon shared truths and the expression of those truths, and the belief that such truths contribute to the welfare of the community and to the individuals who compose it. That most vital of instruments in the upholding of truths – social pressure – is thrown out of the window. Individuals are encouraged not to reproach or to rebuke, to control or to monitor, to hinder or to impede. This amounts to a refusal of responsibility and of participation. It means a depletion of community – to be indifferent to what others do in the moral sphere is in itself a distancing from other people, a lack of involvement, an act of isolation. If I am indifferent to what is done I withdraw from seeking to achieve and maintain authentic society; I retreat into my selfish individualist world. But it also involves lending a helping hand to those who live on the dark side. In desocialised culture when relativist arguments are employed to justify silence in the face of wrong-doing there is a parallel with the putting up of shutters in order not to see the crimes of the secret police in a totalitarian State. If I keep quiet about the wife-beating or the cruelty to children which takes place next door, I am in fact helping the culprit. After all, the indifference of others is one of the things criminals like best.

Wrong-doing is also aided by the opportunities provided by relativism's legitimation of 'diversity'. Relativism constantly affirms that a point of view, an action or a lifestyle with which we disagree is not right or wrong – it is merely 'different'. It is not to be evaluated, or condemned, but to be seen solely as an example of diversity. This offers a wonderful defence for those who live on the dark side. It removes controls on their misdeeds and allows them to do as they please – what they do is not a matter for reprobation or intervention but toleration and acceptance. They become shielded by an indiscriminate respect for what is different. This contemporary cult of diversity has other deleterious consequences. It provides an obvious route by which the wrongly discontented can assault a healthy human environment. Those who live on the dark side may resent what their context does to them. They can respond by being different from it, by adopting alternative modes, mores and morality, and by declaring their divergence from its central axioms and tenets. They can then defend their destructive dissent by invoking the legitimacy of diversity. Moreover the idea of being different, of standing out, of being special, greatly appeals to pride and vanity. At times it becomes merely a means by which to draw attention to oneself and thus an exercise in self-importance. The constant striving to be 'original' (one of the curses of modern scholarship) – quite irrespective of whether that originality is grounded in truth or not – forms another facet of this process. Lastly, the cult of diversity (which is often intimately bound up with selfish individualism) impedes the agreed search for that shared ground with others which forms the basis of any real community. The single common project becomes torn apart by a host of different personal projects.

Relativism also offers a splendid shield and weapon for the practice of envy. As will be discussed in greater detail in chapter nine, sick spirits have a natural hostility to quality in all its forms. Superiority in its various expressions is always resented by those who are ill in their souls. The principle that prizes and prestige within a human society should accrue to those of worth and merit is particularly opposed by those who suffer from spiritual ill-health. Relativism undermines the very concept of quality or superiority and thus provides the envious with a wonderful instrument by which to attack such worth and merit. From stressing that there is no objective truth it is a very simple step to asserting that there are no true standards – an attitude, as we have seen, powerfully present in modern art and aesthetics. (Indeed, the decline of the discipline of aesthetics may in part be attributed to the impact of relativist thought). By this route it becomes very easy to propose that quality and superiority do not really exist but are merely points of view or constructs of some external force or system of power. This can also join up with sameism – being 'equal' or the 'same', others cannot be 'better'. Armed with such a destructive line of thought, those who suffer from envy can deny the greater ability, talent or quality of another person and thereby undermine the latter's rightful claim to reward, position or admiration within a community. Although such envy is in itself a recognition of such superiority, and thus a sign that its bearer is engaging in some kind of discriminating perception, this does not matter. What counts is that the envious person has found a theoretical weapon with which he can justify his own resentments and promote an attack on those of whom he is envious.

Irresponsible Freedom

'They promise them freedom' (II Pt 2:19). Once again baiting its hooks with great skill, relativism often presents the abandonment of divine law and the embrace of the dark side as a positive act of liberation – the individual is promised the prospect of becoming 'free' in his actions. The actual exercise of liberty is what is said to matter, not the specific content of what is done. In this scheme of things no ethical and moral impediments, or possibilities of divine judgement, exist to impede such freedom. Has not man the right as a free agent to pick the fruit from any tree he likes? We can thus understand why relativism is so often dressed up and espoused in terms of liberty and why its hostility to objective ethical and moral thought is expressed with reference to the need to be free. Again and again we hear individuals declare that they must be free to do as they see fit and that we have no right to condemn, constrain or interfere. After all is not their 'opinion' said to be as good as ours? Any such intrusion is said to be an imposition, a constraint and a restriction. What relativism – although it often does not admit to the fact – is really proposing is that man should break free from objective morality in order to do what he wants. He is to be liberated into a state of freedom where he can act as he wishes. Any internal impediments such as shame, remorse, regret or guilt are to be dismissed on the grounds that they do not derive from a non-existent soul or conscience but are externally imposed or the result of some other source which has no real validity. Equally, the external constraints of authority within society are dismissed as a mere exercise in power and not the valid expressions of ethical and moral truths. What is really being offered here is the freedom of the void – that fateful liberty to which Lucifer aspired. For without love and truth what life and fulfilment can there be for man? Such liberty leads only to the vacuum of deprivation. Tempted by the freedom to break all rules, man, as Dostoevsky well recognised, does indeed become 'done for'. Relativism has been a revolution in favour of nothing.

The champions of relativist culture habitually assert that its liberty and variety attest to a readiness to search for the truth. It is said to bestow the benefits of free inquiry and investigation upon its members. Here we encounter an authentic deception if ever there was one, a 'Big Lie' of which Joseph Goebbels (1897-1945) himself would have been proud. In reality this culture's diversity of approach, individual variation and plurality of thought all mask – and by a broad number of mechanisms actually encourage – a striking uniformity, homogeneity and conformity at one essential level. Through all the variety a marked absence is conspicuous by its presence – there is a recurrent refusal to perceive the spiritual dimension to the cosmos, to recognise that within man there is a soul and outside him God, and to accept that as a result there are imperative truths which must inform the way we think and behave. The rejection of objective points of reference may well permit endless inquiry and investigation – something which can be very congenial to intellectuals and artists – but it also rules out inquiry and investigation into those very points of reference. Within the existing plurality there are major barriers to going beyond the accepted paradigms. Because of this we often encounter a dreary and soulless sameness from Left to Right, from rich to poor, and from north to south. What diversity there is often amounts to mere variation on a theme. Beneath the surface cacophony the melodies are frequently the same. We have before us a stagnant whirlpool. For without an appreciation and recognition of certain essential truths what real life can there be in all this variety?

Deculturalisation

Just as relativism immobilises the moral personality and eats away at its inner core, so is it also a great deculturaliser. It is a giant rodent which gnaws away at the anthropological pillars and beams which uphold the edifice of community. Through the denial of fixed bases it removes the props which support the life according to the Spirit which in turn permits a socialising culture. The individual is neither to guide himself nor rebuke others, exercise self-control nor provide help, feel responsibility nor face up to sacrifice. He is placed in a no man's land of nothing, left without maps or a compass and condemned to uncertainty and confusion. At the same time relativism is a creed which undermines the certainties of our civilisation, declares that there are no shared bases upon which to act, and affirms that there are no true goals for which to strive. Relativism refuses all notions of 'normality' and the normal – these, too, are deemed to be mere constructs. Similarly, all received notions about what is right and noble or what is admirable and worthy – the very sheet anchors of our shared experience – become subjected to doubt and called into question. Thus, for example, we have been often told (at times by such liberationist psychiatrists, criminologists and anthropologists as Laing, Foucault and Lévi-Strauss) that distinctions between the mad and the sane, between the criminal and the honest, and between the savage and the civilised, are in fact the mere decisions of those who are in a majority or in positions of power. All in all, under this constant relativist barrage we may become confused about what our real purpose in life is and what should form the guidelines for our behaviour together in society. All this acts to pour acid on the received certitudes of inherited culture which thereby becomes subject to a process of withering.

In Great Britain and the West the religious core of that culture has been an especial target of this operation. From a historical perspective, relativism should thus also be seen as a device by which to deconstruct Christian civilisation. In this it links up with the rest of the materialist matrix's assault on the Christian world-view. The central thrust has been to deny that there are objective ethical or moral truths and to suggest that everything is merely relative – the creation of society, of a class structure, of the psyche, of biological programming, of language, of the brain, of this and of that – but never something which is true in itself. The objective and imperative truths of God and of the soul simply do not exist because such non-material realities are deemed to be mere ghosts of the human mind – constructs of the beholder and nothing else. To put it another way, and in a form which echoes the humanist perspective, we ourselves are the creators of God and the soul. Similarly, relativism constantly reiterates that Christianity is just one of many faiths in the world, just another form of religious perception, just another outcome of the particular historical evolution of a people. It is as right as the other faiths and as wrong as the other faiths, and no other judgement can be made. It is also implied that just as we create Christianity so too can we rid ourselves of it. In this we detect a major aspiration of the liberationists and their doctrinal lodestar – to 'liberate' modern man from traditional religion, its fixed beliefs and their enforcement, and set him up in a brave new world crowned by the freedom to choose. But with relativism can anything really in an authentic sense be chosen?

The Attack on the Common Project and the Sacred

In its strident emphasis on subjective perspective and individual choice, its refusal of inherited convention and its endless encouragement of doubt, this creed also places heavy explosive charges under the concept and reality of the common project. Relativism is selfish individualism run riot: rather than searching for solid axes around which a society could revolve, this creed promotes the principle of every man for himself. Instead of helping us to look for points of contact which could enable a community to function, relativism generates a purely personal perspective. In the place of agreed adherence to received wisdom and practice bequeathed by previous generations, this outlook substitutes an endless questioning of all shared notions and principles. In addition, its assault on the life according to the Spirit is an attack on the vital point of departure for the achievement of real human society; its rejection of the anthropological inheritance involves a massive removal of social cement; and its refusal of the truths of the Christian message is a direct repudiation of what lies at the base of an integrating cultural system. So from any point from which one approaches the aspirations and implications of relativism, one detects a creed which assaults the very idea that people should act together within a society in line with certain common principles and beliefs which are then expressed in behaviour. It is a direct attack on the fundamental social contract of any group of individuals – the expression and promotion of spiritual health. Seen in this light, relativism is an attempt to blow the common project to smithereens. And in this endeavour this revolution in favour of nothing has achieved remarkable success.

In its discrediting and its debunking relativism constitutes a major attack on the sacred. (The same may be said of rationalism's constant propensity to call everything into question and subject what is accepted to debate). If nothing can have real worth then what is handed down by previous generations as being of supreme value becomes devalued. This decline of the sacred is one of the increasing characteristics of contemporary society and here relativism joins up with other forces to form a major assault. To what other factors can this decline be attributed? First of all, the denial of God and the soul removes a perspective of holiness on human affairs. In seeking to obey divine will or acting in favour of illuminated spirituality we impart the sacred to our surroundings. All elements within society or individual thought and behaviour which conduce to these ends acquire a holy connotation. Where such a perspective is absent the sacred fades. Secondly, the very realities of a loss of community mean that people decreasingly subscribe to sacred institutions and conventions which were once surrounded with a halo akin to that of totems. The decline of parental guidance and instruction is a part of this process in that children fail to receive certain fixed unquestionable lessons about the world around them. Thirdly, selfish individualism tends to dismiss the value of elements which are not of direct utility to personal gain and to feel no feelings of loyalty towards such elements, stressing instead the paths of personal liberty and development. This decline of the sacred is one factor behind another increasing phenomenon of our times – the decline of authority. Exactly the same forces working for the former work in favour of the latter. The 'freedom' to which the lifestyle of personal autonomy aspires is an especial force in this direction.

The Relationship with the Materialist Matrix

The role of relativism in the removal of condemnation and in the bestowal of an illusory freedom links up very well with the other visions of man of the materialist matrix. We gain insight into why they are so often invoked together and espoused at the same time. The other false anthropologies of post-modernity remove God and the soul from the universe and encourage the dark side latent in human spirituality. They tend to argue that there are no spiritual truths to follow and to leave man to what it is alleged that he is – that whole range of impulses, aspirations and trajectories which lead to the drive for power, pleasure, wealth, sexual satisfaction and all the rest. Such activities are not seen as a 'moral' area to be discussed in 'moral' terms because they are said to be determined by human nature and to form an inevitable feature of the human condition. They are like the weather – an inescapable part of life. The great point is that here relativism's assault on morality cannot function. Because such elements are determined they cannot be touched by relativist discrediting – they are there because they are there. However, relativism does attack and undermine that objective morality of authentic spiritual life which is the only true enemy of the practice of the dark side. We can thus perceive a remarkable joint operation – the other false anthropologies of post-modernity produce a range of ways of living which cannot be criticised by relativism and at the same time relativism wards off any attack on those ways by attacking their great enemies – objective ideas of right and wrong. This is a very remarkable action of very deep purpose, rooted in the combined action of approaches which are united in their rejection of God and the soul. We encounter a very dark process of mutual support.

However, beyond the ethical and moral sphere relativism is in reality an adversary of the rest of the materialist matrix, although this point is rarely recognised. After all, if nothing is really true then nothing really true can be said about man. For all its intertwining with the materialist matrix and its support for the attacks which that matrix launches against the spiritualist outlook, this central doctrine of post-modernity in reality has a radical incompatibility with humanism, rationalism, societalism, rightsism and all the rest. In the relativist perspective everything is questionable and there are no fixed points of comprehension. Why then should we really believe anything which is affirmed by such anthropologies about *homo sapiens* and the human experience? Exactly the same observation may be made of the postmodernist outlook and the contemporary liberationist practitioners of cultural politics. If relativism is sound why should equality ever be adopted as a first principle? What are the fixed criteria for any statements about race, gender or class? Where are the underlying bases for believing in any of the information gathered or marshalled to support the liberationist project? And if deconstructionist thinking, rooted in relativism, is applied to traditional culture, why should it not also be applied to postmodernism? Paradoxically enough, and almost in whimsical fashion, these kind of objections are often simply shrugged off. Tarnas himself observes that 'Implicitly, the one postmodern absolute is critical consciousness, which, by deconstructing all, seems compelled by its own logic to do so to itself as well'.[46] But if this is so, why should anyone ever proclaim himself the exponent of such a philosophy? Unless, that is, we are dealing with an explicit or implicit act of dishonesty. The observation of R. Scruton is prescient: 'The very reasoning which sets out to destroy the ideas of objective truth and absolute values imposes political correctness as absolutely binding, and cultural relativism as objectively true'.[47]

As this paradox would suggest, at a general level the employment of relativism is marked by a devastating lack of coherence and a staggering divorce from empirical realities. Those who use it to discredit and undermine are never consistent in applying it to their own declarations. When assailed by the frequent relativist refrain 'who are you to say that?', few dare to counter with the obvious answer 'who are you to ask that?' And who replies to the great contemporary observation 'that's only your point of view' with the affirmation 'and that's only your point of view'. The whole approach simply does not stand up. Placed under the most elementary of logical microscopes, relativism becomes rapidly untenable. Furthermore, as is more than evident in the case of determinism, anybody who took this creed seriously as a way of governing their lives would soon encounter massive difficulties. If ever there was an example of common sense being ridden over roughshod this is it. For example, if I cannot really trust to my perceptions what bases do I have for taking decisions about what I should do? The dilemma is rather like that of determinism – if everything is determined why should I ever reflect upon how I should act; indeed, why should I ever engage in decision-making? What we seem to have before us is a veritable agenda for paralysis. Surveying these realities one readily intuits that those who embrace relativism often employ it merely as a device.

Acid on the Soul and the Community

With such a long line of negative features and consequences it is not surprising that all relativist roads lead to desocialisation. It is at one and the same time both acid on the soul and acid on the community. It discourages the input of the socialising potential of the healthy soul into human culture and favours the dissolving impact of its dark side. In addition, it eats away the core beliefs and practices of a people's inherited culture and erodes the whole range of moral tenets and axioms developed over time to ensure social cohesion (which in the case of the West and Great Britain are of a strong Christian imprint). And having destroyed it cannot construct because by its very nature it can engender only doubt. Relativism is thus a major engine of negativity, but an engine decked out in all kinds of superficially attractive flags. Its ceaseless assault on the idea of truth produces vast swathes of the opposite of what there should be or great areas of emptiness. Neither the individual nor society are to contain what they require according to the purpose of man – there is either a negation or a mere absence. Thus the freedom to engage in untruthfulness, insincerity, dishonesty, double-dealing, deception and lying which is supplied by an attitude which discourages the idea of truth, reduces humans to a social form of existence which creates distrust and suspicion rather than co-operation and shared initiative. Men in this way become prised apart and separated from one another. But of course it is not only truth in the sense of honest speech and conduct which is so assailed by relativism. It is also moral truth in a wider sense. Love for one's neighbour, and all the virtues associated with that truth, are also of vital importance to the achievement of community. Here relativism links up with the central impulse of the rest of the materialist matrix. In this context it is more than fitting that deconstructionism has been a recent feature of the post-modern intellectual thrust. Do we not see all around us things which have been deconstructed (or destroyed)? The ironic statement on nihilism of one of the protagonists of Turgenev's *Fathers and Sons* (1862) becomes of striking contemporary relevance: 'We shall see how you manage to exist in a void, in an airless vacuum'.[48]

*

The movement of modernity in the direction of nothingness encouraged by relativism and the other false anthropologies of post-modernity has been sensed and predicted – and at times encouraged – by many a prominent artist and thinker. No comprehensive survey of the last two hundred years is possible here, but when we cast our eyes over such prominent features of the terrain as Surrealism and Dadaism, Munch's 'Scream' and Bacon's 'Pope Innocent X', Kafka's novels and Beckett's plays, the concerns of Dostoevsky's *The Devils*, James's *The Turn of the Screw* (1898) or Conrad's *Heart of Darkness* (1902), we come face to face with a massive pull towards negativity. In the 1930s T.S. Eliot was even moved to refer to 'the intrusion of the diabolic into modern literature'.[49] When we extend our glance to the rock music of more recent times we become aware that writers have not been alone in such a sensibility. Films represent a new art form of the twentieth century, at times involving writers and singers. With their ability to impinge on millions across the world they also constitute a mighty instrument of cultural influence. Hollywood now demonstrates, in the words of one observer, a receptivity to 'dark and disturbing material':[50]

> The Oscar nominations of February 1992 (for movies released in the course of 1991) again displayed the Academy's ferocious fascination with the dark side. Consider the anointed candidates for Best Actor: three of them played murderous psychotics (Anthony Hopkins in *The Silence of the Lambs*, Robert De Niro in *Cape Fear*, and Warren Beatty in *Bugsy*); one of them played a homeless, delusional psychotic (Robin Williams in *The Fisher King*); and one of them played a good, old-fashioned manic-depressive neurotic (Nick Nolte in *The Prince of Tides*) who is the product of a viciously

dysfunctional family background. On the industry's "night of nights", this collection of decidedly downbeat antiheroes is played before the public as the representatives of the most noble and notable characterizations of which the acting craft is possible.[51]

And let it be remembered that the void and horror are realities that are often linked.

This focus on negativity is also found in many philosophical currents of the modern age – Marx's ideology of alienation, Nietzsche's nihilism, the horrors of Nazi racism, the despair of existentialism, the insecurity of postmodernism, and the emptiness of deconstructionism. R. Scruton's observations are incisive:

> We encounter here a peculiar modern phenomenon, which might be called the religion of alienation, the religion whose posture is defined by negation of 'the Other'. Turgenev gave an inkling of it in *Fathers and Sons*, as did Dostoevsky in *The Devils*, and Conrad in *Under Western Eyes*. But its manifestations are more varied than those writers discerned. The religion of alienation has been the motivating force behind much of modern art and politics, and is the spiritual bond which unites the romantic and the modernist against the bourgeois normality. It is the force that leads people so readily to accept what would otherwise appear preposterous: the Marxian theory of ideology, for example, Nietzsche's 'genealogy of morals', Foucault's heresy of domination, and the structuralist criticism of Barthes. Deconstruction inherits from these prophets a store of religious feeling already accumulated in the name of its deity. Like its predecessors, the new religion sanctifies the rejection of the existing order, and at the same time forms a congregation of rebels, armed for the assault, and ready to possess the citadels of power. It also promises the supreme benediction, which is the revelation of the god himself. So who or what is this god? The god of deconstruction is not a 'real presence', in the Christian sense, but an absence: a negativity.[52]

For this, and other reasons, one can well understand the background to an observation of John Paul II of great relevance to this and other chapters:

> One thing however is certain: the currents of thought which claim to be postmodern merit appropriate attention. According to some of them, the time of certainties is irrevocably past, and the human being must now learn to live in a horizon of total absence of meaning,

where everything is provisional and ephemeral. In their destructive critique of every certitude, several authors have failed to make crucial distinctions and have called into question the certitudes of faith.[53]

It is, indeed, to the long-term withdrawal of Christian culture that we now turn our attention.

Chapter Six

DeChristianisation

From his Nazi prison in the early 1940s the German Christian thinker
Dietrich Bonhoeffer uttered the following cry of intellectual pain:

> The movement that began about the thirteenth century (I am not
> going to get involved in any argument about the exact date) towards
> the autonomy of man (in which I should include the discovery of the
> laws by which the world lives and deals with itself in science, social
> and political matters, art, ethics, and religion) has in our time reached
> an undoubted completion. Man has learnt to deal with himself in all
> questions of importance without recourse to the 'working hypothesis'
> called 'God'. In questions of science, art, and ethics this has become
> an understood thing at which one now hardly dares to tilt. But for the
> last hundred years or so it has also become increasingly true of
> religious questions; it is becoming evident that everything gets along
> without 'God' – and, in fact, just as well as before. As in the scientific
> field, so in human affairs generally, 'God' is being pushed more and
> more out of life, losing more and more ground.[1]

Bonhoeffer was right: the withdrawal of Christian culture has been one
of the most conspicuous features of Western society during the modern
era. As John Paul II observed:

> Whole countries and nations where religion and the Christian life
> were formerly flourishing, and capable of fostering a viable and
> working community of faith, are now put to a hard test, and in some
> cases, are even undergoing a transformation, as a result of a constant
> spreading of an indifference to religion, of secularism and atheism.

This particularly concerns countries and nations of the so-called First World, in which economic well-being and consumerism, even if coexistent with a tragic situation of poverty and misery, inspires and sustains a life lived "as if God did not exist".[2]

In Great Britain – during the nineteenth century perhaps one of the most religious countries in Europe – this development has been especially marked. Over the same period this process of deChristianisation appears to have been intimately bound up with the rise of the materialist matrix and the advance of desocialisation. The decline of ideas which work powerfully in favour of true community seems to have been paralleled by the affirmation of beliefs which work in the opposite direction. The chronology is suggestive and indicates a causal connection.

However, religiosity in individuals, as in societies, is hard to monitor. It is difficult to probe the presence of religious beliefs, the intensity with which they are held, the way in which they are put into practice, or the impact that they have on the lives of individuals or cultures. For example, a man may well go to church every morning, but does this mean that he is really religious? The opposite is equally the case – do believers necessarily go to church? At a more general level, do proclaimed principles conform to real commitment? We are dealing here with areas which are difficult to analyse not least because we are probing the realm of the inner man and intimate relationships. Moreover, if the task is difficult in relation to the present, it becomes even more so when applied to the past. But despite these caveats, all the indicators we have available suggest that British society has been heavily deChristianised over the last hundred years. When we survey such factors as levels of church attendance, people's connections with organised Christianity, the importance of religion in politics, and a whole range of contemporary comment, we encounter the most tangible expressions of perhaps the greatest social transformation of our times. The deChristianisation of British culture is no peripheral subject.

1800-1914

During the first part of the nineteenth century Great Britain had the greatest plurality of denominations in the whole of Europe. In historical terms, religious liberty was bound up with political liberty, and the Protestant inheritance was expressed in a broad range of different denominations. In England and Wales the established Church of England was flanked by a large number of Nonconformist Churches. Scotland had its own special traditions, its own Church of State, and its own dissenting denominations. The Catholic Church, after centuries of Protestant ascendancy, was very much a minority force, although its small numbers on the mainland were bolstered by immigration from Catholic Ireland. How many people were actually regular churchgoers? The question is very difficult to answer. In 1851 a special religious census set out to provide an answer to this question. A great deal of debate exists over its findings and conclusions but some general interpretations seem to be possible. On 30 March of that year an official census indicated that perhaps about a half of the population of England and Wales of ten years and over went to a church service on that day. It seems that Nonconformists and Anglicans divided roughly equally, with Catholics making up perhaps about 4% of this category.[3] One historian of late-Victorian and Edwardian Britain suggests that regular affiliation was significantly lower.[4] But whatever the case, church attendance and membership constituted a very major feature of Victorian life. Moreover, significant decline does not seem to have set in before the Great War. In 1910, as a proportion of the adult population, the combined membership of the 'established churches of England and Scotland and of the Protestant Nonconformist churches was still 3 per cent higher than it had been in 1860'.[5]

As might be expected given these figures, the Victorian clergy had a high public profile. 'Clergymen were called upon to add religious seriousness to every sort of public occasion', we are told, 'from prize-givings and cattle shows to ratepayers' meetings and political protests'.[6] Indeed, in the 1880s Britain had more clerics of various kinds than any other country in Europe except Italy and Spain.[7] Substantial religious commitment and involvement were expressed in Victorian society in a whole host of ways. The Churches and the myriad of organisations to which they gave rise were active in a wide range of areas, ranging from the missionary to the charitable, and from the recreational to the educational. Religious-inspired public activity reached far and wide and left a very deep capillary impress on the life of our Victorian forefathers. The wide-ranging activism of church and chapel is brought out in microcosm by the observations made in 1859 by John Angell James, the dynamic head of Carr's Lane Chapel:

> We have now an organisation for the London Missionary Society...
> the Colonial Missionary Society...our Sunday and day schools...We

support two town missionaries...Our ladies conduct a working society for orphan mission schools in the East Indies...They sustain also a Dorcas Society for the poor of the town; a Maternal Society, for visiting the sick poor. We have a religious Tract Society, which employs nearly ninety distributors...Our Village Preachers' Society, which employs twelve or fourteen lay agents...We have a Young Men's Brotherly Society, for general and religious improvement, with a library of two thousand volumes. We also have night schools for young men and women...and Bible classes...In addition to this, there are in all our congregations, many and liberal subscribers to our public societies, such as the Bible Society, the Society for the Conversion of the Jews, and all other objects of Christian zeal and benevolence.[8]

Educational activity was referred to by this Birmingham activist and this was a sphere where organised religion was very active throughout the whole of the century. This role of the Churches deserves special attention, not least because it played a crucial part in the support and inculcation of Christian belief. The religious revival of the late-eighteenth century and early nineteenth century gave an especial impetus to activity by the Churches in the sphere of popular instruction. The British and Foreign School Society (1808, Nonconformist) and the National Society for Promoting the Education of the Poor (1811, Church of England) were the backbone of the voluntary school movement (made up of schools that were founded and financed by private initiative). They sought to provide cheap education for the masses and achieved very rapid growth. By 1851 they had over 18,500 schools and nearly 1.4 million pupils between them; by 1860 they taught perhaps a half of all children at school in England and Wales.[9] Central to their activity was a strong commitment to specifically religious instruction. 'Their activity and role', observes F.M.L. Thompson:

> were founded in religious convictions and belief in the necessity of providing a godly and religious upbringing for the children of the working classes. Religious instruction was central to the voluntary schools, doctrinal and catechismal in the National schools; more neutral scriptural teaching in the British schools; and the school day was likely to have a religious rhythm of prayers and hymns.[10]

The increasing role of the state in education after 1870 was a challenge to the voluntary school movement. But nonetheless this latter force retained significant influence for many decades to come. Sunday school enrolments in England and Wales paint a similar picture of church activism in education: 12% of the population under 15 in 1818; 38% in 1851; and 53% in 1901.[11]

Victorian religious commitment was also expressed in a marked adherence to the Sabbath day. The Sunday Observance Act of 1677 remained on the statute book and theatres and places of entertainment which charged entrance had been closed on Sundays since 1781. The Lord's Day Observance Society belonged to that section of national opinion which pressed for even greater severity. In 1850 there was a reduction of Sunday postal services and certain commercial activities and in 1856 the playing of military bands in parks was curbed. A year earlier there had been popular disturbances against legislative proposals to close London's pubs and shops on Sundays.[12] The dullness of the Victorian Sunday was a noted source of especial boredom for the Queen herself and visitors from the Continent were often much struck by the British adherence to the day of rest. J.C. Fischer left this memorable account of a London Sunday in 1851:

> Today is a Sunday and I...walked down Cheapside which is quite a long street. I would have liked to have gone into a coffeehouse for a glass of ale or claret but all the shops were hermetically sealed... Even the front door of my own hotel was locked and only if one knew the secret could one turn the right knob and effect an entry... On returning to my hotel I asked for my bill as I have been accustomed to settle my account every day. But the innkeeper politely asked me to wait until Monday...I got into an argument with a young lady who strongly criticised Parliament for allowing trains, omnibuses and cabs to run on Sundays. She explained that her own pious family always observed the Sabbath strictly.[13]

Religion also played an important role in political life. For example, the Palace of Westminster opened its days with prayers and religion played a prominent part in ceremonies of state, whilst such leading statesmen as William Gladstone (1809-1898) and Lord Salisbury (1830-1903) were deeply committed to the Christian world-view. More generally, religious issues could generate great friction and controversy. The emancipation of Catholics in the late 1820s was a major issue (Jews were only allowed into the House of Commons in the 1850s), as was the question of the disestablishment of the Irish Church (finally achieved in 1869). The debates over the divorce bill of 1857 provoked major debate in parliament and during the 1880s there were sustained attempts to prevent an atheist from taking his seat in the House of Commons. From 1870 to 1914 the educational question was bedevilled by denominational friction. Anti-Catholicism continued to be a keenly-felt sentiment, sometimes giving rise to rioting, most notably in Lancashire. Furthermore, denominational ties were bound up with party ties. With the advance of the Victorian age there was an increasing tendency for the dissenting vote to be identified with Liberalism and for the Anglican vote to be attached to Conservatism. When it came to political controversy and affiliation, religious identity and feeling counted.

This importance of religion in the society of our nineteenth-century forbears often emerges from the autobiographies which describe the Victorian and Edwardian period. We are often given illuminating entrées into a world which has certainly passed, perhaps never to return. Jack Lawson (1881-1965), who was later to become a Labour MP, reminisced on his mining district at the end of the nineteenth century. He was particularly keen to stress the role of Christianity as a source of social communion and solidarity:

The chapel was their first social centre. Here it was they drew together, found strength in their weakness, and expressed to each other their hidden thoughts and needs. The chapel gave them their first music, their first literature and philosophy to meet the harsh life and cruel impact of the crude materialistic age. Here men first found the language and art to express antagonism to grim conditions and injustice.

Their hymns and sermons may have been of another world, but the first fighters and speakers for unions, Co-op. Societies, political freedom, and improved conditions, were Methodist preachers. That is beyond argument...

There was a spirit of *camaraderie* among the young people I have never seen equalled. Every house was an "open" house. There were spontaneous suppers, when a lot of us drifted in by chance. We were not "invited"; we invited ourselves. We talked pit-work, ideals, the Bible, literature, or union business.[14]

Other autobiographies give us glimpses into the presence of an adherence to Christian culture within Victorian and Edwardian society which was not expressed in church attendance. Indeed, there was often a gap between the two. How widespread this was it is difficult to determine but it is probable that this was a major area of the religious experience which by its very nature escaped the net of statistical investigation. This non-institutional Christianity may have operated in particular at a popular level where there was a frequent hostility to clerical structures because of their identification with the class structure. We find this element mentioned in R. Roberts' memoirs of Salford life. He recalled of the Edwardian period:

> In the decade before 1914, whilst organized religion still kept a hold on some from the upper working class (the undermass had defected generations before) a drift towards secularism was already well on the way, though backsliders salved their conscience by strict insistence on their children's attending Sunday school. Very few people would, in fact, admit to not being Christians: one merely 'disliked' the church, the parson or the congregation. In pub and workshop outright atheists were looked upon as tempters of Providence, very odd fish indeed. The *Freethinker* was banned from the public library.[15]

Flora Thompson (1876-1947), in her memoir on late-Victorian and Edwardian life in a rural village, communicates a very similar message. She recalled that few of the villagers 'went to church between the baptisms of their offspring'[16] but that Christian precepts and vocabulary played an important part in their moral code. They regarded Catholicism as a form of heathenism and 'what excuse could there be for that in a Christian country?'[17]

1914-2008

Against such a background the twentieth century appears as a period of retreat and withdrawal. Again it is difficult to give a precise idea of church attendance or the actual presence of religious belief but certain facts are very suggestive. Such an eventuality, indeed, had been sensed at the end of the nineteenth century, a period when some currents of thought – most notably Darwinism – seemed to many to pose a real threat to the Christian tradition. Matthew Arnold (1822-1888) was moved to declare in 1882: 'whereas the basis of things amidst all chance and change has in Europe generally been for ever so long supernatural Christianity, and far more so in England than in Europe generally, this basis is certainly going'.[18] The years 1914-1945 seem a period of marked decline for organised religion and perhaps the trauma of the Great War was one factor behind this loss of faith. The statistics tell their own story. In 1920 perhaps about 23% of the adult population were active members of the Protestant Churches of Great Britain; a figure which had dropped to roughly 18% by 1945.[19] In the major provincial town of York regular church attendance fell from 35.5% in 1901 to 17.7% in 1935, and to 13% in 1948.[20] The number of civil marriages in England and Wales rose from 16% in 1901 to 31% in 1952.[21] Sunday school enrolments in the same home countries fell from 51% of the population aged under 15 in 1911, to 46% in 1931, and to 20% in 1961.[22] 'Some time during the 1920s', we are told of organised religion in industrial Yorkshire, 'the local religious classes lost heart. They ceased to believe in their mission to evangelise the nation...It no longer seemed possible. And it had become a burden'.[23] During these decades religious sentiment also lost much of its power to generate political controversy and to act as a determinant of party allegiance. Equally, the Churches lost much of their capillary presence within the many spheres of public activity. At a variety of official levels Christianity still seemed well established but, as an official Church of England report acknowledged at the end of the war, realities belied appearances:

> The ceremony of the Coronation, the regular openings of the sittings of Parliament with prayer, the Mayor's Chaplain, the provision for religion in the services and in all State institutions, the religious articles in popular periodicals, the Religious Department of the British Broadcasting Corporation, and many similar phenomena, go to show that the ethos of the State remains Christian...the Established Church is 'still entwined by countless subtle threads around the life of the realm and the nation'...But behind the facade the situation presents a more ominous appearance.[24]

The decline seems to have accelerated after 1960. The statistics are unequivocal. By 1974 only 53.5% of marriages in England and Wales were performed in a place of worship, a figure that had declined to 45.1% by 1995;[25] and by 1989 'only 14 per cent of the under-15s attended church or Sunday school'.[26] What about religious observance? It is estimated that in England in 1967 only about 15% of the population attended a religious service on a Sunday and only 25% went to church at least once a month.[27] By 1975 only 11.3% of the adult English population were committed churchgoers and by 1989 only 9.5%.[28] Recent decades have seen an especial collapse. Trinitarian Churches fell in active membership from 9.1 million adults in 1970 to 6.4 million in 1995.[29] In England in 1979 5.4 million people attended church on a Sunday; by 2005 that figure was down to 3.2 million, and the largest percentage decrease was amongst the young.[30] A Church of England account of the 1989 census on church attendance concluded its analysis in the following melancholy fashion:

'Christian' England? With only two-thirds of the population claiming some allegiance to the church, however faint, 14% active members, and 10% regularly attending, the claim to call England Christian looks thin. The UK community figure is much lower than the figures of other Western European countries.[31]

However one interprets such figures it seems reasonable to suppose that they indicate a fading of Christian religiosity. They correlate with the fact that there is now a broad area of non-belief within British society. Surveys carried out in 1991 revealed that a third of those interviewed never prayed and 40% of the respondents declared that religion made no difference to their lives. In the same year only 7% of those interviewed declared that they were 'extremely' or 'very' religious.[32] In 2001 41% of the respondents in a similar survey indicated that they did not belong to any religion;[33] in 2006 this figure was 46%.[34] At a more specific level, whereas in the 1960s 10% of those interviewed declared that they did not believe in God and 22% declared that they did not believe that Christ is the Son of God, in the 1980s 39% declared that they did not believe that Christ is the Son of God and in the 1990s 27% stated that they did not believe in God.[35] This weakening of Christian faith is further confirmed by the fact that denominational loyalties now play little part in party loyalties and that religious issues are largely absent from political debate. This rule, in indicative fashion, is broken by the case of Northern Ireland – a region where Christian commitment remains strong.[36]

One telling manifestation of the decline of Christianity may be found in the commonly held view that religion is, and should be, in some respect a 'private' matter. This development appears to have had two inputs. On the one hand there is the secularist drive, which goes far beyond traditional anti-clericalism, to expunge public life of religious contents and influence. The priorities here range from the non-expression of religious thinking by politicians in the framing of policy and law to the non-participation of confessions in public debate on major issues of the day, and from the removal of chaplains from hospitals to the banning of the wearing of religious symbols. On the other there is the natural response of believers to retreat into a private world in the face of a culture increasingly unsympathetic or hostile to their beliefs. Bonhoeffer detected this dynamic very early on: 'The displacement of God from the world, and from the public part of human life', he wrote in the 1940s, 'led to the attempt to keep his place secure at least in the sphere of the 'personal', the 'inner' and the 'private".[37] The privatisation of Christianity has constituted an instructive sign of its loss of pre-eminence.

This loss has been reflected in another phenomenon of recent decades – the rise of religious substitutes. In the 1980s Peter Clarke of the Centre for the Study of New Religious Movements at the University of Cambridge registered the presence of 450 new religions.[38] Institutions and practices have sprung up which cater to the religious impulse within humans. It seems that the traditional faiths and confessions have entered into crisis in the minds of men and other forces have leapt into the consequent vacuum. A broad range of elements are now evident which purport to offer spiritual cures, or to provide links with the supernatural, or to secure ways of achieving external beneficial intervention. This tendency in human nature was well recognised millennia ago by the ancient Israelites with their prohibitions on recourse to 'a soothsayer, or an augur, or a sorcerer, or a charmer, or a medium, or a wizard, or a necromancer' (Dt 18:10-11). The emergence of weird and often highly dangerous sects, the superficial embrace of Eastern religions, dabbling in the Occult, adherence to the New Age movement, the consultation of wizards and witches, fascination with UFOs, interest in the paranormal (as witness a host of television programmes), astrology, extreme ecologism and psychoanalysis – all these elements belong to a broad spectrum of phenomena whose true breadth and size is still to be analysed but whose significance is not to be underestimated. Such elements attest to a need to satisfy religious needs which are no longer catered to and their increasing prominence in the second half of the twentieth century, a fact full of chronological significance, appears to be intimately linked to the decline of organised religion.

There are no empirical grounds for supposing that the future offers improved prospects for Christianity in Great Britain. Indeed, there are many reasons to suppose that this historic withdrawal may turn into a near disappearance. For those still committed to our ancient religion the outlook appears bleak. The forces working for its annulment seem to become ever more powerful, and there is always a point in all processes at which resistance collapses almost completely. 'We are moving towards a completely religionless time'[39] predicted Bonhoeffer in the 1940s. A YouGov poll commissioned by the Orthodox Jewish organisation Aish reported in 2008 that more than a half of Britons thought that Christianity was likely to have disappeared from the country within a century.[40] Perhaps we now have before us the prospect of a future where Christianity has become largely a matter of the past – a dramatic development which has often been sensed by artists of the modern age. At the beginning of the nineteenth century William Blake observed the trends of his time, sensed the way things were going, and wept for the future:

Are those who contemn Religion and seek to annihilate it
Become... the causes and promoters
Of these religions?...
This Natural Religion, this impossible absurdity?
...O where shall I hide my face?
These tears fall for the little ones, the children of Jerusalem,
Lest they be annihilated in thy annihilation.[41]

At the beginning of the twentieth century the Catholic writer and ecclesiastic R. H. Benson (1871-1914) wrote a novel, *Lord of the World* (1907), in which he looked forward some hundred years to the future state of England. Benson envisaged a European government and then a world government involved in a systematic and highly successful attempt to extirpate Christianity and eliminate the Catholic Church, in particular through the imposition of a new ideology which recognised neither the supernatural nor the soul in man. 'Humanitarianism' in this future society, in the words of one of his characters, was 'an actual religion itself, though anti-supernatural. It is Pantheism; it is developing a ritual under Freemasonry; it has a creed, 'God is man', and the rest. It has therefore a real food of a sort to offer to religious cravings; it idealises, and yet it makes no demand on our spiritual faculties'.[42] In Benson's eschatological dystopia (in which state-sponsored euthanasia figures prominently) only the coming of the Apocalypse interrupts this systematic and highly successful campaign to eliminate Christian faith and its primary organised expression.

And more recently the English poet Philip Larkin (1922-1985) penned the following lines after a visit to an English church:

Yet stop I did: in fact I often do,
And always end much at a loss like this,
Wondering what to look for; wondering, too,
When churches fall completely out of use
What we shall turn them into...?
Power of some sort or other will go on

In games, in riddles, seemingly at random;
But superstition, like belief must die,
And what remains when disbelief has gone?[43]

DeChristianisation has been especially felt by those who remain sincerely committed to Christian belief and culture, and their laments constitute powerful testimony. Those who adhere to the axioms of the Christian world-view and the tenets of its teachings now find themselves often in friction with their human environment. Contemporary materialist culture is frequently at odds with what they are and do. It often happens that their views on the cosmos and man are contested: their notions about the nature and purpose of life are disputed; their morals and ethics are challenged; and their conduct and behaviour encounter disagreement. They often find that they do not belong and that they are on the receiving end of hostile forces. When faced with much that is contrary to what they believe and hold dear, the members of this category at times find themselves in a state of siege. These remnants of a previously entrenched tradition find that there is strong pressure to surrender their positions, to engage in compromise, or to move over to the enemy camp. Furthermore, their forces are not so much concentrated within a united group as dispersed far and wide, and this, in part, is a direct result of the fracturing and isolating impact of the forces they are up against. All in all, commitment to Christianity seems now no easy option and one of the great features of deChristianisation is the current cultural marginalisation of Christians. In this sense, the lament of K. Ward, an Anglican clergyman and eminent Oxford academic, is both characteristic and incisive:

Britain is, in a real sense, a secular society, and any religious beliefs and feelings there are must be fairly well hidden...The scientific world-view seems to exclude purpose from the universe, and thus to deprive traditional values of their basis. It privatises religion and morality, and relegates them to the inner world of personal preference, thus depriving them of authority and absoluteness...the methods of rational criticism seem to have destroyed, not only the arguments for God or for absolute values, but also for any positive views at all, even a faith in reason as ultimately trustworthy. When it is probed more deeply, even the scientific world-view crumbles, exposed as just one more ideology among others; and this leads to a virtually complete nihilism about beliefs. So the decline of Christianity in Britain seems to be part of a wider decline of belief in any values or ideals at all. And this is allied with a general loss of social confidence, the collapse of a coherent and common basis of national life.[44]

*

Surveying the last two hundred years and the facts and statistics to which they have given rise, it seems clear, therefore, that there has been a marked decline in Christian thought and practice in Great Britain. Indeed, from being one of the most religious countries in Europe, Great Britain appears to have become one of the least, an interpretation supported by a recent survey on belief in God in the EU.[45] It seems likely that the interconnected system of beliefs and forms of behaviour which are at the heart of Christianity have been subjected to large-scale erosion and that the Christian vision of the world has become a minority force within British culture. If this is correct, one can readily discern a marked historical failure behind the rise of the materialist matrix and the forms of behaviour it generates. Paul Johnson has observed:

> Our civilisation is unique in that it is the first to exist on a secular underpinning. All previous cultures have revolved around a series of propositions about life and death, the real and the invisible world, magic and spirits; all have had gods or God – that is, an external arbiter. We alone now attempt to carry on our civilisation on the assumption that it is finite and autonomous, and that we are entirely dependent on our resources – an audacious venture. Is it a feasible one? The attempt dates back less than a hundred years.[46]

Even the enemies of Christianity have often conceded that it can act as a powerful social glue. Might not its decline be one of the reasons why we have become unstuck? There is another modern development which appears to have played a major role in the advance of the materialist matrix – the rise of mass society.

Chapter Seven

The Dots of Mass Society

In the film script for *The Third Man* Graham Greene (1904-1991) had Orson Welles (1915-1985) declaim from the Great Wheel in Vienna:

> Look down there. Would you really feel any pity if one of those dots stopped moving for ever? If I said you can have twenty thousand pounds for every dot that stops, would you really, old man, tell me to keep my money – or would you calculate how many dots you could afford to spend? Free of income tax, old man. Free of income tax.[1]

The observation was well made. Distance from people and their reduction to the status of objects promotes indifference. Anonymity can engender disinterest; removal, a lack of concern. Such an attitude is often the antechamber to inhumanity: 'If you want to understand the way the Führer's mind works', observed one of Hitler's inner circle, 'you must look upon the human race as being just a swarm of ants'.[2] In the industrialised world the last two centuries have witnessed the construction of a context which has a natural propensity to such impersonality and to the objectification of our fellow men. The great feature of mass society is to be surrounded by strangers. Not surprisingly, the modern age has been marked by warnings about desocialisation but it has also been permeated by alarm at the dehumanising consequences of mass society. 'The crowd is untruth' proclaimed S. Kierkegaard (1813-1855) over a hundred years ago.[3] Such worry increased after the intensification of the phenomenon towards the end of the nineteenth century. Thus Gustave Le Bon (1842-1931) published *The Psychology of Crowds* in 1895; Freud produced

Group Psychology and the Analysis of the Ego in 1920; and in 1930 José Ortega y Gasset (1883-1955) issued his *Revolt of the Masses*. Concern with the impact of mass society has since proved a recurrent theme of Western preoccupation. In Great Britain itself T.S. Eliot evoked the chilling anonymity of the mass experience in his aptly titled poem 'The Waste Land' (1922):

Unreal City,
Under the brown fog of a winter dawn,
A crowd flowed over London Bridge, so many,
I had not thought death had undone so many.
Sighs, short and frequent were exhaled,
And each man fixed his eyes upon his feet.[4]

Charlie Chaplin (1889-1977) produced his own cinematic warning of the way things were going in *Modern Times* (1936), and both Aldous Huxley (1894-1963) and George Orwell wrote novels about nightmare totalitarian regimes ruling over manipulated mass societies.

So far this volume has discussed the crisis of British society with reference to the impact of what have been designated the false anthropologies of post-modernity, the ravages of relativism, and the withdrawal of Christian culture. Now it is necessary to turn to another key dimension of our contemporary story, although in truth mass society and the materialist matrix should be considered in harness. What involves the mass is not necessarily bad. Like the age of the En-lightenment, mass society has some positive features – the world of consumption, of democracy, of transport and of entertainment, for example, offer a great deal. But mass society also has a natural impulse towards the depersonalised and the impersonal. It generates a context which is in tension with man's biological need for accessible and familiar social contexts – that famous 'need to belong' which figures so prominently in modern discussion. Indeed, it joins with the materialist matrix in promoting the objectification of our fellow-men, and in this it also engenders conditions which favour the embrace of that matrix and the perspectives and lifestyle it encourages. But at the same time the materialist matrix has itself promoted and shaped mass society and worked through many of its features. It is not surprising that at times they both lie behind the same specific phenomena. In truth, the two cannot be discussed separately. They have interacted and worked together to promote our cultural breakdown, continue to reinforce each other, and seem well set to carry on in their destructive ways. We are now faced with an anonymous mass context drained by the materialist matrix of much of its traditional cultural content and of those inputs which act to unite people in authentic society. This chapter analyses the contours of mass society; the next investigates its symbiotic relationship with the false anthropologies of post-modernity. Firstly, however, some considerations on the biological nature of man. Polar bears might like the solitary life; human beings have rather different inclinations.

The Human Scale

Without entering the troubled debate about the origins of the universe, life and man, it seems likely that humans by their biological natures were made for small-scale, tightly-knit communities. The studies of man in the less technological stages of his existence – those which represent the greatest part of his permanence on earth – indicate a creature created for life in narrow and well-known social contexts. His emotions and impulses, his instincts and needs, his reflexes and reactions, and his talents and capacities, seem closely tied to a way of life based not upon mass contexts but upon personal society. Perhaps in an enterprise which can never really succeed because of the immense empirical obstacles in its path, recent decades have witnessed a series of attempts to understand human nature through exploration of our primordial origins. To prove many a controversial point, primitive man has been constantly disinterred, metaphorically speaking as well, from his archaeological resting places.[5] Views and opinions differ in this debate – as they do about the origins of man – but there is general agreement on the intense sociability of *homo sapiens* and the strong tie which exists between his biological nature and the propensity (and need) to live in a familiar and accessible setting of face-to-face relationships. Man's great characteristic of being a cultural animal (and his capacity for language) seem strongly bound up with this reality. Thus the anthropologist M. Harris tells us that:

Most primates spend their lives as members of groups...and these groups cooperate in finding food and in defending themselves against predators. Group life is facilitated among primates by relatively complex communications systems consisting of signals which indicate the presence of food, danger, sexual interest, and other vital matters. Primates need social companionship not only to survive physically but to mature emotionally. Many studies have shown that monkeys brought up in isolation display severe neurotic symptoms such as excessive timidity or aggressiveness...The unique features of human languages...arise from genetic adaptations related to the increasing dependence of the earliest hominids on social cooperation and on culturally acquired modes of subsistence...We share the following traits with other primates: intense social life... The most distinctive feature of the hominids – at least of *homo sapiens* – is the capacity for language and culture...This dependence on culture is closely related to the distinctive human capacity for language, and both of these are related in turn to the manual dexterity achieved through bipedalism, the substitution of tools for jaws and teeth, and long-term and intense social cooperation based on male-female sexual bonds...There is nothing in the fossil record to indicate that it is human nature to be a 'killer ape'. Rather, it is human nature to be the animal that is most dependent on social traditions for its survival and well-being.[6]

This intense sociability of man is borne out by what happens when it is systematically frustrated. Down the ages those engaged in the business of human torture have been only too aware of the traumatising effects on individuals to be achieved by enforced isolation. To deprive a person of human companionship for long periods of time constitutes a severe attack on the individual which strikes at the very heart of what he is as a living being. Those who have wielded the weapon of solitary confinement well knew what they were about. The psychologists Berelson and Steiner write that 'total isolation is virtually always an intolerable situation for the human adult – even when physical needs are provided for'.[7] But it is not only such an extreme condition which throws light on what we are. At a far wider level we are constantly struck by how man needs close social ties for his development and well-being. The natural need for parental affection, for love with a member of the opposite sex, for authentic friendship, and for wider networks of belonging, would be denied by very few. 'Individuals are not able to function effectively without deep links to others', observes Etzioni, 'without deep, continuous, and meaningful bonds, individuals risk losing their humanity'.[8] The disturbance which is often caused by desocialisation bears witness to this reality – the loss of such bonds provokes unhappiness. We now have a cultural system on our hands which often imposes forms of solitary confinement or deprivation without any need for guards, cells or prison walls, and it is all the more insidious for that. Both spiritually and biologically we are made for community, and the frustration of this feature of humanity is fraught with dangers, as Isaiah Berlin (1909-1997) recognised only too well:

When men complain of loneliness, what they mean is that nobody understands what they are saying: to be understood is to share a common past, common feelings and language, common assumptions, possibility of intimate communication – in short, to share common forms of life. This is an essential human need: to deny it is a dangerous fallacy. To be cut off from one's familiar environment is to be condemned to wither.[9]

The Contours of Mass Society

At a detailed level what do we mean by the term 'mass society'? At the time of the industrial revolution many European thinkers picked up on its early stirrings and they often accurately predicted what its main features would be. In 1859 the English liberal rationalist John Stuart Mill (1806-1873) reflected upon the emergence of the phenomenon in Great Britain. He recognised the breaking down of differences and the move towards uniformity, and feared that this process would produce the smothering of constructive personal dissent. Mill's list of many of the key features of mass society was predictive indeed:

Europe...is decidedly advancing towards the Chinese ideal of making all people alike. M. de Tocqueville, in his last important work, remarks how much more the Frenchmen of the present day resemble one another than did those even of the last generation. The same may be said of Englishmen in a far greater degree...The circumstances which surround different classes and individuals, and shape their characters, are daily becoming more assimilated. Formerly, different ranks, different neighbourhoods, different trades and professions, lived in what might be called different worlds; at present to a great degree in the same. Comparatively speaking, they now read the same things, listen to the same things, see the same things, go to the same places, have their hopes and fears directed to the same objects, have the same rights and liberties, and the same means of asserting them. Great as are the differences of position which remain, they are nothing to those which have ceased. And the assimilation is proceeding. All the political changes of the age promote it, since they all tend to raise the low and to lower the high.

Every extension of education promotes it, because education brings people under common influences, and gives them access to the general stock of facts and sentiments. Improvement in the means of communication promotes it, by bringing the inhabitants of distant places into personal contact, and keeping up a rapid flow of changes of residence between one place and another. The increase of commerce and manufactures promotes it, by diffusing more widely the advantages of easy circumstances, and opening all objects of ambition, even the highest, to general competition, whereby the desire of rising becomes no longer the character of a particular class, but of all classes. A more powerful agency than all these, in bringing about a general similarity among mankind, is the complete establishment, in this and other free countries, of the ascendancy of public opinion in the State. As the various social eminences which enabled persons entrenched on them to disregard the opinion of the multitude gradually become levelled; as the very idea of resisting the will of the public, when it is positively known that they have a will, disappears more and more from the minds of practical politicians; there ceases to be any social support for nonconformity... The demand that all other people shall resemble ourselves grows by what it feeds on. If resistance waits till life is reduced nearly to one uniform type, all deviations from that type will come to be considered impious, immoral, even monstrous and contrary to nature.[10]

With the benefit of hindsight it is perhaps possible to offer a more detailed description. Certainly no discussion of modern times is complete without reference to the increasing super scale of society and the consequences at a human level of such elephantiasis. One of the great tendencies of the last two centuries has been to subject individuals to ever wider frames of reference and to push them towards uniformity and anonymity in their life experience. Stripped to essentials, the rise of mass society has involved the replacement of small communities, narrow horizons and local variability with a national social aggregation, distant lines of focus, greater sameness and less belonging. At a more specific level, it has been marked by a move towards a giant population, urban conurbations, standardised language, mass education, large economic units, a national market, mass recreation, the mass media, the big state, centralised government, mass politics, the erosion of class differences, the weakening of the profile of the family, greater exposure to international influences, the decline of manners, cultural homogenisation, and the loss of meaningful interaction and identity. Observing the travails of the way we live now, how many people would deny that big is ugly?

Population and Cities

The growth of a mass population has been a major force behind the creation of the mass environment. We are constantly surrounded by people we do not know and who have as much relationship to each other as the dots of Welles's speech – a point well captured by the wonderful paintings of L.S. Lowry (1887-1976). Demographic expansion has been one of the great features of the last two hundred years and has been a major generator of larger frames of reference. The figures are striking – in 1801 the United Kingdom counted 15.8 million souls; in 1871 31.6 million; in 1921 47.1 million; in 1961 52.7 million; and by 1998 there were more than 59 million inhabitants in the realm – all-in-all nearly a fourfold increase.[11] This process has involved a movement away from hamlets, villages and small towns towards a world of huge cities and sprawling urban conurbations. At the end of the eighteenth century William Wordsworth (1770-1850) referred to the 'increasing accumulation of men in cities'[12] and by 1871 about a third of the population lived in the ten largest cities of the United Kingdom.[13] The process continued apace thereafter[14] and the British are now a nation of urban dwellers (about 90% of the population of England and Wales in the early 1990s[15]) – giant London (with over seven million inhabitants[16]) being a fitting symbol of this transformation in modern lifestyles.

City-dwelling has become integral to the mass lifestyle. 'The industrial metropolis is the biggest artefact humankind has ever built', observes Theodore Roszak:

No other form of bigness – the bigness of modern nations, corporations, plants and factories, military-industrial complexes, bureaucratic institutions – would be conceivable without the city, and the city is taking over everywhere...Megalopolis presides over the gargantuan expansion of contemporary society in all its aspects. It is not merely the container of big things; it is our collective commitment to bigness as a way of life. It is the daily pressure of city life that turns people into masses, crowds, personnel...Of all the hypertrophic institutions our society has inflicted upon both the person and the planet, the industrial city is the most oppressive.[17]

Against such a background it is hardly surprising that complaint about the anonymity of urban life has become one of the recurrent themes of contemporary conversation: not knowing who one's neighbours are; the dangers of high crime rates and suspicion of strangers; the harshness of the 'rat race' and the inhumanity of the 'asphalt jungle'; the impersonality of the supermarket and the rootlessness of the modern shopping centre – these are just some of the more obvious features of a loud and widespread lament. R. Weatherill cites one typical account of what desocialised urban life can be like, a description which also touches upon the consequences of the decline of the family as an economic unit:

> I was in my home town walking down the main street looking in the shops...Nobody knows anybody here. We are all independently walking around and doing our business. Then I remembered how this street used to be with family businesses and names on the shopfronts that never changed, where people spoke to each other. I used to go round with my father and people would speak to him. You always went to certain shops: this was called loyalty...Each shop was different; some had their own particular smell. Always somebody spoke to you, spoke to me, knew my name...[18]

There is one feature of urban life which has made an especial contribution to this anonymity over the fast fifty years – massively impersonal forms of town planning and architecture combined with an attack on the traditions of the urban landscape. This is yet another example of our national failure over recent decades. Desocialised culture involves a natural propensity towards the 'de-aestheticisation' of experience and here we encounter a classic illustration of that tendency. Glass and concrete, tower blocks and council estates, suburban sprawl and commercial city centres, inner ring roads and demolished historic buildings – these are just some of the features of a modern urbanism which has betrayed fundamental human needs. It is also an area where state planners or economic interests have ridden roughshod over popular opinion, thinking that they know best or immersed in the pursuit of their own selfish ends. To see what has happened to the centre of Leeds, to pass down today's Victoria street, to contemplate the centre of Worcester, or to stand in front of Liverpool's tower blocks, is to walk into a world of imposed depersonalisation and to survey a standardised urban landscape where people have been reduced to objects, almost the ants of Hitler's demonic mind. In the same way the destruction of historic buildings and districts, and the refusal to build in harmony with inherited architectural patterns, has constituted a vital break with tradition and contributed to the impoverishment of personal identity. As the poet John Betjeman (1906-1984) was reported as saying in 1973: 'destroying the surroundings in which people live – and which they like, and are accustomed to – amounts to straightforward robbery'.[19] The urban environment, like the Creation, the roads, the sea, and our inherited institutions and shared conventions, belongs to us all. Why should we have to endure this feature of mass society which so conspicuously fails to respect our humanity?

Language and Education

Cultural homogenisation has expressed itself in a long-term drive towards uniform language. Mass society has worked in favour of a common national idiom. With the exception of Welsh, the historic Celtic languages had been largely swept aside by 1900, and at the beginning of the twenty-first century only a much reduced proportion of the Principality speaks its ancient tongue. The future belonged to standard English. As the novels of such writers as Thomas Hardy (1840-1928) and D.H. Lawrence (1885-1930) well illustrate, at the end of the nineteenth century a majority of the British population still spoke in heavy dialects. But such rich and identity-conferring linguistic forms were to decline greatly during the twentieth century – a development accompanied, especially in the decades which followed 1945, by a similar retreat of local, regional and class accents. A number of factors have lain behind this drive towards linguistic standardisation. The growth of the state and its vastly expanded role in society has acted as a major promoter of standard English – its natural idiom. The increased internal movement of the population and greater travelling, and the communications and advertising needs of an ever more national economy, have worked in the same direction. But perhaps the rise of the mass media – of newspapers, magazines, radio, television and cinema – has been the greatest force at work in encouraging people to speak the same kind of language. The television, in particular, has been a steamrollering linguistic leveller.

Mass education has been another major factor in this move towards uniform language and has itself constituted a principal feature of mass society. It has broken down many a local barrier and subjected students to similar kinds of cultural moulding. Prior to the reforms of the 1870s there were no state schools but this did not mean there was no schooling.

The voluntary school movement, which took off in the first part of the nineteenth century under the direction of the Churches, achieved a major impact and by the late 1860s a large proportion of the nation's children were receiving elementary education. From 1870 to 1918 a series of Acts extended state-funded compulsory elementary and secondary schooling. The process was continued during the inter-war period and further developed by the 1944 Education Act. Since that time mass education has continued to be an entrenched part of social life.[20] Higher instruction, on the other hand, was for long the preserve of the very few. Following the Robbins Report of 1962, however, there was a veritable boom in university and polytechnic education which lasted well into the 1970s, and a much larger proportion of the population was receiving a university education by the late 1990s.[21] Naturally enough, this development has increased the power and influence of the academic elite and the educated classes.

Economic Giantism

The rise of mass society has been characterised by the spread of elephantiasis in the economic sphere. The workplace, the size of firms, the financial sector, the retail trade, trade unions and business associations have all been marked by a move towards concentration and the grand scale. In the world of work and consumption individuals have found themselves immersed in ever larger units. William Blake greeted the industrial revolution with the famous phrase 'dark Satanic mills'[22] but in the employment of this image he was ahead of his times. During the Victorian and Edwardian period manufacturing industry – a key area of the economy – remained dominated by low-scale units of production. Small workshops in which employer and worker were linked by strong personal ties set the tone for the industrial environment. The family concern was conspicuous by its presence. 'In spite of the growth in the size of firms', we are told of the period 1870-1914:

> the gigantic industrial complexes envisaged by Marx in 1866 remained wholly untypical of British industry. Only six industrial firms employed more than 10,000 workers in the year 1900, and most of these were scattered among numerous small factories and workshops. Moreover, large firms grew in tandem with rather than at the expense of small workshops, many of the latter newly emerging in the last quarter of the nineteenth century to supply

accessories and unfinished goods to larger establishments. Coal companies often employed thousands of men, but within those companies the typical individual colliery employed about 300. Smallness of size was often accompanied by archaic and piecemeal methods of organization.[23]

All this was to change during the course of the twentieth century. The great trend was the move away from small family-run concerns to large professionally-managed companies. Giantism reared its impersonal head. The hundred largest manufacturing firms in Great Britain accounted for 21% of net manufacturing in 1948 but held 47% in their hands by 1976. Families were losing their commanding grip – the boards of the top hundred such companies owned less than 0.5% of shares in 1972.[24] In the same year 45% of manufacturing employees worked in concerns of 5,000 workers or over and some 60% worked in plants of 500 employees or more.[25] 'We have long seen the old family business, where the master was in direct personal touch with his workmen', observed Churchill in the middle of the century, 'swept out of existence or absorbed by powerful companies, which in their turn are swallowed up by mammoth trusts'.[26] The nationalised industries, which grew rapidly in number after 1945 and rose to occupy a major position on the industrial landscape before the Tory privatisation programmes of the 1980s, were another fertile field for giantism. Although now in private hands, they often remain vast concerns. Recent decades have also witnessed the growth of the multinational – a repudiation with a vengeance of the Victorian tradition of the small workshop.

But industry has not been the only sector to undergo a dramatic process of concentration. The world of finance has also become a land of giants. At the beginning of the nineteenth century a wide net of locally based country banks existed in England and Wales, numbering perhaps some 800 in 1810. The system of joint-stock banks took off in the middle of the century and by 1914 there were twenty such banks in these two home countries and only a handful of country banks.[27] By the late 1960s the descendants of such credit institutions had reduced their number to eleven and by 2008 they amounted to a handful. Such giant firms as Lloyds and Barclays now stand astride the banking scene like many an imposing colossus, exerting at times what looks very much like monopoly power. Insurance companies have followed a similar path. The history of the retail trade tells the same tale. In 1950 organisations with ten outlets or more (excluding the co-operatives) were responsible for 22% of Britain's retail trade – by 1971, for example, that proportion had risen to 39%.[28] The rise of the supermarket and the decline of the corner shop have been signs of these times – by 1987 five distribution chains alone accounted for 57% of all food sales in the United Kingdom.[29] This long-term move towards concentration throughout the economy has been accompanied by the rise of the managerial class and a concomitant decline in family direction. 3.4% of the occupied workforce of Great Britain were 'managers and administrators' in 1911; 5.5% in 1951; and 15.1% in 1991.[30]

Such concentration and growth of size in the economy has promoted impersonality in two principal contexts. Firstly, there is the world of the work environment. Within the firm greater gaps have opened up between employers and employees. The small-scale workshops and their family framework offered possibilities for face-to-face contact and the extension of familial culture to work relationships which became ever less viable with the emergence of the professionally-managed large company. The ties between work colleagues themselves have become weakened by the consequences of the increase in the size of the workforce. At the same time, the very vastness of the internal context has pushed towards anonymity, a tendency frequently supported by the impersonality of mass production methods, giant buildings, and modernist architecture. Secondly, there is the world of consumption. From fast food chains to giant banks, from supermarkets to media conglomerates, and from mighty insurance companies to industrial multinationals, the citizen as consumer is constantly face to face with entities from which he is distant in his personal life, over which he has almost no control, and with whose representatives he has a highly impersonal relationship. Indeed, he seems to be frequently on the receiving end of a depersonalising system: he is subject to mass advertising, with all its cynical manipulation, almost everywhere he goes; he is reduced to the level of a dot-like purchaser where the only nexus is that of buying and selling; and he has to face the fact that the political influence and cultural power of these large entities dwarfs his own beyond all measure. When Schumacher wrote his best-selling book *Small is Beautiful* in the early 1970s he was, in part, responding to exactly these kind of long-term developments in the world of manufacturing and business. The widespread popularity of his work attested to a diffuse anxiety about the implications, in human terms, of such developments:

Almost every day we hear of mergers and takeovers, Britain enters the European Economic Community to open up large markets to be served by even larger organisations...The great majority of economists and business efficiency experts support this trend towards vastness. In contrast, most of the sociologists and psychologists insistently warn us of its inherent dangers – dangers to the integrity of the individual when he feels he is nothing more than a small cog in a vast machine and when the human relationships of his daily working life become increasingly dehumanised; dangers also to efficiency and productivity, stemming from ever growing Parkinsonian bureaucracies.

It is clear, however, that there is now another trend underway which goes in the opposite direction to the giant place of work, without, however, offering any prospects for less impersonality: the move – greatly facilitated by the communications and information revolution – towards self-employment, outsourcing and downsizing. We are now faced with the prospect of a specific shift of people out of the factory or office and into the home or similar context as a place of work. 'The old "work ethic" that modern industrial societies sought to inculcate in their workers', observes David Lyon:

> assumed that work was a matter of spending time on a daily, routine, full-time and long-term basis, in paid productive activity usually in the company of the same group of people, in the same place. Would-be workers today are encouraged to forget just those habits and assumptions in the name of "flexibility"...Work at the start of the twenty-first century is characterized by its mutability in time and space...You are more likely to be working on your own.[32]

This trend is intimately bound up with many other configurations of desocialisation which it reinforces and supports, as the French economist Edmond Malinvaud has observed:

> A very significant and disturbing trend, in many regions and parts of societies, is decreasing social integration caused by the nature of employment. It is linked with other aspects of cultural, social, and technological change: the glue of social cohesion weakens, mutuality and trust are less widespread, and family links decline. In many cases relations at the workplace become more impersonal and new flexibilities in the management of firms are deemed to be required.[33]

It may be that we are moving towards a polarity of work situations: atomism on the one hand and giantism on the other.

It would be a mistake to assume that such giantism is an inevitable feature of advanced economies. In the contemporary age a great deal of what is comes to be deemed that which must be – existence is often convincing. But just as many of the components of mass society are interlinked and reinforcing, so size in the economy is itself connected to cultural factors. Italy, for example, a land of very different anthropological configurations, diverges very markedly from the British experience. In 1950 the Italian economy was very much weaker than that of the UK; today, and without North Sea oil, its GDP is not so distant from the British GDP.[34] Even more significantly, the GDP *pro capita* of both nations today is more or less the same.[35] At the heart of the dynamism of the contemporary Italian economy has been the vitality of what are usually family-owned and directed small- and medium-sized businesses, especially in the North. Strongly underpinned by local and regional loyalties, and by a family culture deeply rooted in the Catholic inheritance, this alternative model of development has been characterised by notable flexibility, adaptability and inventiveness. The family presence also seems to have played a marked role in humanising work relationships and in the transmission of managerial skills. 'Small firms form the backbone of the Italian economy', it was observed in the 1990s, '1 per cent of Italian firms have over 500 workers whereas 90 per cent have under 100 workers' and these firms 'are mostly run by families.[36] It is almost as if the British Victorian model, abandoned by its natural creators, has been developed and improved upon by Mediterranean heirs, and to their very great advantage. Of course this has only been possible because of the maintenance of the family as a living social unit.

The move towards the grand scale in the world of industry and business has been bound up with another great feature of mass society – the rise of a national economic market. During the nineteenth century the economy became increasingly national in character and there was a marked erosion of local and regional frameworks. This process was to advance in leaps and bounds during the twentieth century – the passing of provincial stock exchanges being one of its many symptoms. The greater mobility of the workforce and the opportunities for wider markets opened up by the transport and communications revolution were integral features of this process. One of the great aspects of this move towards the 'nationalisation' of the internal market (a development which prepared the ground in an important way for the recent doctrine of marketism) was the emergence of mass-produced products sold across the country in capillary fashion

– a reality very favourable to large-scale companies. The fact that we now have the national advertising of products on television and billboards well illustrates how these goods are available at a national level and form a part of a national market. Some local and regional variation undoubtedly remains but this is of nothing compared to the reality of a consumer's world all of its own which is marked by a homogenisation of possessions and a drive towards uniformity in tastes. If we take the case of food we encounter a striking example of such unification. What does McDonald's represent after all?

Yet concentration has not only been a phenomenon of the world of economic production, distribution and exchange. It has also been a feature of organised labour and business associations. Workers have had to undergo the impact of size in the field of representation as well. For most of the nineteenth century trade unionism was very much a minority experience in working-class life – in 1888 perhaps 5% of the national workforce belonged to a trade union.[37] These associations were largely small craft-based unions which were local and personal in tone and character. But from the 1890s onwards there was a sustained move towards unionisation and the creation of large national associations. By 1893 about 10% of the occupied civil workforce of Great Britain and Northern Ireland was unionised; by 1933, 23%; by 1946, 43%; and 54% by 1979 before stabilising at about 33% in 1995.[38] In this area, too, the trend was towards concentration – in 1918 there were about 1,241 trade unions in the United Kingdom; by 1945 only 963; and by 1997 just 75.[39] A parallel concentration in the representation of business interests has also taken place. Victorian local organisations were superseded by the National Association of British Manufacturers (created in 1915), the Federation of British Industries (1916), and the British Employers Federation (1919). In 1965 these bodies united to form the mighty Confederation of British Industry, the famous CBI.[40] Such developments, naturally enough, have had major implications for the workings of our national polity – no discussion of the recent history of modern politics would be complete without reference to the role of the CBI and the Trades Union Congress (TUC).

Recreation and the Mass Media

The process of 'assimilation' or uniformity detected by Mill has also manifested itself in the world of recreation. Towards the end of the

nineteenth century there was a major expansion in the mass
commercialisation of leisure. Football, cricket and rugby joined
horseracing and boxing in belonging to a panorama of mass recreation
which extended to seaside resort towns, music halls, pubs and (before
the Great War) cinema. Improved systems of transport and raised levels
of popular prosperity gave a major impetus to these moves towards
mass forms of recreation between 1850 and 1914. This period also
witnessed a boom in mass national newspapers and magazines, elements
which were joined by the spread of the paperback during the inter-war
years. Some changes have occurred since the Great War. The radio took
off in the 1920s and the cinema gained hugely from the invention of the
talkies in the 1930s. Both seaside towns and music halls were already in
serious decline before 1939. Newspapers and books have retained their
hold. In the 1950s music began its climb to dizzy heights, pushed
forward by the transistor radio, and since that time pop and rock music
have remained a dominant feature of youth culture.[41] In the same decade
another form of mass recreation arose which was to outshine all the rest
and constituted a major challenge for such rivals as radio and cinema
– the television. It was estimated that in Great Britain in 1995 people of
the age of 16 or over watched an average of 19 hours a week and those
of 60 or over watched 26 hours.[42] In recent years the habit of spending
hours in front of the television screen has been reinforced by the boom
in videocassettes and DVDs, a development which, like video games
and surfing the internet (nearly 60% of households in Great Britain
had an internet connection in 2006),[43] acts to further close people up
within the walls of their homes. Here we are light-years away from
how seventeenth-century peasants in their villages, or our primordial
ancestors at their fires, spent their free time.

The relationship between television and our spreading loss of ties
deserves special comment. In many respects the impact of this new
phenomenon symbolises what has happened to us, although the depths
of its deleterious influence have probably yet to be fully understood.
Certain key features stand out. The large-scale watching of television
precludes interaction with others. Traditional sources of amusement
based upon shared activity with other people – with all the socialising
mechanisms that they involved – have been severely compromised by
the passive watching of the video screen. The television confines
individuals even more to the home, a process reinforced by the cult of
privacy and by the advance of other such home-based forms of recreation

as 'do-it-yourself'. Interaction within the family and between friends has been sharply undermined by a practice which in itself works in favour of distance and isolation. When people lament the decline of conversation are they not in part referring to the impact of the desocialising box? In this area the watching of television also has major consequences for the development and growth of children.

Secondly, the television creates a 'virtual' pseudo-social world with which the individual interacts. He is not engaging in genuine social relationships, or experiencing feelings through authentic contact with others, but participating in a mock reality. This technological substitute for social life is pre-eminently desocialising in character. Furthermore, we are now faced with the frequent imposition of virtual reality onto actual reality. There is a growing tendency to see the real world in terms of the perspectives of the screen – people become objectified by being equated with the images of the television world. Humans come to be seen as they are seen on the screen. The TV virtualises that which is not virtual. Have we not been told that 'the world is your film'? Similar comments may be made about the increasing presence of the personal computer, and its system of outside communications, within the home. The individual's employment of such elements as internet with which to interact with the human environment has many of the same desocialising features of the TV, and if work becomes increasingly home-based through the utilisation of the domestic computer then this will be a further factor working for social isolation.

The television is a conspicuous part of a dominant feature of contemporary mass society – the mass media. Mill observed of the mid-Victorians: 'they now read the same things, listen to the same things, see the same things'. The TV, radio, and newspapers, pushed forward by forms of technological advance which Mill could never have foreseen, are now a major force in achieving such uniformity. The mass media are not only important focal points in the nation's shared recreational activity, they are also major elements in the dissemination of information and the reproduction of culture. They communicate knowledge about, and to, the whole of society, or to large parts of it, and thereby act to aggregate individuals together in a shared mass context. They reach out far and wide, breaking down all kinds of barriers, whether of region, age, class or religion, and sweep people up into large frames of reference where solid links between people are weak. It is true that the mass media often provide the idea of participation in community, but in fact they deal in descriptions and expressions of a mass society which lacks an authentic social anchorage. From this point of view, radio, television and the press are often the opium of desocialised man – providing the illusion of participation but not the reality; offering a virtual substitute for genuine belonging; and supplying the image but not the substance of membership of a community. Furthermore, the mass media are able to transmit and engender change with great speed, and thus bear much responsibility for that frenetic rhythm and lack of continuity which so marks contemporary lifestyles.

The Big State and Centralisation

The rise of mass society has been bound up with the emergence of the big state. Citizens now have to deal with a system of government which is on a mammoth scale and which is strongly stamped by centralisation. In this sphere, too, do we encounter size and remoteness, the large-scale and the anonymous. The vastness of government has created an impersonality symbolised and generated by bureaucracy, distant ministries, and far-off decision making.

At the beginning of the nineteenth century Great Britain was the land of low government and local government. All that was to change over the next two centuries. To cite just one indicator: in 1831 central and local government expenditure accounted for about 16% of UK GNP – by 1979 that figure was over 50%.[44] Public expenditure was 44% of GDP in 1979-1997; 43% during the years of Conservative government 1992-1997, and 38.9% in the years 1998-1999.[45]

Higher levels of state interference in the economy and in society have taken three main forms – public ownership; regulation and direction; and the providing of social services. Up to 1900 moves in these directions were rather limited, although the Victorians were by no means prisoners of a narrow *laissez faire*. Thereafter the Liberal reforms of 1906-1914 greatly developed government-funded welfare policy. In the inter-war period such steps forward were continued and there was far greater state interference in the economy, in particular through the rationalisation of certain sectors of heavy industry. The Labour governments of 1945-1951 greatly extended public ownership and created the welfare state, albeit on previously constructed foundations. Over subsequent decades government extended its role in these three principal directions and by the 1970s Great Britain was a highly governed society with a function performed by the state which would never have been dreamed of in the 1870s. A reaction set in during the 1980s, but even after the Thatcher experiment and its highly successful reduction of the province of public ownership, government still retained a very high profile – a fact represented in particular by the maintenance of a still vigorous welfare state.[46]

The story of state expansion contains within it another story of great importance – the rise of centralisation. Concentration within the economy has been matched by concentration within government. Today it is often forgotten that our nineteenth-century forefathers largely trusted to the localities for the government of our country. Here was an authentic Victorian value if ever there was one. Throughout the nineteenth century local authorities outstripped Whitehall in levels of domestic spending and central grants remained on a small scale. The power of local authorities to levy their own taxation – the famous 'rates' – was the key to this financial independence. Energised by high levels of civic identity, town councils were often a principal force for innovation and advance. Many on the Left wanted to build on these foundations to promote the collectivist state. Sidney Webb (1859-1947) was one of them:

> The individualist town councillor will walk along the municipal pavement, lit by municipal gas and cleansed by municipal brooms with municipal water and – seeing by the municipal clock – in the municipal market, that he is too early to meet his children coming from the municipal school, hard by the county lunatic asylum and the municipal hospital, will use the national telegraph system to tell them not to walk through the municipal park, but to come by the municipal tramway to meet him in the municipal reading-room, by the municipal museum, art-gallery and library, where he intends...to prepare his next speech in the municipal town hall in favour of the nationalization of the canals and the increase of Government control over the railway system. 'Socialism, Sir', he will say, 'don't waste the time of a practical man by your fantastic absurdities. Self-help, Sir, individual self-help, that's what has made our city what it is'.[47]

It was this localism of the Victorian polity which so attracted the admiration of those Continental liberals such as Alexis de Tocqueville who were hostile to the centralised and bureaucratic methods to be found throughout the major States of Europe. Victorians themselves tended to unite in praise of this feature of the British system of government. As an official report of 1871 declared:

LOCAL SELF-GOVERNMENT ESSENTIAL TO ENGLAND. The principle of local self-government has been generally recognized as of the essence of our national vigour. Local administration under central superintendence, is the distinguishing feature of our governments. The theory is, that all, that can, should be done by local authority, and that public expenditure should be chiefly controlled by those who contribute to it.[48]

Similar sentiments were expressed far and wide across the political spectrum. The common idea was that a localist state based upon effective local government created national cohesion and a well-anchored polity. Personal links between the governed and their governors were considered essential to such an outcome. Remoteness was what was especially feared. 'The life and spirit of free Institutions must depend wholly upon the consciousness of their reality', declared Toulmin Smith in 1851, 'That consciousness, can only spring from constant personal experience'. Local government in his opinion provided exactly that:

True patriotism finds in Local Self-Government its constant nurse... Local Self-Government does not serve to stir up class against class, and interest against interest...It draws all classes nearer in kindliness and in daily life to one another...It will not let the festering places of society lie hidden and unknown.[49]

In 1861 Mill declared that the British system of government was 'the least centralized in Europe'. In discussing the 'public education of the citizens' he argued that 'of this operation the local administrative institutions are the chief instrument'.[50]Accompanying fears about the consequences of centralisation were widespread. In 1848 David Urquhart MP expressed the common view that a shift towards the centre promoted social dissolution:

Centralisation dissolved the bonds of society...It was a usurpation by the Government of the powers of local bodies, and a destruction by the general Executive of local rights. The people of England loved and possessed municipal government...he would adduce as an instance the late Government of France, the fate of which should be a warning to the would-be-centralisers in this country...He resisted this Bill because it was un-English and unconstitutional – corrupt in its tendency – it was an avowal of a determination to destroy local self-government, and, if carried would be to pass a roller over England, destroying every vestige of local pre-eminence, and reducing all to one dull and level monotony.[51]

Notwithstanding such eloquent warnings, the last hundred years have witnessed a major assault on this tradition. He who pays the piper calls the tune. Increased levels of central grants-in-aid have been a major factor in increasing Whitehall (the location in London of government ministries and departments) control over local government. From the abortive 1914 budget to the Thatcher legislation of the 1980s and beyond, the great trend has been for local authorities to become ever more subject to central direction and supervision. Ministerial orders and edicts have been one marked feature of this process. At the same time central government has taken upon itself responsibility for areas which were previously in the hands of local government. For example, during the Victorian period poor relief was administered by self-financing and elected local boards of guardians. During the twentieth century the emergence of the welfare state involved central government shouldering the responsibilities for this important service. Furthermore, the increasing role of government in society and the economy, which grew apace after 1900, has acted to alter the internal balance of state responsibilities – in large measure it is Whitehall rather than town and county councils which has been entrusted with these new tasks. Bureaucracy has grown in vigour as a result of these developments, although it is certainly true that we have by no means yet reached the levels of our Continental counterparts.

The rise of the big state has had another result which is not often commented upon – emphasis upon the use of law, and upon certain forms of law in particular. This development has not been without its consequences for social ties. From the early decades of the nineteenth century parliament emanated increasing quantities of statute law and thereby subjected society to an ever more elaborate net of direction. Reflecting the orientations of the Victorian state, a great deal of local legislation (*ad hoc* measures for the needs of specific localities) also reached the statute book – an element which was to wane markedly during the next century. During the Edwardian period, however, there was a marked leap forward in bestowing subordinate legislative powers upon government departments and officials. This development of 'administrative law' was to prove one of the great features of modern legal evolution. These two key developments (the growth of statute law and administrative law) undermined the common law tradition – an inheritance rooted in custom and precedent which was highly expressive of the shared cultural heritage. Common law was an integral feature of the living organic community and its long-term erosion is an example of how desocialisation has also manifested itself in the legal sphere. The legitimacy of state institutions and the much commented upon popular respect for law meant that this process of ever greater legal regulation has met with little opposition. We now face a situation where in assessing courses of action individuals are naturally inclined towards considering what the state dictates through legislation. The orientation towards state regulation rather than self-regulation, and to statute and delegated legislation rather than shared custom and practice, has not only encouraged a shift away from personal moral reflection but also diminished the role of shared rules enshrined in general acceptance. These, too, have proved important factors working against community.

The historic movement within the state towards the administrative offices of Whitehall has been matched by a long-term shift in power towards those at the top of the ministerial tree – the prime minister and the Cabinet. From Waterloo to the third millennium the history of the British Constitution has been marked by a movement towards the placing of ever greater power in the hands of those who control the majority party in the House of Commons. The hybrid and varied polity characterised by a mixture of separate power points of the early nineteenth century has been replaced by a more uniform and vertical structure based on dominance by those at the head of the Executive. In the 1970s many commentators even began to assert that a new 'corporatist' system of government had emerged composed of the top of the Executive and such extra-parliamentary power centres (themselves marked by a process of concentration) as organised labour, big business, the City and the mass media – a development which would not have been possible without such concentration.[52] Clement Attlee (1883-1967) declared that the British were good at putting 'new wine into old bottles',[53] but in reality most centres of power within the constitutional settlement have been drained of much of their content. Although the modern British Constitution has been praised for its adaptive continuity, beneath the surface very profound changes have taken place in the structure of our national polity. Another layer of remoteness has been added to the experience of the ordinary citizen.

From 1798 to 2008 the Executive has had a field day and like a cuckoo in another bird's nest has greatly reduced the role of other power points within the constitutional system. During the last two hundred years the

Executive has greatly increased its mastery over the House of Commons. This has been achieved by a number of routes. Party loyalties and identity hardened during the nineteenth century and mass parties had emerged into the light of political day by the 1870s. Power tended to be concentrated at the apex of those institutions and they were characterised by strong systems of internal discipline – party leaders thereby gained ever greater ascendancy over what happened in the lower chamber. Minor parties, potential obstacles in this path, have habitually been discouraged by an adverse electoral system which has favoured the big groupings. Beginning with the reforms of the 1870s, governments of the day have been able to establish marked control over the procedure and business of the House of Commons. At the end of the eighteenth century the Crown still exercised significant influence in matters of state – it has since become marginal. The House of Lords – a real second chamber during the Victorian period which left a deep imprint on the nature of legislation – lost its effective veto in 1911 and has since been largely peripheral. The independence and importance of local government has been greatly reduced during the last hundred years, a development crowned by the massive levels of centralisation promoted during the years 1945-1997. At the same time no written Constitution existed which could prevent this long-term concentration of power in the hands of the Executive. With such developments it is hardly surprising that by the 1980s and 1990s many observers were detecting the presence of a 'prime ministerial' form of government – a kind of presidential system under a different guise.[54]

The Political World

The move towards a remote centralised big state marked by the concentration of power in the hands of those in charge of the Executive has been matched by a trend towards an ever more impersonal system of national and local politics. This is another major feature of mass society. Today the individual often feels himself merely another number in electoral aggregates or opinion poll percentages; his vote just another cross to be sought after by people he does not know who appear in calculated form on a television screen. He seems very far from being a member of an integrating community which governs itself by participatory mechanisms. G.D.H. Cole (1889-1958) sensed some of this in the 1920s:

democrats set out to strip the individual naked in his relations to the State, regarding all the older social tissue as tainted with aristocratic corruption or privileged monopoly. Their representative democracy was atomistically conceived in terms of millions of voters, each casting his individual vote into a pool which was somehow mystically to boil up into a General Will. No such transmutation happened, or could happen. Torn away from his fellows, from the small groups which he and they had been painfully learning to manage, the individual was lost. He could not control the State: it was too big for him. Democracy in the State was a great aspiration; but in practice it was largely a sham.[55]

This distance and impersonality of Western mass politics was one of the factors behind Solzhenitsyn's admiration for canton democracy in Switzerland:

Closely packed on the town square stood all those with a right to vote ("those capable of bearing arms", in Aristotle's formulation). Voting was conducted by an open show of hands. The head of the canton government, the *Landammann*, was re-elected easily and with an obvious show of affection. But of the bills he then introduced, three were immediately voted down. We trust you, the voters seemed to be saying, to govern us, but without those proposals.[56]

At a national level, a mass population has produced a mass electorate endowed with national perspectives with all the problems of scale that such a development implies. In the first part of the nineteenth century the guiding idea of the electoral system was that the House of Commons was an assembly of the representatives of local communities. For this reason the idea of constituencies of equal size was resisted for a long time and even in the 1990s this guideline was still not fully applied. Parliamentary constituencies were small and MPs were frequently closely connected to their locality, often being bound to their area by occupation, upbringing or family ties. Successive measures of parliamentary reform greatly increased the number of voters and also encouraged the formation of mass parties with national organisations and orientations. By the end of the nineteenth century a national stage had been created marked by competing party programmes and policies – a process which brought with it the erosion of local and personal dimensions to political life. Politicians were becoming much more the expressions of party ideologies and banners than the delegates of local communities. By 1900 the chief points of contact between the voters and politicians were the platform and the press but in the long run the radio and later the television were to command the stage. Today the voter finds himself in a mass constituency relating to mass parties which conduct mass politics through the mass media. We are very far from the world of the Swiss Landammanns or the localist politics of the early nineteenth century.

The impersonalisation of national politics is not only the outcome of scale – it has also arisen from changes in the conduct of politics. There has been a long-term move towards a system of electoral buyers and sellers. Reflecting the spirit of the times, politics now contains an impulse to marketing. Where now is the real community governing itself according to a common project? From many points of view the adversarial two-party system has become a struggle to convince the electorate of one party's ability to deliver material well-being. Indeed, one of the great political trends of the last hundred years has been an increasing emphasis on material and economic issues. One of the signs of such times is the way in which the parties, armed with opinion polls, now seek to target their appeal to groups which are defined in socio-economic terms; another – the frequent employment of pre-electoral budgets. This impersonal system of targeting is matched by impersonal methods. Manipulation through the television, the employment of public relations techniques, the ceaseless concern with 'image', and the impulse to oversimplification, if not outright deception, all involve a propensity to objectify the voters. At the same time the growth of government has made a great deal of political concern and debate too remote from common knowledge – another alienating force. The technicalities of policy are a further creator of remoteness. Furthermore, politicians now have a strong 'professional' dimension. In the early nineteenth century many MPs had no ambition and never spoke in the House of Commons – as members of established elites they were there because they were there. Nowadays MPs are often career politicians who look to politics for material gain, social prestige and the conquest of power. Their approach to the electorate seems often to involve the belief that the voters are instruments to such ends. For such reasons electors are frequently nothing more than dots on the political landscape.

There is one aspect of the modern British political system which for all its positive achievements has played an important role in removing many a personal tie between a politician and his electorate. In much of Southern Europe political 'clientelism' – the use of the state apparatus to secure favours and concessions for political supporters – continues to constitute a major link between individuals and their governors. However much an integral and reprehensible part of corruption, this system serves to create a personal and often local dimension to politics which is no longer evident in our television-dominated mass democracy. Such a background was precluded by our Victorian forefathers. In Great Britain between 1800 and 1850 there was a strong and successful attempt to cut back sinecures and patronage in central government. The professionalisation of the Civil Service during the years 1868-1920 continued the process. Legislation in the 1880s strove to curb electoral bribery and corruption. Low government and local government, in conjunction with the rectitude and public service ethos of the Victorian governing classes, were further factors which worked against clientelism in nineteenth-century British politics. That achievement has remained a prized part of our national political culture, notwithstanding the recent appearance of 'sleaze'. But it is nonetheless a remover of many a potential personal bond between MPs and voters. If anything, clientelism in Britain has taken an impersonal form, with parties seeking to gain the support of specific groups and interests with general policies.

The rise of mass politics has been characterised by the spread of distance and remoteness within local government. During the nineteenth century local democracy came to be a vital and energetic feature of the national polity. Various kinds of local authorities based on different kinds of ratepayers' franchises proved important and dynamic centres of initiative and participation. The local sphere often paved the way for the national sphere when it came to policies and democratic participation. Such localism was often bound up with a strongly felt sense of urban identity – in a very real sense people were Mancunians, Liverpudlians or Glaswegians. We are now faced with a very different picture and local government has become yet another area of lost belonging. This growing gap between local government and local people has been promoted by a number of factors: the impact of centralisation; the creation of large and unwieldy authorities; the identification of local government with unpopular urban planning; and the decline in civic identity. Points of contact are now decidedly weak. In the 1980s turnout in local elections was about 40% and some 40% of council seats were uncontested. During the same decade it was estimated that only about 15% of the electorate ever made contact with their local councillors and in a district of Manchester in 1974 only one person of the hundred interviewed in a survey knew the names of the three councillors of their area.[57] The 1990s, as has already been observed, witnessed a yet further decline in levels of local election turnout. What many Victorian theorists feared has come to pass – the localist dimension of our national polity has been severely compromised. It remains to be seen how far the recent instalment of regional parliaments in Scotland and Wales will really act to combat these processes of centralisation and remoteness and undo a great deal of the damage which has been done. Their establishment has been, in part, a response to exactly such processes.

Class and the Family

The erosion of class differences has been another feature of the rise of mass society. Mill's perceived process of assimilation has been at work in this area with a vengeance. The decline of local identity has been matched by a fall-off in personal identification with a specific social grouping. During the nineteenth century British society was very complicated in class terms with all kinds of sub-categories, gradations and shades of membership. But certain core groups had a high profile and constituted important poles of belonging and differentiation. For example, the industrial working classes had an evident physiognomy and constituted the driving force behind the structures and culture of mass trade unionism, the co-operative movement and the Labour Party. During the second part of the twentieth century, however, this group was reduced in proportionate size by the growth of employment in the service sector. Greater levels of homogeneity have also been promoted by the expansion of the middle classes and a decline in the working classes – a reality expressed in the long-term fall-off in manual labour.[58] Whatever happened, for example, to that community with the highest of high profiles – the miners? Equally, there is nothing now to compare with the landed elite of the Victorian age. George Orwell was sensitive to these general developments and in the early 1940s correctly linked them to the rise of mass society:

> One of the most important developments in England during the past twenty years has been the upward and downward extension of the middle class...In tastes, habits, manners and outlook the working class and the middle class are drawing together. The unjust distinctions remain, but the real differences diminish. The old-style 'proletarian' – collarless, unshaven and with muscles warped by

heavy labour – still exists, but he is constantly decreasing in numbers; he only predominates in the heavy-industry areas of the north of England.

After 1918 there began to appear something that had never existed before: people of indeterminate social class. In 1910 every human being in these islands could be 'placed' in an instant by his clothes, manners and accent. That is no longer the case. Above all, it is not the case in the new townships that have resulted as a result of cheap motor cars and the southward shifts of industry. The place to look for the germ of the future England is in light-industry areas and along the arterial roads. In Slough, Dagenham, Barnet, Letchworth, Hayes – everywhere, indeed, on the outskirts of great towns the old pattern is gradually changing into something new. In those vast new wildernesses of glass and brick the sharp distinctions of the older kind of town, with its slums and mansions, or of the country, with its manor-houses and squalid cottages, no longer exist. There are wide gradations of income, but it is the same kind of life that is being lived at different levels, and in labour-saving flats or council houses, along the concrete roads and in the naked democracy of the swimming-pools. It is a rather restless cultureless life, centring round tinned food, *Picture Post*, the radio and the internal combustion engine.[59]

What about the family in this move towards the mass? Certainly it is a unit which can work against becoming lost in the modern crowd, swept up into large impersonal frameworks, or processed into uniformity. The family, as the European totalitarian systems found out and as Southern Europeans will often tell you, can be a powerful source of resistance to wider processes which oppress and undermine individuality. Mass society has weakened the role and profile of this institution in a number of ways and very great tension now exists between the familial and the super scale.

At the most obvious level mass society has created contexts which dilute the emphasis placed upon the family by its members. Located within far broader frameworks, individual orientations shift away from the immediate environment. Attention becomes directed away from the family towards other concerns and priorities. As a part of this process, information and influences coming in from such frameworks undermine the specific impact and range of control of the family. To listen to the radio is not to listen to relatives; to be interested in national politics may divert attention away from the home. More specifically, the reality of parental guidance can be weakened by external mass influences, whether in the form of educational structures, the television, or rock music. Higher rates of mobility in places of work and residence involve a shift away from proximity to relatives in the village or neighbourhood. The push towards large professionally-managed companies means the decline of family-based small firms and thus of the role of the family as a principal factor in the shaping of economic experience. And big state welfare assistance can render the need for familial care and responsibility redundant or discourage their provision.

International Horizons

An increasing exposure to wider international influences has been another key feature of the rise of mass society. The domestic enlargement of horizons has been matched by the extension of anthropological borders. Over the last thirty years the individual's frame of reference has been extended deep into the United States of America and Europe. Since 1945 the USA has been the world's foremost power and has exercised a massive cultural influence on other nations, especially within the West. 'The impact of American culture on Europe during the twentieth century, the "American century"', we are told by students of the phenomenon, 'has been of as profound in importance as the knowledge of the discovery of the new world had been in the fifteenth century'.[60] A shared language has made Britain particularly vulnerable to the impact of American thought and practice, a development further aided by special and long-standing historical ties. 'Americanisation' now seems to be an accelerating process in the British Isles. Cinema and television have provided a very direct channel of influence, placing the individual in an American context in very immediate fashion. To watch a TV programme or see an American film is to be transported to New York or California. Youth culture, especially in the form of rock music, has flowed over from the Atlantic. American currents of thought have penetrated through strong intellectual and artistic contacts. Business methods and practices have also been copied in Britain. Is not concentration a typically American model? The political world has also been open to the American influence: ideas and policies have certainly left their mark, but it is perhaps in the sphere of presentation and propaganda – with all their impetus to superficiality – that the American political system has been most imitated by its British counterpart. Thus real debate and the exchange of points of view is now often subsumed in importance by fine hairstyles, improved teeth, and the public hugging of wives.

But our mental horizons have not only extended beyond the Atlantic – they have also gone beyond the Channel. In part this is a process which has arisen from the general mechanisms behind the emergence of the global village. The Continent forms the closest part of that village. But, in part also, it has been a natural outcome of British membership of the European Union from the 1970s onwards. The fact of electing a European parliament, or of obeying European law, or of being subject to the European Commission, or of participating in a move towards some kind of political confederation are all elements which have acted to draw Great Britain more tightly into a Continental frame of reference. At the very moment at which Americanisation has reached its height, the British are becoming more European. At one level this development has added yet another layer of impersonality and remoteness to how the British are governed. Our countrymen feel distant from European institutions as is well borne out by the devastating fact that in the 1999 European elections, for example, there was a UK turnout of 24.1%.[61] At another, the impulse towards greater uniformity (or 'assimilation' to use Mill's term) within the European Union, often expressed by the worrying semi-euphemism 'harmonisation', and the British participation in the various bodies and organisms of this proto-confederation, necessarily have the effect of exposing the individual citizen and our national culture to a broad range of Continental influences. At the moment these are largely of an institutional character and are connected in particular to law and legislation, but there is no reason to suppose that in the future they will not also bear powerfully upon beliefs and behaviour, and that there will be a 'Europeanisation' of our cultural realities on a scale to match Americanisation. This remains a part of our national future which has still to be experienced. The danger exists that Europeanisation, like Americanisation, will lead to further deculturalisation.

Manners

De Tocqueville believed that the 'influence of the social and political state of a country upon manners' was 'deserving of serious examination'.[62] The decline of manners (forms of greeting, expressions of gratitude, gestures of regard, rules of hospitality) which seems to have accelerated since the 1960s (another telling chronological fact) – like references to stress or the oft-posed question 'has the world gone mad?' – is often a feature of common conversation, especially amongst the elderly. Rather hollow public relations techniques seem to have displaced previous courtesies. When one surveys 'road-rage', the decline of the queue, and the general spread of incivility, one is very far from that emphasis on good behaviour which was once deeply rooted in British society and crossed many a class barrier. Memoirs bring out the point. 'Two generations afterwards, when I taught, in prison, the grandsons of some of my Edwardian contemporaries, the same attitude persisted', recalled R. Roberts, 'in hundreds of essays on 'Bringing up Children' students cited 'good manners' above all else as a virtue required of the young, followed by "kindness".'[63] It is a sign of the times that in September 1996 the nation's schools had to be instructed by the School Curriculum and Assessment Authority to inculcate 'good manners' in their pupils.[64]

This decline arises naturally from mass society which with the rationalised, mechanistic and remote kinds of contact it engenders between people has little need for manners. The kinds of relationships it favours tend to reduce human points of interface to a minimum. Furthermore, the settled and personal lifestyles encouraged by small-scale local ways of living engender the promotion of manners by providing systems of control and encouragement and by requiring greater oiling of wheels which are far more intimate – the super scale has swept this aside. Equally, with mass society's closing up of individuals within themselves and its associated processes of atomisation, shared agreement over manners becomes less viable. De Tocqueville believed that manners would suffer from a certain 'incoherence' because they would be 'molded upon the feelings and notions of each individual rather than upon an ideal model proposed for general imitation'.[65]

But at the same time the decline of manners arises naturally from the processes of desocialisation. Manners attest to shared ideas within a group or a society about right behaviour in certain contexts; they are transmitted from generation to generation, especially by means of family instruction; they facilitate social interaction and promote community; and with their affirmation of respect and concern for others they contain a moral content. Far from being a matter of mere *politesse*, manners can be valuable indicators of levels of social cohesion; their decline, a sign of the times. Incivility is indicative.

This is fully realised by Lynne Truss in her recent *Talk to the Hand*.

The Utter Bloody Rudeness of Everyday Life (2005), the author of a previous bestseller on the decline in punctuation: 'just as the loss of punctuation signalled the vast and under-acknowledged problem of illiteracy, so the collapse of manners stands for a vast and under-acknowledged problem of social immorality'. The author declares that a principal aim of her book is to mourn 'the apparent collapse of civility in all areas of our dealings with strangers'. Thus it is that in its pages we are offered a panorama of the poor state of manners in post-modern Britain and the author is keen to stress that we are dealing with a development of recent decades. The analysis focuses on six principal areas 'in which our dealings with strangers seem to be getting more unpleasant and inhuman'. Referring to contemporary social alienation, the author speaks of the 'current climate of unrestrained solipsistic and aggressive self-interest'. 'This is an age of social autism', she goes on to declare, 'in which people just can't see the value of imagining their impact on others'. Hence the key observation that the loss of social ties is intimately connected with the loss of good manners and that both of them do us no good: 'cut free from any sense of community, we are miserable and lonely, as well as being rude'.[66]

Uniformity and Anonymity

Mill believed that the central dynamic of mass society was a drive towards assimilation which created uniformity amongst its members. The homogenisation of the cultural system and of conditions of life has indeed been one of the striking features of recent British history. The loss of the Celtic languages and of dialects; the waning of class identities; and the demise of local and regional loyalties have all worked in this direction. The movement away from local politics, local trade unions, local markets and local government towards national frameworks in all these four areas has underpinned the process. The mass media, mass forms of recreation and mass education have been other factors which have worked for the standardisation of our experience. The dilution of the individuality of families, the move away from the peculiarities of small firms, and shared subjection to Americanisation and European-isation have had the same effect. The buying of the same products and common participation in similar urban contexts are further parts of the picture. And huge institutions such as those of central and local government, trade unions, large companies, TV, radio, the national press and cinema, and political parties, because of their mass frameworks of reference, tend to treat us all in the same way. They address themselves to the crowd and make us listen to the same speech. They look at us as Welles looked at his dots, and in this they make us alike.

This push towards uniformity has been accompanied by a drive towards anonymity. The very vastness of the contexts of mass society, whether in the form of supermarkets or cities, companies or national politics, systems of government or international frameworks, works against the individual's capacity to identify. Things are simply too big. The human cannot belong to that which is not on a human scale. Anonymity precludes membership. This is one reason why the phrase 'identity crisis' is so often to be found on contemporary lips. Man is not happy being a dot. The ordinary citizen's encounter with giant firms, the big state, huge trade unions, the mass market, the mass media and centralisation naturally tends to involve an experience directed towards our reduction to the level of objects and the neglect of what we are as humans. Few people actually welcome this state of affairs, but it now seems widely accepted as being somehow a part of 'progress'. 'Are we moving towards an age of colossal organizations and collective institutions', Bonhoeffer wondered to himself in the 1940s, 'or will the desire of innumerable people for small, manageable, personal relationships be satisfied?'[67] Surveying the scene at the beginning of the millennium we can provide an answer to this question, and it is not one which exudes satisfaction. As Roszak observed:

> the *scale* of things can be an independent problem of our social life…It has taken our unique modern experience with public and private bureaucracies, the mass market, state and corporate industrialism to teach us this lesson. We have learned that human beings can create systems that do not understand human beings and will not serve their needs…we live in an age of gargantuan institutions whose vastness makes pygmies of us all…Even where we deal with public institutions whose intentions are benign and which make no effort to exploit us for private advantage, we are nevertheless weighed down by the facelessness and rigidity which are the inescapable results of mass processing.[68]

But it is not only the citizen on the receiving end who gets drawn into this process. Those working on the inside are also encouraged to behave in impersonalising ways, and here we encounter Weber's fears about 'rational bureaucracy'. Roszak again:

As those who work in the system are screened off from the results of their action, their human sympathy and ethical sensitivity are deadened; their sense of personal responsibility fades into an infinite regression of delegated authority. Bigness encourages me (even forces me) to treat you like a cipher, an inconsequential fraction of the masses I must deal with...So we become unreal to one another, mere phantoms moving through a maze of impersonal rules and statistical formulas. All this is familiar enough. It is the common-place, Kafkaesque nightmare of modern industrial life which fills so much of our literature and art.[69]

*

Such are the contours of mass society. After analysing in chapter four how the materialist matrix brings about desocialisation in a direct and personal fashion by attacking the life according to the Spirit and encouraging the dark side, we will now analyse how contemporary mass society interacts with that matrix in various ways to being about a loss of ties on a wider collective canvas. A dark symbiosis is placed under the microscope.

Chapter Eight

A Dark Symbiosis

The anonymity and alienation promoted by mass society creates an environment which constitutes very unfavourable terrain for the generation of values, ideas and attitudes which help people to live together in a condition of authentic community. In being separate from each other, in their distance and detachment, in the *anomie* of their vast contexts, and in their dot-like existence, the citizens of mass society are naturally impeded in their capacity to develop and sustain a culture which generates and promotes social communion. Where gaps have grown up it becomes more difficult to bridge those gaps. In becoming the silent figures of Eliot's London Bridge, how can we develop methods by which to establish interaction? If the supermarket requires that I never greet those who pass me by, how can I establish links with those who go where I shop? If my neighbours in my apartment block never talk to me, how can ways of living be developed which would enrich discussion? In this way authentic Christian culture – or other cultures which share many of its truths – find it very difficult to achieve grip and purchase. At the same time, the turning of people into objects naturally encourages an embrace of the materialist matrix. Without love between people – because the conduits are not there in the first place for its expression – the spiritualist perspective seems not to correspond to the human experience. The false anthropologies of post-modernity, with all their emphasis on distance and separation between individuals, appear much more convincing. By these two routes mass society lends a powerful hand to the materialist matrix as well as producing similar ends. We must now turn our attention to how the materialist matrix works with and through mass society to engender a loss of ties at more specific levels. The topography is complicated, but much can be understood by an examination of such key subjects as the family/gender crisis, big government, the mighty market, politics, the mass media, Americanisation, uniformity and deculturalisation.

The Crisis of the Family and of Male and Female Identities

In discussing the 'increased fragmentation of modern and postmodern culture, the crumbling of the old order, the loss of a frame of reference, and the pervasive and accelerating tendency towards splitting', R. Weatherill observes that 'the crisis in our culture is most clearly marked in the relationship between men and women'.[1] The family/gender crisis is so much at the heart of what has gone wrong in our country, and so illuminates the origins and character of our plight, that it must be understood to the full. We are observing here the direct result of recent decades of erroneous historical evolution and the (at times intended) deconstruction of vital areas of our cultural heritage, for which such groups as those plunged into loneliness against their wishes, the elderly, the young, children, humans at the foetus stage of their existence, humans at the embryo stage of their existence, and the not yet conceived, in particular, have had to pay a very heavy price.

The Crisis of the Family

The preservation of a healthy family structure is a potent barrier against the forces of mass society. It can be a focus for belonging and identity, a unit which can personalise whole areas of human activity, and a place where levelling uniformity can be resisted. Where individuals participate in viable family contexts the pulverising effects of mass society can be opposed, attenuated and perhaps reversed. Such realities are only to be expected given the biological origins of man, which seem to require close patterns of kinship. Similarly, the family is a natural locus for the cultivation of living according to the Spirit. It provides a context where love for love and love for truth find their most natural points of potential expression and encouragement. Where this is achieved the materialist promotion of the dark side can be effectively combated. 'In the revolutionary times ahead the greatest gift will be to know the security of a good home', predicted Bonhoeffer. 'It will be a bulwark against all dangers from within and without'.[2] Mass society and the false anthropologies of post-modernity have joined together to weaken this basic, and sacred, social unit.

The statistics are there for all to see. Only 6% of the marriages of England and Wales of 1936 had ended in divorce after twenty years and in the 1930s and 1950s 'marriages enjoyed a stability without precedent in history'.[3] Historical reminiscence gives us glimpses into these times gone by. When reading R. Roberts's moving account of working-class life in Salford during the Edwardian period it is worth bearing in mind that in Great Britain in 1995 at least 300,000 of our young people were at one time sleeping rough on the streets:[4]

> The Edwardian slum child, like his forbears, felt an attachment to family life that a latter age may find hard to understand. Home, however poor, was the focus of all his love and interests, a sure fortress against a hostile world. Songs about its beauties were ever on people's lips. 'Home, sweet home', first heard in the 1870s, had become 'almost a second national anthem'. Few walls in lower-working class houses lacked 'mottoes' – coloured strips of paper, about nine inches wide and eighteen inches in length, attesting to domestic joys: EAST, WEST, HOME'S BEST, BLESS OUR HOME, GOD IS MASTER OF THIS HOUSE (though father made an able deputy); HOME IS THE NEST WHERE ALL IS BEST. To hear of a teenager leaving or being turned out of it struck fear in a child's mind. He could hardly imagine a fate more awful.[5]

But by 1993 there were seven times more divorces in the United Kingdom than there had been in 1961.[6] In 1938 in England and Wales there was one divorce for every fifty-eight weddings – by the mid-1980s the corresponding figure was one for every 2.2.[7] For the same home countries trends suggested that the divorce rates of 1979 would terminate 33% of marriages by 25 years duration and 56% of teenage marriages over the same period.[8] In such a context it is hardly surprising that in 1985 more than a third of all weddings in England and Wales involved at least one formerly married person.[9] Today one in three marriages finishes in divorce.[10]

However, these figures tell us only one part of the story. Divorce requires the prior contraction of a marriage but the very institution has lost appeal. Since the early 1970s there has been a marked decline in nuptiality rates: in 1971 71% of men and 65% of women in Great Britain were married; in 2000 the respective figures were 54% for men and 52% for women.[11] This appeal seems destined to wane still further. 'The proportion of the adult population that is married', we are told in relation to England and Wales, 'is projected to fall from 57 per cent in 1992 to 49 per cent by 2020'.[12] In addition, the number of people cohabiting has increased dramatically: between 1979 and 2000/2001 the number of cohabiting unmarried adults rose from 11% to 30% of the total adult population.[13] However, these kinds of relationship appear to be notably unstable and involve their own kind of rapid divorce: it was calculated in 1992, for example, that only 16% last more than five years.[14] Marriage as an agreed context for the bearing of children has also lost ground. Whereas live births outside marriage in the United Kingdom were under 10% of the total at the beginning of the twentieth century, they had passed that level by the mid-1970s, and by 1994 they were over 30%.[15] By 2005 they had gone beyond 40%.[16] Such realities lie behind the massive increase in one-parent families, and again we are dealing with rapid recent change: the proportion of children in Great Britain living in families headed by a lone parent nearly tripled from 7% in 1972 to 23% in 2003 and lone mothers headed around nine out of ten lone-parent families.[17]

The decline of the family also constitutes a background to the massive increase in the number of people living alone. This situation is unprecedented in the history of human society and confirms that post-modern culture is something radically new. It has already been observed that it has been estimated that in England and Wales by 2016 36% of all homes will be inhabited by one person but it should also be emphasised that whereas in 1971 a quarter of men were single and a fifth of women, by 2000 a third of men and a quarter of women were in this condition.[18] In such a context it comes as no surprise that whereas there were three million people living alone in Great Britain in 1971, by 2005 that figure had risen to seven million.[19] Such realities also lie behind the rise of the figure of the 'single', a figure explored, for example, in *Bridget Jones's Diary* (1996): over the last two decades the proportion of people living alone in Great Britain has doubled from 7% to 14% of men aged between 25 and 44 and from 4% to 8% of women in this age group.[20] Naturally, the frequently unwanted status of being single is in part directly attributable to the imposition of social conditions that make the forming of contacts between the sexes increasingly arduous. With the decline of natural networks of contact that previously existed through such institutions as the family, the churches or neighbourhood life (with their presence of a shared culture that made the codes of courtship recognised and thus communications as to feelings and intent accessible), the search for contact now often has to take place in relatively unknown territory, with all the risks that this involves. One instructive symbol of this development is the explosion on the internet of much-used sites for singles in search of a partner, 'virtual' courtship so to speak, the full ramifications and consequences of which remain to be investigated.

When we survey what has happened to the family in British society we study in microcosm what has happened to us on much broader canvasses. We perceive fracture at a whole host of levels. We now employ the phrase 'nuclear family' – the wider family, that whole constellation of grandparents, aunts and uncles, cousins and all the rest, has often been fragmented. The very high levels of divorce bear witness to the dissolution of family units. And the increasing number of so-called 'one-parent families' (another significant phrase) involves a desocialising of children through their being deprived of the company of another parent and of the relatives of that parent.

These are very tangible elements but fracture is also to be found at a deeper and less measurable level – in the very texture of relationships between men and women and between parents and children. The lack of love between marriage partners, or between those men and women who cohabit – a reality more than evident from divorce, separation and 'break-up' levels – is at the core of this spreading dissolution. Rising rates of violence within the family (whose levels are probably much higher than is commonly thought) add further dark colours to this picture. This lack of love is also to be found between parents and children and is reflected in the frequent abdication of parental guidance. The same observations may be said about relationships with the elderly. Is not the old people's home a chilling modern symbol of family ties which are absent? In 2004 it was calculated that the number of lonely and isolated elderly people in Great Britain would increase by a third to 2.2 million in 2021, principally because of high divorce levels and a short-age of children,[21] a development that provokes horror in anyone of compassion. In its failings in this whole area British society not only breaks with its own past but also distinguishes itself from the experience of many peoples across the globe. A jet flight to the Far East or to Southern Europe confirms the point in dramatic fashion.

It is certainly true that in part the decline of the family is to be read within the context of the rise of mass society. Vast frames of reference draw attention away from the family setting; the impact of giant contexts diminishes the prerogatives of family influence; and a whole host of phenomena, such as movement away from one's place of upbringing for reasons of work (in 2000/2001 at least one home in every ten in Great Britain had been inhabited by its occupiers for less than a year)[22] or the destruction of family-based small businesses by huge firms, undermine the viability of this basic social unit. Equally, the decline of the family has itself acted to diminish a natural area of resistance to the rise of mass society. Were the family (both 'nuclear' and 'wider') more effective, a powerful force would exist which would sustain the personal face-to-face world against the impact of an anonymous mass framework.

The Soul and Sexuality

But at the same time, at the heart of the crisis of the family is the assault on the soul. Here, too, a spiritualist reading is required of the way we live. Indeed, we cannot understand what has happened to us in this vital area if we do not turn to the impact of the materialist matrix. However, to comprehend the nature and results of the assault we first have to understand the target, and here an exposition of doctrine is required. To comprehend the family as a human phenomenon (and thus the causes of its decline) we must first grasp its central place in the purpose of man ordained by God. Once again we find that to understand daily phenomena we must lift our gaze to broad horizons.

At conception the soul is fused with sexuality. Gender is thus an integral part of the vocation of each individual. Authentic love between a man and a woman involves the soul and is a sign that they are called to engage in sexual union within marriage to bring other souls into the world. The love felt by a man and a woman not only binds them together both in spirit and in body, and promotes their spiritual health, but also (and most importantly) produces a context in which new souls, united to their parents and other relatives by love, can grow up in a context which conduces to their spiritual health. As a part of this love, parents are to instruct their children in those elements of the shared culture of society which works for such health. Love within the family is thus a gigantic generator of the well-being of the soul within society, a major creator of community, and a vital expression and promoter of the kingdom of heaven amongst and within men. The family, obviously enough, has other more mundane purposes, not least the provision of those material resources which are necessary to the maintenance of life. Written within us is thus perhaps the greatest socialising force known to the human experience – the potential for love between a man and a woman. But how many now, with the endless cacophony about sex, talk about this gift? In this sublime sphere, as well, love seems often no longer loved.

The feelings of true love between men and woman, which have been celebrated and evoked by artists down the centuries for their celestial quality, throw important light on this potentiality of the human condition. A veil is drawn back on a very deep inner reality. Love provokes rich spiritual perceptions; heightens aesthetic sensitivity (a telling sign of the link between the condition of the soul and awareness of beauty); produces a complementation of the sexes and an accompanying achievement of sexual identity; heightens and enriches the nature of physical desire and union – love, indeed, is the one true aphrodisiac; and spontaneously activates a number of mechanisms within the partners – most notably a desire to generate children and to love and protect them. When a man and a woman love each other they know what to do; their purpose and role within the cosmos become self-evident; the divine plan unfolds before their eyes without their needing to search for it. Equally, the two sexes have certain different responses to love which throw light on their respective vocations.

However, the materialist matrix attacks this target with an astonishing and revealing ferocity. The intensity of its assault tells us that it is combating one of its principal enemies and that we are touching upon a vital front of a much broader war. Its first great step is to pervert our understanding and practice of sexuality. By denying the existence of the soul and inhibiting the life according to the Spirit, it drains sexuality of the spiritual; divorces sex from love; provides an erroneous picture of this essential feature of our make-up; and renders us ignorant of a vital generator of community. We become turned away from our purpose as sexual beings, and the family as a generator of love and spiritual health becomes severely weakened. Secondly, let us not forget that true love can only take place where there is spiritual well-being – the sun can only come into the room if the shutters are opened. Thus the failure to steward the soul and the move towards the dark side which is encouraged by the materialist matrix rules out the pre-condition to the arrival of love. Thirdly, this matrix places sexuality firmly within the practice of selfish individualism and the lifestyle of treating others as objects – 'sex objects' to use the contemporary phrase. An alternative anti-spiritualist approach to sexuality becomes installed which inculcates a way of living which betrays how this dimension to our lives should be managed. A barrage of arguments encourages the exercise of crude selfishness in the sexual sphere. In the main what becomes important is the purported 'satisfaction' of the individual, not his responsibilities towards others or the impact his behaviour has on the community more generally. Indeed, if there is one thing which characterises the contemporary 'me generation', with all its fall-out from the 1960s (which more and more appears a decade full of error), it is this impoverished view of man's sexuality.

All these elements are brought out by an analysis of the details of this assault. Feelingism lays stress on the selfish pleasure to be gained from the feelings of sexual activity. The societarist impulse towards the adoration of society promotes objectification by turning members of the opposite sex into instruments of self-importance – they become expressions of status, signs of prestige, or mere decorations to be admired. Animalism tends to see sexual activity as the outcome of an inner impulse directed towards the reproduction of the species or of one's own genes. Justifying and sanctioning sexual activity connected without reference to a spiritual anchorage, this creed provides a kind of deterministic licence to do whatever you please which is manufactured by the location of man within the animal kingdom. Psychism parallels some of this approach when it emphasises the dangers of the frustration of man's sexual urge – indulgence is said to be necessary and is even seen as the outcome of an inner psychic structure which exists beneath and beyond the individual's will. Concurrently, in deterministic fashion, both animalism and psychism provide a system of exculpation for forms of sexual activity which are practised without reference to ideas of good and evil. They also enjoin the 'satisfaction' of basic urges which are erroneously said to constitute the real component elements of man's sexuality.

Relativism parallels the deterministic influence of animalism and psychism by stressing that there is no fixed purpose to sexuality, no path to follow, no guiding truths. Talk of what is right and wrong in the sexual sphere is simply thrown out of the window. Determinism declares that things are inevitable; its sister creed proclaims that reflection has no purpose. However, the end result is always the same – the neglect of the spiritual dimension of our sexual natures. Relativism casts man adrift and offers him no anchorage by which to manage this vital part of his nature. It also erects barriers to the correction of error. It declares that the truth about sexuality is what the individual believes it to be, it is a question of point of view, it is each person who decides, and each individual is sovereign.

Such a line of reasoning is bound up with the post-modern adherence to indiscriminate freedom – it is said to be up to each individual to practise his sexuality as he sees fit and nobody should interfere in the exercise of such liberty. Is this not the age of 'free love'? As might be expected, this stance is also defended with reference to notions of privacy – it is argued that the personal life of a person is not a suitable subject for discussion or condemnation. In sexual terms each person may do as he wishes within the sphere of what is deemed 'private'. At times rightsism is also dragged in – each individual is said to have the right to express his sexuality as he sees fit and as he wants. He is deemed to have the right to express his 'preference' – another common word of the contemporary vocabulary of selfish individualism.

The withdrawal of Christian culture has had a major impact on sexuality. This should not surprise us – the materialist matrix has stepped in to promote a process which is antithetical to the principles of the Christian world-view. During the nineteenth century, and for much of the twentieth, religious culture in Great Britain laid great stress upon the family as the essential building block of society and the primary location for the expression of love. The concept of the 'home' was central to this perspective. Marriage, baptism and funerals – the great religious rites of life – were intimately connected with family life and experience. During this period religious culture was intimately connected with, and a principal promoter of, family culture. It is in this light that we should read the great resistance to divorce and adultery, and the intention to place sexual activity within a marital framework, which so characterised the various Christian denominations. Protestant thought and mentality was perhaps not as intense as Catholic attitudes in this whole area but nonetheless proved a vital engine of support for what was one of the great Victorian and Edwardian values – the family. Christian beliefs and ideas rooted family life within a firm framework of the sacred and of respect for divine law. Wherever there was church and clerical activity, or the presence of strong Christian commitment, support for the institution of the family – and a Christian conception of that entity – were conspicuous by their presence. 'The popular estimate of the family is an infallible criterion of the state of society', declared Bishop Westcott a hundred years ago, 'strong battalions are of no avail against homes guarded by faith, reverence, and love'.[23] We now lack an input in favour of the family which at one time was forceful, vigorous and influential.

Reflecting deeper spiritual structures within the cosmos, wherever it passes the materialist matrix produces the opposite of what should occur. When we peer deeply into our present situation of sexuality we detect the presence of a very powerful process of inversion. The removal of the concept of the soul and of love from sexuality produces a 'desexualisation' of man. In the West are we not now surrounded by frequent, albeit usually hidden, complaints about male impotence and female frigidity? The relentless contemporary emphasis on sexuality and the equally insistent constant injunction to engage in sexual activity actually involve a weakening of the erotic impulse. By what routes? In the nature of things, without the presence of love the sexual impulse grows weaker. The use of stimuli in all their forms (ranging from pornography to perversions) is an attempt to counter the dying of the flame of desire but in reality merely sustains a vicious circle which involves its extinction. Exactly the same may be said of the constant use of different 'partners'. The increasing frequency of impotence and frigidity, and the lack of desire between men and women, are authentic fruits of a 'sexual revolution' which has frequently brought not liberation but indifference.

There is a further aspect to this process of desexualisation which requires comment. True sexual identity and authentic sexual fulfilment are obtained through love. They occur because of the operation of the healthy soul, whose condition is expressed in this capacity. When sexual activity takes place where love is not present, the opposite obtains – internal feelings and sensations arise which go in the other direction and disturb sexual identity. The vocation of man is not being fulfilled and what he is internally becomes stressed and deformed. This is a circle which cannot be broken. It should always be remembered that love leads to sex, but sex does not lead to love. The relationship is instructive.

Reference has already been made to the stimuli used to engender erotic feeling because love – that great source-spring of desire – is absent. Pornography (a major growth industry of recent decades and a phenomenon much promoted by the internet) requires a separate paragraph because at many levels it reflects and reveals our desocialised condition. In the first place pornographic images involve a direct objectification of people – they are mere objects on a page or screen. Secondly, and this is especially true of pornography in video form, sexual excitement takes place in relation to humans who are not really there – there is a relationship not with another person but with a disembodied virtual reality. In such a context pornography promotes sexual activity in desocialised form and involves the stimulation of sexual feelings where love cannot be possible. Arousal in front of a video screen or colour pages is one of the more potent symbols of the loneliness of post-modern man. Thirdly, pornography expresses and encourages a great deal of that hedonist thinking which is at the centre of selfish individualism. The great point is to have pleasurable feelings, to indulge, and to experience – the consequences for others are not dwelt upon, indeed do not seem to matter. For these reasons, the perspectives pornography encourages are highly injurious, but criticism of its impact is speedily attacked through the invocation of familiar notions of liberty. Here we encounter a system of defence which is met with at many points within post-modern culture. But, of course, once again it is not freedom which is at stake. This is a complete red herring. What is important is not whether we should have the liberty to see pornography but whether pornography really helps us.

The promotion of sex without love has been facilitated by technological advances which have created possibilities that were absent during the formative stages of man's evolution. Man is in part a material creature and it is therefore possible to interfere directly in this part of his being. Predictably enough, such forms of interference receive legitimacy from the materialist matrix. The employment of these possibilities is now underpinned by man's humanistic faith in himself, which is easily expressed in a belief in the acceptability of such interference in the spheres or sexuality and reproduction. In this area, too – the realm of the transmission of life – man seems willing to take on a divine role. Such possibilities also receive the positive charge now commonly accorded to what are deemed the fruits of scientific progress. They are held to be rational steps forward designed by the beneficial human intellect. At the same time, physiologism – with all its stress on man's corporeality – has prepared the ground for the idea that a path forward for mankind lies in the 'improvement' of his body. Moreover, if man is the outcome of evolution, as animalism asserts, might it not be a good idea to shape him in better form? Relativism, for its part, weighs in by saying that nothing can be condemned.

In Great Britain the contemporary debate over 'bioethics' provoked by these technological advances – which should involve the defence of the dignity of man with regard to conception, abortion, euthanasia and artificial generation – is immensely impoverished by the modern denial of the soul. 'Within the Christian tradition, there is a corpus of thought which is frequently employed to underline the dignity of human beings', writes F.J.E. Basterra in his book *Bioethics*, 'this includes the notion of life as a gift from God, of men and women created in the image and likeness of God, and the presence of a spiritual soul infused by God'.[24] Such an attitude belongs to a minority position in this debate. In this crucial area the deleterious impact of the materialist matrix has been at work with a vengeance.

Contraception is a major feature of the sexual lives of modern Britons. It is estimated that over 80% of women between the ages of 16 and 40 employ some form of 'family planning'.[25] Here scientific discovery has a marked impact. The ingestion of chemicals, for example, can produce a state of controlled infertility in both men and women. But this is not a practice which is without its consequences at the level of attitudes and behaviour. First and foremost, contraception serves to discourage the linking of sexuality to the generation of children. Ideas about the character and significance of the procreative act undergo a change of orientation. It also works to support the constant encouragement of sexual activity by removing the risk of pregnancy – a traditional inhibitor of the practice of 'free love'. Furthermore, the identity of the two sexes is undermined even further by an annulling of the function of impregnating and being impregnated – an awareness of a primary purpose of gender is weakened and discouraged. By subtracting generation from sexuality and the emphasis on love which that perspective should entail; by diminishing the awareness of gender role which the possibilities of generation stimulates; and by favouring the belief that sexual activity is primarily a function involving pleasure, or 'relief', or the removal of 'frustration', contraception proves of great utility in the assault on sexuality which the materialist matrix sustains.

Abortion is another conspicuous feature of today's world of reproduction and sexuality. Abortifacient pills and technical advances in surgery have greatly facilitated this method of ending life. A veritable massacre of the innocents has been underway. Since the legalisation of abortion in 1967 the killing of unborn children has increased by leaps and bounds, a development of horror that is readily perceived by anyone of sensitivity confronted by a picture of an aborted five-month-old foetus. In 1969 there were 62 legal abortions for every 1,000 live births in England and Wales – by 1985 that figure had risen to 215;[26] and the number of recorded abortions in Great Britain nearly doubled between 1971 and 1994 – from 133,110 to 178,200.[27] Since 1994 recourse to abortion has continued to increase.[28] And these figures do not take into account the abortions procured by the morning-after pill, wrongly termed an example of 'emergency contraception' – in reality conception has often already taken place. Indeed, it may be observed that in the whole area of reproduction and sexuality a new and often highly misleading lexicon has been introduced, a fact that should immediately arouse our suspicions as to the true character of what is taking place in this field.

Abortion is often conceived as a sort of contraception – which of course it is not. But in the view that it is a sort of back-up method by which to prevent an 'unwanted pregnancy' it is very similar in its impact on thinking about sexuality, and similar observations may be made about it. However, abortion has two specific features which mark it out from contraception and these bear directly on the concerns of this book. Abortion is a very explicit assault on the soul. The killing of a human being in the very earliest and most vulnerable stages of his existence is a devastating attack – the removal of the body deprives the spirit of its temple. It also amounts to a refusal of the mother to steward the soul of the child which she bears within her, in particular through the defence of his physical integrity. Abortion is, of course, a quintessentially desocialising act – the relationship between the mother and her child is severed beyond repair.

This lack of respect for life is often expressed at two other stages of vulnerability in the existence of an individual – old age and terminal illness. The advance of the philosophy of euthanasia, with its emphatic repudiation of the sanctity of the soul and its readiness to destroy its physical dwelling place, mirrors abortionist thinking and serves to reinforce it. And what could be more desocialising than killing the sick and the elderly? As might be expected, the horror of euthanasia receives important support from the various members of the materialist matrix:

economistic thinking tends to downgrade those who are not economically productive or dynamic; physiologism does the same in relation to those whose bodies are not what they were; rationalism devalues those whose rational faculties are impaired; feelingism refuses the prospect of the physical suffering which old age often brings and underpins much of the insidious euthanistic 'quality of life' argument; and societalism rounds off the barrage by suggesting that old people are often a burden on society. Relativism, for its part, of course, hinders any condemnation of this practice on moral and ethical grounds. In addition, the post-modern concept of liberty (linked to rightsism and the value of privacy) provides a support in this area much as it does in the spheres of contraception and abortion. It is sometimes argued that voluntary euthanasia (in which of course the sick or the elderly must be assisted) is (like suicide) part of the freedom of man, really a private concern, perhaps even a right. The sanctity of the soul is simply left out of the picture.

In discussing the impact of scientific discovery on how sexuality is conceived and practised it may be observed that another inhibitor of sexual activity without love – the risk of sexually transmitted diseases – has been inhibited by advances in the realm of medical science, although the phenomenon of AIDS over recent years has proved a very rude awakening.

Scientific discovery has created another fracture in the chain which links sexuality, love and children. Humans can now be conceived by artificial means. It has for some time been possible to secure the conception of embryos in test-tubes and then implant them within a woman's womb. With this development a future involving the selection of certain types, genetic engineering and gender determination has been opened up. In addition, the cloning of humans for reproductive purposes has become a practical possibility. Within British literature there have for long been warnings about such developments, as Mary Shelley's *Frankenstein* (1818), H.G. Wells's *The Island of Dr. Moreau* (1897) or Huxley's *Brave New World* (1932) well demonstrate. C.S. Lewis, the writer and Anglican intellectual, expressed his warnings in *The Abolition of Man* (1943):

> The final stage is when Man by eugenics, by pre-natal conditioning, and by an education and propaganda based on a perfect applied psychology, has obtained full control over himself. *Human* nature will be the last part of Nature to surrender to Man.[29]

More recently Kazuo Ishiguro has continued this lineage with his warnings about human cloning in *Never Let Me Go* (2005).

The prospects are now very dangerous. God's design by which love (a spiritual reality) is given to a man and a woman as a sign to engage in sexual union which then brings new souls into the world within a spiritually healthy family context becomes blown sky-high by the scientific ability to conceive children without reference to love at all. The association between sexuality, love and children which lies at the heart of the family is further neglected, discouraged and submerged. We have before us the prospect of a sublime dimension of the human world rendered redundant by the appliance of science. Needless to say, the whole natural back-up to sexual identity is also torpedoed by such processes. Furthermore, this artificial process of conception by scientific techniques inevitably reinforces the materialist perspectives on man – in reality, does it not appear from such processes as though humans really are mere constructions of matter? Exactly the same may be said about advances in genetic engineering and the artificial determination of gender. What we are is not seen in terms of the vocation of God expressed in what body He chooses for our soul but with reference to what has been decided by the scientific and all too human hand. Examined closely, the potential ramifications of this whole revolution stagger belief. 'Our post-human future',[30] to employ the phrase of Francis Fukuyama, provokes very great concern and evokes uncharted horrific horizons.

It should be observed, as Angelo Serra, an Italian scholar of international prestige in the field of bioethics, makes clear in his works,[31] that it is in Great Britain that science has been most severe in assaulting the dignity and sanctity of the human person during the first stage of his existence. Indeed, it was in Great Britain that the first child to be conceived in a test tube was born and that a State for the first time allowed the cloning of human embryos (for the purposes of research), not to speak of experimentations on human embryos (and their mass destruction). The black bioethical record of the British plunged to new depths in May 2008 when the House of Commons passed the Human Fertilisation and Embryology Bill. Apart from allowing artificial insemination (wrongly termed 'fertility treatment') for lesbian couples and single women, the creation of saviour siblings (where parents use artificial fertilisation to select an embryo which is a genetic match to a sick older child), this measure also allowed the creation of human-animal hybrid embryos for research purposes – a policy permitted by no other State on the planet and making Great Britain in the bioethical sphere a veritable 'rogue State'. This generation of chimeras, of course, by breaking down the barriers between animals and humans, constitutes yet another assault on the identity of man, an assault already carried forward by the false anthropologies of post-modernity. The reality is that the post-modern culture of Great Britain is no longer able to resist many of the horrors of this kind; indeed, it favours them. It seems that the contemporary British, in this as in many other areas, want to become the sorcerer's apprentices. The wise warnings of their literary ancestors have not been heeded.

Sexual Confusion

A 1980s American film review contained the following instructive lines:

> In the film, Carmen Maura plays a man who's had a transsexual operation and, due to an unhappy love-affair with his/her father, has given up men to have a lesbian (I guess) relationship with a woman, who is played by a famous Madrid transvestite.[32]

Sexual confusion is an integral feature of desocialisation and is at the core of our present-day gender crisis. The post-modern cultural system seems to be producing – albeit by mechanisms which are not yet fully clear but which should certainly be analysed in depth – disorder in sexual identity and orientation. In this sphere the anthropological context is producing developments which restrict the space for love between a man and a women. Contemporary individualist thought is incapable of achieving such a cultural explanation and seeks to locate such phenomena solely within a *personal* framework of causality, but it remains clear that our cultural crisis also involves a crisis of gender.

The *Catechism of the Catholic Church* declares:

> Tradition has always declared that 'homosexual acts are intrinsically disordered'. They are contrary to the natural law. They close the sexual act to the gift of life. They do not proceed from a genuine affective and sexual complementarity.[33]

Homosexuality 'is spreading more and more in urbanised societies'.[34] In 2001 a three-year study by University College, London, the London School of Hygiene and Tropical Medicine, and the National Centre for Social Research found that whereas in 1990 one in twenty-eight men and one in fifty-six women had admitted having a homosexual relationship, by 2000 the respective figures had risen to one in nineteen for men and one in twenty for women.[35] With its positive view of homosexuality, expressed in the slogan 'gay pride', 'homosexualism' is now a distinct force for cultural change within Western society, as the 'gay rights' movement well illustrates. But precisely because people of the same sex together cannot produce offspring (and in this they deviate from the natural trajectory of sexuality-love-children and close the future to kinship ties – a necessarily desocialising step), they challenge the family and structurally reduce the space available for love between men and women. Indeed, the greater the number of homosexuals, the more society is unable to base itself upon a future of souls brought up within a family context infused with the spirit of love.

Furthermore, the high profile of homosexuality and bisexuality (which have gained recent legitimation from the attitudes propagated in books, films and TV programmes and by measures such as the Civil Partnership Act of 2004 which granted same-sex couples rights and responsibilities identical to civil marriage) is a challenge to the self-view of individuals in relation to their own sexuality. In this confused context men and women, and especially young people in the formative stages of their lives, may well be led to ask of their gender (and all it implies): 'who am I?'

The contemporary challenge to sexual identity also finds expression in such realities as 'sex change' operations (in reality a person cannot change their sex; they may be able through surgery and the ingestion of hormones to change the appearance of their bodies, but that is a completely different matter); the 'gender benders' of rock music; and the interest in moving across the sexes which has cropped up in literature or films over recent decades. Indeed in this context it comes as no surprise that the 'transsexual' has become one of the new figures of contemporary mental horizons.

This gender crisis is pre-eminently rooted in the false anthropologies of post-modernity and the contours of the culture to which they give rise. Various elements within materialist thought either deny that there are specifically male and female vocations or attack their manifestations by arguing that they are mere products of external conditioning – the outcomes of historical, societal or cultural contexts rather than inner human nature. Relativism, for its part, asserts that there is no true or natural form of sexuality and that everything boils down to a question of personal perspective or preference. Sameism weighs in by arguing that in fact men and women are in essence the same and that no authentic differences save the physical really exist between them. At another level, diminishing levels of spiritual health and thus of the capacity for love remove a path by which sexual identity is felt. In addition, the general detachment of the individual from his human environment, the very condition of being deprived of authentic community, in itself provides an overall weakening of how we see ourselves in gender terms – we lack a frame of reference and means of measurement. This is reinforced by the processes of deculturalisation which mean that young people do not receive instruction and wisdom about men and women and the differences between the sexes, a practice which has been a principal task of society down the ages. Lastly, the cult of liberty (frequently without responsibility) has encouraged the idea that sexuality is not ontological, indeed vocation, but a matter of personal choice: in some sense it is suggested that individuals are free to decide their own 'gender'.

No analysis of this gender crisis (and of the travails of the family) would be complete without a discussion of feminism – a movement which in chronologically significant fashion has had a major impact on British and Western society over the last four decades. Feminism has been a rather heterogeneous movement made up a variety of beliefs, aims and aspirations which have shifted and mutated over time. On its extreme wing there have been elements which have played an important role in promoting confusion over gender, in disturbing the relationship between men and women, and in undermining the family. Many of the principles, approaches, assumptions and aspirations of *radical* feminism can be taken from the introductory 'summary' to Germaine Greer's *The Female Eunuch* (1970):

> It is impossible to argue a case for female liberation if there is no certainty about the degree of inferiority or natural dependence which is unalterably female…What happens is that the female is considered as a sexual object for the use and appreciation of other sexual beings, men…The compound of induced characteristics of soul and body is the myth of the Eternal Feminine…This is the dominant image of femininity which rules our culture and to which all women aspire. Assuming that the goddess of consumer culture is an artefact, we embark on an examination of how she comes to be made…The castration of women has been carried out in terms of a masculine-female polarity, in which men have commandeered all the energy and streamlined it into an aggressive conquistatorial power, reducing all heterosexual sex to a sadomasochistic pattern… The nuclear family of our time is severely criticized, and some

vague alternatives are suggested, but the chief function of this part, as of the whole book, is mostly to suggest the possibility and the desirability of an alternative...Rather than dwell upon the injustices suffered by women in their individual domestic circumstances, these parts deal more with more or less public occasions in which the complicated patterns of mutual exploitation do not supply any ambiguous context...women ought not to enter into socially sanctioned relationships...The woman who realizes that she is bound by a million Lilliputian threads in an attitude of impotence and hatred masquerading as tranquillity and love has no option but to run away. The revolutionary woman must know her enemies, the doctors, psychiatrists, health visitors, priests, marriage counsellors, policemen, magistrates and genteel reformers, all the authoritarians and dogmatists who flock about her with warnings and advice... Hopefully, this book is subversive. Hopefully, it will draw fire away from all the articulate sections of the community...But if women are the true proletariat, the truly oppressed majority, the revolution can only be drawn nearer by their withdrawal of support for the capitalist system. The weapon that I suggest is that most honoured of the proletariat, withdrawal of labour.[36]

Much of the materialist matrix ties up with radical feminist belief. In the first place, there has been the frequent assertion that traditional ideas about the nature and roles of men and women are mere products of conditioning produced by existing society. This has led to a deculturalising attack on the inherited beliefs and practices which are produced by such ideas. Often little except personal freedom and equal economic opportunities are offered as substitutes for displaced convention. Indeed, there does not appear to be a coherent set of answers as to how men and women should actually see and behave towards each other. This is not surprising because there is a strong impulse within radical feminism to engender conflict between men and women. Rooted in notions of historic unjust male dominance, this perspective has a natural propensity to attack, counter and rival men at a large number of levels. Here one encounters a mighty wedge being placed between the sexes. A gap is being built up where there should be mechanisms to produce harmony in the community at large and in personal relationships more specifically. This lack of a set of answers is also rooted in the frequent radical feminist espousal of sameist thinking in relation to the sexes. If the genders are more or less the same, it is argued, there is no need to reflect upon their special roles, which should not really exist.

Furthermore, and strongly influenced by the economist and powerist contention that society is a place where individuals struggle for money and command, extreme feminism has often encouraged women to direct their attention towards economic activity and careers. This has involved an attempt to downgrade the role of the woman who lays primary value on the expression of love for her children and husband and on the stewardship of her family environment. This line of approach constitutes a very direct challenge to the embattled institution of the family. Naturally enough, the increasing number of working women has major implications for the extended family. In 2004 the Henley Centre published 'The Responsibility Gap – Individualism, Community and Responsibility in Britain' in which it reported that according to its research nearly one in two adults agreed with the statement 'I am so tired in the evening, I often don't have the energy to do much' and working mothers in particular were so busy with their jobs and looking after their children that they could not look after their parents and neighbours as they once could.[37] It also has implications for the special supports available to the non-working mother – she encounters yet another mechanism working for her isolation and the absence of another potential support in the performance of her family role. By this emphasis on the economy, radical feminism has also clearly sowed doubt and confusion within many women as to their true purpose and identity – just one more element in the vast ocean of doubt and uncertainty which surrounds post-modern man. And the very speed of the change in the condition of women over recent decades has been a further factor working for 'culture shock' and for confusion over gender roles.

The frequent impulse of radical feminism to engender conflict and competition between men and women – with all the promotion of the lifestyle of selfish individualism that this produces – clearly plays an important part in bringing about the present-day situation where men and women increasingly do not know how to relate to each other. The loss of old bearings, the emergence of new ideas, the waning of inherited custom, the decline of the culture of courtship and of the family, confusion over the purpose of sexuality, and uncertainty over what gender involves, in addition to the rapidity with which all this has taken place, have all combined to set men and women adrift in uncharted seas. They are increasingly unaware of how to treat each other, how to approach each other (here the decline of the culture of courtship, a significant part of deculturalisation, requires special mention), and how to live with each other. This is especially true in the sphere of intimate relationships, that area which should be the place for the flowing forth of the spring of love – that supreme socialising force of the human condition. And who would deny that the decline of respective roles and recognised differences between the sexes (a development well expressed in changes in styles of dress) constitutes yet another example of those phenomena of homogenisation and identity loss which so characterise mass society?

Radical feminism's frequent downgrading of motherhood has contributed to the modern attack on the family; indeed, it has been one of its chief features. Women by their very natures are especially orientated towards love, and this derives directly from the task entrusted to them by the Creation. It is the woman who carries the child within her and then bears it at her breast. The love of a mother for her child both within the womb and beyond is one of the great socialising aspects of the human experience and a force of the very highest value and nobility. Indeed, of all the forms of love, is not the love of a mother for her child the purest? The physical proximity of the mother to her child, the affection and caresses, the care and concern – not to speak of protection – that she provides are the very highest examples of the social. By directing the woman away from this sphere, by stressing the primary importance of career, by offering all sorts of other goals and prizes, by failing to remind the husband of his very great duties towards the woman who has children with him through many travails, and by frequently producing an isolated context in which the mother fails to receive support and help, post-modern life – influenced by extreme feminism – assaults one of the most vital and integrating areas of the human experience: where maternal love is lacking, authentic community is on the road to disrepair.

At another level, the contemporary attack on the dignity and reality of maternity is rooted in our common mistake about what we are. The sanctity of motherhood has been undermined by the widespread failure to understand humans as embodied spirits. The mother is the special custodian of a new soul brought into this world. She is the sacred vessel of life. Her role is therefore of the very greatest importance. In perceiving the sacredness of the unborn and born child we are able to understand the holiness of her task. But when this perception does not take place because of the thinking of the materialist matrix, that sacredness is severely sabotaged. The woman becomes a sort of test-tube and from this position it is very easy to move towards the idea that test-tubes are just as acceptable as a woman in achieving procreation.

The Attack on Children and the Young

There is another aspect to the decline of the family. 'The fragmented society neither educates nor builds', a leading French social psychiatrist has observed, 'we have observed over the last twenty years that relationships involving upbringing have been increasingly neglected'.[38] The observation is incisive – much of post-modern thought has struck a massive blow at the idea and practice of parental guidance. First of all, we commonly encounter the bizarre idea that in some way children are little adults: sameist thought, notions of individual rights and modern concepts of liberty have all encouraged the idea that children should be treated as though they have already grown up. Furthermore, the principle that wisdom should be imparted to them, that they require direction, and that they need to be instructed, has been eroded by notions that somehow this is an authoritarian and erroneous approach. Here we encounter such ideas as the belief that children should find their own way, that they should not have beliefs 'imposed' upon them, or that they should be autonomous and self-directing in their development. Or to put it in more obviously desocialised terms – that they should be left alone. Relativism has buttressed this process. Parents are encouraged to think that their children have a point of view as well and that this is as valid as their own or that what they themselves believe is not necessarily 'true' – all truth being relative – and that there is thus no secure point of departure for parental guidance. At the same time, the erosion of the concept of personal responsibility has meant that the idea that parents have a duty to bring up their children, to impart wisdom to them, to guide them, and to ensure their inner growth, has been undermined. And all these elements working against guidance, naturally enough, provide a wonderful cloak for those parents who in essence care very little about their offspring. Once again we encounter the phenomenon of doctrines and notions which serve to justify and mask ill-doing. The selfish individualism of parents here finds a ready defence.

There is also the question of the actual feasibility of parental guidance in post-modern society. Responsible mothers and fathers face a by no means easy undertaking in the discharge of their duties. They are often up against forces which mean that their range of influence is reduced and their room for action restricted. Faced with such realities, they are often encouraged to throw in the towel. Children and young people are exposed to influences and formative forces well beyond the control of their families. Within a mass society they are placed within contexts which rival parents in the imparting of ideas, beliefs and behaviour, and where the family no longer acts as the chief conduit for the transmission of culture. For example, children and young people are exposed to television, to radio, to rock music, and to cinema, for which, indeed, they constitute a vital economic market. These aspects of mass society, which are so often associated with youth culture and the famous 'generation gap', involve influences which by-pass and at times counter parental guidance. The same may be said of mass schooling and higher education, and here, too, forces are at work which can relegate parents to a very subordinate role. Universities in particular, with all their rationalist emphasis on the prowess of intellect and the downgrading of inherited wisdom, often act to form young minds in a way which marginalises parental influence. Underpinning this general incursion into the previous realm of parental guidance is the idea commonly communicated to the young by mass-media culture and official education that authority is to be questioned, convention tested, and tradition doubted. The family and its role are often the very special target of such assertions.

Only a fool would be indifferent to the grave consequences for our society of this crisis in the relationship between men and women. The basic social contract of the family – like that of society more generally – should be the expression and promotion of spiritual health. This is a mechanism of the very greatest importance for our general well-being. Both in relation to each other, and in relation to their children, parents should aim to achieve that condition of the soul which expresses the kingdom of heaven and prepares the way for eternal life both for themselves and for others. This must involve a commitment to love and truth. The marriage partners by their marriage are called to be dedicated to each other's highest well-being (of which spiritual health is the utmost expression) and have exactly the same responsibility towards their children – those new souls which they have brought into this world in co-operation with God. Within the family there should thus be a common project which revolves around the achievement of spiritual health. When this common project is adhered to, the community receives a very rich inflow of individuals, whether parents, children or relatives, whose souls have been well stewarded and protected. In terms of the future the family acts as a nursery bed for healthy plants which are then placed around the fields. Wider society becomes built on people who are capable of – and indeed are oriented towards – authentic community. Where this does not take place the opposite occurs and desocialisation receives yet another impulse.

But the contemporary travails of the family not only erode community by weakening a source of spiritual health – they also create individuals who by personality, emotions and mentality are ill-prepared for life with other people. The impact of broken homes, of single-parent families, of unhappy family backgrounds, and of parental indifference or cruelty stare us in the face as we cast our eyes over post-modern life. Individuals increasingly lack that formation within the family which prepares them for their later lives. Their development and growth are often compromised by having undergone the trials of a familial background disturbed by disorder. Their characters thereby become stamped by an inability to achieve community with others. This, of course, is a process which feeds on itself. A failed family background can encourage the repetition of such an experience in those who have been marked by its injurious impact. On a broader canvass the failure of the family often helps to create a desocialised kind of person who himself is incapable of effective socialisation; he becomes a bearer of a distinct way of life marked by the absence of capacity for real interaction. There is a very short step from a bad family experience to the desocialised type. Overall, when love for love and for truth withdraws from the family environment other elements enter into the picture which work in the opposite direction and set up various chains of consequences which undermine social cohesion and work against the achievement of community.

In this general context it should be observed that from many points of view post-modern culture is engaged in an increasingly forceful attack on children. The beginning of life seems at times to be a veritable obstacle course: the widespread use of contraceptives impedes conception; abortion means death; and the destruction of embryos within the context of *in vitro* artificial fertilisation techniques destroys life forever. At the same time, homosexuality and bisexuality prevent conception because people of the same sex cannot generate life together. In 2006 the Pontifical Academy of Social Sciences published a detailed work entitled 'Vanishing Youth? Solidarity with Children and Young

People in an Age of Turbulence'. One of its conclusions was that 'Children are quite literally vanishing due to rapidly falling birth-rates in the developed world'.[39] Here, too, we encounter the creation of the void. Then, after birth, children often have to face up to the realities of a single-parent family or the suffering, if not trauma, caused by separations or divorce. There is also the major risk of being exposed to violence and cruelty in the home. In 2006 UNICEF, the United Nations and Body Shop International published a report entitled 'Behind Closed Doors: the Impact of Domestic Violence on Children' which estimated that up to a million children in Britain lived in violent homes.[40] Furthermore, love, care and upbringing within a family environment often seem inadequate if not absent, and post-modern society is increasingly less a 'home' and ever more a place that does not provide a welcome. In this area literature, once again, reflects cultural development, as can be readily grasped from a reading of such novels as *The Cement Garden* (1978) by I. McEwan or *About a Boy* (1998) by Nick Hornby or the many publications of the new and instructive genre of 'misery literature'.

In this area, too, do we not often come up against horror? Some of the statistics on mental malaise amongst children, which should be read in the context of these realities, are deeply disturbing. In 1999 it was reported that up to 20 per cent of children may need help for depression-related problems[41] and in 2004 '10 per cent of 5 to 16 year olds living in private households in Great Britain had a clinically diagnosed mental disorder'.[42] The Children's Society in September 2006 stated that a climate of 'fear and confusion' was contributing to rising levels of child depression in Britain. It pointed to higher levels of depression and mental illness amongst children in the United Kingdom than in any other country in the European Union.[43] And in the same month a group of 110 academics, teachers, psychologists and authors wrote an open letter to a leading national newspaper in which they pointed to the 'escalating incidence of childhood depression'.[44] Here, also, should we not sit down upon the banks of the post-modern river and weep?

Similar observations may be made about what young people have to endure. The condition of teenagers in contemporary Great Britain has features that are equally disquieting. For example in 1999 *The British Medical Journal* published an article that described how British teenagers had the worst record for sexual diseases, pregnancies, abortions and illicit drug-taking in the whole of Europe – elements rightly deemed to be evidence of a 'fundamental malaise in our culture'.[45] The publication of a report on teenagers by the British Medical Association in December 2003 gave rise to the following newspaper article:

Doctors will this week voice unprecedented alarm over the health of teenagers in Britain today. The mental, physical and sexual wellbeing of young people is deteriorating so much that drastic action is needed to defuse a "potential public health time bomb".

The report will show that one in five people aged 13 to 16 is overweight one in five adolescents experiences psychological problems and up to one in ten 16 to 19-year-old women has the sexually transmitted infection chlamydia. It will conclude that "adolescent health paints a bleak picture of the problems facing young people in 2003".

Dr Russell Viner, a consultant in adolescent medicine…who will launch the report, said: "It's not until you take all these figures together that you realise how worrying the situation is. It seems that adolescents are the one group whose health is actually getting worse. Better drugs are protecting older people from disease, and vaccination has brought huge improvements for infants. But for people in their teens, there are social health problems, which mean worrying rates of accidents, suicide, drug use, pregnancy and sexually transmitted diseases".

The statistics are stark: the number of 16 to 19-year-old women diagnosed with chlamydia, which can cause infertility if left untreated, jumped by nearly 300 per cent between 1996 and 2002. The number of 16 to 19-year-olds who have used cocaine rose four-fold, from one in 100 in 1994 to one in 25 in 2000. Since 1980, the number of obese 16-year-olds in the UK has doubled.[46]

In addition, young people are not receiving the education they deserve: standards in schools have reached new low levels, with a half of students taking the primary school-leaving examination in England being below standard in reading, writing and arithmetic.[47] The most extreme examples of teenage malaise provoke authentic horror. 'In many of our larger cities, in areas of extreme deprivation, there are almost feral groups of very angry young people', Barbara Wilding, the Chief Constable of South Wales, told the Centre for Crime and Justice Studies of King's College London in May 2008, 'Many have experienced family breakdown, and in place of parental and family role models, the gang culture is now established. Tribal loyalty has replaced family loyalty and gang culture based on violence and drugs is a way of life'.[48]

What we are also witnessing in the family/gender crisis is the promotion of cultural breakdown through an assault on the inheritance of mechanisms working for social integration. T.S. Eliot observed that 'the primary channel of transmission of culture is the family'.[49] The family is a vital conduit for the communication down the generations of a people's shared beliefs and practices, customs and habits, ways of thinking and forms of behaviour. It is the location where many of the practical realities of the common project are learnt and applied. To put it differently – the family is an institution where shared wisdom and knowledge are imparted over time in a process which sustains and supports the accumulation and maintenance of a community's cultural patrimony. When parents teach their children respect for others, or good manners, or essential moral principles, or how to face up to life, or the history of their people, or how to behave towards others, they take part in a common enterprise of ensuring community. But the break-up of families, the decline of the wider family, the lack of authentic relationships within the family, the weakening of responsibility between relatives, and the erosion of the very idea that the family represents a shared project for its members all act to remove this primary channel. An intense process of deculturalisation is promoted – what was previously transmitted and learnt becomes lost, perhaps for ever. Once again the void rears its ugly head. This can only mean an impoverishment of the means by which a society remembers, embraces and implements the methods and means by which it achieved and achieves cohesion. This has necessarily also had profound implications for the transmission of Christian culture.

Big Government

The materialist matrix has interacted with mass, centralised, interventionist government in a large number of ways. The Conservative view that large-scale state action is a principal factor behind the breakdown of community undoubtedly contains some sound insights. Over the last hundred years the societalist view that man is a product of society and that the road forward lies in major changes in socio-economic structures has been a significant force behind the massive growth in government. Vast new tasks have often been given to the state, and especially to the central state, out of the belief that the changes it would produce within society were the chief path by which to promote the welfare of man. Such an approach has been one of the great innovations of modern Western civilisation. At times it seems as though the exponents of this collectivist approach – often embraced with enthusiasm by social scientists – have believed that the great task of politics is to find an elusive right combination of forms of intervention. Find that, it is assumed, and the answer to our problems has been discovered. Naturally enough, other elements and aspirations have lain behind this historic innovation but there can be no doubt that this materialist model of man has been an energising factor.

The great danger of societalism is that it can alter thought and orientations within a community – away from the soul, the life according to the Spirit, and the cultural forms which express and promote spiritual health. Attention becomes placed exclusively on socio-economic structures to the detriment of the deeper sources of personal well-being and community. It comes as no surprise that the most extreme form of societalism of the twentieth century – Communism – was an atheistic movement which acted to fragment and deculturalise the societies over which it exercised control. In Great Britain the societalist thought and practice which have been expressed in the advance of collectivist institutions and culture have certainly led to a major shift in emphasis within our society. People have been encouraged to think that the way forward and the answer to their troubles lies in the right structuring, adjustment and management of socio-economic realities. Individuals have been led to think about themselves, their problems, and their futures from this kind of perspective. Given this development, it is hardly surprising that national politics during the last century has become increasingly dominated by concern with material issues. The great tragedy of this approach, however, is that it diverts attention away from our spiritual lives and from related paths by which to improve our condition. We have become desocialised in part because of an erroneous emphasis on 'society'.

However, societalism has been a force behind desocialisation in more specific ways. Collectivism, which has received great impetus from societalist thought, has weakened links between people by promoting impersonal forms of care; eroding ideas of direct responsibility at a face-to-face level; encouraging impunity for individual irresponsibility; and undermining self-regulation by placing an exaggerated stress on state regulation. These elements have all helped to produce a severe weakening and draining of interpersonal relationships. Collectivism has also acted to promote deculturalisation by shifting attention away from custom and tradition and by diminishing the profile of personal society. In addition, much of collectivism has involved classist thinking, and this has encouraged the perception of people as societal units rather than spiritual beings – with all the objectification that such a process implies. This perspective has also promoted the idea that society is a place of conflict and struggle. All these points will now be discussed.

A blanket condemnation would not be in order. No extreme marketist position is being propounded here. Big government can claim many positive achievements. It has played an important role in checking the abuses of the market, defending the economically vulnerable, providing essential services such as health, housing and schooling, and combating the severity of poverty. Moreover, as many on the Left have pointed out, this form of solidarity may have acted to integrate certain groups more securely within society and promoted a greater sense of belonging. But there can be no doubt that there have also been deleterious effects which have contributed to our cultural crisis. Collectivism has had a whole host of unforeseen and damaging consequences. Yet there again it would be very surprising if the momentous changes in the modern role of the state were not in some ways intimately linked to the difficulties of contemporary British society. Did not Burke warn, after all, that there were latent dangers in major programmes of great change?

The science of constructing a commonwealth, or renovating it, or reforming it, is, like every other experimental science, not to be taught *a priori*. Nor is it a short experience that can instruct us in that practical science; because the real effects of moral causes are not always immediate; but that which in the first instance is prejudicial may be excellent in its remoter operation; and its excellence may arise even from the ill effects it produces in the beginning. The reverse also happens; and very plausible schemes, with very pleasing commencements, have often shameful and lamentable conclusions. In states there are often some obscure and almost latent causes, things which appear at first view of little moment, on which a very great part of its prosperity or adversity may most essentially depend. The science of government being therefore so practical in itself, and intended for such practical purposes, a matter which requires experience, and even more experience than any person can gain in his whole life, however sagacious and observing he may be, it is with infinite caution that any man ought to venture upon pulling down an edifice which has answered in any tolerable degree for ages the common purposes of society, or on building it up again...[50]

When the state takes responsibility for whole areas of life this can encourage individuals to relate to each other at an impersonal level through the medium and agency of government. Collectivism promotes the idea that the way to help others is through a contribution to state action rather than through personal face-to-face initiative. It also encourages the view that we should turn to government for help in our personal lives rather than to those we find around us. All this involves an impulse to the impersonalisation of the human experience, and the personal input into community is necessarily eroded. The individual gives and receives help not personally but impersonally; his relationships in this sphere are not with people but through institutions. His real social world thereby becomes powerfully depleted. Voting in ballot boxes and the payment of taxes take the place of individual face-to-face duty and care; the receipt of state aid substitutes the acceptance of personal help from those the individual knows. Some empirical flesh may be put on these rather dry abstract assertions. Instead of my family or my friends helping me, I turn to the social security office; rather than taking an initiative to help those near me who are suffering, I expect the state to step in; rather than caring personally for the elderly, I direct my grandparents to a state-financed old people's home; rather than comforting my neighbour, I advise him to talk to a state-paid counsellor; and rather than lending money to a friend in need I urge him to campaign for lower taxes. It is not necessarily that the will to follow personal avenues and paths is lacking – merely that state resources allow them not to be used.

There is also a direct discouragement of the idea and practice of personal responsibility towards others. The individual can be systematically encouraged to think that it is not he who has a duty towards others but the state. It is not for him to lessen suffering, or to offer guidance, or to make suggestions – all that is said to be a matter for government. State responsibility elbows out individual responsibility. Thus, for example, a person does not believe that he must steward his soul, cultivate virtues, or express love for others by direct face-to-face action. He does not conceive of himself as an active participant in a community where he helps his family, his friends, his neighbours, his workmates or his fellow citizens. He becomes instead the observer of a society where such matters are largely left to the state. It is for government, not himself, to care. Indeed, the growth in the contemporary use and importance of the notion of 'caring' is in part directly attributable to this development. People are said to 'care' not because of initiatives in their personal province but because they promote state action to solve certain problems. Of course this shifting of responsibility onto government and its organs is mightily convenient to the selfish. Individuals become absolved from their immediate social duties – at a personal level they need to do very little. Selfish individualism is thus strongly reinforced. But of course it is not enough to argue that society cares for others solely through government – the community exists at a capillary level and looks after its members through face-to-face action in a variety of forms as well. Such salient features of desocialisation as the erosion of family responsibilities and of personal commitment to public service are partly rooted in the idea encouraged by collectivism that we should leave a great deal to the state. 'Social policy' has many unforeseen anti-social consequences.

Thirdly, the action of the state can involve the removal of impediments to irresponsible behaviour. The erosion of personal responsibility is accompanied by the indirect encouragement of individual irresponsibility. This works at two levels – in relation to a person's behaviour towards others and in the sphere of the individual's self-management. By providing financial support to those who are in economic difficulty the state runs the risk of removing an inhibition to injurious action – the person who has caused such hardship is not made to be economically responsible for what he does. Thus he who mindlessly makes a woman pregnant finds that the state bears the burden; she who unthinkingly brings an illegitimate child into this world receives benefit; and the person who evicts or sacks unjustly perceives certain safety nets being provided to those he has wronged. Numerous other examples of not having to face the consequences for one's actions could be cited. Similarly, the person who makes no effort to work, or to improve himself, or who runs irresponsible risks, finds that in some way he will be bailed out by the state. He will not have to pick up the bill. In the final resort the penalties he incurs are by no means a deterrent. This is one route to what is now termed 'welfare dependence'. It is hardly surprising that many commentators are now beginning to perceive in the workings of the welfare state mechanisms which reproduce poverty by sanctioning acts of personal irresponsibility. And where all this is encouraged social bonds can only be further drained of their rightful content.

But faith in the big state and a much-governed society has struck a blow at personal responsibility at a more subtle level – that of individual self-regulation. One of the great features of British society – certainly until the emergence of our crisis over recent decades – was the legitimacy of state institutions. Respect for law and order, a commitment to the paying of taxes, and a belief in the due processes of government all attested to a deeply-rooted respect for the state. Collectivism's advance was partly facilitated by this reality – the prestige of government paved the way for the acceptance of policies which urged an expansion of its role. One consequence of this expansion of government activity has been a shift away from self-regulation towards state-regulation. The idea emerged that the points of reference for what could and could not be done, and for what should and should not be done, were not personal perception and assessment but the decisions and dictates of legislation – government, not personal conscience, was to be the arbiter of individual behaviour. This encouraged two elements, both of which have undermined personal responsibility and the living of a conscious moral life. On the one hand, there is a lack of thought and reflection about individual action because the onus for decision has been shifted onto the directive role of government. On the other, those crucial areas not covered by state regulation diminish in importance and come to be perceived as a province where personal responsibility is not very relevant. It was almost as if crime is believed to stop at the criminal code. Furthermore, in this stress upon the directive role of the state we touch upon yet another mechanism working for the loss of the cultural inheritance – there has been a shift away from the role of social pressure, custom, convention and tradition in directing and governing the behaviour of individuals towards entrusting such tasks to legislation and government action.

However, this is only one feature of the process by which collectivism has acted to promote deculturalisation. The erosion of the notion, practice and habit of personal responsibility (caused by many other factors as well) has meant that people have been directed away from the world of the face-to-face and the interpersonal. Not living the personal world, or living it in a highly depleted fashion; not being oriented towards interaction at individual points of contact; and not being accustomed to thinking and acting in person-to-person terms, individuals produce an empty space around them – the societal comes to replace the social. In not being directly responsible towards other individuals and placing themselves within an impersonal collective framework, people lose the need for, and interest in, those mechanisms which favour the sound working and functioning of the face-to-face and the personal. This means that there is far less requirement for all those features of inherited culture which over the generations have been accumulated to help and sustain this vital dimension of society. Such mechanisms become lost like water flowing into the sands of a desert – they no longer serve a purpose. Much of the cultural patrimony no longer becomes transmitted because a state of affairs has arisen which renders it inappropriate. Subsequent generations become born into a culture which has been thinned in relation to its provisions for the face-to-face. In a certain sense people no longer know how to behave towards each other at a personal level; they no longer know the ropes. A great deal of inherited wisdom designed to secure community thereby becomes lost.

The impersonality (and depersonalisation) provoked by societalist thought and practice arises from yet another process: that of conceiving of the human environment not in terms of an interaction of souls – with all the perspectives that this approach involves – but from the point of view of an aggregation of units or more usually of sets of units. The big state, the world of interventionist government, and the practice of collectivism (which is often imbued with social science thinking) all have the implicit effect of encouraging people to refer to each other in highly impersonal terms. It is noticeable, for example, that much of the societalist thrust has revolved around class perspectives. It is often asked which class gains and which loses within society and in this way people are encouraged to see each other, indeed to assess and evaluate each other, as units within an impersonal category. At another level a great deal of the conduct of politics, and the actual practice of big government, is carried out with reference to groups – groups which should be taxed and groups which should be helped, categories which should be advantaged and categories which should be penalised, interests which should be protected and interests which should be checked. When reference is made to the working classes or to the middle classes, to women or to ethnic groups, to the City or to trade unions, and policies and laws are framed accordingly, individuals are necessarily encouraged to see each other in terms which do not emphasise or favour individuality or spirituality but which stress group membership and promote abstract forms of relationships. People become groups of dots in an impersonal framework.

This implicit tendency within big state culture to see others in terms of categories not only impersonalises the human experience. It also involves the generation of conflict. When the state becomes a source of gain, an instrument for the redistribution of wealth, a force which adjusts and allocates material advantage between different categories, there is a natural propensity to see government as a terrain for conflict-ridden encounter between different interests. Individuals are encouraged to see themselves as members of categories whose battleground in their struggle for advantage is the forum of state action. Legislation and public policy become features of a form of collective spoils system. And all this engenders and sanctions our old friend envy. This overall process feeds on itself – once government becomes such an arena for the conquest of gain people do not want to be left out of the race. Some people want to bear a lighter tax burden; others, to receive specific benefits. One group wants favourable laws; another, special treatment. Politics thus become conceived as a site where such claims are disputed and resolved, and the state emerges as an arbitrator between competing sets of aspirations and ambitions. So not only does collectivism engender the impersonality involved in seeing others as units who belong to rather abstract categories, it also compounds such distance between people by placing such units in frequent competition. By these routes do individuals become more tightly drawn into a mindset of conflict in relation to their fellow men. And where there is such friction and antagonism authentic community becomes ever more difficult to achieve.

In Great Britain in recent years the big state has been increasingly identified with the implementation of the modern secular theory of natural rights. This is part of the general shift away from trusting to tradition and convention and towards approaching problems from the perspective of innate entitlements. Such a process will probably be accelerated by the further doses of Americanisation and European- isation which seem to await us. Such a development conforms very well to the dynamics of mass society with all their impetus to uniformity and the breaking down of difference. In this case all people are said to be the same in the rights they have. Mill himself observed some hundred and fifty years ago how people were acquiring 'the same rights and liberties, and the same means of asserting them'. Nowadays rights are increasingly *à la mode.* It is very significant that contemporary public debate in Great Britain about reform of the Constitution has included proposals to introduce some kind of bill of rights and that in 2000 the government incorporated the European Convention for the Protection of Human Rights and Fundamental Freedoms into British law. In the same way we constantly hear talk of the 'rights' of certain groups, interests or lifestyles. Given these realities, there are good grounds for believing that rightsism will increasingly shape and mould public policy in the constitutional, economic, social and legal spheres. This will also probably act to sustain the policy of the big state. In the light of this history and this prospect, exploration of the desocialising impact of rightsist thought is more than incumbent. Here we probe the consequences of one of the most successful of all the false anthropologies of post-modernity.

The modern secular theory of natural rights is by no means all bad. It offers a series of safeguards against tyranny, an important framework for individual liberty, and a route by which to guarantee certain levels of material well-being. But as is the case with so many other post-modern doctrines, rightsism has a number of unforeseen consequences which work to fracture community. This is rooted in its theoretical point of departure. The age of Enlightenment push towards natural rights theory built upon previous Christian notions of natural law which involved very different philosophical bases and practical expressions. Indeed, to a certain extent such theory constitutes a heresy which betrays the parent from which it partly sprang. What modern rightsism has done is to promote rights against a background without God or the human soul. As these previous Christian notions argued, our rights derive from divine law, which requires that we behave in a way which conduces to our spiritual health and to that of others – a highly socialising imperative. It imposes a compelling duty upon us – to God, to ourselves, and to our neighbour – which involves obedience to divine law. Such law bestows upon the individual the 'right' to be treated by others in a way which conforms to that law – namely, in a way which promotes the well-being of his soul. Divine authority confers this central entitlement (from which other rights flow) which might be termed 'innate' in that it is natural to the laws of the cosmos, although in this tradition far more emphasis is placed upon obligations and responsibilities than upon entitlements. The contemporary secular theory of natural rights, however, neglects this spiritualist line of reasoning. Indeed, rightsism, as it is currently usually propounded, acts in subtle but forceful fashion to divert attention away from a spiritualist approach to rights which works more towards duties and in favour of community. At the same time, like collectivism, it shifts attention away from the soul, its stewardship, and the role of culture in expressing and promoting spiritual health. Such processes in themselves work for social fragmentation. But the modern secular theory of natural rights has other corrosive effects.

At a general level rightsism is a creed which tends to neglect the community and to place exaggerated emphasis upon the individual. This is implied in its conceptual point of departure. The great rightsist thinkers from Locke to Rawls usually begin by asking themselves what individuals would insist upon before agreeing to participate in society. But in reality we are born into existing communities and cultures – with all the roles and relationships that this condition implies. Rightsists thus often have the habit of failing to dwell upon the texture and character of existing community; they direct their gaze away from what helps to bind men together within society; and they frequently fail to explore the needs and requirements of man's social nature. The spiritual dimensions of life in community are frequently just swept under the carpet, if recognised at all. Instead, such thinkers often formulate theories and proposals which approach society from an individualist point of view and then proceed to draw up principles which involve people relating to each other in terms of respect for personal rights. In fact what is often being encouraged is a mutual agreement to pursue private interest. There is frequently an impulse towards the drawing up of reciprocal accords to engage in egoism. Selfish individualism here finds a powerful doctrinal champion. By such routes rightsism acts to undermine the associations and connections, the shared tissues and binding links, and the cultural girders and struts of society which permit the flourishing of human nature. This, indeed, is one of the primary criticisms levelled at the post-modern theory of natural rights. It has been observed that such critics believe that:

> we should relate to each other in a spirit of solidarity and mutual caring, of readiness to offer help whenever it is needed. Such a spirit binds us together by ties of 'community', without which human life is shallow and even unnatural. A culture of rights, they claim, is a culture of strangers. Humanity cannot live by rights alone.[51]

One result of this rightsist individualism is to provide yet another impulse to deculturalisation. The loss of emphasis on the dimension of community, the stress on each individual person, the relative lack of interest in what actually binds people together within a living society – all these weaken those components of the inherited cultural patrimony which are designed to ensure social cohesion. Rightsism involves a shift in orientation away from tradition towards a theoretical framework; a move from what has been tried and tested over time to an abstract approach; and the supplanting of inheritance by a highly intellectualised set of organising principles. Habit, custom and convention lose ground to novel points of departure. Much of what previously kept society together, that which was implicitly shared as part of a common project, is made redundant. The cultural constellation made up of the shared tissue and binding links of society is rendered obsolete by what from many points of view appears indeed to be a 'culture of strangers'. A people becomes deprived of its anthropological heritage. Once again we encounter the deleterious process of cultural drainage. And because contemporary rightsism is not rooted in perceptions of God and the soul, this creed necessarily involves an assault on what remains of Christian culture.

At a more specific level, rightsism desocialises in two special ways. Firstly, the individual is encouraged to see society as something which gives him things and which supplies him with advantages. He is not encouraged to see it in terms of a living community to which he must contribute and in which he must participate. There is little idea that at a personal level he fashions the context in which others must live – the whole emphasis is on what is done for him and not on what is done by him. Once again we come across the attitude that society is a sort of dispensing machine. In this sense it is highly suggestive that few talk about 'innate duties', which perhaps would be an equally valid concept. In addition, because resources are always limited and there is no clear agreement as to where these rights stop, rightsism as it is presently conceived is a direct invitation to conflict – citizens are prompted to struggle to persuade the state to satisfy their specific needs and wants. Such conflict is also expressed in the struggle between different groups to ensure their specific 'rights' – a process which involves a sectionalist fracturing of community.

So although rightsism in its best form is designed to project and advance the fulfilment and dignity of the individual, it can in reality act to deprive him of one his most precious possessions – community.

Many of these deleterious effects are described by the American legal
scholar M.A. Glendon:

> Our rights talk, in its absoluteness, promotes unrealistic expectations,
> heightens social conflict, and inhibits dialogue that might lead
> towards consensus, accommodation, or at least the discovery of
> common ground. In its silence concerning responsibilities, it seems
> to condone acceptance of the benefits of living in a democratic
> social welfare state, without accepting the corresponding personal
> and civic obligations. In its relentless individualism, it fosters a
> climate that is inhospitable to society's losers, and that systematically
> disadvantages caretakers and dependants, young and old. In its
> neglect of civil society, it undermines the principal seedbeds of
> civic and personal virtue. In its insularity, it shuts out potentially
> important aids to the process of self-corrective learning.[52]

The Mighty Market

What of the mighty market? Economism has been intimately bound up
with the giant economy and the impersonal market. In recent decades
political debate (and policy) have been strongly shaped by a conflict
between various forms of collectivism and an approach which places
immense emphasis on the benefits of the free market. 'Marketism'
might be a suitable appellation for this latter creed (one might also
employ the phrase 'market correctness'). This time we are dealing with
sympathies largely to be found on the political Right. Marketism made
rapid progress in the Anglo-Saxon world during the 1980s and was able
to secure a strong footing in many countries of Eastern Europe after the
fall of the Berlin Wall, leading at times to a mistakenly hurried
transformation to market methods. Much of this doctrine is to be found
in the pages of a book by two British exponents which bears the highly
significant title 'The New Enlightenment'(1986):

> We are on the way to a liberal state. Some would call it a 'minimal'
> state, or a 'night-watchman' state. It is inspired by the notion that
> the peaceful enjoyment of our own property and the free pursuit of
> our own ends, in communities in which others are likewise free,
> comprise the highest political good. The scenario above shows how
> this state grows logically from a negative right: the right of
> individuals to use their own property for their own purposes without
> interference from others...Not all New Enlightenment thinkers

agree that we want a 'minimal' state. They all agree, however, on the importance of the tradition of the 'limited' state, whose job it is to safeguard the rights of individuals. This tradition says that a state is no more than the individuals who compose it.[53]

As a current of intellectual theory, the marketists cannot rival the postmodernists in size and influence but they nonetheless have a significant presence in the right-wing intelligentsia and the disciplines of economics and political science. Although the point is hard to prove, it is likely that the marketist outlook is perhaps now most embraced and implemented by managers, entrepreneurs and businessmen in the world of manufacturing, commerce and finance. Marketism usually involves the idea that what is of primary importance within a society is a free enterprise economy; that what the market promotes is bound to be largely valuable; and that the future of civilisation is to be secured by an adherence to market principles. The orientation is clearly economistic in that it is the economic dimension of man and of society which is deemed to be of primary importance. The central concern in this outlook is the world of wealth and property. From many points of view marketism, like collectivism and rightsism, becomes a kind of philosophy of life, shaping behaviour, values and attitudes, personal identity, and collective perspectives. Like them, too, it is not all bad. There can be no doubt that free market methods can be very effective generators of wealth; that economic enterprise forms an important part of individual human expression; and that general innovation and advance receive valuable impetus from the pursuit of personal gain. Equally, the big state by a variety of mechanisms can indeed dull and stunt economic growth – as witness the effects of the dead hand of bureaucracy. But in this sphere, as in so many others within modernity, the road to hell is paved with good intent. Marketist thinking and practice acts to erode community in a large number of ways. Here, too, we encounter some of the key origins of our cultural crisis. It is surely no surprise that this creed emerged with greatest force in the last quarter of the twentieth century, when this crisis really began to bite.

Firstly, some comments on the general damaging effects of market correctness. Like societalism and rightsism, it is deculturalising in impact. This development was foreshadowed in the writings of the great classical economists of the eighteenth and nineteenth centuries – figures like Smith, Ricardo, Nassau Senior, Mill and Marshall – and of their various popularisers. Such thinkers tended to conceive of the economy as a kind of detached machine somehow working autonomously within society. They tended to neglect the role of beliefs, habits, mentalities, customs and convention in shaping the economic experience of individuals and of nations. Much of their thought and analysis was marked by a conspicuous aculturalism. In perceiving the economy, or the market, as an independent machine, and in advocating policies and principles by which it could be defended and assisted, these thinkers – and their descendants – greatly underestimated the importance and value of a society's anthropological inheritance for the economy and for the community as a whole. This was an elementary error which looked at from a distance defies belief. Anyone who travels can see how culture leaves a very deep mark on the world of wealth and its generation. One need only go to Italy and perceive the galaxy of family-based small- and medium-sized businesses or to Japan with its ideas of corporate unity to grasp the point. A similar neglect of wider features of society which is implicit in much contemporary marketism necessarily encourages a weakening of those very features. A destructive orientation is at work. There may well be high salaries and abundant goods because of marketist policies, but the traditions which sustain community can become abandoned and lost. Marketism can encourage a kind of fixation on the economy to the detriment of the stewardship of other vital elements of our life together. It, too, can boil down to nothing more than a tawdry social contract based upon a reciprocal hands-off agreement to engage in the pursuit of private personal gain.

This encouragement of deculturalisation is underpinned by a related feature of marketism – the belief that the future of our national civilisation lies in the achievement of economic growth and prosperity. Marketism constantly informs people that what really matters, what is of paramount importance, what towers above everything else in significance, is to ensure that the market so functions as to provide us with a ceaseless fountain of wealth and riches. In this it is intimately bound up with what is now termed 'consumerism' – itself a marked feature of mass society. We are not told to look to the soul, to dwell upon spiritual health, or to form authentic community. We are directed to very different ends, to the things of this world. But, to repeat a famous phrase, can man live by bread alone? Will the success of the market really bring him happiness? Can the economy truly supply man with what he needs? Should we really frame our life in society predominantly with reference to economic achievement? Of course resources are important and there is no need to engage in some sort of extreme neo-puritan reaction. Poverty and want are evils to be eliminated; economic opportunity and work form an important part of human fulfilment. But from many points of view and in many ways the exclusive pursuit of material wealth provokes the loss of social riches. The great risk of marketism is that we lose sight of other elements which are of essential importance to our purpose in this world. 'Neither a market economy nor even general abundance constitutes the crowning achievement of human life', warned Solzhenitsyn, 'The purity of social relations is a more fundamental value than the level of abundance'.[54]

Marketism also promotes, supports and legitimates an approach to the affairs of men which is highly characteristic of the lifestyle of selfish individualism – the placing of primary value on money and success. People are understood not in terms of their spiritual condition, or their virtues, or their talents, but with reference to their worldly achievements. In this outlook, in a very intense way, what becomes important is not what an individual is but what he has. In a sense a man becomes his property. This kind of perspective is ever present in the world of advertising – that instructive mirror of the way we live now. Every day we are bombarded by the idea that the possession of certain goods is what is to be really admired; that wealth and power are the real litmus tests of success in life; and that the models to be followed are those of economic acquisition. There is a habitual stress on the social prestige and approval which accompany such achievements. The rich man wins the beautiful girl; the well-dressed girl wins the handsome man; the expensive car draws admiring glances; the well-heeled couple have flocks of friends; and people of wealth receive the esteem of all. Conversely, economic humility is depicted as a humiliation; modesty of riches, a malediction; poverty, a denigration. In essence: not to have is not to be. Of course such models and ideas can only have appeal and be effective if they fall on fertile ground. It is because so many of us accept this vision of things that sellers use these techniques. Such models and ideas are found far and wide in contemporary society, are prominent in the mass media and films, present in conversation and thought, and expressed in plans and behaviour.

This massive emphasis on money and success pours barrels of dissolvent on the bonds of community. We are led to see people not as individuals but as kinds of wallets; not as persons but as the bearers of wealth. We are encouraged to relate to others not in terms of love but with reference to what they possess. Emphasis on consumer goods turns people into objects, and humanity becomes lost behind a giant screen constructed out of banknotes. But this is only one part of the story. Marketism's stress on wealth in the perception and treatment of others is also a mighty excluder and marginaliser. It leads to those who are not prosperous, or who are not capable of becoming rich, becoming distanced or shunted aside. Here one notices a reason for the widespread use of the horrible contemporary term 'loser'. There is a lack of interest in such members of society, a lack of concern, a lack of contact. Like the famous untouchables of India, they are to be deprived of the company of the successful. So it is that the sick and the handicapped, the elderly and the weak, the poor and the injured, those of few gifts or modest abilities, the unfortunate and the unlucky, the attacked and the wounded, the hungry and the needy, strangers and orphans – in short, all those whom these perverse modern anti-values dismiss as being of little interest – become ignored and avoided. Such people are not integrated into society, helped to participate, aided in contributing to the community, but subjected to a process of desocialisation which compounds their suffering. The Christian concept of the neighbour is murdered; and the Good Samaritan is strangled within us.

In a very direct way marketism sustains and promotes the lifestyle of selfish individualism. It is argued that the free enterprise economy is a place where each person should pursue his own material gain and that the great point of existence is to accrue wealth within and through the market. The person who is solely concerned in life with his own economic enrichment receives sanction; other individuals are encouraged to embrace his position; and the sin of greed gains massive legitimacy. But we are not dealing here with a simple question of compass-directions and an impulse towards egoism. There is also the idea that the market is a place of competition and struggle between people; a place where the stronger survive. Once again, we encounter a source of conflict generation. The market becomes an aggressive place where every man is to fend for himself. Responsibilities towards others, concern for fellow citizens, worry about the consequences of one's actions – all these elements become relegated to a lowly position of importance. In this outlook it is further urged that what the market allows is somehow 'right'. Just as societalism turns society into a sort of a God – the great point of reference for human affairs – so marketism involves a form of implicit worship of the economy. If the workings of the free market permit something, then it is somehow thought to be acceptable. If a man evicts, or sacks, or exploits, or speculates, then this is somehow legitimate because it is allowed by the 'free' economy. There thus emerges a discouragement of any kind of moral or ethical approach to individual economic activity which by its nature parallels the impact of determinism and relativism. By these various mechanisms, marketism drives wedges between people and promotes social fracture. A splendid critique of free market motivations without reference to authentic ethics, and of how they can be combated by economic initiatives centred around a sense of social responsibility, is to be found in Frank Capra's cinematic masterpiece *It's a Wonderful Life* (1946).

No analysis of marketism would be complete without a discussion of its interaction with consumerism. The mass market and the giant economy lay enormous stress upon the acquisition and the possession of commodities. We are constantly encouraged to consume, to purchase, to throw away, and to renew. Is not the gigantic industry of advertising directed towards this end? It is hardly surprising that the term 'consumer' now occupies such a prominent position in the post-modern vocabulary. What we are repeatedly told is that these material goods are of the very greatest importance in our lives and that we should place great value upon them. Indeed, we are invited to judge ourselves and others by the nature of the relationship we have with them. The feelings and sensations which they can provoke are held to be valuable in the extreme. The more we have, the 'better' we are said to be. The whole orientation of this emphasis is to direct attention away from God, the soul, and union with others, towards products and services. We are led to worship things and to steward commodities, to live the life of the consumer and to commune with what we possess. Here we see a very direct link between materialist thought and adherence to the narrowly material. Human relations become directed away from relationships with other people towards relationships with objects. Community becomes supplanted by personal ties with mere possessions. At this point we are not far from the syndrome of the miser – the pitiable and lonely rich man who finds company in gold coins he talks to during the night.

Overall, as John Paul II stressed:

A *disconcerting conclusion* about the most recent period should serve to enlighten us: side-by-side with the miseries of underdevelopment, themselves unacceptable, we find ourselves up against a form of *superdevelopment*, equally inadmissible, because like the former it is contrary to what is good and true happiness. This superdevelopment, which consists in an *excessive* availability of every kind of material goods for the benefit of certain social groups, easily makes people slaves of "possession" and of immediate gratification, with no other horizon than the multiplication or continual replacement of the things already owned with others still better. This is the so-called civilization of "consumption" or "consumerism", which involves so much "throwing-away" and "waste"...All of us experience firsthand the sad effects of this blind submission to pure consumerism: in the first place a crass materialism, and at the same time a *radical dissatisfaction*, because one quickly learns – unless one is shielded from the flood of publicity and the ceaseless and tempting offers of products – that the more one possesses the more one wants, while deeper aspirations remain unsatisfied and perhaps even stifled.[55]

One aspect of the culture of consumerism requires special comment. Personal debt in Great Britain has reached historically high levels. Mortgages, credit cards, bank overdrafts and other instruments led to the accumulation of a total personal debt of over three trillion pounds by 2004.[56] Post-modern man is also indebted man. The constant encouragement to consumption, which is so rooted in contemporary culture, has been a powerful factor in generating such high levels of debt, now well beyond annual GDP. Another factor has been that the old cultural resistance to the contracting of debts much rooted in Christian ethics, previously much communicated through the family, has been severely eroded through deChristianisation and the decline of the family. Of course the problem with debts is that they have to be paid – a reality that produces further stress (indeed the mass stress caused by mass indebtedness is a further new phenomenon of our epoch) and is yet another factor that helps to make the post-modern age the age of anxiety. This very high level of debt was one of the factors behind the banking crisis of the second part of 2008. This crisis revealed on the part of many leaders of the financial sector an extraordinary neglect of the common good, a striking absence of moral self-regulation and a devastating lack of a sense of ethical responsibility, all elements natural to the post-modern culture rooted in the materialist matrix analysed in the pages of this volume. This crisis also raised very serious questions about the wisdom of the contemporary doctrine of market correctness.

Economism has very injurious effects in the sphere of another economic feature of mass society – the huge firm or giant place of work. This sphere is very favourable to its damaging impact. Giantism produces an environment where the individual has to deal with a context which is marked by the impersonal. The sheer size of factories, companies, offices, supermarkets, state departments and all the rest creates a framework where the individual often lacks personal ties with the large numbers of people with whom he comes into contact. The lack of identity produced by such a situation naturally encourages a sabotaging of the idea of a shared project. In such a context it becomes much easier to believe the economistic tenet that others are objects with whom it is necessary to compete; that in reality economic life is chiefly a struggle between selfish individuals; and that what people are doing in their work is solely a question of making money, acquiring power, or achieving status. Powerism, too, finds fertile terrain in the harsh and often anonymous world of economic giantism. Personal and friendly ties and a shared sense of belonging and participation are not present to counter the notions and sentiments connected with the judgement that the human experience is essentially about power.

Very similar observations may be made about the world of consumers, where economism also makes its presence felt. The individual finds himself in front of huge banks, or massive retail stores, or vast companies. His relationship with them is highly impersonal and based almost exclusively on purchase. One need only compare the experience of the familiar corner shop with what happens when a person buys from a supermarket to grasp the point. And if there is only purchase then of course it becomes very easy to believe the economistic assertion that money alone is what is of importance. Mass advertising reinforces this whole process by making consumers into manipulated objects whose sole function is to buy.

Politics

The materialist matrix and mass politics have had a very intimate relationship. The political world has been a major force behind the materialist locomotive, and the materialist matrix has left a deep imprint on the character of national politics. Given the notable importance and influence of politics in modern society, the vital role of this area of national life in shaping the way people think and behave is *a priori* likely to be of major consequence. Although there have been great differences between the political parties, there have also been great affinities at certain key points. As with our wider national culture, marked variety and variegation conceals deep levels of uniformity – non-spiritualist approaches to man and the human experience are thick on the ground. What can be said about this relationship *at the level of thought*?

Certainly a notable force in the diffusion of the materialist matrix within mass politics has been supplied by secular and non-religious intellectuals. From Karl Marx and Henry George (1839-1897) to many of today's social scientists, and from the classical economists to Keynes and Friedman, theorists have done much to shape the way politicians think. This process has been strengthened by the expansion of universities which has taken place in recent decades and the increased exposure of future politicians to the ideas and attitudes circulating in the world of higher education. Through publications, direct advice or indirect influence, thinkers wedded in one form or other to the materialist matrix have done much to shape the beliefs, language, and orientations of politics. The secularisation of the intelligentsia over the last hundred years has necessarily meant a secularisation of their input into politics and policy. Christian thinkers such as T.S. Eliot or R.H. Tawney (1880-1962) have been far and few between. There have been very few in Great Britain to match the vast array of Catholic theorists who provided supports to Continental Christian Democracy.

The political parties have done a great deal to promote the false anthropologies of post-modernity and their associated ways of thinking and acting. Humanism and rationalism have been conspicuous by their presence. During the last hundred years politicians have often argued that they have the cures for the nation's ills. They have claimed that it is through political action that real advance for the nation can be achieved. The individual citizen is to look to them, to parliament, and to government for his future. This involves an encouragement of humanism in that it suggests that human understanding, control and direction are what constitute the key to success. Divine power, intervention and initiative do not get a look in. Equally, all this is to be done rationally and through the use of the rational faculties, and is based on the belief that reason is capable of understanding (and reforming) something so immensely complicated and intricate as the workings of human society. Mass politics have also been increasingly imbued with relativism, which has thereby found expression and support. The observation that each voter has his opinion, that politics are made up of different opinions, that each party perspective is neither right nor wrong but another point of view, that every person has the right to his opinion, that what matters is not the opinion itself but the freedom to express it, and that each opinion is of equal value because each individual has equal rights – all this is meat and drink to the relativist perspective. There are also constant references within mass politics to the relativist 'virtues' of the balanced view, the moderate approach, tolerance and compromise. And in significant fashion, whether in good faith or not, there is today a great deal of political shying away from the rejection of a point of view on the grounds that it fails to reflect moral and ethical truth. Economism has also made its presence felt. There has been a mounting emphasis within national politics on the need to secure economic welfare and prosperity for the people. Whatever their location on the party spectrum, politicians have increasingly presented themselves as the generous operators of state levers who will provide prosperity to the voters. Against this background it is hardly surprising that to listen to contemporary political debate is to encounter endless references to tax rates, growth levels, wealth distribution, help for specific groups, social security, and all the rest.

The ways in which this prosperity is to be achieved also reflect the thinking of much of the materialist matrix. The societalist perspective has received great support and expression from a constant emphasis on the importance of promoting a reform of socio-economic structures. It has been repeatedly argued that the way forward for man lies in 'changing society'. The same may be said of economistic marketism with its exaggerated praise for the free market economy. And rightsism is of course a quintessentially political doctrine which in its various different forms finds expression in – and is promoted by – the world of mass politics. It is also a creed which in recent decades has become much concerned with economic questions.

What about this relationship at the *level of practice*? The conduct of mass politics has been intimately bound up with the various phenomena and manifestations of the culture of the materialist matrix. The use of opinion polls, public relations techniques, mass media advertising, and all the other methods of manipulating and moulding public opinion, are part and parcel of the treating of people as objects. Furthermore, mass politics often involve behaviour on the part of politicians and parties which tends to see people as impersonal units or groups of units. In the same way their point of contact with the electors is very much a question of television and its images. In front of the camera they cannot even see the people they are addressing. At least on the late-Victorian and Edwardian platform there were visual points of connection. By such routes voters have come to resemble the dots of Welles's Great Wheel speech.

At the same time – and this is a phenomenon much aided by relativism – political life is characterised by a great deal of lying. Much of this is implicit in modern techniques of presentation which reflect the impulse to dissimulation to be found in modern methods of advertising (one need only think here of the figure of the 'spin-doctor' or such infamous practices as 'burying news')[57] but it is also powerfully encouraged by the common idea that there is no such thing as objective truth or at least that it is a more than elusive entity. Thus consciously untruthful statements are often defended with the facile assertion that they are somehow legitimate 'points of view'.

Mass politics have acted to generate and sustain conflict, and thus division, within our national community. It is worth recalling that at the end of the eighteenth century the concept of party was frequently criticised on the grounds that it was divisive of the nation. Today, politicians frequently appear as adversarial and hostile agents engaged in a perpetual and often aggressive struggle. Television confrontations, infantile slogans and puerile advertising campaigns (so reminiscent of the competitive commercial world) bear ample testimony to this reality. By such routes, and others, the political parties have done a great deal to polarise opinion and encourage friction between the voters. Indeed, they often draw electoral lifeblood from the very systems of antagonism which they do so much to engender. So often nowadays people vote 'against' a party rather than 'in favour' of another. All this has been encouraged by our antiquated two-party system, which has been kept alive by a grossly unrepresentative electoral system. Since 1979 no governing party has achieved a majority of the popular vote, but nonetheless the days after have been marked by preposterous 'victory' celebrations – an act full of connotations of conflict. The habit of seeing the electorate in terms of competing groups, of striving to secure the support of rival categories, has been a further factor in the dissolution of our national polity, and testifies to that 'gradual fragmentation of the body politic into a variety of special interest groups that no longer define their political objectives in terms of a better society, but rather in terms of narrow self-interest'.[58]

In addition, political life at the summit seems increasingly separate from the rest of the community. More and more remoteness characterises the relationship between the governed and the governors. Part of this springs from the very mentality of those who participate in national politics. If liberationists are present in the power points of cultural formation and marketists in the world of business, perhaps powerists naturally gravitate towards the world of political power. Many politicians seem to be convinced that politics is essentially a matter of career, of self-advancement, and of acquiring power (a telling expression of powerism) – and act accordingly. Such an attitude, and the propensity to lie and to engage in conflict at a variety of levels, can only widen the fissures within the British *polis*.

The Mass Media

Mill observed of the Englishmen of his time 'they now read the same things, listen to the same things, see the same things'. With their capacity to bear directly and concurrently upon vast swathes of the population, the mass media now constitute a mighty instrument of cultural moulding which is located at the heart of mass society. What is beamed across the airwaves, set up in newspaper print, projected on the silver screen, or pumped down the ubiquitous 'box', has scant regard for social or regional variation. Because of this vast and unprecedented power the mass media are able to shape and influence thought and behaviour in a way which Mill himself would never have been able to imagine. A mass impact on mass life is constantly at work, and we are now light-years away from the eighteenth-century world of distant villages and slow-travelling news. The totalitarian regimes were acutely aware of the importance of this modern phenomenon and paved the way in developing innovative techniques and forms of propaganda. Such governments were ruthless and relentless exponents of cultural politics but at times found themselves on the receiving end of what the mass media could do – in the 1980s the Eastern European Communist regimes were hit hard by TV and radio transmissions beamed from beyond their borders.

A simple question naturally poses itself – what is the relationship between the mass media and contemporary culture? In Great Britain such forces are able to reinforce and reproduce existing cultural patterns. Of course, they are not alone in this function and they are by no means homogenous as a grouping – they are connected in various ways to different parts of society and often perform rather different roles. But they are certainly united in their general adherence to the materialist matrix. So if we want to understand a feature of mass society which is intimately connected with the generation and maintenance of our contemporary form of national civilisation, the mass media should be subjected to very close scrutiny.

The world of the television, the press, the radio and cinema is a constant promoter and reflector of the false anthropologies of post-modernity. This largely acts at an implicit and unconscious level, but the process is powerfully present nonetheless. Naturally enough, the sets of attitudes and forms of behaviour which spring from these materialist visions of man also receive repeated exposition. This should not surprise us in the least – much of the time the mass media are merely describing and reporting what goes on within contemporary society. They act as mirrors which reflect back how we are. Yet at another level they behave like magnifying lenses and act to enlarge common features and elements. In their emphasis on wealth and power, violence and destruction, science and technology, the successful and the beautiful, sexuality and eroticism – much of which is animated by a desire to capture attention, secure sales and increase viewing levels – the mass media act to raise the profile of a number of phenomena powerfully promoted by the materialist matrix. When one observes how sexuality is portrayed in Hollywood films, wealth is admired in advertising, or success is worshipped in soap operas, one comes across many of the features of this process. At the same time, the ideas and tenets of relativism are constantly showered down upon us. In converse fashion, all sorts of other values and perspectives are markedly absent. Traditional Christian culture, for example, is weak and its influence slight. A few special columns or peripheral programmes on Sunday attest to a long-term process of marginalisation.

There is one input of the materialist matrix into the mass media – or into much of the world they represent – which requires special exploration. Mass systems of communication and of cultural formation have opened up new opportunities for intellectuals and the educated classes. A great many representatives of this category now occupy positions of power and influence within the mass-media galaxy. From the age of the Enlightenment onwards thinkers and men of learning have played an important role in redefining man. In the past they relied upon the written word and rather narrow audiences. Today they have vastly more powerful instruments to hand. Moreover, the great expansion of universities from the 1960s onwards, with their important role in the promotion of the various forms of the culture of the materialist matrix, has provided a significant training ground for those who now work in the various sections of the mass media. The fact that that section of the political spectrum known as the 'politically correct' lays great stress upon the practice of cultural politics, and exercises a notable influence within the media and its higher education supports, well reveals how this area of mass society is intimately connected with the promotion and reproduction of the materialist matrix. The mass media now offer opportunities to the intelligentsia by which to influence people in a way which was unimaginable three hundred years ago. TV screens, for example, at times have become the pulpits of today's world – and not without the desired results. And what is preached involves, whether implicitly or explicitly, very distinctive ideas about man and his condition. Paul Dacre's comments on the ideological orientations of the BBC, for all their polemical character, deserve to be read with attention:

> BBC journalism starts from the premise of leftwing ideology: it is hostile to conservatism and the traditional right, Britain's past and British values, America, Ulster unionism, Euroscepticism, capitalism and big business, the countryside, Christianity and family values. Conversely, it is sympathetic to Labour, European federalism, the state and state spending, mass immigration, minority rights, multiculturalism, alternative lifestyles, abortion, and progressiveness in the education and the justice systems...Thus BBC journalism is presented through a leftwing prism that affects everything – the choice of stories, the way they are angled, the choice of interviewees and, most pertinently, the way those interviewees are treated. The BBC's journalists, protected from real competition, believe that only their worldview constitutes moderate, sensible and decent opinion. Any dissenting views – particularly those held by popular papers – are therefore considered, by definition, to be extreme and morally beyond the pale.[59]

Another observation should be made about the mass media and the materialist matrix. Language reflects culture. Anthropologists are more than aware of the vital role which language plays in transmitting and shaping the shared sets of perceiving and acting which characterise a society. The language we inherit and we develop expresses and moulds ways of understanding, reacting and evaluating. The mass media have certainly played an important role in the erosion of the Celtic languages and our regional dialects – a rich inheritance of wisdom, identity and belonging has thereby been lost. Forces which played a vital part in expressing local community, and in imparting ideas and attitudes which worked in its favour, have been steamrollered. Indeed, the national cultural revivalism now to be found in Scotland and Wales may in part be seen as a reaction to this development. At the same time our contemporary language, which has been so heavily shaped by the mass media, has helped to promote the materialist matrix. It contains words, terms and meanings which are rooted in post-modern perspectives. This is especially true of the world of moral discourse. Where now is the language of God and the devil, good and evil, right and wrong, the virtues and the vices? Today we are much more immersed in a vocabulary of 'caring' and 'welfare', 'points of view' and 'opinions', or 'values' and 'attitudes'. The very concepts expressed and encouraged by our standardised language – which in turn is so shaped by what is churned out daily by the mass media – bear witness to a transformation in our civilisation. They also act to reinforce and underpin these changes. The dominant culture of post-modernity has produced its own diction.

Americanisation

The mass media are intimately connected to another area of cultural change – Americanisation, a phenomenon which is receiving increasing study. 'To what extent', ask some scholars, 'has the Americanisation of the global village changed the lives, including the hearts and minds, of the inhabitants of that village?'[60] 'The confrontation between fundamentalism and enlightenment values is a battle that is being joined', observe others, 'and it is one in which resistance to perceived Americanisation, or at another level, the forces of modernity, takes the form of turning back to or re-inventing the traditions of a pre-enlightenment past'.[61] The presence of a shared language and the large role played by the USA in British mental horizons have meant that this superpower has spread waves of influence deep into the contours of our national culture. These waves have in particular been transmitted through films, television and rock music (although one may also think of the importation of political and business practices and the transfer of ideas from the academic and intellectual world). We have also taken on some of the language of our transatlantic cousins with all the impact on our way of thinking that this implies.

A facile and superficial anti-Americanism still has a certain residual purchase in Western countries. However, it cannot be denied that the United States of America has made a vital contribution to modern Western civilisation. Two world wars and a tenacious commitment to democratic methods, for example, bear testimony to this truth. Our hemisphere, and the world, would be immensely impoverished without the existence of this extraordinary nation, with which Great Britain, to an extent greater than any other country, has had an intimate historical relationship. Yet, at the same time, it must also be conceded that America, which is many things and has great riches of the spirit, also has within it prominent cultural currents that are closely bound up with the materialist matrix. This does not mean to say, of course, that within the USA there are not other major tendencies as well – religious sentiment, for example, with all its community-generating effects, remains high. We would, indeed, have done much better to import realities from this sphere.

Three cultural currents intimately connected with the materialist matrix have wielded especial influence from America – the modern secular theory of natural rights, market correctness and political correctness. Rightsism has come across with increasing vigour from the land of the American Declaration of Independence and during the 1980s a number of thinkers, especially the so-called 'monetarists', were able to achieve an audience for their marketist views in much of right-wing England. The postmodernists, however, have perhaps proved the most influential. Was not the phrase 'politically correct' originally coined in liberal America? Academic and intellectual circles have been one principal channel of influence of this outlook; the world of TV programmes and films, another. 'The power of American culture to influence ideas, attitudes, tastes and desires', it is observed, 'is contained most directly in the images which Hollywood conveys'.[62] One detailed study of the American film industry reveals how a very small band of people have sought to implement a clear programme of cultural politics. We are told that they have been engaged in an 'ongoing war on traditional values' and a 'war against standards' in which an 'assault on organized faith' plays a central part. This involves a 'preference for the perverse', a 'glorification of ugliness', and a 'bias for the bizarre'. This exercise in cultural politics has at times been conducted against Hollywood's economic interest – an idea 'so revolutionary, so disturbing, counter-intuitive, that most analysts refuse to take it seriously – despite an overwhelming accumulation of evidence'.[63]

Uniformity

Sameism threads its way in and out of the materialist matrix and mass society itself has close reinforcing links with this way of thinking. By various routes the impulse towards uniformity and shared experiences acts to give credibility to sameism and to turn people naturally towards its tenets. In homogenising culture and promoting assimilation, mass society provides very fertile ground for the belief that in reality we are the same. Looking around him in such a context, the individual is spontaneously encouraged to believe that men by nature are indeed more or less 'equal' or the same. 'What is' often has the habit of being seen as 'what must be', and this rule applies very well in this instance. Mill himself perceived this process when, in describing mass society, he bracketed shared conditions with shared aspirations and ambitions. In reciprocal fashion sameist thought has the effect of encouraging and reinforcing those aspects of mass society which work towards uni-formity of condition amongst individuals. This is especially true in the political and constitutional spheres (one thinks of the idea of one man, one vote) but it has also been at work within areas of social and government policy (one thinks of the idea of equal access to health care). Mass society and sameism have had a potent symbiotic relationship of no peripheral significance.

Mill also predicted that the dynamics of mass society would produce a sameness which would rule out constructive individual dissent – everyone would become a kind of conformist dot. He also feared that 'all deviation from that type will come to be considered impious, immoral, even monstrous and contrary to nature'. From one point of view this prediction was exaggerated. Despite the impulses towards assimilation, there remains great variety within mass society in terms of beliefs, party loyalties, lifestyles and interests. Pluralism certainly involves marked plurality. Do we not live, for example, in the age of sub-cultures? However, from another angle, albeit in a way that he did not intend, Mill possessed an accurate crystal-ball. The uniformity he predicted is to be most found at a spiritual and moral level. This is what Solzhenitsyn seems to have had in mind when he asserted that Western society 'moves along rigidly defined channels in generally accepted directions'.[64] Moulded by the impress of the materialist matrix, and interacting with it at a whole number of points, mass society is increasingly inhabited by people who frequently tend to think and act within the parameters, patterns and framework of that matrix and its associated universe. There may be variety, but it is often a variety which takes place within certain limits – the zebras may have different markings but they are always zebras. What is increasingly absent within mass society is a commitment to the soul, an embrace of the life according to the Spirit, and the promotion of ways of living which express such attitudes. Indeed, such elements are subject to precisely the pressure of elimination which Mill so feared. It is in spiritual ill-health that our society is increasingly expressing a propensity to uniformity and at the same time it is becoming increasingly characterised by an attack on the opposite of spiritual ill-health – as healthy souls can often testify only too well.[65] Herein is to be found much of its real underlying sameness.

Deculturalisation

In many respects mass society produces an environment marked by transience, the instant and rapid change. People daily come across individuals they will never meet again; products, TV programmes and buildings come and go with rapidity; individuals change their friends, partners and spouses; people are mobile in relation to their occupations and place of residence; what is news on the mass media today is forgotten tomorrow; and we seem perpetually locked into a permanent technological revolution. All this is compounded by, and at times linked to, the rapid cultural changes encouraged by the materialist matrix over the last four decades. Divorce and crime, feminism and homosexuality, the continuing decline of Christianity and the crisis of institutions, alterations in manners and the independence of youth, and all the beliefs and attitudes connected with such areas are part and parcel of a hurtling velocity in alterations in our human environment. Furthermore, desocialisation itself seems to be a rapid process and part of that rapidity of evolution which characterises the cultural crises that peoples sometimes have to undergo. But our biological origins would suggest that man is not made for such endemic and constant transience. 'We create an environment so ephemeral, unfamiliar and complex', Alvin

Toffler warned, 'as to threaten millions with adaptive breakdown'.[66] The disorientation induced by this rapid change has as one of its natural features a growing inability on the part of individuals to know how they should react and respond to what they encounter in their human context. They are uncertain, hesitant, unsure as to forms of communication and behaviour. Increasingly, people do not know how to treat each other, and thus they are inhibited in interaction. This is a propulsive force behind our loss of ties.

The reality and consequences of transience form a part of a much wider process integral to desocialisation to which this study has repeatedly drawn attention – deculturalisation. Mass society, with its impulse towards the impersonal, has been an integral part of this process. A massive process of cultural deconstruction has been at work, and over a very short space of time, which now means that at all sorts of levels people do not know how to behave towards each other, act for each other, and live with each other. In our family experience, in our courtship patterns, in the relationship between men and women, in our friendships, in how we approach neighbours and those we work and do business with, and in our more collective lives in relation to institutions, government, politics and law, we are often at a loose end. We may have great individual autonomy and freedom, but we increasingly find that we no longer know how to live with others. ('How-to' books are needed because people do not know how to). We take part together in mass society, but a deeper shared experience fades ever more into the background. In proposing a programme of 'humanistic communitarianism'[67] in order to combat this development, Erich Fromm (1900-1980) wrote:

> We are a culture of consumers. We "drink in" the movies, the crime reports, the liquor, the fun. There is no active productive participation, no common unifying experience, no meaningful acting out of significant answers to life...what help is it to have almost no illiteracy, and the most widespread higher education which has existed at any time – if we have no collective expression of our total personalities, no common art and ritual? Undoubtedly a relatively primitive village in which there are still real feasts, common artistic shared expressions, and no literacy at all – is more advanced culturally and more healthy mentally than our educated, newspaper-reading, radio-listening culture.[68]

All this in itself produces loneliness and aloneness within the crowd, but it also opens up perilous prospects and risks. The inherited cultural system produced by many generations of evolution was not only designed to keep us together and foster life in society – it also had the function of avoiding grave errors. In this kind of new vacuum all sorts of dangerous elements can leap into the breach. An in-built and inherited resistance to them is increasingly no longer there. This is one way of understanding the contemporary emergence of the bizarre and the horrific, or the presence of forms of conduct which were once banished by mechanisms of social pressure. Perhaps in this sense there is much to be said for the 'conservative sensibility'. In this outlook there is not only a wish for the settled, the continuous and the ordered, but also a propensity to have faith in handed-down methods and notions. Oakeshott wrote that the 'man of conservative temperament believes that a known good is not lightly to be surrendered for an unknown better'.[69] 'We are afraid to put men to live and trade each on his own private stock of reason', affirmed Burke, 'because we suspect that this stock in each man is small, and the individuals would do better to avail themselves of the general bank and capital of nations, and of ages'.[70] Burke stressed the importance of taking received wisdom and behaviour seriously and emphasised that their value could often escape immediate rational analysis. It was the outcome of generations of experience, produced by the learning of ancestors. And Maritain for his part observed:

it is normal that in the political community the customs, the established traditions, the hereditarily developed instincts, the stock of experience accumulated in the unconscious, co-operate with the regular play of institutions for the purpose of giving direction to and stabilising the work of the consciousness and reason, and for the purpose of sparing men from the fluctuations and wanderings to which their intelligence is exposed when it is not rooted in firmly set tendencies.[71]

But when such an inheritance has gone, such checks are removed and grave risks are run. Toffler understood this very well and provided us with an incisive warning about the hazards of deculturalisation:

Take an individual out of his own culture and set him down suddenly in an environment sharply different from his own, with a different set of cues to react to – different conceptions of time, space, work, love, religion, sex and everything else – then cut him off from any hope of retreat to a more familiar landscape, and the dislocation he suffers is doubly severe. Moreover, if this new culture is itself in constant turmoil, and if – worse yet – its values are incessantly changing, the sense of disorientation will be still further intensified. Given few clues as to what kind of behaviour is rational under the radically new circumstances, the victim may well become a hazard to himself and others.[72]

*

By a whole host of routes, therefore, mass society and the materialist matrix have worked side by side, and with each other, to produce a weakening of bonds between people. Post-modern man increasingly finds himself in a context which systematically assaults his spiritual and biological nature. Called by his innate structures to community, he often finds, instead, that he has to face up to the realities of non-membership. The mind, the emotions and the spirit of man now find themselves under strain, as the frequent employment of the word 'stress' demonstrates only too well. Human beings are often deeply discontented at what the post-modern world has built for them, even though, paradoxically enough, they act collectively to sustain it. Despite the suffering, the post-modern building remains upright – indeed, it seems to become ever more solid with the passing of time. To explain this paradoxical state of affairs we must now turn our attention to how desocialisation reproduces itself – a by no means easy undertaking.

Chapter Nine

A Self-Reproducing System

Hitherto the forces which have worked for desocialisation have been subjected to examination. Now it is necessary to take the analysis a step further and to explore the mechanisms by which this dark cultural pattern reproduces itself. One of its great features is that despite the unhappiness it generates, it nonetheless manages to remain alive and kicking – and with a vengeance. Indeed, it seems to grow stronger as years pass. This chapter examines these mechanisms of self-reproduction and inquires into the deepest purpose of desocialisation. What we have before us is a process which systematically encourages ill-health in the souls of those who come into contact with it. Conversely, this cultural pattern is itself directly promoted by those who live on the dark side: like the shapes formed by searchlights on the night sky, its forms and character are moulded by the orientations, priorities and behaviour of sick souls. In this duality we encounter the supreme self-reproducing mechanism – desocialisation is both a product and a producer of spiritual ill-health. The implications of what has been constructed are dramatic: eternal life, the purpose of human life on earth, is countered. The soul is assaulted at its most important point – its rightful destiny.

No exhaustive account of these self-reproducing mechanisms is possible here but perhaps it is possible to capture the salient features of the terrain. Desocialisation reproduces itself in a number of principal ways, all of which are tenacious in the extreme. First of all, following the immutable spiritual structures of the cosmos, unhealthy souls themselves are naturally drawn towards the materialist matrix, act as its promoters, and thereby contribute to a system which generates the spiritual condition they represent. Secondly, the materialist matrix creates ways of thinking and behaving within post-modern British culture which provide a seeming empirical basis for believing that its tenets are correct. Thirdly, the ruthlessness of selfish individualism – especially as regards the pursuit of power and money – encourages people to adopt its methods out of the belief that this is the only way by which to avoid being left out of the race. Fourthly, deepening spiritual impoverishment means that people are faced with a lack of spiritual leadership which itself means that no directions are given to the exit doors. Fifthly, the anomic condition produces a spiritual ignorance which means that individuals tend to be unaware of the nature of their condition, the alternatives to it which exist, and the ways by which it might be changed. Accompanying this lock-in mechanism is another – the widespread suffering, anxiety and stress provoked by the loss of ties often reinforces selfish individualism by promoting an exaggerated concern with personal worries and welfare. In parallel fashion, desocialisation engenders a high level of social insensitivity which renders the individual increasingly incapable of forming and sustaining community. At the same time, the harsh conditions of anomic life favour the emergence to positions of influence of certain types of individuals who by their very nature cannot promote a culture of community.

On top of all these elements, the very orientations of desocialisation act to create a kind of individual who is incapable of achieving a wider collective and anthropological perspective. He is naturally distanced from that spiritualist approach which alone would supply remedies. In addition, once a society has lost the bulk of its mechanisms of social cohesion, once it has become heavily deculturalised, the inability to sustain community becomes, as it were, built into its genetic code. Furthermore, the mind-set of desocialisation is encouraged by the language people now use. This language has often been shaped and moulded by the contours of the anomic condition and acts to reproduce the very mentality which lies behind our present crisis. Concurrently, the atomised and fractured condition in itself produces a propensity to embrace relativism. If all this were not enough, the standard responses to the suffering caused by desocialisation often lead the individual to turn to pseudo-solutions which only make things worse and which reinforce our present plight. Then we come to the most powerful mechanism of self-reproduction of them all – the attempt to eliminate the existence or influence of healthy souls. Looked at in terms of the functioning of a system, such individuals are the deadly enemies of desocialisation and the removal of their presence and role is an integral element of self-perpetuation. These mechanisms will now be analysed in the order in which they have just been listed.

Ignorance, Selfishness and Fear

The ways of approaching man and living the human experience typical of the materialist matrix are naturally embraced and promoted by those who live on the dark side. In a classic example of an anthropological vicious circle, spiritual ill-health is encouraged by a cultural pattern based on perspectives which are naturally embraced by unhealthy souls. As J.B. Coates observed in discussing the decline in the belief of God: 'we have seen a great outcrop of philosophies which are conscious or unconscious rationalisations of the instinctive urges of their begetters'.[1] Well might one say – 'tell me your conception of man and I will tell you who you are'. It is a feature of human nature that individuals tend to understand human reality with reference to their own internal experience; they have the habit of attributing to others their own consciousness and motives; and they often see their fellows as they see themselves. Thus those who live on the dark side, because they neglect the soul and refuse the life according to the Spirit, naturally tend to subscribe to the models of man and the tenets of behaviour of the materialist matrix. They naturally see man and society in terms (for example) of power, wealth, conflict, pleasure, sex and selfishness. This is because they themselves are actually like this, and so tend to comprehend others and the human environment as they understand themselves. Their own internal ignorance acts to produce erroneous perspectives about the world around them. They are like colour-blind men whose vision of reality is distorted by their own physical defect. Their implicit or explicit failure to steward their souls naturally leads them to leave spirituality out of the equation when they come to consider the nature and experience of man. In so doing they become constant promoters, in various ways and forms, of the outlook and way of living of the materialist matrix. They are the products and agents of this self-reproducing system – and the more there are of them, the stronger this system becomes.

There is often something massively compelling about what exists. The observation of the way things are often gives rise to the conviction that 'life's like that'. In the desocialised condition the individual encounters ways of thinking, being and behaving which suggest to him that such, indeed, is the way man and life must be. He seems to have before him the empirical evidence for the models of man and their associated forms of conduct provided by that context. In seeing people animated by the desire for power or money, moved by their feelings or their sexual impulses, engaged in self-gain and selfishness, not believing in truth or responsibility, and all the rest, the individual is naturally led to the conclusion that in essence the analysis of the materialist matrix is correct. He is encouraged to embrace that perspective because of his own personal observations of the world around him. Thus the visions of man and of the human experience characteristic of the false anthropologies of post-modernity lead to a cultural condition which by the sheer weight of fact and evidence render those visions plausible and convincing – the case produces the proof which corroborates the case.

One aspect of this process deserves special comment. It is a frequent view that although on the surface people may appear to be something else, in actual fact they conform to the apparatus of understanding of the materialist matrix. The belief is often held that, whatever the appearances, whatever the evidence which points to other conclusions, people deep down are in fact as the materialist matrix really paints them. The rest is held to be merely tactical, or window-dressing, or idle convention. So it is that facts to the contrary – the activity, for example, of those individuals who live their lives according to the Spirit – are written off as mere facades. This propensity to dismiss evidence which disproves the thesis of the materialist matrix as mere camouflage is underpinned by a common anxiety not to be deceived – an element which itself is engendered by the widespread practice of deception.

The rooted practice of selfish individualism encourages the belief within people that they are faced with an everyday situation of 'sink or swim'. The idea naturally arises that life is really about the individual pursuit of selfish gain – whether one likes it or not – and that the only way to survive in such a context is to act as others do, namely selfishly. Jungle practices produce a jungle mentality which in turn produces jungle practices. For example, the individual comes to say to himself that he must gain money and power by severe methods or he will lose out; he believes that unless he uses others for sexual pleasure, he will be left without sexual opportunity; or he concludes that he must engage in false friendship or he will be left completely alone – and so the sad litany continues. Thus the compromising of moral truth is constantly encouraged by a context which is often severe and deprivational in its impact. The fundamental notion is that the individual must do as others do if he does not want to be swept under. We are dealing here with something akin to the mentality of war: harsh actions are necessary because the consequences of not acting in such a way are too serious to contemplate – thus many an inhabitant of our increasingly severe society now embraces the ancient Roman policy of 'my life, your death'. The lack of belief in the possibility of divine intervention reinforces the choice of this all-too-human response. In addition, once individuals become accustomed to such forms of behaviour, they readily lose the capacity to reject them on spiritual grounds. Moreover, reflecting natural emotional reactions, the aggression which the individual often experiences at the hands of his desocialised environment provokes an all too predictable response – further aggression. Violence breeds violence. People are paid back in kind. This, too, forms an integral part of responding to selfish individualism by adopting its characteristics and methods.

Leadership or guidance is important in any human community. Power should involve responsibility; wisdom must be transmitted; advice is of the utmost. But post-modern Britain is now faced with a notable crisis of spiritual leadership. This operates at many levels, from the family to the Churches, from the workplace to parliament, from schools and universities and from newspapers to television. The widespread cynicism which now exists in relation to public life attests to this crisis. The attack on authority which has been underway for many decades, associated with a refusal of tradition and convention, has been one factor in undermining the reality of any kind of leadership at all. But far more important is the fact that our spiritual impoverishment may well be especially felt amongst the privileged, the powerful and the prominent, as is suggested, for example, by a cursory reading of Woodrow Wyatt's decadent diaries.[2] Equally, love for love and for truth appears to be much more felt amongst those distant from the glittering prizes of this world. Have the rich become the shame of the poor? A major consequence is that in the present state of confusion and uncertainty people often do not know to whom to turn; voices of sound direction are increasingly thin on the ground; and constructive role-models frequently fail to be in the offing. This means that people ever more are not directed in a healthy way towards their spiritual selves or are actually encouraged to live on the dark side.

Existence is compelling, but so, too, is the void. The man kept in the dark knows very little about the light. It is rather difficult to have cognisance of something which has never been encountered. The anomic condition creates an ignorance about other ways of living which in itself constitutes a self-reproducing mechanism. The spreading lack of love for love and for truth, the progressive depletion of authentic spirituality, and the growing absence of community which all increasingly mark our culture, create an environment which renders people ever more ignorant or uninformed about possible alternative ways of being and thinking. The anomic condition creates people whose frame of reference is the contours of that condition; a necessary instructive input is lacking, and correct awareness thereby becomes sabotaged.

But not only are individuals often surrounded by a world which tells them very little about the soul and living according to the Spirit, or which fails to present models of being and behaving which are alternative to the universe of the materialist matrix, they also frequently live within a context which fails to provoke within them a consciousness of such realities. Vital inner elements within man fail to be activated. The receiving of love engenders an experience of love and an encounter with truth provokes a perception of truth, but these routes to awareness are impeded by a context which fails to provide such a stimulation. To express the point differently, that which is healthy in the spiritual realm has within it the capacity to reproduce similar health in those with whom it comes into contact – perceiving what is good involves in some way that good entering into our inner experience. But where that good does not exist externally, how can we be helped by it? Exactly the same may be said of community. The provision of help, solidarity, support, care and concern, the expression of good will, and the realities of belonging and participation – all these inform people about the workings and advantages of community. Yet when such elements are not present how can people sense and experience the benefits of such a state within themselves? The void reproduces the void.

Selfish individualism involves a massive propensity to concern with the self. An individual's attention is turned towards himself, towards his own concerns, interests and perceptions. This inward-lookingness is compounded by the consequences of the suffering and anxiety caused by a loss of ties. The worry and care provoked in individuals by the poverty of their own human relationships, by their lack of fulfilment and by their detachment often engenders an inward-looking form of personality which has little time or concern for others. In being desocialised the individual is propelled towards being asocial. After all, when afflicted by a toothache, the human being tends to dedicate much more time to himself than to the trials and tribulations of those around him. He aims to help himself first because his pain is what commands his primary attention. Exactly the same may be said of his reaction to the consequences of the desocialised environment. His general awareness of those around him, his sensitivity to the group to which he belongs, his concern and care for the well-being of the wider community – all these elements tend to become compromised by the self-centredness provoked by the painful and disturbing impact of desocialisation. Indeed, does not the wounded animal isolate itself in order to lick its wounds?

The lifestyle of selfish individualism and the social disengagement which desocialisation generates join to promote a context where individuals lack social sensitivity. Whole areas of their inner selves are either stunted in their growth or not developed at all. A lack of authentic interaction with other people produces a failure to develop a sensitivity to other people. By this route one of the great features of human nature – sociability – becomes assaulted. The anomic experience encourages an in-built indifference towards – and a failure to participate in – the world of others. Just as teeth without a nerve cannot feel, so there is a tendency to become insensitive and indifferent towards the rest of the human environment. This is not only true of such situations as walking down crowded high-streets, or working in giant firms, or shopping in supermarkets, where others are often related to as dots, it is also true as regards relatives, friends and neighbours. The whole sphere of empathy, sympathy and sensitivity – which has often been observed by anthropologists as being highly developed in many so-called 'primitive' peoples – becomes impoverished. Such vital building blocks of society fail to be constructed. In this way, desocialised post-modern man at times appears as a new sort of human, perhaps even a kind of cultural mutation, who has been ripped free from his biological and spiritual origins and set up in a world where he is ignorant and inexpressive of much of his most essential potential. At this point reproduction of our cultural crisis occurs with a vengeance. This ignorance means that the individual does not know what community involves and so he is inhibited in its formation; he is unable to perceive the cultural crisis because his understanding of others and their experience is limited; and he is incapable of grasping the realities to which those who are not dead teeth refer and for this reason he cannot respond to their observations and appeals.

There is another dimension to this creation of social insensitivity and the related incapacity to form community which requires examination. Our society seems to be becoming more 'Darwinian', though in ways and for reasons which are not usually perceived. The harshness and severity of post-modern society may well be increasingly bringing to the fore those people who tend to be the most insensitive and asocial of all its members. It is precisely these individuals who have the highest degree of resistance to what desocialisation imposes and are least impeded and wounded by its knife-twists; it is they who are most directed towards the pursuit of selfishness and are least distracted by concern and care for others; it is these people who are prepared to use methods which damage others and remain unaffected by the suffering they cause; and it is such types who least have their gaze directed towards the collective good and are most uninterested in the wider consequences of their actions. The severe and the deaf, the rhino-skinned and the self-sufficient, the blind and the harsh, the callused and the cauterised – these are the kind of personalities who appear increasingly to occupy positions of influence and power. Naturally enough, the way they live often tends to become a model and an example, a style which becomes diffused and imitated because of their prominence. They emerge as a kind of cultural ruling class whose ideas and attitudes become spread far and wide. Yet such people are the enemies rather than the friends of community – their successful survival of the processes of desocialisation is followed by their becoming some of its most conspicuous subsequent champions.

The anomic condition bears within it a propensity on the part of the individual to neglect the welfare of the general culture. The tunnel vision of the egocentric lifestyle means that little individual attention is paid to the wider cultural context. On the one hand, this means that there is a marked tendency to disregard the impact of personal behaviour on the cultural system and, on the other, that one of the primary routes to understanding the nature of our contemporary crisis becomes obstructed. One of the spreading features of our age is the failure of individuals to realise that what they think, do and say forms a part of the context of others. There is an error at the level of perspective which involves each person neglecting to realise that what he is and how he acts have consequences for the lives of other people. The lifestyle of selfish individualism involves a propensity to understand personal activity solely with reference to its agent and not in terms of its implications for others. In a desocialised context there is an insistent inability to raise horizons beyond the personal world and engage in a wider sweep. But once this way of living becomes established, the culture of a people is constantly vulnerable to damage and injury – in pursuing their own selfishness individuals detract from the welfare of their cultural context. In the same way they are most reluctant to raise their gaze and to ask themselves questions about the general state of the culture they live in, whether it is positive in its impact, and what steps should be taken to improve it or defend it – hardly a positive point of departure.

Desocialisation involves deculturalisation and this hinders any future possibility of achieving a successful exit. By not living together in any authentic way, by not being connected, by generating disengagement, and by neglecting the family and all its potential for the transmission of culture, the desocialised increasingly lose the ability to conserve and promote shared ways of thinking and behaving which conduce to community. The very fact of being separate and distant means that people may not communicate to each other those ideas and beliefs, conventions and customs, wisdom and sagacity, which would bind them together and which could be bequeathed to subsequent generations. They can lose the habit of cultural maintenance and construction. In so doing they become increasingly ignorant as to what these elements could be and so become poor architects and custodians. Necessarily, the very lack of a collective and group perspective also means that the desocialised may not be exercised about the need to maintain and generate a common project within society as a whole. Moreover, the frequent self-centredness of the post-modern lifestyle leads to a neglect of the idea that there is a clear responsibility to those who come afterwards and that successive generations would gain from the bequest of a cultural system which guides, instructs, advises and uplifts.

When discussing America some hundred and fifty years ago, de Tocqueville wrote a section entitled: 'How American Democracy has Modified the English Language'.[3] Reference has already been made to mass society and its relationship to the language we speak. Analysts of culture are more than aware of how the language of a people contains specific and characteristic ways of understanding and perceiving reality. The language of a culture, which is influenced and moulded by that culture, itself becomes an instrument by which that culture is reproduced. In surveying the present-day scene, we see that desocialisation has modified the English language not as regards grammar and syntax but in relation to notions and concepts, the falling out of use of terms, and the bestowal of negative or positive charges upon certain words. It seems reasonable to suppose that the mental thought-world of those who come to use such language becomes influenced and that men's minds become linguistic carriers of what lies behind our loss of ties. No systematic survey is possible here, but the waning of the vocabulary of absolute morality, religious experience, and the vices and virtues; the widespread use of terms such as 'partner', 'neurosis', 'market' and 'preference'; and the connotations of such words as 'tolerance', 'duty' or 'tradition', all speak loud and clear. Desocialisation has shaped the language we use and has thereby become equipped with another instrument by which to perpetuate itself.

The Relativist Vicious Circle

Relativism itself has an inbuilt propensity to self-reproduction. By destroying all certitudes – except that there are no certainties – it leaves behind it no apparatus which can refute it. Similarly, it produces a mechanism which strangles at birth any idea which opposes it – how often today do people say to themselves, 'well, that's just my opinion', and so lack the confidence or the courage to follow the path of truth. But beyond the world of thought-processes, relativism and desocialisation interact at a very practical level to produce a potent system of self-reproduction. The atomised world of anomie creates a social (or rather anti-social) way of living which encourages the relativistic approach, and this in turn acts to promote that lifestyle. By living in an individualistic way and acting along atomised lines the individual is naturally encouraged to look to his own personal perceptions for guidance and instruction. Wrapped up in himself – his own interests, thoughts and feelings – he readily becomes convinced of the exclusive truthfulness of his own perceptions. They easily become the sovereign point of departure for his existence. In the same way, once the anomic condition has been installed, once community has faded, once there is no solid core of true beliefs or practices which constitute a common project, what remains, naturally enough, are the perspectives and interests of the single man. He upholds how he wants to think and behave. He believes that what is truth is his affair, relative to him alone. But of course with such individualism run riot, community in any real sense becomes impossible, as the prophetic Alexis de Tocqueville realised only too well:

> If everyone undertook to form all his own opinions and to seek for truth by isolated paths struck out by himself alone, it would follow that no considerable number of men would ever unite in any common belief.

> But obviously without such common belief no society can prosper; say, rather, no society can exist; for without ideas held in common there is no common action, and without common action there may still be men, but there is no social body. In order that society should exist and, *a fortiori*, that a society should prosper, it is necessary that the minds of all the citizens should be rallied and held together by certain predominant ideas; and this cannot be the case unless each of them sometimes draws his opinions from the common source and consents to accept certain matters of belief already formed.[4]

So desocialisation is generated by relativism, which itself is generated by desocialisation.

This process takes place by another route. Within a relativistic cultural context there is an empirical imperative towards an acceptance of its governing principle. If people believe that truth is what they believe it to be, and if individuals within a society believe in the supreme validity of their own perceptions and act accordingly, then an observer is easily drawn towards the conclusion that 'truth' and especially moral 'truth' is indeed a variable – something which really does depend on the observer. A similar observation may be made about the phenomenon of 'sub-cultures' – a vogue term of recent decades. Here, too, relativistic realities lend credence to the relativist case. One of the characteristics of post-modern Western society is a splitting-off into different groups each of which champions a specific 'lifestyle'. The emergence of such sub-cultures is often a product of the search by anomic individuals for belonging and identity. The very reality of these sub-cultures proceeds to lend weight to the relativist perspective. What happens is that truth becomes related to categories rather than to individuals. The idea is that each group has a way of life and a set of opinions which is as good (or as bad) as any other. Presented with the realities of sub-cultures and their lifestyles, with all their various 'points of view', the observer is induced to believe that experience would suggest that truth is indeed a variable.

Cures which Worsen the Illness

Like the pre-modern physicians who bled their sick patients whose attention they continued to command, desocialisation also reproduces itself by encouraging a series of cures which worsen the illness. The paths which individuals choose – whether consciously or unconsciously – to escape from the loneliness, frustration, unhappiness, discomfort and unease (of which they may or may not be fully aware) caused by their loss of ties often end up by leading them back to where they started or perhaps even further back. The 'answers' they produce to their plight can merely lock them up more securely within the walls of their prison. At the same time, these answers may act to reinforce the cultural pattern which has helped to bring about their initial condition. These are especially vicious circles. This perverse process of escape generating further imprisonment works by two principal routes. On the one hand, in the solutions they choose, people come up against and further absorb the false anthropologies of post-modernity and the ideas and conduct that these anthropologies engender. On the other, they become even more immersed in human relationships which lack authenticity and are rooted in selfish individualism. In an example of inversion which is almost demonic, desocialisation produces personal attempts to escape its clutches which merely reproduce its core realities.

At the deepest level what we are witnessing are erroneous individual answers to the failure to receive love in all its expressions. Thus it is that in their troubles and travails the victims of the anomic condition turn to psychistic and physiologistic remedies; the solace of wealth and power; the world of sensual pleasure; false unions or marriages; empty friendships; the shifting sands of the pseudo-social; the imagined and the fake; or simple aggression and assault. Unaware that the absence of love is what is at the root of their disquiet, the desocialised are frequently unable to produce a spiritual response to their malaise. They turn instead, in erroneous fashion, to cures which worsen the illness. This process will now be subjected to detailed analysis.

The Age of Anxiety

The age of the loss of ties is also the age of anxiety. Ample testimony now attests to spreading mental and emotional distress, disorder and disorientation. The constant use of the word 'stress' is one symptom of a reality which has reached almost plague proportions. Anorexia and bulimia, panic attacks and self-injury (a disturbance that involves over 170,000 people in Great Britain every year),[5] impotence and insomnia, alcoholism and drug-abuse, manic shopping sprees and depression – such are some of the manifestations of this anxiety. Western (and British) man is increasingly sick and his maladies have naturally enough become the subject of scientific inquiry. Reference has already been made to the very high number of people consulting their GP for depressive disorders and the current massive levels of consumption of anti-depressants. To have one picture of this situation, one may refer to the fact that in May 1999 it was reported that 'one in four women and one in ten men in the UK will suffer depression serious enough to require treatment, while up to 20 per cent of children may need help for depression-related problems'.[6]

In response to such alarming developments an international conference (organised by the Pontifical Council for Pastoral Assistance to Health Care Workers) was held at the Vatican in 1996 on 'Disturbances of the Human Mind'. Speakers rose one after the other to draw attention to the high levels of mental affliction to be found in the Western world. One expert referred to the World Health Organisation's judgement that depression was the great illness of the planet's rich countries;[7] another observed that in Germany in 1988 14% of the population suffered from some kind of psychiatric disturbance.[8] Perhaps the most perceptive contribution was that made by Fiorenzo Angelini, the conference's organiser, who declared that: 'at the root of many and new forms of mental disturbance there is a crisis in values and the dominance of anti-values which propel man into increasing loneliness'.[9] In this incisive affirmation is to be discovered the principal cause of the sickness of post-modern man.

In 2003 the same Pontifical Council organised another international conference in the Vatican, this time on the subject of depression. A recurrent theme of the papers and debates was that depression was very much on the increase in the West and was often rooted in the loneliness that afflicts post-modern man. 'Depression, therefore, is a psycho-social malaise', observed the joint authors of one paper, 'that has its roots in a society that excludes rather than includes, that rejects rather than welcomes, and that abandons rather than protects'.[10] 'The absence of ties afflicts with an extraordinary breadth the marital and family universe', observed another speaker, 'we live in a disintegrated society that...fosters...the development of broken-down personalities who encounter great difficulty in unifying themselves psychologically and morally'.[11] 'During our time', declared yet another speaker, 'the most evident symptom of depression lies in the marginalisation of the individual and his non-relevance within society'.[12] In his contribution to the conference, J.L. Barragán emphasised that depression should also be understood with reference to the 'culture of post-modernity' which 'is openly expressed in a whole series of forms of depression'.[13]

Our cultural crisis is a root cause of many of these forms of disorder, disorientation and distress. When faced with a loss of ties, *homo sapiens*, because of his biological and spiritual nature, suffers and worries – something which tells us a great deal about man's purpose in this world. Just as solitary confinement can drive the individual into delirium and madness, so loneliness in all its forms works for imbalance and disorder within the human personality. The absence of authentic community now creates a whole host of phenomena across a broad spectrum which are in a very real sense the symptoms of our cultural breakdown. Without love and truth, without spiritual health, and with the 'dominance of anti-values', the inner man buckles and bends. The very presence of all these phenomena should alert us to the fact that something has gone very wrong in post-modern society – this, indeed, is writing on the wall. It should also lead us to question the path we have taken over recent centuries. One answer to our predicament (that proposed by this work) is to try to analyse it and then to proceed to draw up a blueprint for remedial action. Yet at an individual level people attempt other forms of response which, however, are bound to fail.

The 'Relief' of Pain

In Britain a vast army has sprung up to deal with these various afflictions. The mushroom growth of 'counselling' and 'psychotherapy' – a boom phenomenon of recent decades – has been made possible by a deep and widespread level of suffering within our society. We have before us an imposing array of people of various hues and colours who should perhaps be termed 'pain relievers'. The figures are truly startling. In 1997 there were 'more than 2m workers in the UK whose job formally involves giving counselling; in 1995 there were an estimated 40,000 people earning their living from it and another half a million doing so half time'.[14] The observer encounters a kaleidoscopic world made up of all kinds of figures, practices and methods, an at times uncontrolled jungle of unlicensed practitioners, unproved and tenuous theories and remedies, and uncertain effects and consequences. One thing is clear – this vast army would not be possible without the ravages of desocialisation and deculturalisation. In studying the victims of the loss of ties of modern society who turn to these pain relievers, one is constantly struck by a simple reality – the absence of love, family, friends and community is provoking alarming levels of disturbance and distress. Here, too, one often enters what can only be described as horror. A certain 'Steven', a 45-year-old artist, had received constant 'counselling' from the age of 27, it was reported by a national newspaper in 1997. Here is his horrific account of what his human environment had meant for him:

> I look at it like going to a dentist. I don't have a problem with the stigma, I'd tell anyone. My parents were violent to each other and I learnt to dread hostility; I became a 'pleaser' with violent thoughts. I had a terrible adolescence, I was a depressive with isolationist tendencies. I didn't know how to function in society. I moaned at the therapist for a year, then went into group therapy, which educates you to deal with people.[15]

One Alistair Anderson even founded a company to provide 'mentoring' schemes for the work-stressed:

> who need a friend outside the company, and has talked workers through divorce, alcoholism, family murder and even suicide attempts in the workplace. These are often people whose 16-hour days leaves no time for friends and family, and whose management offers round-the-clock counselling to keep them going...Whatever happened to leaving our personal problems at home? "These people are hardly ever at home!" says Anderson. Or talking to friends? "Their friends are the people they work with."[16]

It is hardly surprising that one of our popular daily newspapers, when publishing an article on this whole galaxy, ran the headline: 'Are We All Going Mad?'[17]

The great problem is that in turning to the vast army of pain relievers people are often merely pursuing a cure which worsens the illness. First and foremost, this world of counselling and psychotherapy frequently fails to get to the heart of the matter. Far from explaining to the suffering individual that his condition may derive from the impact of an unhealthy and inhuman cultural context, it refers him in individualist fashion back to himself. The analysis thus fails at its point of departure. Indeed, looked at from a distance, the suffering reaction of the individual should often not be understood as a sign of inner malady but as an indicator of health. Just as the pain felt by a hand which is put in a fire in reality defends its owner (this is one of the purposes of suffering within the Creation), so the unhappiness and stress which a person feels in an unhealthy environment warns him that there is something wrong with his context. The attempt to work away psychic pain through therapy is in effect often merely the counter-productive cancellation of a vital and instructive warning sign. Attention is being directed away from the real problem – desocialisation and its consequences – and there is an accompanying interference with the defensive faculties of the individual. The person's natural knowledge about the world around him is being disrupted. Exactly the same point may be made about the use of mood-altering drugs which in Great Britain is one of the most conspicuous responses to this age of anxiety. This, too, can be like anaesthetising the hand which has been placed in the flames: it does not remove the injury but deadens the sensation of the injury. In both these ways what is often happening is that no attempt is being made to extinguish the fire itself – our spiritually unhealthy cultural state. Attention is being directed towards the wrong solutions. The real problem remains, and ignorance about it is maintained.

Secondly, the world of counselling and psychotherapy is often impregnated with the erroneous psychist perspective. In this sphere the whole Freudian impulse has left a deep mark. Was not Freud, after all, the guiding founder of the whole concept of psychotherapy through psychoanalysis? The model of man which this world promotes is frequently full of ideas about the 'psyche' and its experiences. There is a great deal of reference to childhood memories, buried recollections, frustrated impulses and all the rest. The person subjected to this 'treatment' is encouraged to look within himself to the alleged psychic structures which purportedly shape and mould his feelings and behaviour. This draws attention away from his soul and its condition and neglects the relationship between the needs of his spirit and his cultural environment. Thus it is that the victim of desocialisation may be encouraged to think in those very terms of the false anthropologies of post-modernity which form a causal background to his predicament.

A similar observation may be made about resort to pharmaceuticals, which is now so commonly promoted by those working in the world of medicine and which frequently amounts to a dangerous medicalisation of unhappiness. In taking drugs to ward off mental and emotional anguish the individual is led to believe that it is indeed his brain and his body which are responsible for his pain. What has gone wrong, he is encouraged to think, is of a physical nature. Does not the cure, therefore, lie in a corresponding ingestion of chemicals? This naturally leads to an embrace and acceptance of the physiologist model of man, which in turn leads back to that materialist matrix which is at the root of our contemporary cultural crisis.

There is little doubt that the psychism and physiologism of the world of anxiety 'treatment' are likely to receive ever-greater promotion with the probable further expansion of the role of counselling, psychotherapy and medicine in the management of personal troubles. A trajectory will be followed which has gathered accelerating pace in recent times. In discussing the Second World War the preface to a recently published history of a famous RAF squadron includes the telling sentence: 'It never occurred to any of us to ask for counselling or claim financial compensation for any stress we suffered'.[18] Times have certainly changed. In addition, the vast numbers of people employed in this variegated world amount to a category which has a vested economic interest in promoting these kinds of 'answers' to the sickness of post-modern man. For example, there are strong pressures to lock counselling and psychotherapy – notwithstanding the great doubts which exist as to their practical effectiveness – into the National Health Service, a process which involves the prospect of a whole host of salaries and fees. In the same way, pharmaceutical companies reap great gains from the sales of their pills, a fact which will hardly lead them to abandon the path they have chosen – 'what seems almost certain is that the use of drugs will increase. It is big business, with the worldwide market for anti-depressants already worth several billion'[19] – while the whole world of psychiatry has a professional interest in expanding the definition of what constitutes mental illness. After all, the greater the need for cures, the more opportunity for the profession. At a general level, the desocialised way of life, which seems well set to generate ever greater anxiety, is likely to provide ever greater space and influence for those groups and interests which claim that they have the answers to such anxiety, and of course the solutions they offer will tend to be based upon the visions of man and the human experience of the materialist matrix.

Other dangers are implicit in this world and all of them run the risk of intensifying the anomic condition. When an individual seeks help for his problems from a counsellor, psychotherapist or medical doctor he turns towards an impersonal world. He affirms that those closest to him – if, indeed, such people exist – cannot provide him with help and consolation. He moves towards figures with whom he has a professional and not a personal relationship. This necessarily involves a confirmation and promotion of the culture of the depersonalised. Seen in this light, this vast array of people offering relief for anxiety constitutes yet another feature of anonymous mass society. Furthermore, this supplanting of the world of family, friends, neighbours, workmates and colleagues has a knock-on impersonalising effect. The approach and practices of counselling and psychotherapy become imitated by members of this personal world when they have to deal with the suffering or unhappiness of those who are near them. A husband, a son or a friend, for example, may become treated in a way which reflects the thinking of counselling and psychotherapy. He becomes not someone who is loved and with whom there is engaged involvement but a kind of 'patient'. Selfish individualism, too, is encouraged by the psychist militia. The suffering person is naturally led to devote his time and his energy to himself; he becomes the person who really matters; he it is who must be the subject of attention. Placed on the self-centred couch or the egotistical easy-chair, the well-being of others can become diminished in importance or marginalised. The concentration on the self leads to selfishness. Lastly, there is an emphasis within the world of counselling and psychotherapy on the need to avoid suffering. But is it not possible that pain is sometimes the path to perception, knowledge and wisdom, especially in the spiritual realm? Does it not, for example, lead to compassion and concern for others – that major ingredient of community?

Wealth and Power

The unhappiness and emptiness of the anomic lifestyle can induce an individual to seek solace in wealth and power. In part this can be a diversion from personal troubles or the striving for substitutes for affection and companionship, but in part, also, it can involve an attempt to secure respect and esteem. How many people now bury their loneliness and their lack of love in a frenzied commitment to work and what it can bring? And is not one of the characteristics of our age widespread admiration for those who have acquired money and command? However, such a solution falls back on itself. The pursuit of wealth and power can lead off into economistic and poweristic ways of thinking and acting, and other people become mere objects to be employed in their attainment. The relationships which the individual thus forms do not offer him community and a cure for his condition – quite the opposite. Indeed, he becomes a promoter of ways of living which lie behind his predicament. Furthermore, he may find himself surrounded by people who are near to him because of what he has and not because of what he is. Their company is self-interested and in this way, of course, he finds himself back at square one. Spouses, companions and friends who are bought are not authentic and never can be – their loyalty is pre-eminently precarious. At a more general level, the mere possession of gold and influence can never bring fulfilment. Who ever met a happy miser or a dictator who was at peace with himself?

Pleasure

The individual whose feelings cause him suffering because he lacks love and community may also be tempted to counter such feelings through the pursuit of pleasure. This is a major motive source of contemporary hedonism. The employment of drugs and stimulants; the turning to drink or eating; exaggerated immersion in films and television; the reading of escapist literature; delight in the pleasures of consumerism; resort to gambling; and indulgence in sexuality – all these forms of behaviour, and many others, characterise much of our present-day style of living. The statistics flow around us. Whether we consider the high levels of drinking – in 1994-5 27% of British males and 13% of females had a 'high' consumption of alcohol – or of drug consumption – in 1992-3 at least 36% of young people between 14 and 25 had taken some kind of drug, with 9% having taken acid/LSD and 7% ecstasy[20] – or of gambling – the Gambling Prevalence Survey of 2007 drew attention to this reality and found that there were some 250,000 'problem gamblers' in the UK[21] – or of obesity – the report of the Department of Health, Forecasting Obesity to 2010, predicted in 2006 that one in three men would suffer obesity, an increase from 4.3 million to 6.6 million, and that more than one in four women would be obese, an increase from 4.7 million to 6 million[22] – we are surveying realities which, although they have a number of causes, are also at times rooted in the pursuit of pleasurable feelings. Lying behind such choices is often an attempt to avoid those sensations of emptiness and sadness which spring from the absence of authentic relationships. Moreover, such responses at times have that most dangerous feature of all forms of drugs – the need to increase the dose to maintain the same effect. In finding that his feelings arrive at a state where they need ever greater stimulation to respond, the individual in fact immerses himself in a process of 'de-feelingisation'. The user finds that he is on a slippery slope which leads ever downwards. However, in responding to his desocialised condition by pursuing pleasure not only is the individual led away from the paths which could actually cure his condition, not only is he led astray from really understanding the origins of his situation, but he also finds himself entangled in a feelingist way of thinking and living of which he himself becomes the promoter. In resorting to hedonism, whether in moderate or extreme forms, the un-happy individual in his own small way sharpens the gigantic knife which has wounded him and will wound him still further.

Empty Relationships

One of the themes of this study is that however much post-modern Western and British man goes against what he should be and however much he refuses his vocation, he finds that he cannot do so with impunity. In one way or another he has to pay the price for the path of disorder he chooses. Loneliness in its *narrow sense* is perhaps the single greatest punishment that post-modern man has to encounter. In order to escape such a condition – which is frequently very severe in its emotional impact – many individuals of today's desocialised world form relation-ships or contract marriages which are not based on love but on self-interest. The idea is to find someone who can be used to provide company and to end the state of being alone. Perhaps this is one of the commonest of all contemporary social errors. But such a choice is no answer at all. Indeed, it may compound the problem. The other person is being used as an instrument, a means to an end, and there is nothing authentic about the relationship. As love does not exist, real spiritual and physical union – the real antidote to loneliness – cannot take place. No real solution has been achieved by this act of opportunism. Even worse, the individual may be constantly reminded of what he really lacks because he is repeatedly faced with the reality of something which is not there. Far from having escaped loneliness and resolved his problem, the individual has leapt from the frying pan into the fire. He now finds that he has to live a lie, to endure what is false, to experience a relationship which at heart is empty – all elements which illuminate his real state of not having love. He has before him the very opposite of what he needs. He has not only returned to square one but also entered the minus signs.

The desire to escape loneliness in its narrow sense can also lead to the formation of insincere and artificial friendships. Friendship, like love, is as old as the hills. It is perhaps the second cornerstone of human community. Friendship is a location for the expression of virtues, the pursuit of the common project and the achievement of belonging. Good company, mutual help and participation in shared culture are some of its principal benefits. Human history has been marked by its constant presence, although strangely enough its evolution and development has rarely commanded the attention of historians. It has, however, been the repeated subject of literary and artistic evocation and proverbs; precepts and principles have habitually surrounded it with received wisdom. A key feature of the anomic condition has been the loss of the ties of friendship. It appears that a great deal of the knowledge, practice and conventions of what constitutes friendship has been lost and here we encounter yet another form of deculturalisation. The formation of pseudo-friendships to counter loneliness has many features in common with the contracting of false relationships between men and women. There is the same engagement in what is not authentic and the same emptying of vital points of potential human contact. Equally, what is missing and what led to this false step in the first place become emphasised and highlighted by the presence of what is false. Moreover, the ending of friendships and their transitory quality is as much a feature of the way we live now as divorce in marriage and those transient 'partnerships' which so come and go. The same process is often at work – a selfish flight from isolation engenders the creation of fragile self-interested relationships which merely lead back to the original point of departure, and even farther back.

Escapism

Reflecting their spiritual and biological natures, human beings, whether knowingly or otherwise, tend to feel discomfort, unease and disaffection when placed within a human environment which fails to supply them with a sense of belonging and identity. One common reaction to such a condition is the creation of artificial roles and images which act as mechanisms of consolation. The anomic lifestyle is resonant with the playing of parts. People become what they are not because their cultural context does not allow them to be themselves. There is a search for consolation through invention. Such a response is underpinned by the ideas and attitudes promoted by the world of films, television and virtual reality. It forms a part of that taste for fantasy (expressed in literature as well) which has become a feature of post-modern man. But this propensity to act a part, to invent a role and to project an image flies in the face of authenticity. It involves the creation of relationships – and thus of an environment for other people – which are not based upon truth but upon what is false, upon what is performed. It engenders constant artifice which strikes at the heart of community. Rather than life between individuals being based upon what is real, it comes to be infused with what is phoney. The person who adopts this response in order to escape his loss of ties merely returns to his point of departure because he fails to relate to others in an authentic way. At the same time, like the false spouse, 'partner' or friend, he acts to desocialise those he comes into contact with by depriving them of the possibility of authentic interaction. Being an actor, he draws others into a precarious play which offends reality. And by not being true to himself he also comes by various mechanisms to strain and damage his innermost self – that vital departure point for wider social well-being.

Narcissism

Who can deny that we live in an age of narcissism? Paradoxically enough, one of the characteristics of the desocialised condition is a tendency to live in the eyes of others. Other people become mirrors by which individuals observe and admire themselves. This is a common escape response to the lack of love and community. Not supplied with the consideration, esteem or respect he requires or would like, anomic man may embark on a deceitful project to present himself to others in such a way that they will see him in a favourable light. He falsifies what he is in order that he may gain admiration and thereby secure personal satisfaction. In managing to deceive others as to his nature, character or attributes, he gains gratification from their erroneous perception of what he is. He comes to live in what is said and thought about him (rather than in the truth about himself) and his great point of reference becomes how he is perceived in the points of views of others (an important link-up with relativism). This response ties up with the societalist perspective because in essence what is happening is that what the human environment holds to be reality is deemed to be reality – appearance becomes substance and the mask supplants the countenance. Humanism also weighs in because the views of this world, rather than the truths of the other, are what count. Naturally enough, this whole practice – which is nowadays so common – involves an impulse to the deformation of reality, to the changing and altering of the way things really are. Whether a person is talented or beautiful, honest or intelligent, thoughtful or able, rich or powerful, does not matter – what really counts is whether in the eyes of other people he is thought to be such. This is a denial and betrayal of truth and involves the construction of a lifestyle of deception. Thus, at the heart of selfish individualism, we encounter a propensity to pretence. This is yet another reason why we find ourselves constantly surrounded by the fake.

Aggression

There is another personal response to desocialisation which is of a hostile and destructive character and involves a series of forms of aggression. When the individual feels isolated, neglected and not valued he may, be encouraged to reject and attack the world around him. In feeling belittled and downgraded, his natural reaction may be to assault his context much as the troubled dog bites the postman. Resentment finds an outlet in a policy of aggression. If the human environment does not provide the individual with what he wants, then for him that world must be changed, altered or reconstructed (or deconstructed) so that he no longer feels an absence of esteem or regard. Here wrath finds an important energiser. This kind of response often operates at an individual level but it can also find expression in collective action, for example through political ideologies. But the great problem with this kind of response, whether expressed personally or collectively, is that it springs from an aggressive impulse and lacks an authentic positive perspective. The main aim is to remove a grievance rather than to improve what exists. And the consequences can often be dire: much of what holds a society or a culture together – the texture and tissue of cohesion – can become subjected to assault and attack.

Self-isolation

There is another response at a personal level to the desocialised environment which involves a kind of anti-initiative – the withdrawal from contact and the reduction of the contents of interaction to a minimum. People deliberately desocialise themselves in order to diminish the actual or potential painful impact of their social surroundings. Three chief motivations lie behind this stance, all of which serve to lock up anomic man even more securely within his lonely cage. Firstly, there is a fear of the aggression, inconstancy, exploitation, unhappiness, criticism and severity which relationships with others can bring. A very simple answer is simply not to engage in contact at all or to ensure that such contact operates at a very superficial level. The danger becomes avoided. Secondly, the desire for self-importance can lead to a reluctance to engage in relationships because they could threaten that self-importance or to an attempt to make sure that they are so drained of content as to prevent the emergence of any elements which might involve such self-importance being challenged. Thirdly, because there is a lack of common agreement about how relationships should be formed and sustained, and because they involve such high levels of risk and danger, the idea of engaging in contact and the actual practice of such contact engenders insecurity and uncertainty. An obvious reaction to such unease is to steer away from personal relationships altogether or to confine them to the heights of shallowness. What is happening here is that the illness is being chosen to counter the illness; the plague is employed to ward off the plague.

The Attack on Healthy Souls

'I have given them thy word; and the world has hated them because they are not of this world, even as I am not of the world' (Jn 17:14). These telling words bring us to the difficult part. We now come to the final stage of the assault on the soul – aggression against those whose spirituality is alive and against all the potential good that they could do. Once a cultural pattern has become committed in its workings to the expression and promotion of spiritual ill-health, it must necessarily seek to corrupt, marginalise, neutralise or eliminate those who by their very natures engage in the opposite. Indeed, one of the ways we can understand what has happened to us as a people is to observe the fate of those individuals who – whether implicitly or explicitly – seek to steward their souls and to achieve eternal life for themselves and for others. Their fate is a revealing litmus test for the well-being of any society of men. It should be made clear, however, that in order to describe and bring out the key dynamics here the analysis is limited to what happens to people who are spiritually healthy when they are subjected to the most extreme features of this cultural pattern, that is to say desocialisation in its radical form. Obviously, I am not describing here the 'normal' experience of all men and women of good will who live today in post-modern Great Britain.

The first form this assault can take lies in the spiritually healthy person being placed in a cultural context with which he is in friction and disagreement. Such a condition involves a continual attempt to dissuade him of his position, but it also means that he becomes disheartened by being denied legitimacy and support for the way in which he sees the world and his fellow-men. At the same time he is subject to the demoralisation of having to constantly witness that which he believes to be wrong. Some of this process was described by the American sociologist Peter Berger with the concept of 'cognitive deviance',[23] a condition full of high risk for those who belong to it:

> those to whom the supernatural is still, or again, a meaningful reality find themselves in the status of a minority, more precisely a cognitive minority – a very important consequence with very far-reaching implications...a cognitive minority is a group formed around a body of deviant 'knowledge'...The status of a cognitive minority is thus invariably an uncomfortable one – not necessarily because the majority is repressive or intolerant, but simply because it refuses to accept the minority's definitions of reality *as* 'knowledge'...such supernaturalists as may still be around will find their beliefs buffeted by very strong social *and* psychological pressures.[24]

What is the nature of these kinds of pressures for healthy souls who are subject to desocialised culture in its extreme form – figures who constitute an authentic cognitive minority? First of all, the viewpoints the spiritually healthy individual, if a religious believer, receives from the human environment around him constantly tell him that he is in error – man does not have a soul (and thus God does not exist), but is to be understood in other terms; the authentic spiritual life is a fiction and other paths in life should be followed. Furthermore, whether a religious believer or not, he finds himself surrounded with thought and practice which goes against his innermost nature. His thought-world, his attitudes and values, and his way of living are denied legitimacy. This involves a massive process of dissuasion which seeks to encourage him to stop being what he is. This in itself is debilitating enough, but a natural concomitant of this state of affairs is that he receives little back-up and reinforcement from those around him. He is not supported and encouraged in what he is and does – he becomes the victim both of dissuasion and of an absent input. In addition, there is the impact of the constant presence of what is wrong, what is false, and what is inverted. This causes pain and stress in the healthy soul. Sorrow, and even horror, are provoked by the constant contemplation of error. By these various routes his energy and will are sapped and he thereby becomes a far less dangerous adversary.

But we are not dealing only with disheartenment. The person of good will is also beset by disorientation and disturbance. The spiritually healthy person is not only saddened, he is also placed in a condition where he cannot be himself – he is denied fulfilment and condemned to frustration. This places a massive strain upon the most essential parts of what he is. By what mechanisms does this take place? The spiritually unhealthy are unable to form authentic community; they cannot produce love for love and love for truth. If surrounded by them the healthy soul finds himself unable to engage in that which he is called upon to sustain – authentic relationships. This is something which is especially painful for him because it is that which he is naturally propelled to do, it is that which he wants, and it is that which he needs. His desire for love and for truth means that he feels their absence in an especially intense way and their deprivation affects him much more than those who have chosen to live on the dark side. Just as a fish is called upon to swim in water, so he is made to live within authentic community, in a context of spiritual health, in a cultural system which works to the benefit of spirituality. When he is unable to do this he suffers like a fish floundering in a drained pond. He finds that he cannot express himself, he has to suffer the pains of frustration, and this acts to disorientate and disturb him. His inner balance and equilibrium and his capacity for action, at all sorts of points, become undermined. Like the man compelled to walk for days without water in a desert, the spiritually healthy person becomes subject to a hugely disruptive climate. He is like a compromised oasis inundated with sand which finds it ever harder to sustain life – that life which opposes the desert.

The man who safeguards his spirituality is also subjected to the pains of not being understood by those around him, and this forms a conspicuous feature of the attack which he must endure. His perspectives, outlook, reflexes, reactions and systems of comprehension are those of the life according to the Spirit. His adversaries live in a very different universe and the way they experience the world is of an altogether different order. As a consequence, not only is he unable to achieve community with spiritually unhealthy people (because this is something they do not want and of which they are not capable) but he also finds it almost impossible to make himself understood – a human condition not to be wished on anyone. Communication, that most vital element of community, becomes powerfully compromised. The person of good will finds himself almost in another dimension where others are like ghosts – he moves his lips and makes gestures, but they cannot really hear or see him. He is referring to realities, and employing language which describes them, of which unhealthy souls have devastatingly little cognisance. This inability to communicate is one of the cruellest of the conditions the good man has to experience. Not only does this condition increase his demoralisation and disorientation (and thus weaken him further), but it may also encourage him to give up the unequal struggle and throw in the towel – in the face of a lack of a response he may choose to adopt a policy of silence. What is the point of talking to walls? Thus the voice of truth becomes extinguished and a light goes out. Such is another route by which this cultural pattern in its radical form counters the input of those who are spiritually alive. Candles are obscured.

The healthy soul is not only encouraged to keep quiet – there are also strong forces operating on him to change his ways. It is certainly true that the false anthropologies which surround him, the kinds of ways of living to which they give rise, and the false values that they generate are direct invitations to live and behave differently. He is encouraged by the natural processes of cultural pressure to conform to dominant practice. But this system of pressure does not stop there – his condition of deprivation involves the temptation to embrace compromise. When faced with the demoralisation and disorientation of desocialisation, the healthy soul may be encouraged to adopt the ways and behaviour of the world around him. In order to alleviate his suffering and unhappiness he may be tempted to take what appear to be obvious ways out, at least in the short term – responses which are especially encouraged by the fact that they are approved and practised by much of his human environment. They are, after all, constantly suggested to him by the world with which he is surrounded. For example, faced with poverty or economic difficulties, he, too, may be tempted to remove them by dishonesty, or cheating, or exploitation. Faced with loneliness, he, too, may be tempted to cancel it by entering into insincere or false friendships. Faced with sexual frustration, he, too, may be tempted to eliminate it by treating somebody else as an object. Faced with imposed insignificance, he, too, may be tempted to engage in the immoral pursuit of power. Faced with boredom, he, too, may be tempted to make it disappear by descending into the pursuit of pleasure at other people's expense. But if he does all these things, he runs the risk of damaging his own spirituality. Of course this is exactly what the spiritually unhealthy people around him want – he is no longer an adversary but has passed over into the enemy camp.

The pressure of desocialisation in its extreme form on the person of good will, which at times makes him feel as though he is being crushed a hundred fathoms below the surface of the sea, involves another line of attack. There is the burden of receiving the epithets of rejection. The man who lives according to the Spirit finds himself subjected to all the difficulties of not fitting in and of being the odd-man-out. He is seen – and may even come to see himself – as not being 'normal'. He is vulnerable to being labelled by others as eccentric, unusual, strange, perhaps disturbed, perhaps mad, not to be trusted, not to be integrated. Such are some of the bitter fruits of the friction he encounters. The man who by his nature yearns for community finds instead that he must experience the realities of rejection. For all the contemporary cult of tolerance for what is different, the person of good will often finds himself the victim of a barrage of refusal and repudiation. The deleterious effects on his self-esteem, morale and self-confidence are obvious. But of course it is not he who is abnormal. In these relativistic days the great tendency is to define what is normal in terms of what is the human norm. What society decrees and what is established convention is deemed 'normality'. Yet what happens if disorder reigns within a human environment? In truth, normality should be given a very different definition – that which a spiritually healthy person would think and do in whatever culture or context he finds himself. The thoughts and actions of such an individual should be seen as conforming to the 'norms' of divine law. Within desocialisation, however, what is normal often becomes abnormal and vice versa. So it is that the man who is committed to spiritual health finds that he must bear the cross of the various forms of denigration which arise from him being different.

There is another body-blow which the spiritually sound receive from desocialised culture – the demoralisation caused by deceit. There are few things more demoralising than betrayal. Those who live on the dark side regard others as instruments by which things can be obtained. In their outlook people are objects to be used in the practice of selfishness and in the acquisition of rank, power, wealth, prestige and pleasure. For them it is far better to take than to give and to this end they engage in deception. Fake good will, the mask of friendship, the employment of lying, the practice of duplicity all these phenomena of deceit are considered acceptable if they secure personal gain. The spiritually healthy person becomes a special target of such a mentality and a special victim of this process. The man of spiritual health has a natural propensity towards helping, giving and providing. This is a part of his yearning for community. Consequently, he is a rich potential source of gain – such a yearning is vulnerable to exploitation. What good would it do to knock at the door of the selfish man? Similarly, the spiritually healthy person wants to respond to calls based on principle, to behaviour rooted in what is good, and to appeals launched by the virtuous. For such reasons he is approached by those who want to exploit his generosity and do so by wearing a disguise which will induce his trust and kindness. Subsequent discovery of such a betrayal is a bitter experience. What is sacred has been profaned and distress is provoked. Furthermore, such memories often remain and can constitute a recurring source of sorrow.

Duplicity contributes to another condition which the good spirit must endure and which compounds the sufferings caused by disheartenment, disorientation and demoralisation – insecurity. Desocialisation often provides the opposite of a safe and ordered human environment for the spiritually healthy person. The failure of the cultural context to express the kingdom of heaven in itself means that there is no reinforcement for living according to the Spirit. In addition, relativism in thought and practice constantly erodes any fixed and rooted points of reference – secure bearings become challenged or lost, and what is assumed to be right is perpetually questioned. The widespread practice of duplicity, for its part, means that there is a lack of constancy in thought and action, that positions repeatedly change, and that people are not to be trusted or relied upon. As in a constant earthquake where walls and pavements always move and shift, the human environment is in a perpetual state of motion because it is not built upon secure foundations of truth. If this were not enough, contemporary mass society, as we have seen, has a propensity to generate rapid change and instability in a person's individual and collective environment – what is familiar and known is subject to constant alteration. To make matters even worse, the process of deculturalisation in all its forms means that anthropological continuity becomes increasingly elusive. Faced with all these realities – which are often interconnecting – the spiritually healthy person is afflicted by uncertainty and a lack of trustingness. Such a condition of insecurity applies yet further pressure and adds to a strain which is already intense.

Desocialisation in its radical form often counters the spiritual health which the good man bears within him in a far simpler way. The good man wants to be a good neighbour, but what happens when neighbours are not there? Place a man who can do a great deal of good on a desert island and his actions will amount to very little. Deprive a great pianist of a piano and he is unable to play his music. The spiritually healthy person expresses love and truth. He thereby works to the benefit of the spiritual health of those around him and contributes to the construction of community. But if he is deprived of family, friends, neighbours and all the rest (or if these relationships are drained of their authentic content), then all this becomes countered. Desocialise the good man and his positive input into the human environment becomes hindered or negated. His beneficial effects can become cancelled because he has been placed in a kind of social vacuum or void. So this cultural pattern not only involves the demoralisation and disorientation of the spiritually healthy person, the draining of his energy, and the weakening of his will, it also, by means of its own processes of the isolation of that individual, works against the contrary and opposing effects of those who are committed to spiritual health.

Desocialisation in its radical form not only works to isolate the man of spiritual health, it also hinders him from encountering and acting in union with his spiritual fellows. Unity is strength and the common action of those who live according to the Spirit not only provides mutual support but also secures an increase in the good that can be done. The pooling of resources achieves a multiple increase in the overall value of assets – individuals fighting alone can be picked off one by one; armies acting together are quite another proposition. It is clearly in the functional interest of this cultural pattern to prevent such a process of common action. Moreover, union between spiritually healthy people, and their co-operation, amounts to the formation of exactly that kind of true community which is anathema to desocialised culture. It constitutes a deadly enemy similar in character to anti-bodies within a sick body. When good people by the natural processes of desocialisation are isolated, when they lack points of social access, when they are checked in the creation of connections with others, it becomes very difficult for them to come into contact with their own kind. The paths of the dispersed army of healthy souls do not meet because the jungle is constantly wiping out the tracks which would permit their encounter. Furthermore, the temptation to keep silent, the reluctance to speak out, the experience of betrayal, the suspicion of others, the sapping of initiative, and the draining of energy – all elements encouraged by the anomic condition – make it much harder for healthy souls to recognise one an-other and come into contact. By such routes, the forces of spiritual health are subjected to processes which work for their separation and fragmentation. In this way, too, they become far less dangerous adversaries.

However, the assault on the healthy soul goes far beyond demoralisation, disorientation and isolation. It also involves constant and endemic aggression. In order to understand this process it is necessary to probe deep into the realities of the dark side – a by no means pleasant undertaking. A hostility to love and to truth, a refusal to be inferior, a drive for power, and a rejection of community – all these features, and others, mark out the man who lives in the spiritual shadows. There is thus a naturally aggressive attitude towards those who live according to the Spirit – they are disliked *a priori*. In addition, there is a hostility towards their presence and role. Those who seek to construct the kingdom of heaven (implicitly or explicitly) within the affairs of men are working in favour of structures and processes which necessarily inhibit and impede those who do the opposite. This innate spiritual struggle within culture must mean that healthy souls come under attack from their counterparts – these last want to be free to be what they are and to do what they want and are hostile to any kind of interference. Indeed, they often attack anything which goes against them, or might go against them, with astonishing ferocity. It is now necessary to explore these forms of attack in depth and to understand the reasons that lie behind their being launched.

There is a paradox on the dark side. However much unhealthy souls have embraced the darkness, they rarely want to be reminded of what they are. Darksiders seem not to want to perceive the depths into which they have descended and they would like to ignore or to forget what they have become. Similarly, they prefer not to remember what wickedness they have done in the pursuit of their own narrow selfishness. Seen from this perspective of not wanting to be exposed, the healthy soul constitutes a very serious challenge or threat to his counterpart. The man who lives the life of the Spirit bears that light within him which illuminates the wrongdoing and spiritual sickness of others. As St. Paul observed:

> Take no part in the unfruitful works of darkness, but instead expose them. For it is a shame even to speak of the things that they do in secret; but when anything is exposed by the light it becomes visible, for anything that becomes visible is light (Eph 5:11-13).

So it is that just as the dirtiness of a filthy rag becomes greatly emphasised when placed next to a clean cloth, so the spiritually fallen comes to see what he really is in all clarity when he encounters the man who has safeguarded his soul. Like a whiplash, the truth of his condition strikes him full in the face. He becomes like the bat who was secure in the darkness of the cave until a torch was introduced. To use another image – he is like a monster in an underground tunnel who only observes the horror of his body when a man bearing a lantern draws near. In such a context the unhealthy soul reacts in a spirit of aggression – he must distance or destroy his opposite in order to remove the crisis of truth which afflicts him and causes him pain. He must attack precisely that reality which reveals him for what he is. And let us not forget, in addition, that aggression is the natural emotion of humans who have something to hide. Thus it is that the good man, in being true to himself, becomes the victim of aggressive assault perpetrated by those who do not want the light he bears within him to be shone upon them.

This reaction is paralleled by another – that of resentment at being spiritually inferior, which, in turn, is accompanied by envy at the achievement attained by the spiritually healthy person. Another of the paradoxes of evil is that it rejects good but at the same time senses its superiority. The darksider, when placed next to his healthy counterpart, is more than conscious of a lack, an absence and an inadequacy. Whether he likes it or not, light in the dark is always preponderant. Such a condition provokes a feeling of inferiority, of subordination, and of being second-rate. This sensation is especially discomforting because it is held by a being who naturally aspires to importance and power. An obvious reaction to such a condition is aggression – the immediate provoker of such feelings has to be seen off much as a dog barks furiously at an intruder. This resentment at spiritual superiority is accompanied by the destructive impulses of envy. The unhealthy soul perceives that the man who lives according to the Spirit has that which he does not have and he may also recognise that this has been achieved through sacrifices which he has not been prepared to make. Perhaps deep within himself he even perceives the supreme future prize of eternal life which will be gained by the man who has illuminated spirituality. Feelings of envy arise spontaneously and aggression is the obvious response – the anger and rage which are felt are given expression and the object of such feelings becomes the victim of an assault.

But such resentment should not be understood merely in terms of a kind of gut-reaction, something similar to the shrieks of a bat or the barking of a dog. It should also be placed within a wider and more worldly context. The dark spirit naturally senses that the qualities of those who are spiritually superior have implications for what he may have to experience within human society. In all sorts of ways the healthy soul is a very serious threat to what he wants to be and do. First and foremost, given that a culture should express and promote spiritual health, it is only natural that those who steward their souls will seek to enforce this process. They strive to uphold certain truths, principles, values and forms of behaviour; they are the guardians of the true social contract; and they are the champions (whether knowingly or unknowingly) of the tenets of divine law. But such a stance is a constraint on the man who lives on the dark side because it impedes him in his aspirations. It is a check on his immorality and a threat to his potential or actual worldly gains. Such authority and constraint has to be thrown off, and aggression is the most obvious course of action. Secondly, the presence of the spiritually enlightened involves the constant danger that the deceit of their counterparts will be detected and exposed. The healthy soul is sensitive to when truth is being betrayed – after all he has the internal instruments for such a judgement – and because such betrayal is something which is of the greatest importance to him, he protests against it and works against it. This, too, is a very great threat to those who live on the dark side – their posing and fakery may be unmasked; their guile and cunning, uncovered; their lies and deception, revealed. What, then, will happen to all their worldly gains? The successful criminal risks being deprived of the fruits of his work. Aggression is the obvious response.

However, there is more, much more, when we focus in on rank and money. Within society, prizes and approval should accrue to the virtuous and the talented. Rewards should go to those who do things well. The historian who is more capable than the dunce should occupy the professorial chair; the honest public figure rather than the scoundrel deserves popular trust; and the mother who loves her children rather than the wastrel should win our esteem. But this general principle is unacceptable to the darksider, who by his very nature longs for power, prestige and riches. What matters to him is not so much how these things are attained, but that they are attained. To employ the famous phrase, the ends justify the means. Indeed, if there is one thing which marks out the dark side, it is this drive to be 'important' in one way or another, something which is linked to a corresponding readiness to be dishonest in its attainment. Again and again, it is evident that those who live on the dark side do not act or think with reference to the truth, the soul or God. They live within the parameters of this world. What really interests them is that society should consider them 'important', whether such a judgement is accurate or not. From here there is a natural leap to deception. Such people want the prizes and prestige which should really accrue to those who deserve them. They are impostors who are all too ready to defraud the deserving.

In this light, one easily grasps that the presence of talents and virtues in other people is a threat to the unhealthy soul – if rewarded, they could deprive him of what he wants. Quality in others is something which threatens his potential acquisition of gain. This is so in two areas in particular – that of power and that of work. Command at all levels within a community should be in the hands of those who have the spiritual quality to guarantee sound and beneficial decisions. Their power should be employed for the benefit of others. This is as true of prime ministers as of station masters. But the darksider wants such command because of the importance and material rewards that it bestows upon him. His is a predominantly selfish perspective where wider responsibilities towards the community are not perceived. The man who lives according to the Spirit, because he has a superior claim on power, thereby becomes his deadly rival. The man who wants to govern well, or wants trains to run on time – because these are good things in themselves – becomes an enemy who should be attacked.

Indeed, when people today talk in marketist terms about the legitimacy of competition, are they not often merely constructing a cover for assault on the talented? And when it is asserted that we are all equal, is this not a way of dismissing the claims of the more capable?

Secondly, quality in economic activity and in the world of work should bestow rewards on its protagonists. Talents are widely distributed, but those who steward their souls have the natural tendency to defend and promote their talents. The guardianship of such gifts is a part of their virtue. Indeed, for the spiritually healthy person labour is an expression of his spiritual state – in performing honest work to the best of his abilities he promotes that which is intrinsically good and he acts to the benefit of others. Indeed, labour has immense social responsibilities and a strong creative role. For example, the man who makes a good chair provides something which is what it should be and which well supports the human body. One of the features of desocialised life is the constant denial of these dimensions to labour and the repeated idea that work is to be seen solely as a source of gain to its performer. Not only does the unhealthy soul resent the talents of others which place him at a disadvantage in the acquisition of gain and prestige, but he is also inherently opposed to that impulse to good work which is latent in people who live according to the Spirit. Conversely, the spiritually healthy are naturally opposed to those who aspire to prizes and approval without deserving them or who neglect their responsibilities to others or do not do things well. For all these reasons, the man who lives on the dark side finds people of good will naturally obstructing his path. They are rivals to him in his struggle for worldly advance and they are opposed to his illegitimate gains.

The natural reaction of the darksider to this rivalry and opposition at the level of money and success is to attack his spiritual counterpart. The frequent intensity of this reaction reflects the immense importance which is attached to such prizes. This assault is expressed in four principal forms – disguise, isolation, dominance and corruption. Let disguise be considered first. To achieve their ends those who live on the dark side engage in imitation, fakery and deceit. They pretend that they have virtue and talent; they put on the act of working well and for the benefit of others. A great deal of deception is put into the pretence of being worthy. People of good will, being in favour of truth, have a natural propensity to spontaneity. Unhealthy souls, in contrary fashion, lean towards calculation. The great hope is that through dissimulation, wealth and worldly success will be achieved. In this way the spiritually healthy person can be knocked out of the race and removed from the field. His clothes become donned in order to deprive him of his birthright.

Secondly, the person of good will becomes the victim of a process of isolation. One of the best ways to counter his role and impact, and to remove the challenge and competition he represents, is to deprive him of company, points of contact, and possibilities of participation. He must be desocialised. As a result of the practice of such a policy he comes to lack space in which to move, a context in which to operate, water in which to swim. By moving away from the man who lives the authentic spiritual life, by abandoning him to an authentic no-man's-land, and by depriving him of a theatre for his actions, unhealthy souls well realise that for all his virtue and his talents their spiritual counterpart will encounter massive difficulties in expressing his quality. His range of opportunities has become severely restricted. The pianist cannot play his admirable music because he no longer has a piano, or, if he does have one, it lacks large numbers of keys. In such a situation those who play badly, for all their faults and poor quality, have an immediate advantage. The whole strategy is fiendishly simple – isolate the good man and he becomes a much less dangerous competitor. Indeed, he may even disappear from the scene altogether.

Thirdly, power is employed to keep the good man down. He becomes subjected to dominance. If through wealth, or political control, or economic pressure, or many other mechanisms, the spiritually healthy person is subordinated and subjected to direction, then the threat that he represents can be reduced, perhaps even neutralised for ever. He can be prevented from expressing what he is; his potential becomes countered and checked. This is yet another reason why those who live on the dark side have an inordinate appetite for power – they know that it is a mighty weapon by which to fend off the threat posed by those who bear the light within them. This exercise of power, which is often economic in character, is frequently accompanied by aggression, defamation, deceit and denigration, which at times can even become sadistic. Indeed, a pleasure is often enjoyed in the practice of this subordination – the sense of inferiority of the man who lives on the dark side in relation to the man who lives according to the Spirit can be reduced. In attacking his spiritual superior, the spiritually unhealthy person gives vent to his anger and resentment at what he is. This exercise of dominance has one distasteful characteristic which requires comment. The wielding of power involves a natural sensitivity to strength and weakness. In the attack on the spiritually healthy person those who live on the dark side try to engender weakness or wait for weakness before attacking. Like hyenas who first seek to damage the legs of the antelope, or vultures who draw near a dying animal, darksiders sense that their assault must be launched when their prospective victim is debilitated – by the imposition of poverty, for example, or the suffering of loneliness, or by frustration in career.

Fourthly, there is the attempt by the spiritually unhealthy to corrupt the man who stewards his soul. Were that man to embrace the dark side, the dangers of his virtue and talents would be removed – he would have shifted over to the other camp. The threat which is posed would have disappeared because its bearer has changed. Within desocialised culture, at the level of conversation and action, by persuasion and example, and by pressure and prompting, the healthy soul is often encouraged to abandon what he is. This process of corruption takes a whole host of forms. The good man is told, for example, that man and the human experience conform in one way or another to the framework of analysis of the materialist matrix and that he should embrace its approach. He is thus beckoned towards ways of behaving and thinking which lead deep into the dark side. He is encouraged to compromise himself and to depart from his principles. Overall, darksiders aspire to the vampire effect in relation to those who live according to the Spirit – they seek to suck out the life-blood and transmit their characteristics. And this is mightily convenient to them from one specific point of view – good men with crosses, after all, not other vampires, are a danger to the living dead. This tactic of corruption is perhaps the most dangerous and potent of them all. Whereas in the other three principal forms of attack the main idea is to constrain and impede the spiritually healthy person, and to keep him down or to marginalise his role, in this case the goal is to change his nature. The vampire bite, after all, has a devastating effect. The victim passes over to a different dimension. He ceases to be a danger and will never be so again.

As is to be expected, many of those attacks on the spiritually healthy person are legitimated (and promoted) by the materialist matrix. Once again one sees how the inner features and mechanisms of desocialisation are interconnected by all kinds of routes. The launcher of those attacks finds a ready defence and self-exculpation for his aggression and he is both encouraged and justified in his various forms of assault. For example, he can say that his actions are determined and that he is not responsible for what happens – a licence to do as he pleases; or that truth is relative and that his view is as good as anybody else's – another licence to do as he pleases. In the same way, his rage and his anger can be legitimated with reference to his animal character or to his inner psychic impulses. Equally, his use of power in all its forms – but especially his use of economic power – to keep down a person of good will can be sanctioned with powerist or economistic arguments – is he not merely doing what is natural to man? At the same time the use of the specious and the fake as an instrument of deception can be upheld with reference to relativist ideas which remove any objective bases for quality or real standards. In addition, what happens to the spiritually healthy person, his suffering and his unhappy destiny, and the waste of his potential, can be shrugged off with reference to determinist ideas that this is what happens in life, and that this is the outcome of various impersonal forces such as society, the economy, the struggle for power...

Chapter Ten

A Crisis Foreseen: Melting into Air

The modern sensibility has frequently perceived the way modernity was going; there has been an intuitive recognition that a new epoch was on the way. From various perspectives it has been thought that society was 'melting into air'. In the same way there is now increasing comment on community breakdown, and this contemporary debate is itself a testimony to the presence of desocialisation. Past and present observation lends force to the contention that we are now undergoing a cultural crisis rooted in a move towards social atomisation. This book, therefore, presents no idiosyncratic or 'paranoid' point of view; this is no example of some kind of 'moral panic'; the previous chapters do not belong to a removed limbo all of their own. No comprehensive survey of modern Western or British thought is possible in these pages, although an attempt to approach thinkers from the point of view of their interest in the loss of community would certainly provide instructive and innovative perspectives. Hitherto no such project has ever been attempted and here merely an illustrative glance must suffice – *a tour d'horizon* which may, however, stimulate more detailed studies. Such a survey places this book, and the ideas it proposes, in an (albeit variegated) lineage which has all too often been overlooked and lends credence to much of its argument. It also involves a study of various explanations of our present predicament, all of which, however, because of their non-spiritualist interpretation, cannot really get to the root of the question. This glance falls first on the West and then on Great Britain.

The West

Max Stirner (1806-1856) was an obscure Berlin man of letters, principally a translator, a *habitué* of café society. In 1844 he published a work whose importance was to remain neglected for many decades. In this strange anarchist tract – and anarchism takes individualism to extremes – Stirner envisaged a 'union of egoists' atomised within a society dominated by selfish individualism and drained of its religious content. Although this is a work of propositive theory, it nonetheless contains accurate insights into future developments. Stirner could feel the future in his bones and should be read from this point of view. The move from Christian thought to the objectification of man is very well perceived:

> If community is once a need of man, and he finds himself furthered by it in his aims, then very soon, because it has become his principle, it prescribes to him its laws too, the laws of – society. The principle of men exalts itself into a sovereign power over them, becomes their supreme essence, their God, and, as such – lawgiver...and Christianity is the religion of society, for, as Feuerbach rightly says, although he does not mean it rightly, love is the essence of man; that is, the essence of society and of societary (communistic) man. All religion is a cult of society...Let us therefore not aspire to community [*Gemeinschaft*], but to *one-sidedness* [*Einseitigkeit*]. Let us not seek the most comprehensive commune, 'human society', but let us seek in others only means and organs which we may use as our property...In opposition to this I am told that I should be a man among 'fellow-men': I should 'respect' the fellow-man in them. For me no one is a person to be respected, not even the fellow-man, but solely, like other beings, an *object* in which I take an interest or else do not, an interesting or uninteresting object, a usable or unusable person.[1]

At the same time as Stirner was gazing into his accurate crystal ball, the great French liberal historian and cultural observer Alexis de Tocqueville was investigating what seemed to be the most advanced and modern nation on earth – the United States of America. When this author published his pioneering *Democracy in America* in the middle of the nineteenth century he was to a certain extent mapping out the future of the Western world and exploring the evolution of mass society in advanced industrialised countries. De Tocqueville envisaged the emergence of societies atomised by the triumph of a spirit of selfish individualism which he perceived as being rooted in the latent egalitarianism of the democratic outlook:

> I have shown how it is that in ages of equality every man seeks for his opinions within himself; I am now to show how it is that in the same ages all his feelings are turned towards himself alone. *Individualism* is a novel expression, to which a novel idea has given birth. Our fathers were only acquainted with *égoisme* (selfishness). Selfishness is a passionate and exaggerated love of self, which leads a man to connect everything with himself and to prefer himself to everything in the world. Individualism is a mature and calm feeling, which disposes each member of the community to sever himself from the mass of his fellows and to draw apart with his family and his friends, so that after he has thus formed a little circle of his own, he willingly leaves society at large to itself. Selfishness originates in blind instinct; individualism proceeds from erroneous judgement more than from depraved feelings; it originates as much in deficiencies of mind as in perversity of heart.
>
> Selfishness blights the germ of all virtue; individualism, at first, only saps the virtues of public life; but in the long run it attacks and destroys all others and is at length absorbed in downright selfishness. Selfishness is a vice as old as the world, which does not belong to one form of society more than to another; individualism is of democratic origin, and it threatens to develop in the same ratio as the equality of condition.[2]

Other thinkers of the time maintained that modern economic processes were the real agents of social dissolution. One of de Tocqueville's most famous contemporaries, Karl Marx, believed that the modern economic system, which he described with the term 'capitalism', was destined to break down community bonds. In *The Communist Manifesto* (1848), which he wrote with Friedrich Engels (1820-1895), Marx argued that wherever the 'bourgeoisie' had gained the upper hand the individual was left with 'no other nexus between man and man than naked self-interest' and that all 'fixed, fast-frozen relations, with their train of ancient and venerable prejudices and opinions, are swept away'. Marx's general vision of the path modernity was taking was expressed in a phrase which was to become famous: 'All that is solid melts into air'.[3] And after a visit to London, Engels was moved to write that 'the dissolution of mankind into monads, of which each one has a separate principle, the world of atoms, is here carried out to its extreme'.[4] The

French positivist philosopher and proto-sociologist Auguste Comte (1798-1857) also believed that modern economic processes contained great dangers. He warned that work specialisation would produce social separation. The individual would be directed towards his own special activity and thus constantly reminded of his own personal interest. For this reason 'the same principle which alone permitted the development and extension of society in general threatens...to split it up into a host of incohesive corporations'.[5]

De Tocqueville, Marx, Engels and Comte all gave a major impulse to the development of sociology. The later founding fathers of this discipline shared many of their anxieties. At the end of the century Emile Durkheim (1858-1917) warned that the 'division of labour' – a process which he believed was of decisive importance in the shaping of modern society – could have very damaging consequences for social ties within a community: 'If normally the division of labour produces social solidarity, it can happen, however, that it has entirely different or even opposite results'.[6] Another of the founding fathers of sociology, Max Weber, was deeply worried about the desocialising effects of modern 'bureaucratic' methods – a term he employed in a very broad sense. We are told that he identified 'bureaucracy with rationality, and the process of rationalisation with mechanism, depersonalisation, and oppressive routine'.[7] For such reasons Weber was very pessimistic about the direction Western society was taking:

> No one knows who will live in this cage in the future, or whether at the end of this tremendous development entirely new prophets will arise, or there will be a great rebirth of old ideas and ideals, or if neither, mechanised petrification, embellished with a sort of convulsive self-importance. For the last stage of this cultural development, it might well be truly said: "Specialists without spirit, sensualists without heart; this nullity imagines that it has attained a level of civilisation never before achieved."[8]

In recent decades the description of the breakdown of community has been a characteristic of the work of many authors in the United States of America. Because of the affinity between modern American and British society, and because of the impact of Americanisation on the way we live on this side of the Atlantic, their observations are of especial interest to this study.

In the late 1960s Alvin Toffler observed high-speed cultural change in American society and believed that this was disturbing modern man.

The key phrase he employed was 'future shock' – 'the shattering stress and disorientation that we induce in individuals by subjecting them to too much change in too short a time'.[9] Mobility of work and residence, rapid changes in products and buildings, the presence of the instant, and high velocity alterations in beliefs and conventions were creating an environment that brought with it the dynamics of adaptive breakdown. All this meant that 'many members of the super-industrial society will never "feel at home" in it. Like the voyager who takes up residence in an alien country, only to find, once adjusted, that he must move on to another, and yet another, we shall come to feel like "strangers in a strange land"'.[10] A few years later, in *The Pursuit of Loneliness. American Culture at Breaking Point*, Philip Slater dwelt upon the widespread loss of social ties, observed that a life based upon competitive individualism was destined to be a 'lonely one',[11] and declared that 'we less and less often meet our fellow man to share and exchange, and more and more often encounter him as an impediment or a nuisance'.[12]

Another American thinker, Theodore Roszak, in his book *Person/ Planet. The Creative Disintegration of Industrial Society*, published a few years later, argued in Weberian style that the massive scale of modern society (and he was chiefly referring to American society) and the processes its institutions promoted was dehumanising society and creating an atomised way of living. 'At work, at school, in the streets, in the market place we are ciphers and masses', he observed, 'and so we come to know ourselves and one another – as manpower units, welfare loads, unemployment statistics, public opinion polls, media ratings, body counts, computer print outs...rarely as you and me'.[13] In *The Culture of Narcissism. American Life in an Age of Diminishing Expectations* (1979), Christopher Lasch describes a society atomised and rendered inhuman by a form of selfish individualism which carries egoism to monstrous extremes: 'To live for the moment is the prevailing fashion – to live for yourself'.[14] Such a context means that 'social conditions today encourage a survival mentality'[15] which in turn produces 'men and women who are at heart antisocial'.[16] The picture he presented is familiar:

> Our society, far from fostering private life at the expense of public life, has made deep and lasting friendships, love affairs, and marr-iages increasingly difficult to achieve. As social life becomes more and more warlike and barbaric, personal relations, which ostensibly pro-vide relief from these conditions, take on the character of combat.[17]

Many of these strands were built upon by the Communitarian movement which emerged in the United States in the 1980s. It has since achieved a notable impact in the Anglo-Saxon world and beyond, and has given rise to intense debate within the university forum. Inspired by the political theorist Amitai Etzioni, this movement has achieved major insights into the nature of desocialisation and the devastation it has caused. It is perhaps the first scholarly attempt to provide a systematic account of our present predicament and our debt towards this movement is thus very great. Etzioni places the blame for the fall of community principally at the door of government intervention and the rise of selfish individualism. In these strictures on the lifestyle of egoism he echoes the sentiments of de Tocqueville:

> It is my thesis that millions of individual Americans, the pillars of a free society and a vigorous economy, have been cut off from one another and have lost their effectiveness. Many Americans...are no longer willing or able to take care of themselves, and each other. Indeed, the rise of ego-centred individuals has paralleled the rise of big government. Both constitute a retreat from community, from family, from schools, and neighbourhoods, and from a viable and effective self.
>
> To put it differently, we have experienced a hollowing of America, in which community was whittled down. Greater reliance on government has been accompanied by promotion of a particular brand of individualism best labelled egotism, sometimes referred to as "me-ism" or hedonism.[18]

And in the year 2000, in his *Bowling Alone. The Collapse and Revival of American Community*, R.D. Putnam wrote in the introduction:

> For the first two-thirds of the twentieth century a powerful tide bore Americans into ever deeper engagement in the life of their communities, but a few decades ago – silently, without warning – that tide reversed and we were overtaken by a treacherous rip current. Without at first noticing, we have been pulled apart from one another and from our communities over the last third of the century.[19]

There have also been overviews of the West. In 1975 R. Nisbet published his *Twilight of Authority* and declared that a crisis of civilisation was in progress. The 'rootlessness of our age'[20] was expressed in the decline of authority, the waning of patriotism, the diminishing legitimacy of public institutions and 'the decline – even disappearance in spreading sections – of the local community, the

dislocation of kinship, and the erosion of the sacred in human affairs'.[21]
His general overall picture, with its reference to the rise of individualism,
hedonism, relativism and egalitarianism, is highly instructive:

> Periodically in Western history twilight ages make their appearance.
> Processes of decline and erosion of institutions are more evident
> than those of genesis and development. Something like a vacuum
> obtains in the moral order for large numbers of people. Human
> loyalties, uprooted from accustomed soil, can be seen tumbling
> across the landscape with no scheme of larger purpose to fix them.
> Individualism reveals itself less as achievement and enterprise than
> as egoism and mere performance. Retreat from the major to the
> minor, from the noble to the trivial, the communal to the personal,
> and from the objective to the subjective is commonplace. There is a
> widely expressed sense of degradation of values and of corruption
> of culture. The sense of estrangement from community is strong.
>
> Accompanying the decline of institutions and the decay of values
> in such ages is the cultivation of power that becomes increasingly
> military, or paramilitary, in shape...The centralization and,
> increasingly, individualization of power is matched in the social
> and cultural spheres by a combined hedonism and egalitarianism,
> each in its way a reflection of the destructive impact of power on the
> hierarchy that is native to the social bond...So, I believe, is the
> twentieth century in the West a twilight age.[22]

In 1984 R. Lowenthal published *Social Change and Cultural Crisis*.
In it he analysed 'the cultural crisis of the industrially advanced
democracies and the "Western civilization" common to most of them'.[23]
At the heart of this crisis he detected the '"loss of world orientation"
and the "loss of ties"' caused by the inability of our civilisation to
reinterpret our basic values and adapt the norms of our conduct and our
institutions to 'processes of long-term social change'. The loss of world
orientation was said to be rooted in a 'shattering of the faith in a
recognizable meaning of human life and of social evolution in general'
and the loss of ties 'has resulted from the increasing difficulty of
socialization and identity-formation produced by accelerated change in
the conditions of life'. Part of this loss was to be found in 'the weakness
of the tie to the national or political community resulting from the
absence of historical identification with it.'[24]

Surveying the evolution of Western societies from the 1960s onwards,
Eric Hobsbawm has provided us with penetrating insights into the

modern condition. 'The drama of collapsed traditions and values lay not so much in the material disadvantages of doing without the social and personal services once supplied by family and community' but 'in the disintegration both of the old value systems and the customs and conventions which controlled human behaviour'.[25] Hobsbawm's critique of the thought and practice of selfish individualism, and his stress on the fundamental affinity between such apparently opposing creeds as postmodernism and marketism, should be read a thousand times over:

> The old moral vocabulary of rights and duties, mutual obligations, sin and virtue, sacrifice, conscience, rewards and penalties, could no longer be translated into the new language of desired gratification. Once such practices and institutions were no longer accepted as a way of ordering society that linked people to each other and ensured social cooperation and reproduction, most of their capacity to structure human social life vanished. They were reduced simply to expressions of individuals' preference, and claims that the law should recognise the supremacy of these preferences. Uncertainty and unpredictability impended. Compass needles no longer had a North, maps became useless. This is what became increasingly evident in the most developed countries from the 1960s on. It found expression in a variety of theories, from extreme free-market liberalism to 'postmodernism' and its like, which tried to sidestep the problem of judgement and values altogether, or rather to reduce them to the single denominator of the unrestricted freedom of the individual.[26]

In his work *The Great Disruption* (2000), the American sociologist and cultural analyst Francis Fukuyama analyses in detail the 'seriously deteriorating social conditions in most of the industrialised world' that took place 'from roughly the mid-1960s to the early 1990s'.[27] Observing 'crime and social disorder', 'the decline of kinship as a social institution', declines in fertility, rising rates of divorce, the increasing number of children born outside marriage, and a deep decline in 'trust and confidence in institutions', he also stresses that 'the nature of people's involvement with each other changed as well…their mutual ties tended to be less permanent, less engaged, and with smaller groups of people.'[28] Fukuyama identifies these processes closely with the emergence in the West of the 'information society':[29]

> Was it just an accident that these negative social trends, which together reflected weakening social bonds and common values

holding people together in Western societies, occurred just as economies in those societies were making the transition from the industrial to the information era? The hypothesis of this book is that the two were in fact intimately connected...The connections were technological, economic, and cultural...And the culture of intensive individualism, which in the marketplace and laboratory leads to innovation and growth, spilled over into the realm of social norms, where it corroded virtually all forms of authority and weakened the bonds holding families, neighbourhoods, and nations together.[30]

More recently Z. Bauman has described the absence, weakness and transience of social ties in the West in his *Liquid Modernity* (2000) and A. Touraine has detailed the configurations of the breakdown of social belonging in our hemisphere in his *Can We Live Together. Equality and Difference* (2000), attributing the phenomenon to the dual processes of globalisation and particularisation.

The ravages of desocialisation in post-modern French society have been described in detail by the novelist Michel Houellebecq, although the observations he makes are of far wider application. In his aptly titled work, *Le particules élémentaires* (translated into English with the title 'Atomised'), this author describes a world well-known to Western postmodern man: isolated individuals, unhappy and fractured families, men and women who cannot relate to each other, mental disturbance, and above all else profound loneliness. Sketching a cultural panorama made up of 'social breakdown', 'the destruction of Judeo-Christian values', 'the inexorable rise in the divorce rate', 'the cult of the body', 'the suicide of the West', and having one of his protagonists ask the question: 'how long could Western civilisation continue without religion?',[31] Houellebecq, with a cultural perceptiveness that echoes that of his countryman de Tocqueville, is more than aware of how changes in anthropological models form an important background to this disaster:

> Christian doctrine, which had for long been the dominant moral force in Western civilisation, accorded unconditional importance to every human life from conception to death. The significance was linked to the belief in the existence within the body of a *soul* – which was by definition immortal and would ultimately return to God. In the 19th and 20th centuries, advances in biology gave rise to a more determinist anthropology, radically different in its assumptions and significantly more moderate in its ethical counsel. On the one hand, this meant that the foetus...was no longer

recognised as a viable individual except by consensus (absence of genetic defects, parental consent). On the other hand, the new concept of *human dignity* meant that the elderly, a collection of steadily failing organs, had the right to life only as long as they continued to function. The ethical problems posed by the extremes of youth and age (abortion, and some decades later, euthanasia) would become the battleground for different and radically antagonistic worldviews.

The agnosticism at the heart of the French republic would facilitate the progressive, hypocritical and slightly sinister triumph of the determinist worldview.[32]

Houellebecq belongs to a lineage that is by now well consolidated within Western (and British) literature and art. Indeed, during the contemporary age the themes of actual or impending loneliness, disaffection and alienation, detachment and estrangement have made themselves increasingly felt. From the bewildered victims of Kafka to the outsider of Camus, from the discontented figures of Bataille to the troubled personalities of Grass, from the alienated individuals of Céline to the isolated heroes of Conrad, from the unhappy spirits of Virginia Woolf to the lost souls of Samuel Beckett, from the autobiographical rebel hero of Joyce to the tribulations faced by the characters of William Golding, not to speak of the horrors described in the novels of I. McEwan, emphasis has been increasingly placed on individuals immersed in a loss of ties. Such social dislocation is often connected to personal disintegration and it is for this reason that mental disturbance has often been a chosen area of exploration – elements much anticipated in the pioneering work of Dostoevsky. 'Poets and novelists today', observed Lasch, 'far from glorifying the self, chronicle its disintegration'.[33] Painting has followed similar paths, as the works of Munch or Bacon illustrate, and the visitor to the National Portrait Gallery in London can now pass through gallery after gallery of pictures of subjects separated from others and often bathed in a strangely disturbed light. 'Revolt, anomie, alienation, and other expressions of individual dislocation in the cultural realm are apparent enough', observed R. Nisbet, 'the uprooted or lost individual is surely the dominant figure of contemporary art, letters and philosophy'.[34]

Great Britain

What about commentary on desocialisation in Great Britain? On the whole, views about the breakdown of community have fallen into two camps which reflect party allegiance and political point of view. On the Left, there has tended to be the belief that the economic system is to blame, that unfettered market forces or 'capitalism' act to dissolve social ties, and that deep-lying economic processes drive people into opposing and hostile classes or into a condition of competitive rivalry. Hence a frequent intention has been to analyse and then reform the underlying economic structures of society. On the Right, the Left has often been held to be responsible – this very intention is said to be at fault. It is argued that left-wing state intervention in the workings of society and the economy acts to disrupt mechanisms of unity and cohesion. It has also been stressed that the radical proponents of change erode those inherited values and practices which sustain community. A frequent aim has been to inhibit such intervention and to defend such values and practices. These two approaches emerge very clearly from the following brief survey of the last two hundred years. Attitudes towards community, and explanations as to its decline, turn out to constitute a major line of party demarcation, even though, paradoxically, these opposing strands are often moved by the same deeply-felt concern to keep people together. Let the Right be considered first.

In the 1790s Edmund Burke, the Anglo-Irish politician and philosopher, was much perturbed at Continental developments. He believed that the dislocation caused by the French Revolution was a direct outcome of attempts to experiment on a society without respect for its cultural heritage. 'It is with infinite caution', he warned, 'that any man ought to venture upon pulling down an edifice which has answered in any tolerable degree for ages the common purposes of society'.[35] He laid especial blame at the door of the deleterious impact of a group of French intellectuals – the famous *philosophes*. In *Reflections on the Revolution in France* (1790) Burke sought to prevent his fellow-countrymen from following in the footsteps of their neighbours across the Channel. In his judgement the effectiveness and wisdom of a culture were the outcome of generations of experiment, and this viable common project had to be stewarded with trusting wisdom by its contemporary guardians. Mere reason was no secure basis for plans of radical reform. To tamper with cultures was to play with fire, and disintegration was one of the great risks run:

Society is indeed a contract...it is not a partnership in things subservient only to the gross animal existence of a temporary or perishable nature. It is a partnership in all science; a partnership in all art; partnership in every virtue, and in all perfection. As the ends of such a partnership cannot be obtained in many generations, it becomes a partnership not only between those who are living, but between those who are living, those who are dead, and those who are to be born. Each contract of each particular state is but a clause in the great primeval contract of eternal society, linking the lower with the higher natures, concerning the visible and the invisible world, according to a fixed compact sanctioned by the inviolable oath, each in their appointed place. This law is not subject to the will of those, who by an obligation above them, and infinitely superior, are bound to submit their will to that law. The municipal corporations of that universal kingdom are not morally at liberty at their pleasure, and on their speculations of a contingent improvement, wholly to separate and tear asunder the bands of that subordinate community, and to dissolve it into an unsocial, uncivil, unconnected chaos of elementary principles.[36]

Benjamin Disraeli (1804-1881), the Conservative leader and novelist, had an especial sensitivity to the new problems created and promoted by the industrial revolution. In the 1840s he had one of his literary characters declare:

"These is no community in England; there is aggregation, but aggregation under circumstances which make it rather a dissociating than a uniting principle...It is a community of purpose that constitutes society...without that, men may be drawn into contiguity, but they still continue virtually isolated."

"And is that their condition in cities?"

"It is their condition everywhere; but in cities that condition is aggravated. A density of population implies a severer struggle for existence, and a consequent repulsion of elements brought into too close contact. In great cities men are brought together by the desire of gain. They are not in a state of cooperation, but of isolation, as to the making of fortunes; and for all the rest they are careless of neighbours. Christianity teaches us to love our neighbour as ourself, modern society acknowledges no neighbour."[37]

Some decades on the third Marquess of Salisbury (1830-1903) was alarmed at the advance of collectivist thought and proposals within the

British Isles. Salisbury, leader of the Conservative Party and four times prime minister, was also a political thinker of note. Throughout his public career he feared the disruptive consequences of political radicalism and voiced many of his apprehensions in a famous article entitled 'Disintegration', published in 1883. Salisbury believed that during cycles of economic depression that 'organizer of decay, the Radical agitator' arose to persuade the people that politics was the cure for their ills. This set in motion a struggle between rich and poor which 'slowly kills by disintegration. It eats out the common sentiments and mutual sympathies which combines classes into a patriotic State'.[38] Salisbury's successor, Arthur Balfour (1848-1930), also believed that one of the chief tasks of the Conservative Party was to 'resist the disintegrating forces of modern Radicalism'.[39] In the 1930s T.S. Eliot, a thinker clearly within the traditionalist orbit, warned in *The Idea of the Christian Society* (1940) that 'modern liberalism' acted to destroy the 'traditional social habits of the people' and thus worked to dissolve 'their natural collective consciousness into individual constituents'.[40]

The Austrian philosopher F.A. Hayek, another naturalised British subject, expressed the belief in the 1940s – and repeatedly thereafter – that collectivist-inspired state intervention was striking a mighty blow at the nation's cultural inheritance. In *The Road to Serfdom* (1944) he detected a change in moral values caused by an advance of left-wing thought and practice which was destroying 'almost all the traditions and institutions in which British moral genius has found its most character-istic expression, and which in turn have moulded the national character and the whole moral climate of England'.[41] Hayek was to prove an important source of inspiration for the 'New Conservative' experiment of the 1980s, and Margaret Thatcher herself was another proponent of the view that the nation's anthropological heritage had been severely compromised:

> I was brought up by a Victorian grandmother. You were taught to work jolly hard, you were taught to improve yourself, you were taught self-reliance, you were taught to live within your income, you were taught that cleanliness was next to Godliness. You were taught self-respect, you were taught always to give a hand to your neighbour, you were taught tremendous pride in your country, you were taught to be a good member of your community...I was brought up with a very strong sense of duty...You don't hear so much about

those things these days, but they were good values and they led to tremendous improvements in the standard of living.[42]

In part the Thatcher governments may be seen as a neo-Burkean attempt to revitalise this lost cultural legacy by reducing the role of the state within the economy. In this they may also, in part, be seen as a direct response to desocialisation. Mrs Thatcher herself declared:

What's irritated me about the whole direction of politics in the last thirty years is that it's always been towards the collectivist society. People have forgotten about the personal society. And they say: do I count? Do I matter? To which the answer is, Yes. And therefore it isn't that I set out on economic policies; it's that I set out really to change the approach, and changing the economics is the way of changing that approach. If you change the approach you really are after the heart and the soul of the nation. Economics are the method; the object is to change the heart and soul.[43]

Her successor also lamented the decline of community and also linked it to the advance of state intervention. In a significant speech in 1992 John Major drew attention to widespread anxiety caused by threats to the values which were at the basis of British society: 'People are not certain. They feel uneasy; they feel threatened; they lose their bearings as a result of that uneasiness'. The prime minister called for a 'reinforcement of the social cement that binds us together'. He had especial praise for the 'little networks and small communities – Burke's 'little platoons', if you like – that are the tent-pegs securing our wind-blown society to the ground'. Social cohesion, in his view – and here he expressed a long-standing Tory contention – had been undermined by state intervention: 'It is not where the free market pervades that ties of community are under threat; it is where the State owns and controls to the greatest extent that you find great difficulties and great threats'. Local communities had been hit hardest where the state had been most interfering. In addition to reversing such government-induced dislocation, it was necessary to uphold 'our belief in community and in tradition' by encouraging 'the habit of volunteering, which cements together our society and is one of the great glories of our national life' and by promoting 'those institutions which give continuity and a framework to our national life: the monarchy, Parliament, our churches'.[44]

In 1999 a journalist and intellectual of the Right, Peter Hitchens, published a work entitled 'The Abolition of Britain'. In this volume, in which the author refers to the 'cultural revolution'[45] and the 'atomization of society'[46] that have taken place during the post-modern period, we are presented with a long litany of the symptoms of cultural decomposition and the loss of social ties. In the conclusion Hitchens declares:

> We tore up every familiar thing in our landscape...life is no longer so safe, so polite or so gentle as it once was...bureaucratic law rather than the spirit of an agreed and respected moral code...the collapse of the family...the decay of authority and the withering away of common citizenship...the spread of illegal drugs...the explosion in petty theft...all this is taking place in a landscape of change, change and more change...The reforms and feverish, unsettling change which have continued through the whole of the late twentieth century have...weakened the people's attachment to their traditions and institutions, their liberties and their independence...We have abolished the very customs, manners, methods, standards and laws which for centuries restrained us from the sort of barbaric behaviour that less happy lands suffer...the future is worrying and uncertain.[47]

More recently the leader of the Conservative Party has declared that we now have to face the realities of a 'broken society' and in typically Conservative style David Cameron has drawn attention to the decline in the moral underpinnings to social cohesion:

> We have seen a decades-long erosion of responsibility, of social virtue, of self-discipline, respect for others, deferring gratification instead of instant gratification. Instead we prefer moral neutrality, a refusal to make judgments about what is good and bad behaviour, right and wrong behaviour. Bad. Good. Right. Wrong. These are words that our political system and our public sector scarcely dare use any more...Our relationships crack up, our marriages break down, we fail as parents and as citizens just like everyone else. But if the result of this is a stultifying silence about things that really matter, we re-double the failure. Refusing to use these words – right and wrong – means a denial of personal responsibility and the concept of a moral choice...There is a danger of becoming quite literally a de-moralised society.[48]

What about the Left? Many alarmed observers were convinced that the industrial revolution was breaking down the ties which bound British society together. William Cobbett (1763-1835), the anti-industrial writer, believed that the new class system was 'unnatural' and accused one of its champions of trying to break the 'chain of connection between the rich and the poor. You are for demolishing all small tradesmen. You are for reducing the community to two classes: Masters and Slaves'.[49] In 1815 Robert Owen (1771-1858), an industrialist who was one of the founders of the co-operative movement, predicted that the new manufacturing system would 'produce the most lamentable and permanent evils' unless legislative action was taken, and asserted that 'all ties between employers and employed are frittered down to the consideration of what immediate gain each can derive from the other'.[50] Thomas Carlyle (1795-1881), the historian and writer, is difficult to place politically, but he, too, railed against the new age:

> We call it a society; and go about professing openly the totalest separation, isolation. Our life is not a mutual helpfulness; but rather, cloaked under due laws-of-war, named 'fair competition' and so forth, it is mutual hostility. We have profoundly forgotten everywhere that cash-payment is not the sole relation of human beings; we think, nothing doubting, that it absolves and liquidates all engagements of man.[51]

John Ruskin (1819-1900), the historian of architecture and proto-socialist intellectual, later gave free vent to similar anxiety:

> It is not, truly speaking, the labour that is divided; but the men: – Divided into mere segments of men – broken into small fragments and crumbs of life...It is verily this degradation of the operative into a machine, which, more than any other evil of the times, is leading the mass of the nations everywhere into vain, incoherent, destructive struggling for a freedom of which they cannot explain the nature to themselves...the foundations of society were never yet shaken as they are at this day.[52]

The artist, writer and Socialist thinker William Morris (1834-1896), an admirer of both Carlyle and Ruskin, confessed that the dominant passion of his life was 'hatred of modern civilisation': 'What shall I say concerning its mastery of and its waste of mechanical power, its commonwealth so poor, its enemies of the commonwealth so rich, its stupendous organization – for the misery of life!'[53] In his utopian tract *News from Nowhere* (1891), he gave voice to the familiar left-wing hope of achieving restored community through a newly-created classless society. G.D.H. Cole was a Christian Socialist whose projected local guild system was designed to give rise to an effective community-based democracy. He aimed thereby to surpass mass democracy, which he asserted was 'atomistically conceived': 'Torn away from his fellows, from the small groups which he and they had been painfully learning to manage, the individual was lost'.[54] And the historian and Socialist thinker R.H. Tawney, in his *Equality* of 1931, declared that:

> What is repulsive is not that one man should earn more than others... it is that some classes should be excluded from the heritage of civilisation which others enjoy, and that the face of human fellowship, which is ultimate and profound, should be obscured by economic contrasts which are trivial and superficial.[55]

Moving to more recent times, Tony Blair, the leader of the Labour Party and three times prime minister, dedicated great thought and consideration to the question of the decline of community. He called for the rebuilding of social cohesion and argued that the 'breakdown in law and order is intimately linked to the breakup of a strong sense of community. And the breakup of community in turn is, to a crucial degree, consequent on the breakdown of family life'.[56] His remedies followed two chief paths. On the one hand there was a call for moral regeneration, for the recognition of personal responsibility towards others, and for reflection upon 'the values and principles we believe in and what they mean for us, not just as individuals but as a community'.[57] On the other, there was a rejection of individualistic market economics and a call for the creation of a society which was effective in its welfare provision and provided a suitable economic framework for personal development. These were deemed the routes to active participation in a viable and regenerated community:

> Successful communities are about what people give as much as what they take, and any attempt to rebuild community for a modern age must assert that personal and social responsibility are not optional extras but core principles of a thriving society today.[58]

Suggested Solutions

In Great Britain, therefore, the causes of our cultural crisis have been chiefly attributed to (1) the workings of the free market economy, which have involved (a) the breaking up of society into separate and hostile classes and groups, or (b) the promotion of a socially acidic selfish individualism (or a combination of both); (2) the large-scale intervention of the state in the economy, which has sabotaged natural organic processes of co-operation and collaboration; and (3) the erosion of moral and ethical values which favour community and cohesion – the causes of which are variously attributed. The solutions seem to boil down to (1) a reactivation of such values; (2) a further reduction of the role of the state and the development of voluntary association and civic initiative; and (3) the achievement of greater social integration through the more effective state provision of social support, economic guarantees, and life opportunity. But however valuable and useful these remedies may be they do not really get to the heart of the matter. This is because in essentials our cultural crisis is principally a *spiritual* crisis, and it is this dimension which must be tackled first. It is to the real solution that we now address ourselves in the conclusion.

Conclusion

A Return to the Soul?

'Today an invasive materialism is imposing its dominion on us in many different forms', wrote John Paul II, 'and with an aggressiveness sparing no one'.[1] Through these pages the reader has been accompanied on a Dantean itinerary of the assault on the soul made up of a series of blows – the idea that the soul does not exist and a consequent discouragement of its guardianship; the attack on key features of the life according to the Spirit and the promotion of the dark side of man's spirituality, in particular through the encouragement of selfish individualism; and the establishment of a cultural pattern equipped with mighty mechanisms of self-reproduction which sustains these processes and systematically generates spiritual ill-health. Other historical developments have aided in this assault, most notably the withdrawal of Christian culture and the rise of mass society. This spiritual condition, which has gained such ground in the way we live now, is the outcome of many centuries of erroneous evolution. The true significance of what has happened should not escape us. As a people we have helped to construct a way of thinking and living – an anthropological process or cultural pattern – which by a whole variety of mechanisms assails the soul: darkening it, deadening it, and depriving it of its true purpose.

The precondition to such success is to be found in a simple point of departure – in the fact that today in human affairs and perspectives, self-analysis and the observation of others, in general thought and moral reflection, in approaching reality and deciding on our purpose, in acting

and thinking, the soul is increasingly left out of the equation. Soullessness advances. As we begin the third millennium we are frequently
unaware of what we are. For all his astonishing scientific and technological knowledge, post-modern man is marked by areas of terrifying
ignorance, especially about himself. He has all too often forgotten what
he is. A regression has taken place. Yet at the same time this fall
constitutes an invitation to reject what has happened, understand its
significance, and move upwards and outwards. After all, divine law is
corrective, not punitive.

This assault on the soul is at the heart of a cultural crisis which centres
around the breakdown of community. The physicist F.A Wolf's
reflections are incisive:

> Our Western approach to life seems to be leading to an ever-growing
> "cool" isolation – this insularity results in many people finding
> themselves only able to communicate with the world from behind
> computer screens or within the confines of an office. We are growing
> apart from one another, and this lack of communion is taking its
> toll...I call this feeling *soul-loss*. I see it as the general malaise of
> Western civilisation – the loss of a sacred sense of life.[2]

The denial of the spirit is reflected in a society which at many points is
marked by fragmentation and splitting, fissures and fault-lines, distance
and gaps, breakage and dismantling. Separation, detachment and disengagement are the spreading lot of contemporary man as he faces
up to the twenty-first century. Fractures abound in our collective
broken home: between men and women, husbands and wives, parents
and children; between relatives, neighbours, and the generations;
between employers and employees, landlords and tenants, politicians
and voters, and governors and the governed; between workmates and
between colleagues; between those who sell and those who buy, and
between professionals and their clients; between teachers and their
pupils, doctors and their patients, and policemen and the public; between
different political persuasions, religious denominations, and ethnic
groups; and between fellow-countrymen. That 'civic friendship'[3] to
which Maritain referred is increasingly thin on the ground. Such
fractures are the substance of desocialisation – wounds produced by
that absence of love for love and for truth which arises naturally when
guardianship of the soul is neglected. This gap which has grown up
between man and man is rooted in the break between the individual and
his soul but it is also to be found in the fracture between man and God

– in turning our backs on the spirit we reject our divine origins, calling and destiny. In distancing ourselves from God we cannot but distance ourselves from each other. 'All the lonely people', wrote Lennon and McCartney, 'where do they all come from?' This book hopes to have supplied some answers.

This process has been marked by a hollowing of our cultural inheritance. Culture loss is ever present. We have also had to endure fractures with our past. In recent times we have been subject to high levels of deculturalisation and have witnessed the (often deliberately engineered) removal of a great many of the shared customs and habits, conventions and accords, and principles and rituals, which previously generated community. At the same time there has been a decline in respect for certain institutions and systems of guidance. The sacred has faded from many a horizon. Of course, this is not only a matter of fractures with our past. We are also dealing with breaks with the future. Burke observed that society is a 'partnership not only between those who are living, but between those who are living, those who are dead, and those who are to be born'.[4] In failing to hand on the cultural bases of true community to the unborn we also compromise our responsibilities to those to come. Indeed, we are engaging in a truly selfish neglect. Here, too, there is a powerful loss of ties – in this case between those alive now and those who will arrive in the future. Overall, therefore, much of the inherited anthropological patrimony working for social cohesion has been dispersed or lost. T.S. Eliot had much to say about this condition and he also warned against the adoption of erroneous answers. He seems to have sensed the future mistaken response of a contrived return to 'roots' or the artificial resuscitation of the dead and buried:

> Tradition is not solely, or even primarily, the maintenance of certain dogmatic beliefs; these beliefs have come to take their living form in the course of the formation of a tradition. What I mean by tradition involves all those habitual actions, habits and customs, from the most significant religious rite to our conventional way of greeting a stranger, which represent the blood kinship of "the same people living in the same place". It involves a good deal which can be called taboo: that this word is used in our time in an exclusively derogatory sense is to me a curiosity of some significance. We become conscious of these items, or conscious of their importance, usually only after they have begun to fall into desuetude, as we are aware of the leaves of a tree when the autumn wind begins to blow

them off – when they have separately ceased to be vital. Energy may be wasted at that point in a frantic endeavour to collect the leaves as they fall and gum them onto the branches: but the sound tree will put forth new leaves, and the dry tree should be put to the axe. We are always in danger, in clinging to an old tradition, or attempting to re-establish one, of confusing the vital and the unessential, the real and the sentimental. Our second danger is to associate tradition with the immovable; to think of it as something hostile to all change; to aim to return to some previous condition which we imagine as having been capable of preservation in perpetuity, instead of aiming to stimulate the life which produced that condition in its time.[5]

British and Western man finds himself in a context where many old cultural and moral landmarks have been swept away by a historical earthquake. Around him in the post-modern landscape he often encounters empty space. Not only is it frequently not clear to him how his human environment expects him to behave, but there is also a common absence of love and truth. In such a deconstructed context there arises a feeling of loss, the unknown rears its head, and unease and anxiety are increasingly felt, if not a sense of horror. Fear is often in the air. The writer on animals, Gavin Maxwell, provided his own description of this kind of experience:

As soon as routine is broken a new element enters, in however minute and unrecognisable a trace – the fear of the unknown which is basic to the behaviour of all animals, including man. Every living creature exists by a routine of some kind; the small rituals are the landmarks, the boundaries of security, the reassuring walls that exclude a *horror vacui*; thus, in our own species, after some tempest of the spirit in which the landmarks seem to have been swept away, a man will reach out tentatively in mental darkness to feel the walls, to assure himself that they still stand where they stood – a necessary gesture, for the walls are of his own building, without universal reality, and what man makes he may destroy.[6]

As we embark on a project of reconstruction we must reflect upon what these new walls should be.

Certainly we are dealing with a transformation of epoch-making proportions. British (and Western) man is facing up to unprecedented conditions which place him in a context which he has never experienced before. The historical perspective employed in this book has constantly sought to emphasise and illuminate this point. That such a titanic change was on the way has been expected by many of the thinkers and observers of modern times. At the same time there have been intuitions as to the future emergence of some great climax or resolution. 'On all sides tyrants tremble, crowns are unsteady, the human race restive, on the watch for some better era, some divine war', wrote Walt Whitman (1819-1892) in the middle of the nineteenth century, 'no man knows what will happen next, but all know that some such things are to happen as mark the greatest moral convulsions of the earth'.[7] Weber envisaged modern man ending up in a cage and wondered what reactions this would produce. In the 1930s the German scientist Max Planck (1858-1947) wrote:

> We are living in a very singular moment of history. It is a crisis in the literal meaning of that word. In every branch of our spiritual and material civilization we seem to have arrived at a crucial turning point. This spirit shows itself not only in the actual state of public affairs, but also in the general attitude towards fundamental values in personal and social life.[8]

'Western civilisation to-day is passing through one of the most critical moments in its history', observed C. Dawson during the same decade. 'In every department of life traditional principles have been shaken and discredited, and we do not yet know what is going to take their place'.[9] In the 1940s Jacques Maritain published *The Twilight of Civilisation*. 'One may ask whether there have ever before in human history been people', observed Bonhoeffer at about the same time, 'with so little ground under their feet'.[10] 'All of us', declared Solzhenitsyn in the 1970s, 'are standing on the brink of a great historical cataclysm'.[11] 'As the twentieth century approaches its end, the conviction grows that many other things are ending too', wrote C. Lasch, 'Storm warnings, portents, hints of catastrophe haunt our times'.[12]

'How many dark movements in the civilized world!'[13] It is the contention of this spiritualist (and counter-materialist) work that our crisis springs from certain fundamental errors of the modern age which themselves are based upon a crucial mistake. As Leo Strauss observed: 'the crisis of modernity on which we have been reflecting leads to the suggestion that we should return. But return to what? Obviously to Western civilisation in its premodern integrity'.[14] This book argues that we must return to the soul and to God. It thus not only takes up the statement of Bonhoeffer – 'The most important question for the future is how we can find a basis for human life together, what spiritual realities and laws we accept as the foundations of a meaningful human life'[15] – but also echoes the thinking of one of the most important Christian philosophers of the last century:

> the drama of the modern democracies has consisted in the unwritten quest of something good, the city of the persons, masked by the error of the city of the individual, which, by nature, leads to dreadful liquidations. It is not for the philosophers to forecast whether they can yet reorientate themselves directly in the direction of the truth which they seek by disengaging the parasitical errors from their quest. Such reorientation would presuppose a radical transformation and a vast return towards the spirit.[16]

Such are the walls. In stressing the key role of the age of Enlightenment inheritance this work also necessarily implies that there is much room for a retrieval of the medieval and a positive appreciation of what was bequeathed to us by the ancient Greeks.

General apprehension is also heightened by a scanning of the signs of the times. We are living in an age when all kinds of worrying phenomena have dovetailed to crowd into a few decades. When we survey the physiognomy of the late-twentieth century experience and the contours of the post-modern we witness a whole host of developments that give rise to deep concern. It is almost as if at a certain hour a large number of vigilant geese had all begun their warning cries. But what does all this mean and can we penetrate the inner meaning of this cacophony? The spread of desocialisation and the advance of deChristianisation; the impact of deculturalisation and the crisis of personal identity; the rise of crime and the ubiquity of stress; the decline of the family and sexual confusion; AIDS and accelerating ecological imbalance; the possibility of human cloning and the dangers of genetic engineering – all these elements, and many others, mark out our epoch as one of menace, insecurity and uncertainty. But whatever the true significance of this crisis, however it may be decoded – in eschatological terms or otherwise – a decisive reaction is imperative. Indeed, the emergence and acceptance of all kinds of errors suggest that even worse is to come – resistance to even more virulent viruses weakens as the malaise advances. A swift response is necessary because trends suggest an accelerating process of decline.

To repeat an earlier phrase of this work, many children of post-modernity are not happy children. Perhaps we should now take a step back from the hurtling speed of change of modern times, the frenetic rhythms of daily life, and the kaleidoscopic processes of constant alteration, to reflect on what this means. Indeed, one way of celebrating the dawn of the third millennium is for contemporary man to take a pause for reflection. Since the age of the Enlightenment new directions have been taken and in surveying the destination we have reached we can take this opportunity to evaluate the wisdom of those choices. The spreading 'loss of ties' and all the suffering that goes with it does not suggest that things have turned out so well. Increasing disaffection, dislocation and disintegration within Western and British society indicate that much of the modern and post-modern direction has proved erroneous: in going against our spiritual and biological selves we have followed paths which go against the human. From this point of view, 'progress' far from necessarily being progressive, has frequently generated the negative, and at times what should really be perceived as horror.

Beyond the sphere of personal and cultural experience there is an area which provides grounds for special reflection. Western man's technological model of development, based upon the humanist-rationalist schema of the ordered dominance and exploitation of nature – a model which has produced such material abundance for our hemisphere – now seems face to face with a rebellion of the planet itself. The greenhouse effect and the ozone hole are the symbols of an ecological deterioration which suggests that our faith in this model has been misplaced. Man has wanted to go it alone but is now finding that the Creation is not so willing. Will he be able to draw the right conclusions?

Today there are various explanations of why desocialisation – in whatever terms the condition is described and in whatever ways it is perceived – lies upon us and is extending its grip. Equally, a large number of solutions are put forward by which to end our present plight. There is a debate in progress which is growing in importance and impact. Political discussion and writing, for example, contain analyses and proposals which (whether it is realised or not) are responses to the increasingly recognised crisis of our civilisation. Some argue that the free market is to blame; others that the interfering state has been the primary culprit. Some propose to revive virtues; others to expand rights. Some want to infuse new energy into community by promoting civic and voluntary initiative; others look to greater societal care and protection. And this is only to mention the most obvious proposed courses of action. No doubt in some way or other, with suitable adjustments and agreements, many of these approaches could have a beneficial effect. And it is also likely that in some form or other they will continue, or start, to be implemented or tested.

But in reality none of these remedies can get to the heart of the matter. With the waning of the concept of the soul it has become ever more difficult to achieve the necessary spiritual (and spiritualist) reading of our situation, and here we see that the cause of the crisis impedes its resolution. Indeed, these various proposals can actually compound the problem by expressing and promoting those very models of man which have caused us so much damage. Moreover, even where the suggestions are to be welcomed and are animated by the noblest of sentiments they will only skate on the surface unless accompanied by a reconstruction of the spiritual supports of society. Furthermore, there is the risk that in embracing remedies which offer an apparent *overall* solution – whether in the form of collectivism or marketism, postmodernism or rightsism – we will make matters even worse and thereby parallel the self-defeating personal responses to a loss of ties discussed in chapter nine. Similarly, there seems to be little mileage in those artificial and sometimes folkloristic attempts to restore or to return to what has passed. The nostalgic aspirations to imitate lost practices are often doomed to failure because they fail to reproduce what was at the base of such elements or because they take place in a context where suitable cultural supports are no longer present.

The incompleteness of many proposals produced by their lack of a spiritualist perspective is borne out by a consideration, for example, of the 'Communitarian' and 'virtues' movements. The former in its manifesto refers to the USA, but it could just as well refer to the UK or to other leading Western nations. The analysis, as far as it goes, is very valuable:

> American men, women, and children are members of many communities – families; neighbourhoods; innumerable social, religious, ethnic, workplace, and professional associations; and the body politic itself. Neither human existence nor individual liberty can be sustained for long outside the interdependent and overlapping communities to which all of us belong. Nor can any community long survive unless its members dedicate some of their attention, energy, and resources to shared projects.[17]

To this end the Communitarians are right to stress the importance of 'moral voices'; of starting 'with the family'; of schools and universities providing 'moral education'; of the role of 'intermediate groups'; of the fulfilment of 'duties to the polity'; and of the recognition of responsibilities – 'the moral commitments of parents, young persons, neighbours, and citizens'.[18] But the natural question arises – from where will such new steps forward spring? People may well be agreed on the need for such building-blocks to community, but is such a shared recognition in itself sufficient? If people are sunk in selfish individualism, will such proposals really find fertile terrain? Can such a programme achieve purchase amongst those who inwardly feel no propensity to love or to truth? What really needs to be done is to rekindle the spiritual flame within individuals; there must be a retrieval of the soul. These policies will then find natural support and secure anchorages – they will be embraced and promoted spontaneously.

Similarly, who could disagree with the following classic statement of virtues thinking? It is made by one of the guiding lights of an important group of Anglo-American intellectuals and academics who have sought to restore virtues to the centre of general thought and behaviour. A sensitivity to the phenomenon of desocialisation is more than evident:

As the second millennium draws to a close the full extent of Western society's moral and social crisis is more and more apparent. America and Britain are indeed lands of plenty, rich countries, technologically sophisticated countries, whose citizens live long and healthy lives. But they are also lands of other and darker plenties, plenty of crime, plenty of gratuitous violence, plenty of children without fathers, plenty of fear, more and more alienation from public institutions such as government and law.

Increasingly, commentators are understanding that these problems will not be fixed by more welfare, higher expenditure on schools, more laws, more promiscuous rights. It is not newer, bigger, and better systems that are needed but better people...So during these years there has been a renewed interest in the role of the virtues in understanding and combating social problems and restoring social order. Words that some had thought and others hoped to see the back of forever are creeping back into social analysis: fidelity, duty, fortitude, toleration, honesty, self-reliance, manliness. And even those who are not ready to stomach the full range of the moral vocabulary are alluding to it collectively and indirectly when they talk of the need to promote 'community'.[19]

The emphasis on the return of virtues and on their vital role in securing social cohesion is welcome. But, again, the obvious question poses itself – how can this be achieved? The champions of the virtues movement trust to persuasion and analysis. They also stress the role of pain, shame and stigma and other instruments of social pressure in achieving a personal commitment to virtues. However, is this really enough? Do not the exponents of this movement, like their Communitarian counterparts, look at the first floor of the building rather than examining the pillars in the basement down below? What one really needs to do is to look to the spiritual columns of community and virtue. It is the well-being of the soul which generates virtues; they are the natural and inevitable expression of spiritual health. Those who bear the kingdom of heaven within them cannot but be virtuous. Stewardship of the soul promotes such a condition. Virtues may be instructed, enforced and upheld, but if the inner man is not maintained, the sources of virtue will inevitably dry up. What needs to be done, therefore, is to unblock the spring of this vital water. And that is something which requires a return to our spirituality.

However, within British Christian circles (an increasingly minority position) there are signs of a move towards an accurate diagnosis. In November 1990 a number of Christian politicians and thinkers approved the 'Westminster Declaration'. This was the manifesto of the 'Movement for Christian Democracy' led by David Alton. In a section headed 'Understanding our Times' the following affirmations were made:

> We believe that under God the wellbeing of society should be judged more by the quality of human relationships than by material attainments, more by the richness of human lives than by the abundance of possessions, and more by the realization of truly human values than by the accomplishments of technology...our nation has failed in many ways to live as God requires. Our society is marred by poverty, homelessness, family breakdown, neglect of the elderly, child abuse, destruction of the unborn, exploitation of women, racism, violence, crime, drug and alcohol abuse, excessive personal debt, complacency about global suffering and injustice between nations, and careless ravaging of the natural world. Ours is a nation where too often selfishness is rewarded and responsibilities are evaded, and where the fear, loneliness and unhappiness of some are met by the ignorance and indifference of others...We have placed our faith in the possibilities of self-sufficient service and technology. We have

invested our hopes in the quest for endless economic growth. And, to give meaning to our lives, we have turned to the promise of individual freedom, happiness and prosperity, or have found our identity in collective groups such as state, nation or class. Beneath it all, we have deceived ourselves into thinking that we can solve our problems without reference to God and His good purposes for us. It is time to break with these false notions and to recognize our need for an individual and corporate change of heart and mind.[20]

Sharing much of this approach, this book seeks to point out the essential path to be taken. What is it?

To adapt a famous phrase of Bill Clinton — 'it's the soul, stupid!' If we recognise the soul within us, steward it through love for love and love for truth, and adhere firmly to the life according to the Spirit, we will start to prise back the fingers of the cruel grip of desocialisation. The crisis of the post-modern can be resolved: after the materialist deconstruction, the spiritualist reconstruction. We need go no further than the teachings of the Gospels to see how this can be achieved. Are they not in essence a manual of soul management? And the more of us who engage in this response, the quicker will be the recovery. Such stewardship will restore community much as that famous breath upon the clay brought life to the first man. At the same time our culture will become ever richer in its content and in its capacity to ensure cohesion. Here the ancient Russian concept of *sobornost* clearly has relevance. Such is the road to peace in life together, to creating a truly conducive context, and to making our society into what it should be – a home.

So in essence the rebuilding of Great Britain must be based upon a reconstruction of the kingdom of heaven amongst us. In this enterprise, however, it is necessary to have a very clear idea of what we are up against. We must realise as individuals and as a people that powerful mechanisms are working against us which strive to obstruct such a course of action. We should engage in a *kulturkampf* which should aim at the extirpation of the thought and practice of the materialist matrix. We have to repudiate the advance of models of man, of the human experience and of the cosmos which have become ever more rooted over recent centuries. There must be a new casting out of devils. Many a post-modern sacred cow must be slaughtered. When all this has been achieved, it will also be necessary to ensure that new errors do not become installed. We must learn the lesson of what has happened to us over these centuries and be fully aware about the real implications and goals of certain key ideas and doctrines. In the future there must be a constant readiness to engage in cultural crimewatch, for cultural crime has indeed been committed.

This return to the soul must also involve a readiness to engage in a spiritual reading of the human world around us. In approaching our experience within society we should try to understand the affairs of men with reference to the soul. Today we are encouraged to think only politically, economically, biologically, sociologically, psychologically, and all the rest. The time has now come to think spiritually, to employ a spiritual intelligence, and to anchor ourselves in spiritual values. First and foremost, we must ask ourselves whether what is said and done conduces to spiritual health – in the family, in friendships, in the neighbourhood, in the workplace, or in society as a whole. This attitude in itself will work against the deleterious impact of the materialist matrix. But, in addition, we should try to see other people as souls and with reference to their spirituality. This is a further vital step towards community because it will remove a whole series of materialist perspectives which erect such potent barriers between us. Thus, for example, we should not evaluate people according, for example, to their jobs, beauty, wealth, bodies, health or age. We should see them in terms of whether they bear the kingdom of heaven within them. So it is that the fractures between individuals caused by erroneous perceptions of what people are can be removed by seeing others for what they really are – souls. This is thus a book that calls for 'spiritual correctness'.

It is important to stress that this should involve a turning away from a common manner of perceiving spirituality – that in some way it largely belongs to church ceremonies, prayer beads, hymn singing, and incense. This 'ghettoisation' of spirituality is of course a natural part of the marginalisation of religion – both a retreat into a safe haven on the part of believers and an ejection from general culture promoted by enemies. 'One of the worst diseases of the modern world', observed Maritain, 'is its dualism, the dissociation between the things of God and the things of this world'.[21] Instead, spirituality must be seen as the expression at every level of life of the safeguarding of the soul. Living according to the Spirit finds its role at every point of a person's existence, and being central to him, must be central to his life. 'The Christian is not a *homo religiosus*', wrote Bonhoeffer, 'but simply a man'.[22]

What lies before us, therefore, is a great and historic work of healing. British man is increasingly ill, sick with the loss of ties in its many expressions. It is our duty to ensure that he recovers from his self-inflicted malady. The ending of the fracture between man and his soul will involve the filling in of the crevasses which divide individuals within our society. The bitter fruits of this fracture, which are expressed in a myriad of forms of social disorder and personal suffering, can thereby become phenomena of an erroneous past, the rejected consequences of having taken a historical wrong-turning. And let it be remembered that healing is a self-generating process – after a while recovery comes to be achieved naturally. But for this to be achieved a certain threshold has to be reached, and in reaching this threshold two categories in particular have a special role to play – those who have healthy souls and the sincere bearers of the Christian message.

This book has made an especial attempt to explain to those who steward their souls, whether implicitly or explicitly, why it is that they are so often on the receiving end of hostile cultural forces. It has sought to describe the forces which work against them and to make clear the nature of their experience. It seeks to tell them that they are not alone, that their condition is not unique, and that what they are doing is right. It tries to convince them that what they experience is not abnormal, or their fault, or to be repudiated, but part of the price to be paid for a lifestyle based upon nobility. The time has come for these people to emerge from their hiding places, to take heart, and to act together. They should seek each other out and become forceful agents of renewal. To these heroes of our time this volume offers a simple thought – although others have sought to abolish the light within you, you must respond by radiating more light. This will both illuminate your surroundings and dazzle your enemies. Surveying the scene, it is clear that what is needed now is an alliance of alive spirits. Whether they are rich or poor; of the Left, the Centre or the Right; white, black, brown or yellow; Scottish, Welsh, English or Northern Irish; old or young, men or women; Christians, Jews, Muslims, Buddhists, Hindus or non-believers; in good health or in poor, those who bear the light within them should engage in their own kind of counter-culture. 'We have been the silent witnesses of evil deeds', reflected Bonhoeffer. 'What we shall need is not geniuses, or cynics, or misanthropes, or clever tacticians, but plain, honest, straightforward men'.[23] To healthy souls this book, therefore, launches a simple appeal: come out, come out, wherever you are!

One special observation should be made to them. It has already been stressed that desocialised culture counters the positive input of spiritually healthy people into the human environment by frequently placing them in a kind of void or vacuum. By often depriving healthy souls of points of contact with other people, our dark anthropological pattern deprives them of space for manoeuvre. Wanting to be noble and to do good, those who live on the bright side at times find themselves deprived of a great deal of the opportunity to give practical expression to this inner impulse. But it is exactly in such arduous contexts that they are most needed – lamps are needed in the darkness and springs are required in the desert. Facing up to the waste land, healthy souls will always find the presence of other humans, however distant that presence may be. Although not necessarily able to do things on the grand scale, there will always be small moments and little spaces. They should grasp the value of how a minor action in such a circumstance can have immense value – indeed will testify even further to the worth of what they want and represent. The soullessness of our desocialised mass world, from this point of view, should constitute a challenge and not a barrier. And quiet positive action in an impoverished context has a dignity all of its own. At times it is necessary to be born into stables. In this sense, healthy souls should always remember that it is they who are especially called to save the city, however daunting the task appears to be:

> So the men turned from there, and went toward Sodom; but Abraham still stood before the Lord. Then Abraham drew near, and said: "Wilt thou indeed destroy the righteous with the wicked? Suppose there are fifty righteous within the city; wilt thou then destroy the place and not spare it for the righteous who are in it? Far be it for thee to do such a thing, to slay the righteous with the wicked, so that the righteous fare as the wicked! Far be that from thee! Shall not the Judge of all the earth do right?" And the Lord said, "If I find fifty righteous in the city, I will spare the whole place for their sake."… "Oh let not the Lord be angry, I will speak again but this once. Suppose ten are found there." He answered, "For the sake of ten I will not destroy it" (Gen 18:23-32).

Given that the Gospels constitute a unique manual of soul management, the clergy, members of religious orders and lay faithful who are the messengers of the message they contain have a very special role to play in this healing, in this process of Christian renewal. The Catholic Church has been planning a 'new evangelisation' to launch the third millennium, and here we have a clear declaration of intent to restore spiritual health. But in this undertaking, aspired to by other denominations as well, it must be realised why the message of the Gospels – of which true Christians are the custodians – finds so much resistance in Great Britain and the West. The sowers may go on sowing but much of the soil remains poisoned. What needs to be done is to peer deeply into the character of our various cultural systems and to grasp what it is that is putting up so much resistance. The way the seed is prepared, the way in which it is thrown, where it is planted, and the way in which the early shoot is tended must all be adjusted accordingly. In the same way, the clergy, members of religious orders and the lay faithful of sincere faith must be amongst people and close to them. Only in this way will it be possible to understand the real state of the soil and sow the seed in the right way. The gap that often exists between the champions of Christian culture and ordinary people is another fracture which must be healed. It is no use retreating into bunkerdom or placing the onus on others to approach the citizenry. The policy of raising drawbridges may offer the security of the castle, but it is the villages round about which have need of help – and other armies are more than active where the Christian militia has withdrawn.

In this project of healing (which imitates a central feature of Christ's ministry) three essential points should be borne in mind. Firstly, people must be constantly told by the Christian spokesmen that they have a soul. This is a point of entry which will form a breach in the wall created by the materialist matrix. They must be told that it is only by this perception that they can understand who they are, what they experience, and what they must do. Three centuries of error must be reversed by a firm restatement of this fundamental truth. Such a primary raising of spiritual awareness is the only way by which our cultural crisis can be met head on. As a part of this process the false anthropologies of post-modernity must be exposed for what they are – errors. In related fashion the life according to the Spirit must be explained and the forms of behaviour produced by the false anthropologies of post-modernity repudiated. Secondly, it must be made clear that people live within a wider cultural context which is itself a great influence on them; they must be made aware of their anthropological ecology. It must be stressed that within society there should be a shared agreement to express and promote the well-being of souls and that the attainment of such health should constitute the common project at the heart of the collective culture. There should be constant emphasis on the fact that people have an impact on the environment of others and that this environment has an impact on them. This parallel raising of cultural consciousness must lead people to understand the evils of much of the present context and engage in a shared attempt to produce a social environment which works to their authentic benefit. Thirdly, and finally, attention must be drawn to the intensity of loneliness and to the ravages of the anomic condition. Emphasis must be placed upon this reality and upon the role of the relationship between the soul and culture in bringing it about. It must be explained that a shared agreement to return to the guardianship of our spirituality will regenerate our culture and push back the incidence of atomisation. If this three-pronged approach is employed by the ordained, the consecrated and the lay faithful, the Word will find much greater purchase.

It should not be thought from these two paragraphs, or this book more generally, that an attempt is being made to replace materialist fundamentalism with Christian fundamentalism. Religious fanaticism and extremism have left far too much blood in their wake to allow repetition. There is much affinity between the major religions of the world and thus there is much which unites them in the rejection of Western materialism. For example, Christianity, Judaism, Islam, Buddhism and Hinduism all hold to the view that man has a soul and dedicate energy and thought to its defence. The search for spiritual health is common to them all and at different points there is a marked convergence of approach. There is important shared ground which could be employed to check many of the deleterious developments which now afflict the modern world. Perhaps it is time to open up a global spiritualist front. Indeed, it should be remembered when considering the other religions that different languages can express the same meanings and that the same rays of light pass through many a different prism. In addition, there are many men and women of good will who live outside the framework of religious thought who could participate in this project. Without sharing the world-view of Christianity or the other major religions, they adhere to certain basic truths and forms of behaviour which reflect and promote inner spiritual well-being. Without believing in the soul or the supernatural, they implicitly strive to live according to the Spirit and to promote the way of life to which it gives rise. These people, too, could prove important allies in resolving our present crisis.

We clearly have great duties to ourselves, but we also have major responsibilities towards those beyond Great Britain and the West. Our spiritual renaissance should involve a far greater sensitivity to the trials and tribulations of the many peoples of the globe. The poverty and disease they have to endure is a challenge to us all. By putting our own house in order we will be in a far better position to provide material aid to those beyond our frontiers. The incredible technological and scientific resources we have available could be used with great intelligence to supply highly strategic answers to the problems with which many emerging societies now grapple. We will also be able to call a halt to the spread of those Western ideas and beliefs – and the lifestyles which accompany them – which are doing so much to compromise the cultural tissue of many a historic community of the planet. During the high years of Western expansion from the sixteenth century onwards immense crimes were committed by the Europeans against vast numbers of often defenceless peoples. Cultural patrimonies of priceless value were often swept away as the societies which sustained them were smashed like matchboxes. This should not be repeated by an exportation of contemporary desocialisation. Similarly, we in the West have very great responsibilities towards the well-being of the planet. Just as the body is the temple of the spirit, so the earth is the sanctuary of our physical selves – after all, we have no other home to go to. Today's alarming signs of ecological deterioration are calls to the rich and technologically advanced nations of the world to react and to defend the Creation.

Yet in order to return to the soul and embark on a more noble journey we must engage in a little humility. This is so from two points of view. Firstly, we must recognise that despite our great powers and capacities, we have much to learn and much to regret. Although we have achieved great scientific progress, we are also handicapped by spiritual regression. A survey of failure should lead to serious self-questioning. Secondly, the stewardship of the spirit must mean ending our fracture with God. The return to the soul involves a return to its source and to its intended destiny. Heaven is its home. Such a return involves an act of humility, for in perceiving the soul we also realise that there is Somebody above us, very much above us, but also near. To our eternal comfort, and despite what the post-modern human environment so often wants to do to us, we are not alone. Expressed in different terms: only those who do not worship themselves are capable of improvement. And by turning to the divine through an embrace of the life according to the Spirit, much as a sunflower turns to the sun, we will receive new and very special energy. For these and other reasons, the words of Solzhenitsyn are of a compelling relevance:

> Just as mankind once became aware of the intolerable and mistaken deviation of the late Middle Ages and recoiled in horror from it, so too must we take account of the disastrous deviation of the late Enlightenment. We have become hopelessly enmeshed in our slavish worship of all that is pleasant, all that is comfortable, all that is material – we worship things, we worship products.

> Will we ever succeed in shaking off this burden, in giving free rein to the spirit that was breathed into us at birth, that spirit that distinguishes us from the animal world?[24]

In these post-modern days, instead of assaulting the soul, we should learn to love it.

Notes

Preface

[1] P. L. Berger, *A Rumour of Angels. Modern Society and the Rediscovery of the Supernatural* (Allen Lane The Penguin Press, London, 1970), p. 19.

[2] T. Hutchinson (ed.), *Shelley, Poetical Works* (Oxford University Press, London, 1967), p. 191, 'Julian and Maddalo'.

[3] *The Sunday Times Magazine*, 2 Sept. 2007, front cover.

[4] J. Owen, 'Community? We Don't Know Our Neighbours', *The Independent on Sunday*, 20 Jan. 2008, p. 26.

[5] *Telegraph.co.uk*, 7July 2008, 'David Cameron Attacks UK 'Moral Neutrality' – Full Text'.

[6] Benedict XVI, 'Mass, Imposition of the Pallium and Conferral of the Fisherman's Ring for the Beginning of the Petrine Ministry of the Bishop of Rome. Homily of His Holiness Benedict XVI, St. Peter's Square, Sunday 24 April 2005' (available on the Holy See web site). Benedict XVI also described this phrase as the 'motto' of his journey to Bavaria of 14-19 September 2006: Benedetto XVI, *Chi crede non è mai solo* (Cantagalli, Sienna, 2006), p. 43.

[7] M. Fforde, *Conservatism and Collectivism 1886-1914* (Edinburgh University Press, Edinburgh, 1990), pp. 42-3, 169-172.

[8] M. Fforde, *Storia della Gran Bretagna 1832-2002* (Laterza, Rome/Bari, 2002), pp. 12, 281, 306-7, 385, 404-5.

[9] E.g., M. Fforde, 'Turnout, Desocialisation and Blairism: a Note on the British Regional and Local Elections of May 2003', in G. Ignesti (ed.), *Annali 2005-2006* (G. Giappichelli Editore, Turin, 2007), pp. 693-7; M. Fforde, 'Western Materialism and the Exportation of Desocialisation', in M. Kuna (ed.), *Slovensko, Materialzmus a Desocializácia* (Katolícka univerzita v Ruzomberku Filozofická fakulta, Slovakia, 2006), pp. 257-274.

[10] E.g. M. Fforde, 'La desocializzazione porta dell'infelicità', *L'Osservatore Romano*, 21 Oct. 2005, p. 3; 'La scomparsa del galateo come indicatore di "desocializzazione"', *L'Osservatore Romano*, 18 Jan. 2007, p. 3.

[11] M. Fforde, *Desocialisation: the Crisis of the Post-Modern. A Spiritual Critique* (Aracne, Rome, 2000).

[12] M. Fforde, *Desocializzazione. La crisi della post-modernità* (Cantagalli, Sienna, 2005).

Introduction: Our Post-Social Future?

[1] J.B. Elshtain, 'What is "Civil Society" and How does it Develop?', in H.F. Zacher (ed.), *Democracy: Some Acute Questions* (The Pontifical Academy of Social Sciences, Vatican City, 1999), p. 210.

[2] G. Cottier, 'Morality and Economics in Health Care', *Dolentium Hominum*, 43, XV (2000), n. 1, pp. 67-8. The journal *Dolentium Hominum* is published by the Pontifical Council for Health Care Workers, the Holy See.

[3] J. Maritain, *The Person and the Common Good* (Geoffrey Bles, London, 1948) p. 70.

[4] The Pontifical Academy of Social Sciences, *X Plenary Session, Intergenerational Solidarity, Welfare and Human Ecology 23 April- 3 May 2004*, 'Conclusions on "Intergenerational Solidarity, Welfare and Human Ecology"' (The Pontifical Academy of Social Sciences, Vatican City, 2004), p. 15.

[5] This question is addressed in relation to Slovakia in M. Kuna (ed.), *Slovensko, Materialzmus a Desocializácia*, which contains the response of some twenty Slovak scholars to my lecture 'Western Materialism and the Exportation of Desocialisation' (published in the same work, pp. 257-274).

[6] See, e.g., John Paul II, *Agenda for the Third Millennium* (HarperCollins, London, 1996), esp. pp. 176-8.

[7] M. Houellebecq, *Atomised* (Vintage, London, 2001), p. 3.

[8] See in particular chapter two, pp. 26-36.

[9] John Paul II, *Fides et Ratio* (Libreria Editrice Vaticana, Vatican City, 1998), p. 3.

Chapter One – Our Cultural Crisis

[1] A. Moorehead, *The Fatal Impact. The Invasion of the South Pacific 1767-1840* (Harper and Row, New York, 1987), p. 208.

[2] *Ibid.*, p. 115.

[3] P. Poupard, 'The Depressive Ideas of the Contemporary World', *Dolentium Hominum*, 55, XIX (2004), n. 1, p. 67.

[4] Social Survey Division of OPCS on Behalf of the Department of Health, *Health Survey for England, 1993* (HMSO, London, 1995), p. 142.

[5] John Paul II, *Novo Millennio Ineunte* (Catholic Truth Society, London, 2001), p. 44.

[6] For a detailed statistical discussion of the crisis of the family see pp. 194-7.

[7] Central Statistical Office, *Social Trends*, n. 26 (HMSO, London, 1996), p. 50.

[8] Office for National Statistics, *Social Trends*, n. 37 (Palgrave Macmillan, Basingstoke, 2007), p. 14.

[9] Office for National Statistics, *Social Trends*, n. 27 (Stationery Office, London, 1997), p. 24.

[10] A. Leve, 'Broken Pieces of a Lost Life', *The Sunday Times Magazine*, 2 Sept. 2007, p. 21.

[11] *The Daily Telegraph*, 5 Nov. 1999, p. 1.

[12] J. Masters, 'Hello, Loneliness', *Telegraph.co.uk*, 13 Aug. 2006.

[13] A. Leve, 'Broken Pieces of a Lost Life', p. 19.

[14] *Telegraph.co.uk*, 2 Jan. 2007, 'Britain Tops European Crime League'.

[15] Central Statistical Office, *Social Trends*, n. 26 (1996), p. 159.

[16] A. Marwick, *British Society Since 1945* (Penguin, London, 2003), p. 348.

[17] Office for National Statistics, *Social Trends*, n. 37 (2007), p. 114.

[18] *Bloomberg.com*, 25 Jan. 2007, 'British Crime Survey Shows Robbery and Violent Crime Increased'.

[19] Office for National Statistics, *Social Trends*, n. 33 (Stationery Office, London, 2003), p. 172.

[20] It is estimated that serious knife crimes in England and Wales are now running at over 20,000 a year: *Telegraph.co.uk*, 12 July 2008, 'Knife Crime Claims 60 Victims a Day'.

[21] Central Statistical Office, *Social Trends*, n. 26 (1996), p.160.

[22] K. Minogue, 'The End of Authority and Formality: And their Replacement by Intrusive Regulation', in D. Anderson (ed.), *This Will Hurt. The Restoration of Virtue and Civic Order* (The Social Affairs Unit, London, 1995), p. 65.

[23] Office for National Statistics, *Social Trends*, n. 37 (2007), p. 118.

[24] *Telegraph. co.uk*, 27 Jan. 2008, 'The Figures Show Labour's Record is Criminal'.

[25] *Timesonline*, 23 Oct. 2008, 'Police Fail to Record Crime Properly, as Violence Rises 22%'.

[26] Office for National Statistics, *Social Trends*, n. 33 (2003), p. 168.

[27] *Telegraph. co.uk*, 15 Aug. 2006, 'One Million People are Living in Violent Homes, Says Report'.

[28] Office for National Statistics, *Social Trends*, n. 37 (2007), p. 121.

[29] *Ibid.*, p. 120.

[30] *Ibidem*.

[31] *Bloomberg.com*, 9 May 2006, 'UK Has Worst Anti-Social Behaviour Problem in Europe (Update 2)'

[32] G. Gorer, *Exploring English Character* (Cresset Press, London, 1955), p. 13.

[33] S. Orwell and I. Angus (eds.), *The Collected Essays, Journalism and Letters of George Orwell*, vol. 3 (Secker and Warburg, London, 1968), p. 6.

[34] *Ibid.*, p. 2.

[35] R. Weatherill, *Cultural Collapse* (Free Association Books, London, 1994), pp. 66-7.

[36] S. Orwell and I. Angus (eds.), *The Collected Essays*, vol. 3, p. 16.

[37] G.A. Almond and S. Verba, *The Civic Culture, Political Attitudes and Democracy in Five Nations* (Princeton University Press, Princeton NJ, 1963), p. 455

[38] J. Curtice and R. Powell, 'The Sceptical Electorate', in Social and Community Planning Research, *British Social Attitudes, the Twelfth Report* (Dartmouth, Aldershot, 1995), p. 141.

[39] *Ibid.*, p. 146.

[40] *Ibid.*, p. 147.

[41] A. Marwick, *British Society Since 1945*, pp. 352-353.

[42] Office for National Statistics, *Social Trends*, n. 33 (2003), p. 20.

[43] *Telegraph.co.uk*, 4 May 2007, 'Scotland in the Balance as Voters Turn on Blair'.

[44] D. Kavanagh and D. Butler, *The British General Election of 2005* (Palgrave Macmillan, Basingstoke, 2005), pp. 203-4.

[45] *Ibidem.*

[46] K. Young and N. Rao, 'Faith in Local Democracy', in Social and Community Planning, *British Social Attitudes, the Twelfth Report*, p. 101.

[47] *The Daily Telegraph*, 26 Dec. 1997, p. 1.

[48] *The Times*, 8 May 1999, p. 47.

[49] M. Fforde, 'Turnout, Desocialisation and Blairism: a Note on the British Regional and Local Elections of May 2003', p. 695.

[50] *Bloomberg.com*, 21 Nov. 2006, 'Sweden Is Top Democracy; Italy 'Flawed,' Study Shows (Update1)'.

[51] *The Daily Telegraph*, 5 Nov. 1999, p. 1.

[52] *Telegraph. co.uk*, 3 Dec. 2006, 'Britain Wants UK Break Up, Poll Shows'.

[53] D. Butler and D. Kavanagh, *Twentieth-century British Political Facts 1900-2000* (Macmillan, Basingstoke, 2000), pp. 141-2, 159.

[54] *Ibid.*, p. 401.

[55] B. Harrison and J. Webb, 'Volunteers and Voluntarism', in A.H. Halsey and J. Webb (eds.), *Twentieth-Century British Social Trends* (Macmillan, Basingstoke, 2000), pp. 597, 603, 605, 607, 613.

[56] P.A. Hall, 'Social Capital in Britain', *British Journal of Political Science*, vol. 29, part 3, July 1999, p. 449.

[57] *Ibid.*, p. 450.

[58] Office for National Statistics, *Social Trends*, n. 33 (2003), p. 20.

[59] *Ibidem.*

[60] For a detailed discussion of the concept of 'spiritual health' see pp. 29-30.

[61] S. Dunant (ed.), *The War of the Words. The Political Correctness Debate* (Virago, London, 1994), p. 72.

[62] M.A. Glendon, *Traditions in Turmoil* (Sapientia Press, Naples, Florida, 2006).

[63] Benedict XVI, 'Message of His Holiness Benedict XVI for the Fourteenth World Day of the Sick', 8 Dec. 2005 (available on the Holy See web site).

[64] *The Times Weekend*, 8 May 1999, p. 18.

[65] Office for National Statistics, *Social Trends*, n. 33 (2003), p. 134.

Chapter Two – Spirituality and Community

[1] *Catechism of the Catholic Church* (Geoffrey Chapman, London, 1994), p. 413.

[2] M. Mack (ed.), *Alexander Pope. An Essay on Man* (Methuen, London, 1982), p. 53.

[3] I. Kant, *Logic* (Dover Publications, New York, 1988), p. 29.

[4] The definition of the soul adopted by this work is that espoused by the Catholic Church, see e.g. *Catechism of the Catholic Church*, pp. 82-3.

[5] F. Nietzsche, *The Gay Science. With a Prelude in Rhymes and an Appendix of Songs* (Vintage Books, New York, 1974), p. 167.

[6] R. Crick, *The Astonishing Hypothesis. The Scientific Search for the Soul* (Simon and Schuster, London, 1994), p. 7.

[7] *The Oxford Paperback Dictionary* (Oxford University Press, Oxford, 1983), p. 153.

[8] R.A. Nisbet, *Twilight of Authority* (Oxford University Press, New York, 1975), p. 112.

[9] R. Williams, *The Long Revolution* (Penguin, Harmondsworth, 1965), p. 57.

[10] R. Williams, *Culture and Society. Coleridge to Orwell* (Hogarth, London, 1987), p. 11.

[11] J. Ratzinger, *Truth and Tolerance. Christian Belief and World Religions* (Ignatius Press, San Francisco, 2004), p. 59.

[12] Cf. J-J. Rousseau, *Discourse on Political Economy and the Social Contract* (Oxford University Press, Oxford, 1994).

[13] See D. Boucher and P Kelly, *The Social Contract from Hobbes to Rawls* (Routledge, London, 1994), esp. pp. 1-29, for an overview.

[14] R.A. Nisbet, *Twilight of Authority*, p. 112.

[15] J-J. Rousseau, *Discourse on Political Economy*, p. 45.

[16] J. Maritain, *The Range of Reason* (Geoffrey Bles, London, 1953), p. 195.

[17] D.W. Hudson and H.J. Mancini, *Understanding Maritain: Philosopher and Friend* (Mercer University Press, Macon GA, 1987), p. 159.

[18] J. Maritain, *The Rights of Man and Natural Law* (Geofrey Bles: The Centenary Press, London, 1944), pp. 11, 24, 27, 35.

[19] J. Maritain, *Religion and Culture* (Sheed and Ward, London, 1931), p. 6.

[20] *Ibid.*, p. 24.

[21] *Ibid.*, p. 31.

Chapter Three – The False Anthropologies of Post-Modernity

[1] R.A. Nisbet, *The Quest for Community. A Study in the Ethics of Order and Freedom* (Oxford University Press, New York, 1953), p. 14.

[2] J. Maritain, *The Range of Reason*, p. 185.

[3] *Ibid.*, p. 188.

[4] John Paul II, *Crossing the Threshold of Hope* (Jonathan Cape, London, 1994), p. 133.

[5] T.S. Eliot, *After Strange Gods. A Primer of Modern Heresy* (Faber and Faber, London, 1934), pp. 24-5.

[6] F. Crick, *The Astonishing Hypothesis*, p. 4.

[7] *Ibid.*, p. 257.

[8] K. Ward, *The Turn of the Tide. Christian Belief in Britain Today* (BBC, London, 1986), p. 21.

[9] R. Tarnas, *The Passion of the Western Mind. Understanding the Ideas that have Shaped our World View* (Pimlico, London, 1996), p. 355.

[10] *Ibid.*, p. 358.

[11] *Ibid.*, pp. 355-365.

[12] P. Johnson, *Enemies of Society* (Weidenfeld and Nicolson, London, 1977), pp. 156-160.

[13] R.B. Johnson, 'Models of Man. 1879-1979', in A.J. Chapman and D.M. Jones (eds.) *Models of Man* (British Psychological Society, Leicester, 1980), p. 2.

[14] *Ibid.*, p. 10.

[15] T.L. Panale (ed.), *The Rebirth of Classical Political Rationalism. An Introduction to the Thought of Leo Strauss. Essays and Lectures by Leo Strauss* (University of Chicago Press, Chicago, 1989), p. 243.

[16] J. Maritain, *Religion and Culture*, p. 19.

[17] H. Jonas, *The Imperative of Responsibility. In Search of Ethics for a Technological Age* (University of Chicago Press, Chicago, 1984).

[18] *The New Encyclopaedia Britannica* (Encyclopaedia Britannica, Chicago, 1983), vol. 15, pp. 527-8.

[19] M. Oakeshott, *Rationalism in Politics and Other Essays* (Methuen, London, 1974), pp. 1-2, 3, 4, 35.

[20] W. Barrett, *Death of the Soul. From Descartes to the Computer* (Oxford University Press, Oxford, 1987), esp. pp. 163-6.

[21] C.B. Macpherson, 'Natural Rights in Hobbes and Locke', in D.D. Raphael (ed.), *Political Theory and the Rights of Man* (Macmillan, London, 1967), p. 14.

[22] E. Burke, *Reflections on the Revolution in France* (Penguin, Harmondsworth, 1987), pp. 152-3.

[23] J. Maritain, *The Rights of Man and Natural Law*, p. 34.

[24] For a survey of modern natural rights theory and its implementation see A.H. Birch, *The Concepts and Theories of Modern Democracy* (Routledge, London, 1993), pp. 113-134.

[25] M.A. Glendon, *Rights Talk. The Impoverishment of Political Discourse* (Free Press, New York, 1991), p. 7.

[26] J. Bentham, 'Anarchical Fallacies', in J. Bowring (ed.), *The Works of Jeremy Bentham* (William Tait, Edinburgh, 1843), vol. 2, pp. 501, 523.

[27] W.L. Miller, A.M. Timpson and M. Lesson, *Political Culture in Contemporary Britain. People and Politicians, Principles and Practice* (Clarendon Press, Oxford, 1996), p. 4.

[28] S. Pinker, *The Blank Slate. The Modern Denial of Human Nature* (Penguin, London, 2002), p. 3.

[29] *Ibid.*, p. 6.

[30] F.A. Hayek, *Studies in Philosophy, Politics and Economics* (Routledge and Kegan Paul, London, 1967), p. 237.

[31] D. Willetts, *Modern Conservatism* (Penguin, London, 1992), p. 48.

[32] K. Marx, *A Contribution to the Critique of Political Economy* (Lawrence and Wishart, London 1971), pp. 20-21.

[33] K. Marx, *The Eighteenth Brumaire of Louis Napoleon* (Progress, Moscow, 1984), pp. 38-9.

[34] I. Kershaw, *Hitler 1936-1945. Nemesis* (Penguin, London, 2001), p. 403.

[35] F. Dostoyevsky, *The Devils* (Penguin, London, 1971) p. 615.

[36] C.B. Macpherson (ed.), *T. Hobbes. Leviathan* (Penguin, Harmondsworth, 1981), pp. 225-6.

[37] C. Gordon (ed.), *Foucault Power/Knowledge. Selected Interviews and Other Writings 1972-1977, Michel Foucault* (Harvester Wheatsheaf, Brighton, 1980), p. 145.

[38] See, e.g., E. Wilson, *Sociobiology. The New Synthesis* (Belknap Press of Harvard University Press, Cambridge Mass., 1975); *On Human Nature* (Harvard University Press, Cambridge Mass., 1978).

[39] C. Sagan and A. Druyan, *Shadows of Forgotten Ancestors. A Search for Who we Are* (Arrow, London, 1993), pp. 4, 6, 7.

[40] *Ibid.*, p. 166.

[41] D. Morris, *The Naked Ape* (Triad Grifton, London, 1977), p. 9.

[42] Office for National Statistics, *Social Trends*, n. 27 (1997), p. 220.

[43] See for example T. Regan, *The Case for Animal Rights* (Routledge and Kegan Paul, London, 1983).

[44] R. Dawkins, *The Selfish Gene* (Oxford University Press, Oxford, 1976), pp. 2-3.

[45] K. Parkhurst Easson and R.R. Easson, *W. Blake. Milton* (Thames and Hudson, London, 1979), pp. 138-9.

[46] F. Crick, *The Astonishing Hypothesis,* pp. 3-6.

[47] D. Goleman, *Emotional Intelligence. Why it Can Matter more than IQ* (Bloomsbury, London, 1996), pp. 4-5.

[48] P. Johnson, *The Birth of the Modern. World Society 1815-1830* (HarperCollins, New York, 1991), p. 611.

[49] B.A. Farrell, *The Standing of Psychoanalysis* (Oxford University Press, Oxford, 1981) p. 190.

[50] P.B. Medawar, *The Hope of Progress* (Wildwood House, London, 1974), p. 68.

[51] E. Gellner, *The Psychoanalytic Movement or the Coming of Unreason* (Granada, London, 1985), p. 5.

[52] *Ibid.*, p. 10.

[53] *Ibid.*, pp. 75-6.

[54] M. Lever, *Sade. A Biography* (Farrar, Straus and Giroux, London, 1993), p. 566.

Chapter Four – Their Fatal Impact

1 *L'Osservatore Romano* (English weekly edition), 21 April 1986, p. 7.
2 See, e.g., A. Etzioni, *The Spirit of Community. Rights, Responsibilities and the Communitarian Agenda* (Fontana, London, 1995), p. 256.
3 E. Bethge (ed.), *Dietrich Bonhoeffer: Letters and Papers from Prison* (SCM Press, London, 1971), p. 298.
4 *Ibid.*, p. 191.
5 R. Scruton, *Untimely Tracts* (Macmillan, Basingstoke, 1987), p. 215.
6 *Catechism of the Catholic Church*, p. 539.
7 E. Bethge (ed.), *Dietrich Bonhoeffer*, pp. 344-5.
8 M. Brando, *Songs My Mother Taught Me* (Arrow, London, 1995), p. 349.
9 C. Lasch, *The Culture of Narcissism. American Life in an Age of Diminishing Expectations* (Norton, New York, 1991), p. 11.
10 I. Kershaw, *Hitler 1936-1945. Nemesis*, p. 404.

Chapter Five – Relativism: an Authentic Philosophy of the Void

1 F. Dostoyevsky, *The Devils*, p. 692.
2 P. Johnson, *Enemies of Society*, p. 177.
3 E. Gellner, *Relativism and the Social Sciences* (Cambridge University Press, Cambridge, 1985), pp. 84-5.
4 J.L. Mackie, *Ethics. Inventing Right and Wrong* (Penguin, Harmondsworth, 1977), p. 15.
5 L. Siedentop, *Tocqueville* (Oxford University Press, Oxford, 1994), p. 80.
6 Plato, *Theaetetus* (Clarendon Press, Oxford, 1973), p. 30.
7 R. Scruton, *Modern Philosophy. An Introduction and Survey* (Mandarin, London, 1996), p. 33.
8 E. Gellner, *Relativism and the Social Sciences*, p. 85.
9 J. Ratzinger, 'Homily of Joseph Cardinal Ratzinger, Dean of the College of Cardinals, Mass for the Election of the Supreme Pontiff, St. Peter's Basilica, 18 April 2005' (EWTN, 'Pontificate of Benedict XVI', www://ewtn.com/pope/words/conclave_homily.asp).
10 A. Bloom, *The Closing of the American Mind. How Higher Education has Failed Democracy and Impoverished the Souls of Today's Students* (Penguin, London, 1988), p. 25.
11 R.A. Nisbet, *Twilight of Authority*, p. 139.
12 G. Himmelfarb, *The De-Moralization of Society. From Victorian Values to Modern Values* (IEA Health and Welfare Unit, London, 1995), p. 241.
13 R. Tarnas, *The Passion of the Western Mind*, p. 239.
14 G. Best, *Mid-Victorian Britain 1851-75* (Fontana, London, 1979), pp. 199-200.
15 P. Johnson, *Enemies of Society*, p. 178.
16 I take the term from R. Scruton, *Thinkers of the New Left* (Longman, Harlow, 1985), p. 2.
17 F. Dostoyevsky, *The Devils*, pp. 661-2.

[18] P. Johnson, *Enemies of Society*, p. 194.

[19] *Ibid.*, p. 176.

[20] *Ibidem.*

[21] F.M. Wilson (ed.), *Strange Island. Britain Through Foreign Eyes 1395-1940* (Longmans, Green and Co., London, 1955), p. 240.

[22] J.B Elshtain, 'What is a "Civil Society" and how does it Develop?', p. 214.

[23] For detailed and penetrating commentary on this current see R. Scruton, *The Politics of Culture and Other Essays* (Carcanet, Manchester, 1981); *Thinkers of the New Left; The Philosopher on Dover Beach* (Carcanet, Manchester, 1990); *Upon Nothing* (University College of Swansea, Swansea, 1993); *A Political Philosophy* (Continuum, London, 2006), pp. 103-117.

[24] E. Gellner, *Postmodernism, Reason and Religion* (Routlege, London, 1992), p. 24.

[25] R. Tarnas, *The Passion of the Western Mind*, pp. 395-6.

[26] *Ibid*, p. 397.

[27] *Ibid.*, p. 398.

[28] *Ibid.*, p. 400.

[29] *Ibidem.*

[30] *Ibid*, p. 398 .

[31] G. Jordan and C. Weedon, *Cultural Politics, Class, Gender, Race and the Postmodern World* (Blackwell, Oxford, 1995), pp. xii.

[32] *Ibid.*, p. 19.

[33] *Ibid.*, p. xi.

[34] *Ibid.*, p. 556.

[35] *Ibid.*, p. 8.

[36] *Ibid.*, p. 265.

[37] *Ibid.*, p. 4.

[38] At a personal level I noticed this in the reactions in books, articles and reviews to my work *Conservatism and Collectivism 1886-1914* (1990). An article by me on these reactions, now that a suitable period of time has elapsed, is currently in preparation and will seek to set these reactions in their wider context.

[39] D. Willetts, *Modern Conservatism*, p. 21.

[40] C.B. Macpherson (ed.), *T. Hobbes. Leviathan*, p. 728, quoted in P. Johnson, *Enemies of Society*, p. 161.

[41] R. Scruton, *The Philosopher on Dover Beach*, p. 289.

[42] M. Medved, *Hollywood Vs. America. Popular Culture and the War on Traditional Values* (HarperCollins, New York, 1992), p. 10.

[43] P. Johnson, *Intellectuals* (Weidenfeld and Nicolson, London, 1989), pp. 1-2.

[44] P. Hitchens, *The Abolition of Britain. The British Cultural Revolution from Lady Chatterley to Tony Blair* (Quartet Books, London, 2000), p. xxii.

[45] F. Nietzsche, *Beyond Good and Evil. Prelude to a Philosophy of the Future* (Penguin, Harmondsworth, 1990).

[46] R. Tarnas, *The Passion of the Western Mind*, p. 402.

[47] R. Scruton, *A Political Philosophy*, p. 117.
[48] I. Turgenev, *Fathers and Sons* (Penguin, London, 1975), p. 94.
[49] T.S. Eliot, *After Strange Gods*, p. 56.
[50] M. Medved, *Hollywood Vs. America*, p. 26.
[51] *Ibid.*, p. 25.
[52] R. Scruton, *Upon Nothing*, p. 30.
[53] John Paul II, *Fides et Ratio*, p. 133.

Chapter Six – DeChristianisation

[1] E. Bethge (ed.), *Dietrich Bonhoeffer*, pp. 325-6.
[2] John Paul II, *Christifideles Laici* (Libreria Editrice Vaticana, Vatican City, 1988), p. 95.
[3] G. Best, *Mid-Victorian Britain 1851-75*, pp. 197-9.
[4] J. Harris, *Private Lives, Public Spirit: Britain 1870-1914* (Penguin, London, 1994), p. 153.
[5] *Ibid.*, p. 154.
[6] G. Best, *Mid-Victorian Britain 1851-75*, p. 194.
[7] J. Harris, *Private Lives, Public Spirit*, p. 151.
[8] *Mid-Victorian Britain 1851-75*, pp. 217-8.
[9] See F.M.L. Thompson, *The Rise of Respectable Society. A Social History of Victorian Britain, 1830-1900* (Fontana, London, 1988), pp. 143-151; T. May, *An Economic and Social History of Britain 1760-1970* (Longman, Harlow, 1987), pp. 140-1.
[10] F.M.L. Thompson, *The Rise of Respectable Society*, p. 144.
[11] R. Gill, 'Secularization and Census Data', in S. Bruce (ed.), *Religion and Modernization. Sociologists and Historians Debate the Secularization Thesis* (Clarendon Press, Oxford, 1992), pp. 96-7.
[12] For Sunday observance see A.D. Gilbert, *The Making of Post-Christian Britain. A History of the Secularization of Modern Society* (Longman, London, 1980), pp. 94-6; F.M.L. Thompson, *The Rise of Respectable Society*, pp. 315-7.
[13] G. Best, *Mid-Victorian Britain 1851-75*, p. 195.
[14] J. Lawson, *A Man's Life* (Hodder and Staughton, London, 1932), pp. 110-113.
[15] R. Roberts, *The Classic Slum. Salford Life in the First Quarter of the Century* (Penguin, Harmondsworth, 1973), p. 173.
[16] F. Thompson, *Lark Rise to Candleford* (Penguin, Harmondsworth, 1973), p. 208.
[17] *Ibid.*, p. 213.
[18] A.D. Gilbert, *The Making of Post-Christian Britain*, p. 1.
[19] P. Brierley, 'Religion', in A.H. Halsey (ed.), *British Social Trends since 1900. A Guide to the Changing Social Structure of Britain* (Macmillan, Basingstoke, 1988), p. 540.
[20] J. Stevenson, *British Society 1914-45* (Penguin, Harmondsworth, 1984), pp. 361-2.

[21] D. Butler and G. Butler, *Twentieth-Century British Political Facts 1900-2000*, p. 564.

[22] R. Gill, 'Secularization and Census Data', p. 97.

[23] S.J.D. Green, *Religion in the Age of Decline. Organisation and Experience in Industrial Yorkshire, 1870-1920* (Cambridge University Press, Cambridge, 1996), p. 380.

[24] P. Hennessy, *Never Again. Britain 1945-51* (Jonathan Cape, London, 1992), p. 438.

[25] D. Butler and G. Butler, *Twentieth-Century British Political Facts 1900-2000*, p. 564.

[26] R. Gill, 'Secularization and Census Data', p. 97.

[27] A.D. Gilbert, *The Making of Post-Christian Britain*, p. 95.

[28] P. Brierley, *Christian England. What the 1989 English Church Census Reveals* (Marc Europe, London, 1991), p. 30.

[29] Office for National Statistics, *Social Trends*, n. 27 (1997), p. 224.

[30] Office for National Statistics, *Social Trends*, n. 37 (2007), p. 182.

[31] P. Brierley, *Christian England*, p. 59.

[32] Central Statistical Office, *Social Trends*, n. 26 (1996), p. 225.

[33] Office for National Statistics, *Social Trends*, n. 33 (2003), p. 226.

[34] Office for National Statistics, *Social Trends*, n. 38 (Palgrave Macmillan, Basingstoke, 2008), p. 189.

[35] P. Brierley, 'Religion', p. 663.

[36] Office for National Statistics, *Social Trends*, n. 38 (2008), p. 189.

[37] E. Bethge (ed.), *Dietrich Bonhoeffer*, p. 364.

[38] K. Ward, *The Turn of the Tide*, p. 20.

[39] E. Bethge (ed.), *Dietrich Bonhoeffer*, p. 279.

[40] *Telegraph.co.uk*, 21 June 2008, 'Christianity 'Could Die Out Within a Century''.

[41] K.P. Easson and R.R. Easson, *W. Blake. Milton*, p. 128.

[42] R.H. Benson, *Lord of the World* (The Echo Library, Cirencester, 2005), p. 8.

[43] A. Thwaite (ed.), *P. Larkin. Collected Poems* (Marvell Press and Faber and Faber, London, 1988), pp. 97-8, 'Church Going'.

[44] K. Ward, *The Turn of the Tide*, pp. 22, 26-7.

[45] Office for National Statistics, *Social Trends*, n. 38 (2008), p. 190.

[46] P. Johnson, *Enemies of Society*, p. 117.

Chapter Seven – The Dots of Mass Society

[1] G. Greene, *The Third Man* (Faber and Faber, London, 1988), p. 97.

[2] D. Irving, *The War Path. Hitler's Germany 1933-1939* (Macmillan, London, 1978), p. 171.

[3] For Kierkegaard's views and those of other critics of mass society see H.N. Tuttle, *The Crowd is Untruth. The Existential Critique of Mass Society in the Thought of Kierkegaard, Nietzsche, Heidegger and Ortega y Gasset* (P. Lang, New York, 1996).

[4] T.S. Eliot, *The Waste Land and Other Poems* (Faber and Faber, London, 1972), p. 25.

[5] See T. Megarry, *Society in Prehistory. The Origins of Human Culture* (Macmillan, Basingstoke, 1995), esp. pp. 1-17, 64-90, 91-153 and his bibliography pp. 356-386.

[6] M. Harris, *Culture, People, Nature. An Introduction to General Anthropology* (Harper and Row, New York, 1980), pp. 23, 35, 36, 66.

[7] A. Etzioni, *An Immodest Agenda. Rebuilding America before the Twenty-First Century* (New Press, New York, 1983), p. 29.

[8] *Ibidem.*

[9] C.J. Calipeau, *Isaiah Berlin's Liberalism* (Clarendon Press, Oxford, 1994), p. 149.

[10] J.S. Mill, *On Liberty* (Penguin, Harmondsworth, 1982), pp. 138-40.

[11] B.R. Mitchell, *British Historical Statistics* (Cambridge University Press, Cambridge, 1988), pp. 11-12; D. Butler and G. Butler, *Twentieth-Century British Political Facts 1900-2000*, p. 347.

[12] W.J.B. Owen (ed.), *Wordsworth and Coleridge. Lyrical Ballads* 1798 II edn. (Oxford University Press, Oxford, 1969), p. 160.

[13] B.R. Mitchell, *British Historical Statistics*, pp. 25-7.

[14] J. Harris, *Private Lives, Public Spirit*, pp. 42-5; B. Wood, 'Urbanisation and Local Government', in A.H. Halsey (ed.), *British Social Trends Since 1900*, pp. 325-330.

[15] B. Wood and J. Carter, 'Towns, Urban Change and Local Government', in A.H. Halsey and J. Webb (eds.), *Twentieth-Century British Social Trends*, p. 416.

[16] *Ibid.*, p. 419.

[17] T. Roszak, *Person/Planet. The Creative Disintegration of Industrial Society* (Granada, London, 1981), pp. 253-4.

[18] B. Weatherill, *Cultural Collapse*, pp. 46-7.

[19] M.A. Wiener, *English Culture and the Decline of the Industrial Spirit 1850-1980* (Cambridge University Press, Cambridge, 1982), p. 165.

[20] See F.M.L. Thompson, *The Rise of Respectable Society*, pp. 140-151; M. Cruickshank, *Church and State in English Education 1870 to the Present Day* (Macmillan, London, 1963); and G. Smith 'Schools', in A.H. Halsey and J. Webb (eds.), *Twentieth-Century British Social Trends*, pp. 179-220.

[21] See A.H. Halsey, 'Further and Higher Education', in A.H. Halsey and J. Webb (eds.), *Twentieth-Century British Social Trends*, pp. 221-253.

[22] K.P. Easson and R.R. Easson, *W. Blake. Milton*, p. 62.

[23] J. Harris, *Private Lives, Public Spirit*, pp. 127-8.

[24] S. Pollard, *The Development of the British Economy 1914-1990* (Edward Arnold, London, 1992), p. 254.

[25] *Ibidem.*

[26] W. Churchill, *Thoughts and Adventures* (Odhams Press, London, 1947), p. 194, from the essay entitled 'Mass Effects on Modern Life'.

[27] P. Mathias, *The First Industrial Nation. An Economic History of Britain 1700-1914* (Methuen, London, 1983), pp. 148-159, 320-323.

[28] S. Pollard, *The Development of the British Economy 1914-1990*, p. 254.

[29] *Ibid.*, p. 406.

[30] G. Gallie, 'The Labour Force', in A.H. Halsey and J. Webb (eds.), *Twentieth-Century British Social Trends*, p. 288.

[31] E.F. Schumacher, *Small is Beautiful. A Study of Economics as if People Mattered* (Vintage, London, 1973), p. 202.

[32] D. Lyon, 'The Changing Meaning and Value of Work in a Globalized Information Society', in M.S. Archer (ed.), *Towards Reducing Unemployment* (The Pontifical Academy of Social Sciences, Vatican City, 1999), p. 269.

[33] E. Malinvaud, 'A Synthesis', in E. Malinvaud and M.S. Archer (eds.), *Work and Human Fulfillment* (Sapientia Press, Ypsilanti, Michigan, 2003), p. 287.

[34] For the GDP of both countries see The Economist, *The World in 2004* (The Economist, London, 2003), pp. 96, 97.

[35] Office for National Statistics, *Social Trends*, n. 34 (2004), p. 91.

[36] H.M. Scobie, S. Mortali, S. Persaud and P. Docile, *The Italian Economy in the 1990s* (Routledge, London, 1996), p. 55.

[37] F.M.L. Thompson, *The Rise of Respectable Society*, p. 241.

[38] Statistics on trade union membership see H. Pelling, *A History of British Trade Unionism*, 4th. edn. (Penguin, Harmondsworth, 1987), pp. 297-330; D. Gallie, 'The Labour Force', p. 309.

[39] D. Butler and G. Butler, *Twentieth-Century British Political Facts 1900-2000*, pp. 399-401.

[40] *Ibid.*, p. 408.

[41] For mass recreation see F.M.L. Thompson, *The Rise of Respectable Society*, pp. 288-306; J. Stevenson, *British Society 1918-45*, pp. 381-411; A. Marwick, *British Society Since 1945* (Penguin, Harmondsworth, 1996), pp. 368-372.

[42] Central Statistical Office, *Social Trends* n. 26 (1996), p. 217.

[43] Office for National Statistics, *Social Trends*, n. 37 (2006), p. 173.

[44] W.H. Greenleaf, *The British Political Tradition. Vol. I. The Rise of Collectivism* (Methuen, London, 1983), p. 33.

[45] P. Stephens, 'The Treasury under Labour', in A. Seldon (ed.), *The Blair Effect. The Blair Government 1997-2001* (Little, Brown and Company, London, 2001), p. 194.

[46] For the rise of the big state see W.H. Greenleaf, *The British Political Tradition*, in three volumes, especially vol. 3, *A Much Governed Nation* (Methuen, London, 1987), Part 1 and Part II, which may be consulted for many of these paragraphs. For Thatcherite spending on the welfare state see Office for National Statistics, *Social Trends*, n. 27 (1997), p. 118.

[47] D. Thomson, *England in the Nineteenth Century* (Penguin, Harmondsworth, 1978), p. 180.

[48] G. Best. *Mid-Victorian Britain 1851-75*, p. 59.

[49] H.J. Hanham, *The Nineteenth Century Constitution 1815-1914. Documents and Commentary* (Cambridge University Press, Cambridge, 1969), pp. 377, 378.

[50] *Ibid.*, p. 380.

[51] *Ibid.*, p. 376.

[52] For the corporatist debate see, e.g., L. Hannah, *The Rise of the Corporate Economy* (Methuen, London, 1983); K. Middlemas, *Politics in Industrial Society. The Experience of the British System Since 1911* (Deutsch, London, 1979); *Industry, Unions and Government. Twenty-One Years of NEDC* (Macmillan, London, 1988); and B. Jones and D. Kavanagh, *British Politics Today* (Manchester University Press, Manchester, 1994) p. 222.

[53] A. Partington (ed.), *The Oxford Dictionary of Quotations* (Oxford University Press, Oxford, 1996), p. 32.

[54] B. Jones and D. Kavanagh, *British Politics Today*, pp. 164-177.

[55] R. Williams, *Culture and Society*, pp. 189-90.

[56] A. Solzhenitsyn, *Rebuilding Russia. Reflections and Tentative Proposals* (Harvill, London, 1991), p. 72.

[57] B. Jones and D. Kavanagh, *British Politics Today*, p. 226.

[58] D. Gallie, 'The Labour Force', p. 288.

[59] G. Orwell, *The Lion and the Unicorn. Socialism and the English Genius* (Penguin, Harmondsworth, 1982), pp. 66, 68-9.

[60] P . Melling and J. Roper, *Americanisation and the Transformation of World Cultures. Melting Pot or Cultural Chernobyl?* (Lampeter, Edwin Meller Press, Lwiston, New York, 1996), p. 13.

[61] D. Butler and G. Butler, *Twentieth-Century British Political Facts 1900-2000*, p. 514.

[62] A. de Tocqueville, *Democracy in America*, vol. 2 (Everyman's Library, London, 1994), p. 217.

[63] R. Roberts, *The Classic Slum*, p. 44.

[64] *The Sunday Times*, 22 Sept. 1996, p. 3.

[65] A. de Tocqueville, *Democracy in America*, vol. 2, pp. 217-8.

[66] L. Truss, *Talk to the Hand. The Utter Bloody Rudeness of Everyday Life* (Profile Books, London, 2005), pp. 13-14, 2-3, 19, 14, 36, 36.

[67] E. Bethge (ed.), *Dietrich Bonhoeffer*, p. 299.

[68] T. Roszak, *Planet/Person*, pp. 61, 149.

[69] *Ibid.*, p. 319.

Chapter Eight – A Dark Symbiosis

[1] R. Weatherill, *Cultural Collapse*, p. 90.

[2] E. Bethge (ed.), *Dietrich Bonhoeffer*, p. 295.

[3] D.A. Coleman, 'Population', in A.H. Halsey (ed.), *British Social Trends Since 1900*, p. 75.

[4] BBC 1 Television News, 16 Sept. 1996.

[5] R. Roberts, *The Classic Slum*, p. 53.

[6] Central Statistical Office, *Social Trends*, n. 26 (1996), p. 57.

[7] E. Hobsbawm, *Age of Extremes. The Short Twentieth Century 1914-1991* (Abacus, London, 1995), p. 321.

[8] D.A. Coleman, 'Population', pp. 80-1.

[9] *Ibid.*, p. 82.

[10] *Telegraph.co.uk.*, 24 Oct. 2003, 'Parents are too Poor to Save for their Children'.

[11] Office for National Statistics, *Social Trends*, n. 33 (2003), p. 45.

[12] Office for National Statistics, *Social Trends,* n. 27 (1997), p. 23.

[13] Office for National Statistics, *Social Trends*, n. 33 (2003), p. 46.

[14] G. Himmelfarb, *The De-moralization of Society*, p. 232.

[15] Central Statistical Office, *Social Trends*, n. 26 (1996), p. 61.

[16] Office for National Statistics, *Social Trends*, n. 37 (2007), p. 22.

[17] Office for National Statistics, *Social Trends*, n. 34 (2004), p. 27.

[18] Office for National Statistics, *Social Trends*, n. 3 (2003), p. 45.

[19] Office for National Statistics, *Social Trends*, n. 27 (1997), p. 16.

[20] Office for National Statistics, *Social Trends*, n. 38 (2008), p. 19.

[21] *Guardian Unlimited*, 30 June 2004, 'Older People Face a Lonely Future, Thinktank Warns'.

[22] Office for National Statistics, *Social Trends*, n. 33 (2003), p. 187.

[23] M. Fforde, *Conservatism and Collectivism 1886-1914*, pp. 30-1.

[24] F.J.E. Basterra, *Bioethics* (St. Paul's, London, 1994), p. 39.

[25] D.A. Coleman, 'Population', p. 57.

[26] *Ibid.*, p. 60.

[27] Central Statistical Office, *Social Trends*, n. 26 (1996), p. 62.

[28] Office for National Statistics, *Social Trends*, n. 37 (2007), p. 23.

[29] C.S. Lewis, *The Abolition of Man* (HarperCollins, London, 1999), pp. 36-7.

[30] F. Fukuyama, *Our Posthuman Future. Consequences of the Biotechnology Revolution* (Profile Books, London, 2003).

[31] Cf. A. Serra, 'La rivoluzione gnomica. Conquiste, attese e rischi', *Civiltà Cattolica*, 152, II, 3623, 2 June 2001, 439-453; 'La "famiglia" nell'era biotechnologica', *Pedagogia e Vita*, 2, 2002, 99-112; 'Le cellule staminali embrionali. Problemi e prospettive', *Civiltà Cattolica,* 158, II, 3767, 2 June 2007, 433-446.

[32] E. Hobsbawm, *Age of Extremes*, p. 320.

[33] *Catechism of the Catholic Church*, p. 505. This work also states that 'men and women who have deep-seated homosexual tendencies... must be accepted with respect, compassion and sensitivity. Every sign of unjust discrimination in their regard should be avoided' (*ibidem*). See also Congregation for the Doctrine of the Faith, 'Considerations Regarding Proposals to Give Legal Recognition to Unions between Homosexual Persons', 3 June 2003, esp. n. 4 (available on the Holy See web site).

[34] The Pontifical Council for the Family, *The Truth and Meaning of Human Sexuality. Guidelines for Education Within the Family* (Libreria Editrice Vaticana, Vatican City, 1995), p. 45.

[35] *The Independent*, 30 Nov. 2001, p. 3.

[36] G. Greer, *The Female Eunuch* (Harper Perennial, London, 2006), pp. 16, 17, 18, 18-19, 19, 20, 21, 22, 23, 24, 25.

[37] *Telegraph.co.uk*, 13 Jan. 2004, 'Adults 'Are too Busy to Help the Vulnerable"

[38] T. Anatrella, 'The Depressive Society', *Dolentium Hominum*, 34, XII (1997), n. 1, p. 91.

[39] M.A. Glendon and P. Donati, 'Towards Achieving Solidarity with Children and Young People in our Globalised World', in M.A. Glendon and P. Donati (eds.), *Vanishing Youth? Solidarity with Children and Young People in an Age of Turbulence* (The Pontifical Academy of Social Sciences, Vatican City, 2005), p. 543.

[40] *Telegraph.co.uk*, 15 Aug. 2006, 'One Million Children in Britain are Living in Violent Homes'.

[41] *The Times Weekend*, 8 May 1999, p. 18.

[42] Office for National Statistics, *Social Trends*, n. 37 (2007), p. 97.

[43] *Telegraph.co.uk*, 18 Sept. 2006, 'Climate of "Fear and Confusion" Leading to Childhood Depression'.

[44] *Ibidem*.

[45] *The Guardian*, 14 May 1999, p. 1.

[46] *Telegraph.co.uk*, 7 Dec. 2003, 'Doctors Urge Drastic Action to Halt Decline in Teenagers' Health'

[47] *Telegraph.co.uk*, 5 Jan. 2008, 'Half of Teens Falling Short on Three Rs'.

[48] *Telegraph.co.uk*, 2 July 2008, 'Gang Culture has Replaced Family Life Among Teens, Warns Police Chief'.

[49] T.S. Eliot, *Notes Towards the Definition of Culture* (Faber and Faber, London, 1962), p. 43.

[50] E. Burke, *Reflections on the Revolution in France*, p. 152.

[51] W.L. Miller, A.M. Timpson and M. Lessnof, *Political Culture in Contemporary Britain*, p. 5.

[52] M.A. Glendon, *Rights Talk*, p. 14.

[53] D. Graham and P. Clarke, *The New Enlightenment. The Rebirth of Liberalism* (Macmillan in Association with Channel Four Television Co., London, 1986), p. 118.

[54] A. Solzhenitsyn, *Rebuilding Russia*, p. 44.

[55] John Paul II, *On Social Concern. Sollicitudo Rei Socialis* (Pauline Books and Media, Boston, n..y), pp. 48-9.

[56] *Bloomberg.com*, 2 Aug. 2004, 'Bank of England may Raise Rate to Highest in Almost Three Years'.

[57] See N. Jones, *The Control Freaks. How New Labour Gets its Own Way* (Politico's Publishing, London, 2002) for one critique.

[58] R. Weatherill, *Cultural Collapse*, p. 63.

[59] P. Dacre, 'The BBC's Cultural Marxism will Trigger an American-style Backlash', *Guardian Unlimited*, 24 Jan. 2007.

[60] R. Rollin, (ed.), *The Americanization of the Global Village. Essays in Comparative Popular Culture* (Bowling Green State University Press, Bowling Green, Ohio, 1989), p. 2.

[61] P. Melling and J. Roper, *Americanisation and the Transformation of World Culture*, p. 24.

[62] *Ibid.*, p. 17.

[63] M. Medved, *Hollywood Vs. America*, pp. 50, 21, 50, 24, 161, 18, 286.

[64] A. Solzhenitsyn, 'Our Pluralists', *Survey. A Journal of East & West Studies*, Summer 1985, vol. 29, n. 2 (125), p. 3.

[65] For a discussion of the attack on healthy souls see pp. 274-288.

[66] A. Toffler, *Future Shock* (Bantam Books, New York, 1971), p. 322.

[67] E. Fromm, *The Sane Society* (Routledge, London, 1991), p. 361.

[68] *Ibid.*, p. 348.

[69] M. Oakeshott, 'On Being Conservative', in *Rationalism in Politics and Other Essays*, p. 172.

[70] E. Burke, *Reflections on the Revolution in France*, p. 183.

[71] J. Maritain. *The Rights of Man and Natural Law*, p. 33.

[72] A. Toffler, *Future Shock*, pp. 11-12.

Chapter Nine – A Self-Reproducing System

[1] J.B. Coates, *The Crisis of the Human Person. Some Personalist Interpretations* (Longmans, Green, London, 1949), pp. 236-7.

[2] S. Curtis (ed.), *The Journals of Woodrow Wyatt*, vol. 1 (Pan, London, 1998); vol. 2 (Pan, London, 2000).

[3] A. de Tocqueville, *Democracy in America*, vol. II, pp. 64-76.

[4] A. de Tocqueville, *Democracy in America*, vol. II, p. 8.

[5] *CityRoma*, 28 July 2004, p. 5

[6] *The Times Weekend*, 8 May 1999, p. 18.

[7] T. Anatrella, 'The Depressive Society', *Dolentium Hominum*, 34, XII (1997), n. 1, p. 88.

[8] J.J. Lopez-Ibor Jr., 'Research in the Field of Neuroscience and Mental Illness', *ibid.*, p. 52.

[9] F. Angelini, 'A New Attitude Towards the Mentally Ill', *ibid.*, p. 11.

[10] F. Deriu, D. Cabezas and R. Merola, 'The Results of a Mental Health Survey: a Focus on Depression', *Dolentium Hominum*, 55, XIX (2004), n. 1, p. 75.

[11] T. Anatrella, 'A Depressed Society?', *ibid.*, p. 35.

[12] A.A. Piatelli, 'The Jewish Vision', *ibid.*, p. 107.

[13] J. Lozano Barragán, 'Aspects of Post-modern Thought and Depression', *ibid.*, pp. 13, 14.

[14] *The Sunday Times Magazine*, 5 Jan. 1997, p. 41.

[15] *Ibidem.*

[16] *Ibid.*, p. 42.

[17] *Ibidem.*

[18] V. Orange *et al.*, *Winged Promises. A History of No 14 Squadron, RAF 1915-1945* (The Royal Air Force Benevolent Fund Enterprises, Fairford, 1996), preface by Lord Deramore, p. [iv].

[19] *The Times Weekend*, 8 May 1999, p. 18.

[20] Office for National Statistics, *Social Trends* n. 27 (1997), p. 132.

[21] BBC.co.uk. World Service, BBC News, 19 Sept. 2007, 'Key Points. Gambling Report'.

[22] *Guardian Unlimited*, 26 Aug. 2006, 'Super-size Britain Must Curb Junk Food Ads, Say Campaigners'.

[23] P.L. Berger, *A Rumour of Angels*, p. 31.

[24] *Ibid.*, pp. 18, 19, 21.

Chapter Ten – A Crisis Foreseen: Melting into Air

[1] D. Leopold (ed.), *M. Stirner. The Ego and its Own* (Cambridge University Press, Cambridge, 1995), pp. 274-6.

[2] A. de Tocqueville, *Democracy in America*, vol. II, p. 98.

[3] D. McClellan (ed.), *K. Marx and F. Engels, The Communist Manifesto* (Oxford University Press, Oxford, 1992), pp. 5, 6.

[4] F.M. Wilson (ed.), *Strange Island*, p. 196.

[5] E. Durkheim, *The Division of Labour in Society* (Macmillan, Basingstoke, 1984), p. 295.

[6] *Ibid.*, p. 291, from the chapter entitled 'The Anomic Division of Labour'.

[7] H.H. Gerth and C. Wright Mills (eds.), *From Max Weber. Essays in Sociology* (Routledge, London, 1991), p. 50.

[8] M. Weber, *The Protestant Ethic and the Spirit of Capitalism* (Unwin, London, 1985), p. 182.

[9] A. Toffler, *Future Shock*, p. 2.

[10] *Ibid.*, p. 187.

[11] P. Slater, *The Pursuit of Loneliness. American Culture at Breaking Point* (Penguin, Harmondsworth, 1975), p. 8.

[12] *Ibid.*, p. 9.

[13] T. Roszak, *Person/Planet*, p. 149.

[14] C. Lasch, *The Culture of Narcissism*, p. 5.

[15] *Ibid.*, p. 49.

[16] *Ibid.*, p. 51.

[17] *Ibid.*, p. 30.

[18] A. Etzioni, *An Immodest Agenda*, pp. 3-4.

[19] R. D. Putnam, *Bowling Alone. The Collapse and Revival of American Community* (Simon and Schuster, New York, 2000), p. 27.

[20] R.A. Nisbet, *Twilight of Authority*, p. 85.

[21] *Ibid.*, p. 78.

[22] *Ibid.*, pp. v, vi.

[23] R. Lowenthal, *Social Change and Cultural Crisis* (Columbia University Press, New York, 1984), p. vii.

[24] *Ibid.*, pp. 35, 39, 35, 37, 38-9.

[25] E. Hobsbawm, *Age of Extremes*, p. 341.

[26] *Ibid.*, p. 338-9.

[27] F. Fukuyama, *The Great Disruption. Human Nature and the Reconstitution of Social Order* (Simon and Schuster, New York, 2000), p. 4.

[28] *Ibid.*, pp. 4, 5.

[29] *Ibid.*, p. 3.

[30] *Ibid.*, pp. 5-6.

[31] M. Houellebecq, *Atomised*, pp. 26, 63, 125, 64, 284, 193.

[32] *Ibid.*, pp. 80-1.

[33] C. Lasch, *The Culture of Narcissism*, p. 30.

[34] R.A. Nisbet, *Twilight of Authority*, p. 133.

[35] E. Burke, *Reflections on the Revolution in France*, p. 152.

[36] *Ibid.*, pp. 194-5.

[37] B. Disraeli, *Sybil or the Two Nations* (The Folio Society, London, 1983), p. 82.

[38] Lord Salisbury, 'Disintegration', in P. Smith (ed.), *Lord Salisbury on Politics* (Cambridge University Press, Cambridge, 1972), pp. 356-7.

[39] M. Fforde, *Conservatism and Collectivism 1886-1914*, p. 96.

[40] T.S. Eliot, *The Idea of a Christian Society and Other Writings* (Faber and Faber, London, 1982), p. 49.

[41] F.A. Hayek, *The Road to Serfdom* (George Routledge and Sons, London, 1944), p. 159.

[42] M. Fforde, *Conservatism and Collectivism 1886-1914*, p. 170.

[43] M. Holmes. *The First Thatcher Government 1979-1983. Contemporary Conservatism and Economic Change* (Wheatsheaf, Brighton, 1985), p. 209.

[44] J. Major, *Conservatism in the 1990s: Our Common Purpose* (Carlton Club Political Committee, London, 1993), pp. 20, 36, 15, 16, 16, 23, 24.

[45] P. Hitchens, *The Abolition of Britain*, p. 341.

[46] *Ibid.*, p. xxxvi.

[47] *Ibid.*, pp. 338, 339, 341, 342, 343, 344.

[48] *Telegraph.co.uk*, 7 July 2008, 'David Cameron Attacks UK 'Moral Neutrality' – Full Text'.

[49] R. Williams, *Culture and Society*, pp. 14-15.

[50] *Ibid.*, pp. 26-7.

[51] A. Shelston (ed.), *Thomas Carlyle. Selected Writings* (Penguin, Harmondsworth, 1971), pp. 277-8.

[52] R. Williams, *Culture and Society*, pp. 141-2.

[53] *Ibid.*, p. 149.

[54] *Ibid.*, pp. 189-90.

[55] D. Willetts, *Modern Conservatism*, p. 110.

[56] P. Mendelson and R. Liddle, *The Blair Revolution. Can New Labour Deliver?* (Faber and Faber, London, 1996), p. 48.

[57] *Ibid.*, p. 47.

[58] T. Blair, *New Britain. My Vision of a Young Country* (Fourth Estate, London, 1996), p. 306.

Conclusion: A Return to the Soul?

[1] John Paul II, *Agenda for the New Millennium*, p. 174.

[2] F.A. Wolf, *The Spiritual Universe. How Quantum Physics Proves the Existence of the Soul* (Simon and Schuster, New York, 1996), pp. 21, 24.

[3] J. Maritain, *The Rights of Man and Natural Law*, p. 22.

[4] E. Burke, *Reflections on the Revolution in France*, pp. 194-5.

[5] T.S. Eliot, *After Strange Gods*, pp. 18-19.

[6] G. Maxwell, *Ring of Bright Water* (Penguin, Harmondsworth, 1974), p. 106, quoted in P. Johnson, *Enemies of Society*, p. 229.

[7] C.J. Furness (ed.), *Walt Whitman's Workshop* (Harvard University Press, Cambridge, Mass., 1928), p. 113.

[8] M. Planck, *Where is Science Going?* (Allen and Unwin, London, 1933), p. 65.

[9] C. Dawson, 'general introduction' to J. Maritain, *Religion and Culture,* p. vii.

[10] E. Bethge (ed.), *Dietrich Bonhoeffer*, p. 3.

[11] A. Solzhenitsyn, *Warning to the Western World* (The Bodley Head and the BBC, London, 1976), p. 45.

[12] C. Lasch. *The Culture of Narcissism*, p. 3.

[13] M.Valtorta, *The Notebooks 1943* (Centro Editoriale Valtortiano, Isola dei Liri, 1996), p. 518.

[14] T.L. Panale (ed.), *The Rebirth of Classical Political Rationalism*, p. 245.

[15] E. Bethge (ed.), *Dietrich Bonhoeffer*, p. 314.

[16] J. Maritain, *The Person and the Common Good*, pp. 72-3.

[17] A. Etzioni, *The Spirit of Community*, p. 253.

[18] See *Ibid.*, pp. 256-7, for the central planks of the Communitarian programme.

[19] D. Anderson (ed.), *This Will Hurt. The Restoration of Virtue and Civic Order* (The Social Affairs Unit, London, 1995), p. xv. For other publications by the virtues movement see D. Anderson (ed.), *The Loss of Virtue. Moral Confusion and Social Disorder in Britain and America* (The Social Affairs Unit, London, 1992) and G. Himmelfarb, *The De-Moralization of Society. From Victorian Values to Modern Values*. Publications by the Institute of Economic Affairs Health and Welfare Unit express much of the thinking of this movement.

[20] *The Westminster Declaration* (leaflet 'endorsed by the first national Rally of the Movement for Christian Democracy, Westminster Central Hall, November 1990'), pp. 1-2.

[21] J. Maritain, *The Range of Reason*, p. 195.

[22] E. Bethge (ed.), *Dietrich Bonhoeffer*, p. 369.

[23] *Ibid.*, pp. 16-17.

[24] A. Solzhenitsyn, *Warning to the Western World*, p. 45.

Select Bibliography

G.A. Almond and S. Verba, *The Civic Culture, Political Attitudes and Democracy in Five Nations* (Princeton University Press, Princeton NJ, 1963).

T. Anatrella, 'The Depressed Society', *Dolentium Hominum*, 34, XII (1997), n. 1, 88-92.

T. Anatrella, 'A Depressed Society?', *Dolentium Hominum*, 55, XIX (2004), n. 1, 32-37.

D. Anderson (ed.), *The Loss of Virtue. Moral Confusion and Social Disorder in Britain and America* (The Social Affairs Unit, London, 1992).

D. Anderson (ed.), *This Will Hurt. The Restoration of Virtue and Civic Order* (The Social Affairs Unit, London, 1995).

F. Angelini, 'A New Attitude towards the Mentally Ill', *Dolentium Hominum*, 34, XII (1997), n. 1, 10-11.

W. Barrett, *Death of the Soul. From Descartes to the Computer* (Oxford University Press, Oxford, 1987).

F.J.E. Basterra, *Bioethics* (St. Paul's, London, 1994).

Z. Bauman, *Liquid Modernity* (Polity Press, Cambridge, 2000).

Benedetto XVI, *Chi crede non è mai solo* (Cantagalli, Sienna, 2006).

Benedict XVI, 'Mass, Imposition of the Pallium and Conferral of the Fisherman's Ring for the Beginning of the Petrine Ministry of the Bishop of Rome. Homily of His Holiness Benedict XVI, St. Peter's Square, Sunday 24 April 2005' (available on the Holy See web site).

Benedict XVI, 'Message of His Holiness Benedict XVI for the Fourteenth World Day of the Sick', 8 Dec. 2005 (available on the Holy See web site).

R.H. Benson, *Lord of the World* (The Echo Library, Cirencester, 2005).

J. Bentham, 'Anarchical Fallacies', in J. Bowring (ed.), *The Works of Jeremy Bentham*, vol. 2 (William Tait, Edinburgh, 1843), pp. 489-534.

P.L. Berger, *A Rumour of Angels. Modern Society and the Rediscovery of the Supernatural* (Allen Lane, The Penguin Press, London, 1970).

G. Best, *Mid-Victorian Britain 1851-75* (Fontana, London, 1979).

E. Bethge (ed.), *Dietrich Bonhoeffer. Letters and Papers from Prison* (SCM Press, London, 1971).

A.H. Birch, *The Concepts and Theories of Modern Democracy* (Routledge, London, 1993).

T. Blair, *New Britain. My Vision of a Young Country* (Fourth Estate, London, 1996).

A. Bloom, *The Closing of the American Mind. How Higher Education has Failed Democracy and Impoverished the Souls of Today's Students* (Penguin, Harmondsworth, 1988).

Bloomberg.com.

D. Boucher and P. Kelly, *The Social Contract from Hobbes to Rawls* (Routledge, London, 1994).

M. Brando, *Songs My Mother Taught Me* (Arrow, London, 1995).

P. Brierley, 'Religion', in A. H. Halsey (ed.) *British Social Trends Since 1900. A Guide to the Changing Social Structure of Britain* (Macmillan, Basingstoke, 1988), pp. 518-560.

P. Brierley, *Christian England. What the 1989 English Church Census Reveals* (Marc Europe, London, 1991).

E. Burke, *Reflections on the Revolution in France* (Penguin, Harmondsworth, 1986).

D. Butler and G. Butler, *Twentieth-Century British Political Facts 1900-2000* (Macmillan, Basingstoke, 2000).

Catechism of the Catholic Church (Geoffrey Chapman, London, 1994).

Central Statistical Office, *Social Trends*, n. 26 (HMSO, London, 1996).

CityRoma

W. Churchill, *Thoughts and Adventures* (Odhams Press, London, 1947).

J.B. Coates, *The Crisis of the Human Person. Some Personalist Interpretations* (Longmans, Green, London, 1949). .

D.A. Coleman, 'Population', in A.H. Halsey (ed.), *British Social Trends Since 1900*, pp. 36-134.

Congregation for the Doctrine of the Faith, 'Considerations Regarding Proposals to Give Legal Recognition to Unions between Homosexual Persons', 3 June 2003 (available on the Holy See web site).

G. Cottier, 'Morality and Economics in Health Care', *Dolentium Hominum*, 43, XV (2000) n. 1, 67-8.

F. Crick, *The Astonishing Hypothesis. The Scientific Search for the Soul* (Simon and Schuster, London, 1994).

M. Cruickshank, *Church and State in English Education 1870 to the Present Day* (Macmillan, London, 1963).

J. Curtice and R. Powell, 'The Sceptical Electorate', in Social and Community Planning Research, *British Social Attitudes, the Twelfth Report* (Dartmouth, Aldershot, 1995), pp. 141-177.

S. Curtis (ed.), *The Journals of Woodrow Wyatt*, vol. 1 (Pan, London, 1998), vol. 2 (Pan, London, 2000).

The Daily Telegraph.

P. Dacre, 'The BBC's Cultural Marxism will Trigger an American-style Backlash', *Guardian Unlimited*, 24 Jan. 2007.

R. Dawkins, *The Selfish Gene* (Oxford University Press, Oxford, 1976).

C. Dawson, 'General Introduction', J. Maritain, *Religion and Culture* (Sheed and Ward, London, 1931), pp. vii-xxvii.

A. de Tocqueville, *Democracy in America* (Everyman's Library, London, 1994).

F. Deriu, D. Cabezas, and R. Merola, 'The Results of a Mental Health Survey: a Focus on Depression', *Dolentium Hominum*, 55, XIX (2004), n. 1, 73-79.

B. Disraeli, *Sybil or The Two Nations* (The Folio Society, London, 1983).

F. Dostoyevsky, *The Devils* (Penguin, London, 1971).

E. Durkeim, *The Division of Labour in Society* (Macmillan, Basingstoke, 1984).

S. Dunant (ed.), *The War of the Words. The Political Correctness Debate* (Virago, London, 1994).

K. P. Easson and R.R. Easson, *W. Blake. Milton* (Thames and Hudson, London, 1979).

The Economist, *The World in 2004* (The Economist, London, 2003).

T.S. Eliot, *After Strange Gods. A Primer of Modern Heresy* (Faber and Faber, London, 1934).

T.S. Eliot, *Notes Towards the Definition of Culture* (Faber and Faber, London, 1962).

T.S. Eliot, *The Waste Land and Other Poems* (Faber and Faber, London, 1972)

T.S. Eliot, *The Idea of a Christian Society and Other Writings* (Faber and Faber, London, 1982).

J.B. Elshtain, 'What is "Civil Society" and How does it Develop?', in H.F. Zacher (ed.), *Democracy: Some Acute Questions* (The Pontifical Academy of Social Sciences, Vatican City, 1999), pp. 207-219.

A. Etzioni, *An Immodest Agenda. Rebuilding America before the Twenty-First Century* (New Press, New York, 1983).

A. Etzioni, *The Spirit of Community. Rights, Responsibilities and the Communitarian Agenda* (Fontana, London, 1995).

B.A. Farrell, *The Standing of Psychoanalysis* (Oxford University Press, Oxford, 1981).

M. Fforde, *Conservatism and Collectivism 1886-1914* (Edinburgh University Press, Edinburgh, 1990).

M. Fforde, *Desocialisation: the Crisis of the Post-Modern. A Spiritual Critique* (Aracne, Rome, 2000).

M. Fforde, *Storia della Gran Bretagna 1832-2002* (Laterza, Rome/Bari, 2002).

M. Fforde, *Desocializzazione. La crisi della post-modernità* (Cantagalli, Sienna, 2005).

M. Fforde, 'La desocializzazione porta dell'infelicità', *L'Osservatore Romano*, 21 Oct. 2005, p. 3.

M. Fforde, 'Western Materialism and the Exportation of Desocialisation', in M. Kuna (ed.), *Slovensko, Materialzmus a Desocializácia* (Katolícka univerzita v Ruzomberku Filozofická fakulta, Slovakia, 2006), pp. 257-274.

M. Fforde, 'La scomparsa del galateo come indicatore di "desocializzazione"', *L'Osservatore Romano*, 18 Jan. 2007, p. 3.

M. Fforde, 'Turnout, Desocialisation and Blairism: a Note on the British Regional and Local Elections of May 2003', in G. Ignesti (ed.), *Annali 2005-2006* (G. Giappichelli Editore, Turin, 2007), pp. 693-7.

H. Fielding, *Bridget Jones's Diary* (Picador, London, 1998).

E. Fromm, *The Sane Society* (Routledge, London, 1991).

F. Fukuyama, *The Great Disruption. Human Nature and the Reconstitution of Social Order* (Simon and Schuster, New York, 2000).

F. Fukuyama, *Our Posthuman Future. Consequences of the Biotechnology Revolution* (Profile Books, London, 2003).

C.J. Furness (ed.), *Walt Whitman's Workshop* (Harvard University Press, Cambridge, Mass., 1928).

C.J. Galipeau, *Isaiah Berlin's Liberalism* (Clarendon Press, Oxford, 1994).

D. Gallie, 'The Labour Force', in A.H. Halsey and J. Webb (eds.), *Twentieth-Century British Social Trends* (Macmillan, Basingstoke, 2000), pp. 281-323.

E. Gellner, *The Psychoanalytic Movement or the Coming of Unreason* (Granada, London, 1985).

E. Gellner, *Relativism and the Social Sciences* (Cambridge University Press, Cambridge, 1985).

E. Gellner, *Postmodernism, Reason and Religion* (Routledge, London, 1992).

H.H. Gerth and C. Wright Mills (eds.), *From Max Weber: Essays in Sociology* (Routledge, London, 1991).

A.D. Gilbert, *The Making of Post-Christian Britain. A History of Secularization of Modern Society* (Longman, London, 1980).

R. Gill, 'Secularization of Census Data', in S. Bruce (ed.), *Religion and Modernization. Sociologists and Historians Debate the Secularization Thesis* (Clarendon Press, Oxford, 1992), pp. 90-113.

M. A. Glendon, *Rights Talk. The Impoverishment of Political Discourse* (Free Press, New York, 1991).

M. A. Glendon and P. Donati, 'Towards Achieving Solidarity with Children and Young People in our Globalized World', in M. A. Glendon and P. Donati (eds.), *Vanishing Youth? Solidarity with Children and Young People in an Age of Turbulence* (The Pontifical Academy of Social Sciences, Vatican City, 2005), pp. 543-558.

M.A. Glendon, *Traditions in Turmoil* (Sapientia Press, Naples, Florida, 2006).

D. Goleman, *Emotional Intelligence. Why it can Matter more than IQ* (Bloomsbury, London, 1996).

C. Gordon (ed.), *Foucault Power/Knowledge. Selected Interviews and Other Writings 1972-1977, Michel Foucault* (Harvester Wheatsheaf, London, 1980).

G. Gorer, *Exploring English Character* (Cresset Press, London, 1955).

D. Graham and P. Clarke, *The New Enlightenment, The Rebirth of Liberalism* (Macmillan in Association with Channel Four Television Co, London, 1986).

S.J.D. Green, *Religion in the Age of Decline. Organisation and Experience in Industrial Yorkshire, 1870-1920* (Cambridge University Press, Cambridge, 1996).

G. Greene, *The Third Man* (Faber and Faber, London, 1988).

W.H. Greenleaf, *The British Political Tradition*, vol. I, *The Rise of Collectivism* (Methuen, London, 1983).

W.H. Greenleaf, *The British Political Tradition*, vol. 2, *The Ideological Heritage* (Methuen, London, 1983).

W. H. Greenleaf, *The British Political Tradition*, vol. 3, *A Much Governed Nation* (Methuen, London 1987).

G. Greer, *The Female Eunuch* (Harper Perennial, London, 2006).

The Guardian.

Guardian Unlimited.

P.A. Hall, 'Social Capital in Britain', *British Journal of Political Science*, vol. 29, part 3 (July 1999), 417-461.

A. H. Halsey (ed.) *British Social Trends Since 1900. A Guide to the Changing Social Structure of Britain* (Macmillan, Basingstoke, 1988).

A.H. Halsey and J. Webb (eds.), *Twentieth-Century British Social Trends* (Macmillan, Basingstoke, 2000).

A.H. Halsey, 'Further and Higher Education', in A.H. Halsey and J. Webb (eds.), *Twentieth-Century British Social Trends*, pp. 221-253.

H.J. Hanham, *The Nineteenth Century Constitution 1815-1914. Documents and Commentary* (Cambridge University Press, Cambridge, 1969).

L. Hannah, *The Rise of the Corporate Economy* (Methuen, London, 1983).

J. Harris, *Private Lives, Public Spirit. Britain 1870-1914* (Penguin, London, 1994).

M. Harris, *Culture, People, Nature. An Introduction to General Anthropology* (Harper and Row, New York, 1980).

B. Harrison and J. Webb, 'Volunteers and Voluntarism', in A.H. Halsey and J. Webb (eds.), *Twentieth-Century British Social Trends*, pp. 587-619.

F.A. Hayek, *The Road to Serfdom* (George Routledge and Sons, London, 1944).

F.A. Hayek, *Studies in Philosophy, Politics and Economics* (Routledge and Kegan Paul, London, 1967).

P. Hennessy, *Never Again. Britain 1945-51* (Jonathan Cape, London, 1992).

G. Himmelfarb, *The De-moralization of Society. From Victorian Values to Modern Values* (IEA Health and Welfare Unit, London, 1995).

P. Hitchens, *The Abolition of Britain. The British Cultural Revolution from Lady Chatterley to Tony Blair* (Quartet Books, London, 2000).

E. J. Hobsbawm, *Age of Extremes. The Short Twentieth Century 1914-1991* (Abacus, London, 1995).

M. Holmes, *The First Thatcher Government 1979-1983. Contemporary Conservatism and Economic Change* (Wheatsheaf, Brighton, 1985).

N. Hornby, *About a Boy* (Gollancz, London, 1998).

M. Houellebecq, *Atomised* (Vintage, London, 2001).

D.W. Hudson and H.J. Mancini, *Understanding Maritain: Philosopher and Friend* (Mercer University Press, Macon GA, 1987).

T. Hutchinson (ed.), *Shelley. Poetical Works* (Oxford University Press, London, 1967).

The Independent on Sunday.

D. Irving, *The War Path. Hitler's Germany 1933-1939* (Macmillan, London, 1978).

K. Ishiguro, *Never Let Me Go* (Faber and Faber, London, 2005).

John Paul II, *On Social Concern. Sollicitudo Rei Socialis* (Pauline Books and Media, Boston, n.y.).

John Paul II, *Christifideles Laici* (Libreria Editrice Vaticana, Vatican City, 1988).

John Paul II, *Crossing the Threshold of Hope* (Jonathan Cape, London, 1994).

John Paul II, *Agenda for the Third Millennium* (HarperCollins, London, 1996).

John Paul II, *Fides et Ratio* (Libreria Editrice Vaticana, Vatican City, 1998).

John Paul II, *Novo Millennio Ineunte* (Catholic Truth Society, London, 2001).

P. Johnson, *Enemies of Society* (Weidenfeld and Nicolson, London, 1977).

P. Johnson, *Intellectuals* (Weidenfeld and Nicolson, London, 1989).

P. Johnson, *The Birth of the Modern. World Society 1815-1830* (HarperCollins, New York, 1991).

R.B. Johnson, 'Models of Man: 1879-1979', in A.J. Chapman and D.M. Jones (eds.), *Models of Man* (British Psychological Society, Leicester, 1980), pp. 1-12.

H. Jonas, *The Imperative of Responsibility. In Search of Ethics for a Technological Age* (University of Chicago Press, Chicago, 1984)

B. Jones and D. Kavanagh, *British Politics Today* (Manchester University Press, Manchester, 1994).

N. Jones, *The Control Freaks. How New Labour Gets its Own Way* (Politico's Publishing, London, 2002).

G. Jordan and C. Weedon, *Cultural Politics, Class, Gender, Race and the Postmodern World* (Blackwell, Oxford, 1995).

I. Kant, *Logic* (Dover Publications, New York, 1988).

D. Kavanagh and D. Butler, *The British General Election of 2005* (Palgrave Macmillan, Basingstoke, 2005).

C. Lasch, *The Culture of Narcissism. American Life in an Age of Diminishing Expectations* (Norton, New York, 1991).

J. Lawson, *A Man's Life* (Hodder and Stroughton, London, 1932).

D. Leopold (ed.), *M. Steiner. The Ego and its Own* (Cambridge University Press, Cambridge, 1995).

A. Leve, 'Broken Pieces of a Lost Life', *The Sunday Times Magazine*, 2 Sept. 2007, pp.19-27.

M. Lever, *Sade. A Biography* (Farrar, Straus and Giroux, New York, 1993).

C.S. Lewis, *The Abolition of Man* (HarperCollins, London, 1999).

J.J. Lopez-Ibor Jr, 'Research in the Field of Neuroscience and Mental Illness', *Dolentium Hominum*, 34, XII (1997), n. 1, 52-58.

J. Lozano Barragán, 'Aspects of Post-Modern Thought and Depression', *Dolentium Hominum*, 55, XIX (2004), n. 1,10-15.

R. Lowenthal, *Social Change and Cultural Crisis* (Columbia University Press, New York, 1984).

D. Lyon, 'The Changing Meaning and Value of Work in a Globalized Information Society', in M.S. Archer (ed.), *Towards Reducing Unemployment* (The Pontifical Academy of Social Sciences, Vatican City, 1999), pp. 269-283.

M. Mack (ed.), *Alexander Pope. An Essay on Man* (Methuen, London, 1982).

J.L. Mackie, *Ethics. Inventing Right and Wrong* (Penguin, Harmondsworth, 1977).

C.B. Macpherson, 'Natural Rights in Hobbes and Locke', in D.D. Raphael (ed.), *Political Theory and the Rights of Man* (Macmillan, London, 1967), pp. 1-15.

C.B. Macpherson (ed.), *T. Hobbes. Leviathan* (Penguin, Harmondsworth, 1981).

J. Major, *Conservatism in the 1990s: Our Common Purpose* (Carlton Club Political Committee, London, 1993).

E. Malinvaud, 'A Synthesis', in E. Malinvaud and M.S. Archer (eds.), *Work and Human Fulfillment* (Sapientia Press, Ypsilanti, Michigan, 2003), pp. 285-299.

J. Maritain, *Religion and Culture* (Sheed and Ward, London, 1931).

J. Maritain, *The Rights of Man and Natural Law* (Geoffrey Bles: The Centenary Press, London, 1944).

J. Maritain, *The Person and the Common Good* (Geofrey Bles, London, 1948).

J. Maritain, *The Range of Reason* (Geoffrey Bles, London, 1953).

A. Marwick, *British Society Since 1945* (Penguin, Harmondsworth, 1996).

A. Marwick, *British Society Since 1945* (Penguin, London, 2003).

K. Marx, *A Contribution to the Critique of Political Economy* (Lawrence and Wishart, London, 1971).

K. Marx, *The Eighteenth Brumaire of Louis Napoleon* (Progress, Moscow, 1984).

J. Masters, 'Hello, Loneliness', *Telegraph.co.uk*, 13 Aug. 2006.

P. Mathias, *The First Industrial Nation. An Economic History of Britain 1700-1914* (Methuen, London, 1983).

G. Maxwell, *Ring of Bright Water* (Penguin, Harmondsworth, 1974).

T. May, *An Economic and Social History of Britain 1760-1970* (Longman, Harlow, 1987).

D. McClellan (ed), *K. Marx and F. Engels. Manifesto of the Communist Party* (Oxford University Press, Oxford, 1992).

I. McEwan, *The Cement Garden* (Cape, London, 1978).

P.B. Medawar, *The Hope of Progress* (Wildwood House, London, 1974).

M. Medved, *Hollywood Vs. America. Popular Culture and the War on Traditional Values* (HarperCollins, New York, 1992).

T. Megarry, *Society in Prehistory. The Origins of Human Culture* (Macmillan, Basingstoke, 1995).

P. Melling and J. Roper, *Americanisation and the Transformation of World Cultures. Melting Pot or Cultural Chernobyl?* (Lampeter: Edwin Mellen Press, Lewiston, N. Y., 1996).

P. Mendelsohn and R. Liddle, *The Blair Revolution. Can New Labour Deliver?* (Faber and Faber, London, 1996).

K. Middlemas, *Politics in Industrial Society. The Experience of the British System Since 1911* (Deutsch, London, 1979).

K. Middlemas, *Industry, Unions and Government. Twenty-One Years of NEDC* (Macmillan, London, 1988).

J.S. Mill, *On Liberty* (Penguin, Harmondsworth, 1982).

W.L. Miller, A.M. Timpson, and M. Lessnoff, *Political Culture in Contemporary Britain. People and Politicians, Principles and Practice* (Clarendon Press, Oxford, 1996).

K. Minogue, 'The End of Authority and Informality: And Their Replacement by Intrusive Regulation', in D. Anderson (ed.), *This Will Hurt. The Restoration of Virtue and Civic Order*, pp. 63-75.

B.R. Mitchell, *British Historical Statistics* (Cambridge University Press, Cambridge, 1988).

A. Moorehead, *The Fatal Impact. The Invasion of the South Pacific 1767-1840* (Harper and Row, New York, 1987).

D. Morris, *The Naked Ape* (Triad Grafton, London, 1977).

The New Encyclopaedia Britannica, vol. 15 (Encyclopaedia Britannica, Chicago, 1983).

J.H. Newman, *The Idea of a University Defined and Illustrated* (Routledge/ Thoemmes, London, 1994).

F. Nietzsche, *The Gay Science. With a Prelude in Rhymes and an Appendix of Songs* (Vintage Books, New York, 1974).

F. Nietzsche, *Beyond Good and Evil. Prelude to a Philosophy of the Future* (Penguin, Harmondsworth, 1990).

R. A. Nisbet, *The Quest for Community. A Study in the Ethics of Order and Freedom* (Oxford University Press, New York, 1953).

R.A. Nisbet, *Twilight of Authority* (Oxford University Press, New York, 1975).

M. J. Oakeshott, *Rationalism in Politics and Other Essays* (Methuen, London, 1974).

Office for National Statistics, *Social Trends*, n. 27 (Stationery Office, London, 1997).

Office for National Statistics, *Social Trends*, n. 33 (Stationery Office, London, 2003).

Office for National Statistics, *Social Trends*, n. 34 (Stationery Office, London, 2004).

Office for National Statistics, *Social Trends*, n. 37 (Palgrave Macmillan, Basingstoke, 2007).

Office for National Statistics, *Social Trends*, no. 38 (Palgrave Macmillan, Basingstoke, 2008).

V. Orange and Lord Deramore, *Winged Promises. A History of No 14 Squadron, RAF 1915-1945* (The Royal Airforce Benevolent Fund Enterprises, Fairford, 1996).

G. Orwell, *The Lion and the Unicorn. Socialism and the English Genius*, (Penguin, Harmondsworth, 1982).

S. Orwell and I. Angus (eds.), *The Collected Essays, Journalism and Letters of George Orwell*, vol. 3 (Secker and Warburg, London, 1968).

The Oxford Paperback Dictionary (Oxford University Press, Oxford, 1983).

L'Osservatore Romano.

J. Owen, 'Community? We Don't Know Our Neighbours', *The Independent on Sunday*, 20 Jan. 2008, p. 26.

W.J.B. Owen (ed.), *Wordsworth and Coleridge. Lyrical Ballads 1798*, II edn. (Oxford University Press, Oxford, 1969).

T.L. Pangle (ed.), *The Rebirth of Classical Political Rationalism. An Introduction to the Thought of Leo Strauss. Essays and Lectures by Leo Strauss* (University of Chicago Press, Chicago, 1989).

A. Partington (ed.), *The Oxford Dictionary of Quotations* (Oxford University Press, Oxford, 1996).

H. Pelling, *A History of British Trade Unionism* 4th. edn. (Penguin, Harmondsworth, 1987).

A.A. Piatelli, 'The Jewish Vision', *Dolentium Hominum*, 55, XIX (2004), n. 1, 106-107.

S. Pinker, *The Blank Slate. The Modern Denial of Human Nature* (Penguin, London, 2002).

M. Planck, *Where is Science Going?* (Allen and Unwin, London, 1933).

Plato, *Theaetetus* (Clarendon Press, Oxford, 1973).

S. Pollard, *The Development of the British Economy 1914-1990* (Edward Arnold, London, 1992).

The Pontifical Academy of Social Sciences, *X Plenary Session, Intergenerational Solidarity, Welfare and Human Ecology 23 April- 3 May 2004*, 'Conclusions on "Intergenerational Solidarity, Welfare and Human Ecology"' (The Pontifical Academy of Social Sciences, Vatican City, 2004), p. 15.

The Pontifical Council for the Family, *The Truth and Meaning of Human Sexuality. Guidelines for Education within the Family* (Libreria Editrice Vaticana, Vatican City, 1995).

P. Poupard, 'The Depressive Ideas of the Contemporary World', *Dolentium Hominum*, 55, XIX (2004), n. 1, 67-72.

R. D. Putnam, *Bowling Alone. The Collapse and Revival of American Community* (Simon and Schuster, New York, 2000).

J. Ratzinger, *Truth and Tolerance. Christian Faith and World Religions* (Ignatius Press, San Francisco, 2004).

J. Ratzinger, 'Homily of Joseph Cardinal Ratzinger, Dean of the College of Cardinals, Mass for the Election of the Supreme Pontiff, St. Peter's Basilica, 18 April 2005' (EWTN, 'Pontificate of Benedict XVI', www://ewtn.com/pope/words/conclave_homily.asp).

T. Regan, *The Case for Animal Rights* (Routledge and Kegan Paul, London, 1983).

R. Roberts, *The Classic Slum. Salford Life in the First Quarter of the Century* (Penguin, Harmondsworth, 1973).

R. Rollin (ed.), *The Americanization of the Global Village. Essays in Comparative Popular Culture* (Bowling Green State University Popular Press, Bowling Green, Ohio, 1989).

T. Roszak, *Person/Planet. The Creative Disintegration of Industrial Society* (Granada, London, 1981).

J.-J. Rousseau, *Discourse on Political Economy and the Social Contract* (Oxford University Press, Oxford, 1994).

C. Sagan and A. Druyan, *Shadows of Forgotten Ancestors. A Search for who we are* (Arrow, London, 1993).

Lord Salisbury, 'Disintegration', in P. Smith (ed.), *Lord Salisbury on Politics* (Cambridge University Press, Cambridge, 1972), pp. 335-376.

E.F. Schumacher, *Small is Beautiful. A Study of Economics as if People Mattered* (Vintage, London, 1973).

H.M. Scobie, S. Persaud, and P. Docile, *The Italian Economy in the 1990s* (Routledge, London, 1996).

R. Scruton, *The Politics of Culture and Other Essays* (Carcanet, Manchester, 1981).

R. Scruton, *Thinkers of the New Left* (Longman, Harlow, 1985).

R. Scruton, *Untimely Tracts* (Macmillan, Basingstoke, 1987).

R. Scruton, *The Philosopher on Dover Beach* (Carcanet, Manchester, 1990).

R. Scruton, *Upon Nothing* (University College of Swansea, Swansea, 1993).

R. Scruton, *Modern Philosophy. An Introduction and Survey* (Mandarin, London, 1996).

R. Scruton, *A Political Philosophy* (Continuum, London, 2006).

A. Serra, 'La rivoluzione gnomica. Conquiste, attese e rischi', *La Civiltà Cattolica*, 152, II, 3623, 2 June 2001, 439-453.

A. Serra, 'La "famiglia" nell'era biotecnologica', *Pedagogia e Vita*, 2, (2002), 99-112.

A. Serra, 'Le cellule staminali embrionali. Problemi e prospettive', *Civiltà Cattolica,* 158, II, 3767, 2 June 2007, 433-446.

A. Shelston (ed.), *Thomas. Carlyle. Selected Writings* (Penguin, Harmondsworth, 1971).

L. Siedentop, *Tocqueville* (Oxford University Press, Oxford, 1994).

P. Slater, *The Pursuit of Loneliness. American Culture at Breaking Point* (Penguin, Harmondsworth, 1975).

G. Smith, 'Schools', in A.H. Halsey and J. Webb (eds.), *Twentieth-Century British Social Trends*, pp. 179-220.

Social Survey Division of OPCS on Behalf of the Department of Health, *Health Survey for England, 1993* (HMSO, London, 1995).

A. Solzhenitsyn, *Warning to the Western World* (The Bodley Head and the BBC, London, 1976).

A. Solzhenitsyn, 'Our Pluralists', *Survey. A Journal of East & West Studies*, Summer 1985, 29, 2 (125), 1-28.

A. Solzhenitsyn, *Rebuilding Russia. Reflections and Tentative Proposals* (Harvill, London, 1991)

P. Stephens, 'The Treasury under Labour', in A. Seldon (ed.), *The Blair Effect. The Blair Government 1997-2001* (Little, Brown and Company, London, 2001), pp. 185-207.

J. Stevenson, *British Society 1914-45* (Penguin, Harmondsworth, 1984).

The Sunday Times.

The Sunday Times Magazine.

R. Tarnas, *The Passion of the Western Mind. Understanding the Ideas that have Shaped our World View* (Pimlico, London, 1996).

Telegraph.co.uk.

F. Thompson, *Lark Rise to Candleford* (Penguin, Harmondsworth, 1973).

F.M.L. Thompson, *The Rise of Respectable Society. A Social History of Victorian Britain, 1830-1900* (Fontana, London, 1988).

D. Thomson, *England in the Nineteenth Century* (Penguin, Harmondsworth, 1978).

A. Thwaite (ed.), *P. Larkin. Collected Poems* (Marvell Press and Faber and Faber, London, 1988).

Timesonline.

The Times Weekend.

A. Toffler, *Future Shock* (Bantam Books, New York, 1971).

A. Touraine, *Can We Live Together. Equality and Difference* (Polity, Oxford, 2000).

L. Truss, *Talk to the Hand. The Utter Bloody Rudeness of Everyday Life* (Profile Books, London, 2005).

I. Turgenev, *Fathers and Sons* (Penguin, London, 1975).

H.N. Tuttle, *The Crowd is Untruth. The Existential Critique of Mass Society in the Thought of Kierkegaard, Nietzsche, Heidegger and Ortega y Gasset* (P. Lang, New York, 1996).

M. Valtorta, *The Notebooks 1943* (Centro Editoriale Valtortiano, Isola dei Liri, 1996).

K. Ward, *The Turn of the Tide. Christian Belief in Britain Today* (BBC, London, 1986).

R. Weatherill, *Cultural Collapse* (Free Association Books, London, 1994).

M. Weber, *The Protestant Ethic and the Spirit of Capitalism* (Unwin, London, 1985).

The Westminster Declaration (leaflet 'endorsed by the first national Rally of the Movement for Christian Democracy, Westminster Central Hall, November 1990').

M.J. Wiener, *English Culture and the Decline of the Industrial Spirit 1850-1980* (Cambridge University Press, Cambridge, 1982).

R. Williams, *The Long Revolution* (Penguin, Harmondsworth, 1965).

R. Williams, *Culture and Society. Coleridge to Orwell* (Hogarth, London, 1987).

D. Willetts, *Modern Conservatism* (Penguin, London, 1992).

E. Wilson, *Sociobiology. The New Synthesis* (Belknap Press of Harvard University Press, Cambridge Mass., 1975).

E. Wilson, *On Human Nature* (Harvard University Press, Cambridge Mass., 1978).

F.M. Wilson (ed.), *Strange Island. Britain Through Foreign Eyes 1395-1940* (Longmans, Green and Co., London, 1955).

F.A. Wolf, *The Spiritual Universe, How Quantum Physics Proves the Existence of the Soul* (Simon and Schuster, New York, 1996).

B. Wood, 'Urbanisation and Local Government', in A.H. Halsey (ed.), *British Social Trends Since 1900*, pp. 322-356.

B. Wood and J. Carter, 'Towns, Urban Change and Local Government', in A.H. Halsey and J. Webb (eds.), *Twentieth-Century British Social Trends*, pp. 412-433.

K. Young and N. Rao, 'Faith in Local Democracy', in Social and Community Planning Research, *British Social Attitudes, the Twelfth Report*, pp. 91-17.